THE TWO MARXISMS

THIS IS PART OF A TRILOGY

The Dark Side of the Dialectic by Alvin W. Gouldner

VOLUME ONE

The Dialectic of Ideology and Technology

VOLUME TWO

The Future of Intellectuals and the Rise of the New Class

VOLUME THREE

The Two Marxisms: Contradictions and Anomalies
in the Development of Theory

OTHER BOOKS BY ALVIN W. GOULDNER

Studies in Leadership: Leadership and Democratic Action

Patterns of Industrial Bureaucracy

Wildcat Strike

Emile Durkheim's Socialism and Saint-Simon

Notes on Technology and the Moral Order
(with Richard A. Peterson)

Enter Plato: The Origins of
Western Social Theory in Ancient Greece

The Coming Crisis of Western Sociology

For Sociology: Renewal and Critique in Sociology Today

THE TWO MARXISMS

Contradictions and Anomalies in the Development of Theory

ALVIN W. GOULDNER

A Continuum Book

THE SEABURY PRESS • NEW YORK

1980 ● *The Seabury Press*
815 Second Avenue ● *New York, N.Y. 10017*

Library of Congress Cataloging in Publication Data

Gouldner, Alvin Ward, 1920-   The two Marxisms.
(His The dark side of the dialectic ; v. 3) (A Continuum book)
Includes index.
1. Communism—History. 2. Socialism—History.
I. Title.   II. Series: Gouldner, Alvin Ward, 1920-
Dark side of the dialectic ; v. 3.
HX36.G68   335.4'09   79-18041   *ISBN 0-8164-9138-0*

Dedicated to
the editorial collegium of
Theory and Society

CONTENTS

Part III: Paradigms and Anomalies in Marxism
The Ordeal of Aborted Creativity

PREFACE

This first section of my study of Marxism begins to redeem a number of promises: first, the promise to contribute to the study of the origins of western social theory outlined and begun in my *Enter Plato* (1965); secondly, the promise made in *The Coming Crisis of Western Sociology* (1970) to conduct a study of Marxism as critically probing as my study of western sociology; and thirdly, the promise made in *The Dialectic of Ideology and Technology* (1976) to develop its analysis as a trilogy. This is that third volume.

Or at least part of it, which is why I remarked that this study *begins* to redeem these several promises. This *first* part of my study of Marxism focuses on its evolution, as generated by its own internal contradictions and emerging anomalies, for the most part during the lives of Marx and Engels. Another volume deals with the effects of these contradictions and anomalies in the work of post-Marxists such as Lenin, Stalin, Trotsky, and Lukács, Gramsci, Althusser, and others. A third part of my study of Marxism will devote itself to its origins, including its technical origins in other social theories, along with an analysis of the problem of theoretical creativity, as well as Marxism's social and historical origins, its *class* basis. The fourth, and hopefully final part, will address the problem of the rationality and the limits of Marxism in terms of its position in the historical evolution of modes of discourse.

Mary Grove has managed our office—three-ring circus that it is—with saintly patience and humor, at once fearless and talented. Vicki Ibera who, along with Mary did much of the typing, was superb. Very importantly, however, I want to acknowledge and thank another kind of "being"—the ancient and yeasty city of Amsterdam, where I began and indeed got quite far into the present work, as well as those students at the University of Amsterdam who listened to this alien American in supportive and stimulating ways. The work on Marxism is basically a product of Amsterdam.

Alvin W. Gouldner

PART I

Contradiction Within Marxism

With all the philosophers it is precisely the 'system' which is perishable; and for the simple reason that it springs from an imperishable desire of the human mind—the desire to overcome all contradictions.

Friedrich Engels

Alas, two souls dwell in his breast, and one seeks divorce from the other.

Johann Wolfgang von Goethe

. . . this struggle is a conflict defined not by the indifference of the two sides in their distinction, but by their being bound together in one unity. I am not one of the fighters locked in battle, but both, and I am the struggle itself. I am fire and water . . .

G. W. F. Hegel

1

INTRODUCTION

Having set out to change the world, rather than produce one more interpretation of it, Marxist theory must ultimately be weighed on the scales of history.

Convention has it that on a blustery October day in muddy St. Petersburg the military forces of the Bolshevik Party stormed the Winter Palace, arrested the Provisional Government that had replaced the Czar months earlier, and took command of the state. Actually, the storming of the Winter Palace was a more confused affair, for many revolutionaries had been infiltrating the great Palace all day through its hundreds of entrances and were already inside when the final assault took place. Indeed, that assault was but the culmination of less dramatic military movements, for the Bolsheviks had, days earlier, already assumed control over most public buildings, the post office, railroad station, telegraph offices, and other vital centers of communication.

In any event, on October 24, 1917 (old style calendar, November 6 new style), the Bolshevik Party that Vladimir Ilyich Lenin had carefully pruned and steadfastly trained to his will for some fifteen years, came to power in Russia. These were indeed, "ten days that shook the world," as John Reed described them, and there is little in the world—within and between nations—that has not felt the impact of this event.

Since that time, many other nations have also come under the governance of Marxist political parties, all of whom have learned from, even if not modelling themselves on, the experience of the Bolsheviks. In addition to the vast Chinese nation, others that have come under the reign of Marxist states are: Afghanistan, Albania, Angola, Bulgaria, Cambodia, Cuba, Czechoslovakia, East Germany, Ethiopia, Hungary, North Korea, Laos, Latvia, Lithuania, Mongolia, Poland, Rumania, Vietnam, South Yemen, and Yugoslavia. Readers will note whether this list has since contracted or expanded. At this time, about one-third of the world's population lives under the governance of states regarding themselves as Marxist, and all this has come about in little more than half-a-century.

Never in world history has there been so profound a change in human lives and social systems among so many nations of people in so brief a time span. Never, for example, has a military conqueror, a religious prophet, or a new way of life spread themselves so far and wide in what, from any historically informed view, must be regarded as the shortest possible time span in which events of such magnitude could have occurred. It has happened within the normal span of a single lifetime. It was a unique event and we all still live in its midst. The historical epicenter of that political earthquake, whose tremors are still felt throughout the world, was the Bolshevik assumption of power in Russia.

"The Bolshevik victory in November 1917 may fairly be described," wrote Merle Fainsod, "as one of the most remarkable triumphs of revolutionary engineering in human history. On the eve of the March revolution [which first overthrew the Czar] the total membership of the Bolshevik Party was generously estimated at 23,600. In the short space of eight months, this small group was able to accumulate sufficient support to seize power in a nation of over 150,000,000."[1] How did this happen? A small question for a great problem. Fainsod notes that during World War I, the Czarist Government had suffered ruinous losses of men, territory, resources, public repute, and legitimacy, and that these losses fostered a widespread desperation. "The Bolsheviks alone among revolutionary parties," writes Fainsod, "were able to turn the resulting disorganization to their advantage. One major source of the strength of the Bolshevik Party was its highly centralized organization, its activist membership, and the determination of its leader, Lenin."

This is substantially correct, yet something of consequence has been left out. It is the unique role of a special social theory, of Marxism, in forging the Bolshevik Party, in endowing it with a dense cohesion, in shaping the Party's tactics and strategy, and in giving it a sense of mission in the making of history. It is the role of this theory about which Fainsod and, indeed a major school of interpretators of the October Revolution, are silent. (I shall return to them later.) Certainly the man who fashioned the Bolshevik Party, who created it committee by committee, congress by congress, almost man by man, who painstakingly blueprinted it in his book of 1902, *What Is to Be Done?*—certainly the Lenin who knew the Bolshevik Party like a Japanese gardener knows the tiny Bonsai plant whose every branch he has trained for fifteen years—was not silent about theory but shouted its importance for his Bolsheviks.

Theory: Changing the World

Lenin began, in *What Is to Be Done?*, by quoting Marx's *Critique of the Gotha Program*. In this, Marx had written to the German party leaders, "If you must combine, then enter into agreements to satisfy the practical aims of the movement, but do not haggle over principles, do not make 'concessions' in theory."[2] Then Lenin himself added:

> This was Marx's idea, and yet there are people among us who strive—in his name—to belittle the significance of theory. Without a revolutionary theory there can be no revolutionary movement. This cannot be insisted upon too strongly at a time when the fashionable preaching of opportunism is combined with absorption in the narrowest forms of practical activity. The importance of theory for Russian Social Democrats is still greater: . . . the *role of the vanguard can be fulfilled only by a party that is guided by an advanced theory*.[3]

Still further, Lenin quoted Friedrich Engels to the same effect:

> It is the specified duty of the leaders to gain an ever-clearer understanding of the theoretical problems, to free themselves more and more from the influence of traditional phrases inherited from an old conception of the world, and constantly keep in mind that Socialism, having become a science, demands the same treatment as every other science—it must be studied.[4]

Lenin insisted, and I shall return to this at a later point, that a *socialist* "consciousness could only be brought to them [i.e., the workers] from without. The history of all countries shows that the working class, exclusively by its own effort, is able to develop only trade-union consciousness. . . . The theory of Socialism, however, grew out of the philosophic, historical and economic theories that were elaborated by the educated representatives of the propertied classes, the intellectuals. The founders of modern scientific

Socialism, Marx and Engels, themselves belonged to the bourgeois intelligentsia."[5]

The Bolshevik Party itself was at first largely conceived as the instrument through which the *teoreticki,* who edited Lenin's newspaper *Iskra,* could imprint a proper socialist consciousness on the working class, and on "practical" organizers. The party's centralized organizational character aimed, in part, to protect the theoretical germ plasm of its leaders, placing the party under the control of the most theoretically informed, ensuring their influence on those less theoretically trained: "belittling the role of 'the conscious element,' " added Lenin, *"means, whether one likes it or not, growth of influence of bourgeois ideology among the workers.* All those who talk about 'exaggerating the importance of ideology,' about exaggerating the role of the conscious element, etc., imagine that the pure and simple labour movement can work out an independent ideology for itself, if only the workers 'take their fate out of the hands of the leaders.' "[6]

Lenin's point, however, was that a serious revolutionary could not overestimate the importance of the theoretical: "a man who is weak and vacillating on theoretical questions, who has a narrow outlook, who makes excuses for his own slackness, . . . such a man is not a revolutionist but a hopeless amateur."[7] Thus while some historians now hold that Bolshevik history was only the result of the force of circumstances, and not of Bolshevik commitment to a specific theory, the man who more than any other shaped these events, tells us, rather, that theory was decisive in forging the Bolshevik organization and without theory there would surely have been no October Revolution.

It is important to understand why these historians minimize the role of Marxist theory. Most generally, theirs was a reaction to the ideologically saturated view which regarded every development in the Russian revolution as the "logical outgrowth" of some theoretical commitment. Thus countless analyses of Stalinism have, for example, held it to be a "straightline," "fulfillment" and "logical" result of Marxism and Leninism. Given such a mechanical view, little attention need be paid to history, to the way events actually unfolded, to what people really said and did, to the confusing circumstances in which they found themselves. One merely has to invoke Marxist theory to account for anything. This model is a form of vulgar idealism, in which history is seen simply as the outgrowth of an idea. It is easy to understand, therefore, that it inhibited serious historical study and deserved to be opposed.

Nonetheless, what has often happened in the heat of the polemic against this vulgar idealism is that some historians overstated their case and assigned no significance at all to Bolshevik theory and to Marxism. Here vulgar idealism was supplanted by an eclecticism no less vulgar: by a tacit emphasis on the insignificance of human rationality; by an overemphasis on the importance of irrationality in human affairs and on the psychopathology of leaders in the making of history. To this extent, however such historians failed in their special obligation to attend to the *uniqueness* of the events. For what was indeed unique about the Bolsheviks, and especially their leadership, was that they were *theoretically* dedicated men; instead they are, in some accounts, treated as if they were recent "end of ideology" pragmatists, concerned only with what "works." Nothing could be farther from the truth. Much more than most other political leaders, the Bolsheviks were defined and shaped by their intellectual commitments to a theory, to Marxism and especially to Lenin's reading of Marxism; they and the things they did are incomprehensible without knowing this theory.

This is not to say that the Bolsheviks were not influenced by other conditions, by the "force of circumstances." This is not to say that they did not sometimes change their theory, or sometimes act in gross violation of it. Still, the central consideration remains: the influence that self-conscious, articulated theory had on them was vastly greater than that which it normally has on politics, and the events ramifying from their deeds will be opaque if the specific theory to which they were committed is ignored or deprecated.

The point is not that everything the Bolsheviks did was done because it was dictated by their theory, or was the mirror image of their Marxist theory. *Some* of it was; for example, the great importance they attributed to the use of the state as an instrument for controlling the economy. In other cases, even where theory's prescriptions were disregarded, the theory continued to have consequences in the same way that a law has consequences, even where—as in a crime—it is broken. To argue that because there are some differences between Bolshevik policies and Marxist theory, that therefore their policies were not influenced by the theory, is like concluding that since a law is broken it is without consequence.

It is uniquely important to know Marxist theory if one wishes to understand the events that have ramified into the world from the

time of the October Revolution. A knowledge of Marxist theory is
an indispensable key to understanding the world-shaking revolutions of the twentieth century, although it is certainly not a substitute for the study of history. Theory becomes a social force when it
finds an organizational instrument as historically remarkable as
the Bolshevik parties who utilize it as the lever to move great
masses. Yet if theory helps to make history, it is also totally impossible to understand that theory except as itself made historically,
and by situating it in its proper historical context. I shall shortly
return to this point.

Why study Marxism? For much the same reason we study ge-
netics. Marxism is the genetic code, the germ plasm of the main
twentieth century revolutions and of the societies they created.
Like any genetic influence, it interacts with its environment and is
only part of what shapes outcomes; but it *is* a vital part, and without understanding it we cannot understand many of the great
events of the century.

The Two-Marxisms Project as Critique

The project here is, at one level, a critique of Marxism which rests
upon some assumptions of Marxism itself and is thus, in part, an
auto-critique of Marxism. Indeed, the very idea of a critique,
originally rooted in Kant's critique of pure and practical reason,
was transmitted and reshaped by Marx. In saying this, however,
no ritual piety is intended and it will soon be plain that I am not
one of those who thinks a critique is something one inflicts on
others. Since the original idea of a critique was never unambiguous, and since my own view of it is what counts here, I had best
turn at once to say what I mean by critique.

1. To understate: Marxism is something concerning which
there are differences of opinion and strong feelings. It is certain
that anyone interested enough in Marxism to read this work will
find things that go against his grain; indeed, I take it as axiomatic
that any reader who works his way through this volume without (at
least) some spasm of irritation is either a saint or has altogether
wasted his time. Yet critique, for me, is in no way an effort to
debunk or unmask a theoretical system, is never undertaken as an
occasion in which the critic outsmarts his subject, and certainly
never views the subject's work as the mere product of an historical
mistake or ignorance.

It would seem—at least to those who do not hold mankind in contempt—that Marxism, which has won fully a third of the world today, could not have done so if it were bereft of all reason; and so a critique searches for Marxism's rationality. At the same time, a critique, seeing a theory as a human product, can have no impulse to canonize it. Conceiving theory as a doing and making by persons caught up in some specific historical era, critique searches for the limits no less than the achievements of a theory. A critique then is a lapidary act: it strives to discern and strike off from Marxism (as from any doctrine) its flawed, erroneous, and irrational parts, so that it may rescue its productive and rational side, polishing and resituating this in a new intellectual setting.

2. To critique a theory is a very active act; engaging the theory in dialogue, it inevitably interweaves commentary with exegesis, paying scrupulous attention to what the theorist's text says, while at the same time recognizing that the meaning of any text (as of any life) is never limited to its author's self-understanding. It must be interpreted, never merely recited. A theory contains a message some part of which is surely the author's and known to him, but another part is only glimpsed and is opaque even to him. It is therefore not rendered altogether intelligible simply by putting down his prefatory explanations of what his work is about. For all prefaces (yes, all) are written only after the fact, are efforts to construct an account of what has already been done, which renders it consistent and acceptable; therefore, they are partly justifications no less than explanations, partly distorting no less than clarifying. An author's own account of himself, then, can never really be altogether superior to someone else's account of him.

To critique a theory, then, is to think about it not as a culturally privileged object but as another object of culture, to be understood as we attempt to understand, say, a novel by William Gass, a cinema by Kirosawa, a play by Pinter, the layout and architecture of Red Square in Moscow, a life such as Antonio Gramsci's, or an event such as Louis Napoleon's coup. Such a view of theory, it must be admitted, is somewhat at variance with theory's own exalted self-conception, which tends to present itself as if it were altogether transparent to itself and knowledgeable about what it is up to. The first commandment of the theorist's guild is, after all, know what you are doing. Critique takes note of this special requirement, sees theorists as bound by such a pledge, but yet as no more capable of living a life without shadows than anyone else. To view Marx or Marxism as having shadows, silences, subtexts beneath the text, is thus in no way to debase it but only to see it as sharing in the common human condition.

3. A critique sees a theory as embodying the unique talents of some intellectual craftsmen, the standards, traditions, and concerns of their craft, and also of the larger society, culture, and historical epoch in which the craft is practised. It is to see theory as a technical product, but never as that alone. To view theory as a craft object is to see it as an object in which both personality and history, individual and group, are blended into focussed statement. To view Marxism from the standpoint of critique is thus to see it as something more than the product of lonely and tormented genius, or as the work of warrior scholars, while at the same time recognizing that, since the life of theory is concerned with transcending the commonplace, it is always a precarious performance.

Although Marxists would be the first to agree that a critique must view theory as a social and historical product—and thus as something more than the result of other and earlier theories, philosophies, or ideologies—they are not particularly eager to do this. Like "normal" academic sociologists, who are often made uneasy by the sociology of knowledge (and downright distraught by a sociology of sociology), Marxists likewise do not hurry to their rendezvous with a Marxism of Marxism; which is in part why, as Perry Anderson writes, "the history of Marxism has yet to be written."[8] For Marxists as for sociologists, reflexive efforts at historical self-understanding are often taken as narcissistic, diverting enquiry from its proper objective of understanding (not to speak of changing) the world.

That Marxism, like academic sociology, is indeed an historical and social product also discomfits those Marxists who think themselves social "scientists." For if it is an historical product, shaped by social needs no less than reason and research, it is part of the tissue of its time, rather than an eruption without precedent or an achievement without peer. This perspective on Marx and Marxism, then, will not be congenial to those like Louis Althusser who celebrate "Marx's discovery as the greatest event in the history of human knowledge, since the appearance of mathematics, somewhere in Greece,"[9] or who like to shroud Marxism's origin in the mystique of an unaccountable *coupure épistemologique*, setting it altogether apart from (and above) other achievements of its time. Critique, however, genuflects to no theory or theorist.

4. If critique views Marxism as the product of need no less than

reason, it also goes one step further, asking *whose* need. Certainly, Marxism never doubted that a critique required an answer to that question. Moreover, any inquiry into social theory that lets matters rest simply by setting theory in its general historical context, without also relating it to the generative interests of some specifiable social group, cannot be deemed a critique in any remotely Marxist sense. The matter, then, will in the end come down to a question that will be viewed either as outrageous or as simple-minded: What is Marxism's *class* grounding? What, in short, is its class origin?

This question will be viewed as simple-minded by those Marxists who, reciting by rote the catechism that "Marxism is the consciousness of the working class," think that this says all that needs saying, conveniently forgetting that Marxism also says: "Consciousness is determined by social being." If that is so, how can the proletarian consciousness of Marxism have been generated by the bourgeois social being of its authors? The question of Marxism's class origins will, however, be viewed as outrageous by those Marxists who suspect that the answer to be given here is not the mechanical and contradictory answer some of them conventionally offer.

5. Although critique views theory as expressing and relying on the needs and standards of the various groups from which it emerges, it does not assume that theory and theorist are related to this social context only in a harmonious or dependent way. On the contrary. Critique also sees theory-work as commonly shaped by a *conflict* with its environment and as proceeding, in particular, by opposing parts of it: elements of its *technical tradition,* on the one side, and of the "common sense," on the other.

Like other social theories, Marxism emerged in an ambivalent relationship—i.e., both relying on and opposed—to different parts of its technical tradition and to the culture of the everyday life around it. Marxism established its own identity only by drawing a line between itself and such technical traditions as Hegel's philosophical idealism or English political economy, as well as elements of the then common sense such as religion or conventional political ideologies. More than most theories, Marxism emerged in the form of a thrusting polemic against other views, as indicated by the very titles of its works: *Critique of Hegel's Philosophy of Law; The Holy Family* (a polemic against Bruno Bauer and others); *Critique of Political Economy; Anti-Dühring; Critique of the Gotha Program.*

To understand Marxism, as any theory, then, requires an understanding not only of the intellectual allies and ancestors from which it draws its resources but also of its intellectual adversaries and the competitors from which it painstakingly sought to distinguish itself. Theory-work is not done just by "adding another brick to the wall of science" but often involves throwing bricks as well; it not only involves paying one's intellectual debts but also (and rather differently) "settling accounts."

6. If the idea of a critique insistently focuses attention on the *con*text of a text—i.e., its historical and technical origins—it also views texts themselves as embodying their own internal contradictions which it insistently seeks to identify and understand. But critique, as understood here, does not assume that only our adversaries are vulnerable to contradictions; it premises that even forces with whom one is aligned—we heroes—also have their own contradictions. From this standpoint, then, Marxism will be seen as possessing its own contradictions, and contradiction will not be understood simply as a stigma of Marxism's enemies.

For some (vulgar) Marxists, to speak of Marxism's own contradictions is to deprecate and even slander it. It seems to say that Marxism shares something of the defective existence of the very life it wishes to abrogate. But who could deny that? A consistent auto-critique of Marxism can do no other; it must insist that Marxism too—*even* Marxism and *even* socialism—has its own internal contradictions. An attempt to take hold of these must deal with Marxism's living contradictions, not simply the vestigial remnants of Marxism's birth, its bourgeois heritage or Victorian prejudices; it must view Marxism's own contradictions as a living part of Marxism even today, and as an essential key to its present condition and future prospect.

6.1 To speak of Marxism's own contradictions is, I am aware, to use a metaphor *insofar* as Marxism is more than a system of propositions, the truth of one of which implies the falsity of another. Yet Marxism is considerably more than a system of propositions or a doctrine; it is a larger organized community of actors pursuing a revolutionary project. Can actors' *actions*, as well as the propositions they utter, also be contradictory? Does it help to look upon them in this way? Certainly it is legitimate to hold that propositions may be contradictory but what of persons' (other) actions?

To speak of actors' actions as "contradictory," is *not*, be it noted, a commitment to a general "dialectic of nature" in which *all na-*

ture is held to be potentially contradictory; my comments only embody a limited dialectic of *social* action and not of Nature. All human conduct may be regarded as embodying messages and meanings some of which are reducible to propositional forms; and so human conduct itself can be contradictory, even in a strict construction of "contradiction." Yet to view social conduct as potentially contradictory or not, is to view persons *as if* they were logicians and rational, which they are, but *only* in part. Contradiction here, then, is indeed, a metaphor.

In this, however, it is not different from other equivalent characterizations of actors and their conduct as, for instance, speaking of their being in "tension," "strain," or as possessing "dissonance." All of these also entail metaphors. If contradiction likens social conduct to logic, "tension" seems an organic (even medical) metaphor likening action to the body's or mind's exhaustion; "strain" seems a mechanical metaphor likening social conduct to the overload, say, on a bridge; "dissonance" seems a musical or accoustical metaphor likening some actions to intolerable sounds. Some such metaphors are inescapable and ought, it seems to me, to be judged largely by their consequences; by whether or not they make it possible to focus systematically on implications of consequence. All these metaphors—contradiction, strain, tension, dissonance—have an overlapping implication, commonly calling attention to the increased probability of change in the actions or persons thus characterized, or to the improbability of such things remaining as they were. If critique commits us to a concern with contradiction, then, it does so because its project is the study of *change* and of its mechanisms.

In viewing Marxism, either as a system of propositions or of actions, as potentially contradictory, my intent is not to render a judgement against Marxism's irrationality but, first of all, to insist: that Marxists are themselves concerned with being and seeming to be rational; that the requirements of rationality are important to *them* no less than to us; that they will not simply be seen here as billiard balls whose movements are produced only by external forces, but as persons attempting to live in conformity with standards they deem proper, including those of rationality; and therefore, they will exert themselves to pursue courses of conduct, partly because those courses are noncontradictory, and they will seek to escape contradiction or the appearance of it. In asserting my interest in the contradictory character of Marxist ideas and actions I am thus asserting my assumption that Marxists are in part actors committed to and capable of rationality, who are in part shaped by their efforts to be or to seem such.

6.2 To make a critique implies a concern with identifying the contradictions, strains, or dissonances embedded in Marxism, with a view to seeing certain other parts of the theory as efforts to reduce, control, or remove these, as well as a concern with the resulting development of the theory. One task of critique, then, is structural: to lay out and exhibit the elements opposing one another. Another part, is dynamic: to explore the results of that opposition.

From the standpoint of critique, both the structure and dynamics of opposition are understood as achievements brought about by those holding the theory, being maintained partly by their commitments and partly by the conditions within which these are lived.

One of the most general consequences of a contradiction in theory is to separate the mutually opposing elements, reducing their mutual interaction by splitting them off from the single system in which they first exist, and segregating them from one another by incorporating each in different (systems or) subsystems that are (at least) partly insulated from one another. In other words, different subsystems may be elaborated through (and result in) a process of increasing *differentiation* of the initial system, so that each of the formerly contradictory elements is now enclosed in boundaries reducing its interaction with the other. It will be my contention that primary Marxism has a "nuclear contradiction," and that this generates and recurrently reproduces (at least) two boundaried subsystems of elaborated theory that I will call Scientific Marxism and Critical Marxism.

6.3 Among other, specific types of contradictions that are discernible in Marxism are those that will be called "anomalies." These may be conceived as observations or assumptions that are at variance with expectations derived from prior theoretical commitments. Nothing, then, is inherently anomalous but only in relation to some theoretically grounded expectation.

It is not supposed that an observation *automatically* generates an anomaly, which, without interpretation, is taken to be divergent from theoretical expectation. Whether or not an observation is anomalous is a definition produced by some interpretation; but any observation can always be interpreted or defined as either conforming to or departing from theoretical expectation. Even when, from some third party's standpoint, a given observation may seem anomalous, the theorist who made it may not see it that way. On the contrary, he often has a strong impulse to "normalize" observations, i.e., to somehow define them as consistent with his expectations, by accommodating observation to theory or by denying the need for an accommodation. I shall return shortly to the problem of normalization. For the moment, however, I simply want to stress that whether or not an observation is anomalous is a produced act, a definition made via interpretation, rather than imposed and dictated by the "data" itself.

6.4 There are at least *two* types of anomalies—research-generated and event-generated anomalies—our study of Marxism will encounter. The first is a divergence from expectations produced by deliberate efforts of scholarship; these research-generated anomalies are produced by scholars' own initiatives and technical interests, and would not have occurred but for some scholar's activity. The second, event-generated anomalies, seem to be produced by "history," i.e., they are not contradictions of theoretical expectation generated by scholarly initiative. In short, they are not "academic problems" arising within scholarly work but "practical" problems arising "outside" a theory. The first, research-generated anomaly derives from reading or observation that may be made only by some scholar; the second, event-generated anomaly refers to *newspaper*-relevant events, hence visible even to "laymen" and all who read newspapers. The event-generated anomaly derives from "practical" events visible to laymen but which do *not* become anomalies unless, additionally, viewed from the standpoint of some theoretical expectation from which they are defined as diverging.

Among the *research*-generated anomalies in Marxism that will be examined are Marx's "observations" on the role of the state in the course of studying *The Eighteenth Brumaire of Louis Bonaparte* and, a few years later, his observation of the Asiatic Mode of Production or Oriental Despotism. The *event*-generated anomalies of most importance to Marxism that will be discussed come in two waves: first, the "observed" failure of capitalism to self-destruct following the long depression of the last quarter of the nineteenth century; secondly, the success of the revolution where it was least expected (in Russia), and its failure where it was most expected (in industrially advanced central and Western

Europe). The first, event-generated anomaly contributed to
Bernstein's "revisionism"; the second accelerated the decline of
"scientific" Marxism and the rise of Critical Marxism.

Critique, then, centers on contradictions: first, contradictions
between a theory, in its "foreign relations" with other views,
whether these are technical theories or assumptions of the "common sense," i.e., the theories of the everyday life; and secondly,
critique focuses on contradictions internal to a theory, whether
those termed here its "nuclear contradiction," or others termed
"anomalies," whether research-generated or event-generated.

6.5 Critique expects theorists will be far more ready to acknowledge (and even accent) contradictions between their own
theoretical expectations and those of other theorists. Correspondingly, critique expects theorists to be far less ready to acknowledge the existence of internal contradictions within their
own theory, or between their theory and their own research observations or with event-generated information.

The Lure of Normalization

External contradictions generate "polemics" that lead theorists to
overstate differences between their own theory and others and to
neglect their similarities, thereby contributing to boundary formations which are identity-defining for a theory. Here the task of
critique is to *resist* the overstatement of the divergence and, also,
the repression of the convergence between a theory and others.
More importantly, critique also resists those deeper and more
powerful impulses to deny, gloss, repress, and conceal internal
contradictions and anomalies in a theory. External contradictions
are more likely to be expected and polemically visible; internal
contradictions, however, constitute improprieties that generate
powerful impulses to conceal them and to resist efforts to uncover
or even discuss them.

6.6 A theory, in short, is expected and permitted to be at war
with other theories but not with itself; thus when internal contradictions are glimpsed, theorists are exposed to powerful pressure to *normalize* their theory. To "normalize" is an effort to reduce the dissonance between how an object is *supposed* to appear
and how in fact it seems to be, by treating it as if it really was what
it was supposed to be; by actually perceiving its traits as they
should be; or by denying or ignoring "improper" traits. Normalization includes all those devices by which disparities glimpsed

between what we see and what we deem right are somehow reduced. The task of the critical theorist is to resist impulses to normalize the world, however comforting they are, and to enable persons to "recover" what they have already noticed but never really assimilated. To paraphrase Alfred North Whitehead, everything of importance has been noticed by somebody who did not see it. The task of the critical theorist, then, is to mediate between persons and their own experience, enabling them to appropriate critically something already a part of them, helping them to make it their own.

Among the important forms of normalizing maneuvers are those induced by disparities between the imputed "goodness" (or badness) of an object and its imputed "power" (or weakness). Commonly, objects perceived as good are normalized by also perceiving them as strong; those seen as weak are normalized by defining them as deservedly so because "bad." Here, to normalize is to attempt to see things regarded as good also as powerful, or to change and make them such if seen as weak; "the bottom rail," it is promised, will in time "become the top." Conversely, the bad but powerful object will and should get its comeuppance, meet its nemesis, have justice inflicted upon it. Thus *it is not that powerful objects are always seen as good* but special tension and remedial efforts are generated if they are not, and these proceed either by reducing their power or enhancing their imputed goodness. Thus "populists" have often seen the powers that be as bad, but what makes them "populists" is their effort to change that.

Again, those powerful in society find the weakness of those beneath them highly convenient, but they do not commonly say that this very weakness of the subjugated is for that reason good; they define it as *appropriate* because the subjugated are imputed to be slothful, untrustworthy, incompetent, cowardly, or dirty, etc., and possessed of other "bad" traits. In short, an imputed lack of goodness makes the subjugated *deservedly weak*—in the eyes of the powerful. Correspondingly, a ruling group may be said to be an hegemonic elite when its power corresponds to a goodness—e.g., competence, bravery, productivity, etc.—imputed to them by the subordinated.

A macho or sexist culture may view feminine "weakness" or that of children as "endearing" not because good but because "natural." In both cases, weakness is defined as appropriate to the *nature* of their being—i.e., as beyond good and evil. The child is expected to overcome this condition—i.e., to equilibrate power and goodness—in time by maturation. The woman is expected to overcome her own *natural* weakness, precisely insofar as she is imputed to be "good," through the deserving protection of powerful males which will overcome or compensate for her natural weakness, thereby achieving a potency appropriate to her goodness.[10]

The young Marx held that the proletariat (feminine in its present weakness)[11] is good, being the bearer of universal interests; but he also maintained that the proletariat is destined to be the new repository of power and to become the ruling class. Marxism thus normalizes history and the working class.

6.7 Critique, however—the kind of critique to which I am committed here—considers all those bearing such glad tidings, in which the (suffering and good) bottom rail must become the top, to be suspect precisely because theirs is such a routine normalization. The critique to which I am committed seeks to make it possible to see whether and when the social world has become "abnormal" and thus recognize those occasions when the powerful are bad and the good weak, and that things may even remain this way, resisting all temptations to exclude them from reality or to compensate for an abnormal present with the guarantee of a normalized future. It is intrinsic, then, to the critique practiced here to reject an account of history that is essentially polyannalike, and to help persons bear bad news concerning their most cherished projects, neither overestimating their own chances nor underestimating the prospects of their adversaries. The critique I practice is stripped of the myth of inevitable progress. It does not believe that the evil are *destined* to lose power, that the good are *fated* to win it, or that we will *inevitably* surpass our ancestors; indeed, the critique practiced here is thoroughly confident that none of this can be improved upon without controlling the impulse to normalize.

The analytic rules by which I am guided, here as in other studies, bear of course upon the question of "objectivity." Most particularly the rules that I obey here call upon me to attend to specially and to bring out those sides of a matter that the participants themselves might prefer to *avoid*. The rule I follow says that, if there is something systematically silenced in an area of discussion, it is the analyst's responsibility to bring it into focus. In this analytic, then, it is a critical theorist's special task to speak the bad news. In the topic at hand, this has various applications but perhaps the most striking will be that I have felt a special obligation to attend most closely to the *limits*—politically and theoretically—of those Hegelian readings of Marxism for which I, like other intellectuals, feel the most sympathy, rather than adding my voice to the chorus of condemnation of "scientific" Marxism, of its authoritarianism and "economism," or of Engels's presumable "vulgarization" of Marx. The critic's special mission, I also hold, is to protect those very intellectual values which are made most precarious in a world of encapsulated specializations, that is, to husband the fading contemporary sense of complexity, reuniting things our culture has already fragmented.

Taking Language Seriously

If the above attempt to clarify my own usage of critique has been successful it needs to be added that, even at its best and most powerful, the idea of critique does not encompass and entirely characterize the resources I propose to use in understanding Marxism. Critique is the center but not the totality of these resources. A fuller account of them includes five other ideas:

1. A proper discussion of a theory, I shall hold, must be textually responsible and should never be so interpretatively arrogant as to neglect questions of what in fact was said in the texts, hurrying on from this presumably simple-minded question to the more exhilarating heights of hermeneutics. I think I yield to no one when it comes to an awareness of the inescapability of interpretation and of the naivete of believing that a text can be rendered without presupposition. Nonetheless, Marxist scholarship faces real problems of tampered and suppressed texts, indeed, of ambiguous and concealed authorship. Moreover, the authors themselves sometimes plant misleading views concerning their own texts, as, for instance, when Marx avers, in his introduction to the second edition of the *Eighteenth Brumaire* that he confined himself to "mere corrections of printer's errors and to striking out allusions now no longer intelligible." Similarly there is no doubt that Engels felt free to revise certain of Marx's own formulations after the latter's death. Again, texts long thought to have been Marx's, including some of the articles for the *New York Herald Tribune,* are now known to have been ghosted by Engels. My intent in mentioning this is certainly not to cast suspicion on Engels for any impropriety or to prepare the reader for an unmasking of his differences with Marx. I mean simply to indicate that there are times when questions of textual authentication are important, both to ground our own interpretations and to evaluate the interpretations of others. There have, for example, been interpretations which have so differed from my own that the first thing required was to establish whether we were really working from the same text.

I have also found it highly valuable to pay close attention to the date when a work was in progress and to distinguish this from its date of publication. It was also useful to discern whether a given work was in fact published by Marx and Engels themselves, whether it was published posthumously, and, if only posthumously, whether they themselves had earlier sought to have it published but, for whatever reason, failed to do so. Thus Marx's famous "Theses on Feurbach," a major early text justifying an interpretation of Marxism as a theory of practice, was written in 1845 but was published posthumously only by Engels in his *Ludwig Feurbach* of 1888; there is no evidence that Marx himself ever sought to have it published. In contrast, Marx and Engels's *The German Ideology,* although first written in the summer of 1846, did seek but could find no publisher and was left to the "gnawing criticism of the mice," only part being published during their lifetimes.

When something was written, whether the authors wanted it published or whether it was published only posthumously but without their permission, are important bits of information for interpreting it. They constitute elemental parts of a manuscript's *con*-text. In the modern period, it is noteworthy that the two most celebrated breakthroughs in Marx-Engels scholarship entailed the new availability of manuscripts that were published only posthumously. The first of these was Marx's "Economic and Philosophical Manuscripts" which, while developed in 1844, were not published until 1932 in Berlin. The second was the so-called *Grundrisse* which, although written during 1857–58 in London, was not widely known until the single volume edition by Dietz Verlag in 1953.

Every writer knows that there are apt to be substantial differences of many kinds between his published and unpublished work. For all manner of reasons, writers often blanch at the prospect of the posthumous publication of their hitherto unpublished manuscripts. The implications of a manuscript's being unpublished at the time of an author's death are not always transparent nor are they always the same. It would be naive to assume, then, that published and unpublished works constitute identical grounds for inferring an author's considered position.

The distinction between published and unpublished work—as distinct from poorly and fully developed work—is important, moreover, not so much for learning what an author actually thought or believed; it may also indicate a difference between positions he was prepared to present publicly and others he may have thought less attractive or defensible. Every published work, like the proverbial tip of the iceberg, is a literary superstructure erected on a substructure of unpublished work and on which it is in many ways grounded, even though the latter, literary "graveyard," may not be as rigorous as the work publicly presented. Much of the dramaturgy of literary production is concerned with making salient, defensible, or attractive things, while concealing—often through not publishing them—the ungrounded or unattractive positions on which they may rest. Published as distinct from unpublished work is a visible indicator (when we have access to the latter) of the values the author wishes to support or with which he wishes to be identified, of the kind of scholar/writer he wishes to be thought of as being, and of the audiences to which he wishes to appeal. Unpublished work is often (not always) a form of self-censorship also indicating, if in its own different ways, the author's commitments.

It is thus important to discern whether an author's unpublished works share any common characteristics differentiating them from those he published, for these may help explain why they had been censored. Marx's unpublished work, then, need not be less indicative of what he "really thought"; but this may suggest that a certain line of thought created important difficulties for him or that he was uneasy about being seen in public with them. When there is a line of thought common to a body of unpublished work it suggests that it is inserted in his work at a special level, not that it is absent from the work, and suggests how the structure of his *oeuvre* acquired its form. To distinguish an author's unpublished work helps us see that certain positions may, indeed, be "his" yet not necessarily exist at the same level in his work as those positions he published. That, to anticipate, is what I shall hold concerning the two different syndromes in Marx's work, Critical and Scientific Marxisms, as I term them here.

2. One important implication of taking texts seriously is that we take *language* seriously. While not in the least imagining that

Marxism is "only" a theory or that its success or failure depends only on its theory, Marxism is still in important part a theory; as a socialism it is distinguished by the importance it attributed to theory (and theorists) and cannot be understood unless its theory is understood. It is on this theory that we focus here. As theory, Marxism is above all language. Whatever our views on Marxism as a "science" and whether science or not, Marxist theory is expressed in language and in a system of communication. Our linguistic perspective disposes us to seek whatever assistance we can derive for an understanding of Marxism from disciplines concerned with the analysis of speech or silence, of texts or subtexts, of spoken and written forms of communication, whether these are a sociology of language, aspects of sociolinguistics, or even elements of literary criticism. An understanding of what Marxism means will be greatly facilitated if we take what it says and how it says this quite seriously.

3. In turn, our language perspective on Marxism indicates that, if we often adopt Marxist assumptions here in attempting to understand Marxism, we will not *confine* ourselves to Marxist precept—and certainly not at all to Marxist self-understanding—in interpreting Marxism. In particular, I have throughout also viewed Marxism from the standpoint of sociology, for each is a sister discipline to the other. Both sociology and Marxism arose in the nineteenth century as part of the emerging naturalistic view of persons and society and, indeed, of the still larger development of the natural sciences. Both Marxism and sociology developed much (and sometimes too much) of their intellectual identity from the larger emergence of natural sciences. Yet if they are sister disciplines, the two are also sibling rivals.

To hear Marxists talk, as they sometimes scoff at sociology's "triviality" and especially its powerlessness in the world, there might seem to be no comparison between the two. On this question of sociology's powerlessness, Marxists are quite right; it is true that sociology—as Stalin once remarked of the Vatican—commands no armies. To this, of course, sociologists might rejoin, that their object was not to be powerful but right, and, if powerless, they at least bear no responsibility for the vast political catastrophes, such as Stalinism, by which Marxism has been tainted.

The point of using sociology here, to understand Marxism, is of course because it provides intellectual leverage. For both Marxism and sociology, having developed partly in polemical opposition to one another, have each developed knowledge and insight the other has neglected. Precisely for that reason, then, each has much to contribute to understanding the other. Since I have already presented my critical account of sociology, in *The Coming Crisis of Western Sociology* (1970), my attention here now turns to the other side of that sibling relationship. I have found it helpful not to limit myself to Marxism's own theoretical perspective but also often use those views it has systematically neglected, the work of Emile Durkheim, Max Weber, and other sociologists. Sister disciplines like sisters know a great deal about each other at the deepest levels and, if listened to critically, may be heard to say incisive things about the other. It is this that gives them the right to participate in the dialogue, not their association with power which only corrodes them both and which, once more, brands them as siblings.

4. Part of taking Marxist theory seriously means that we must not only view it as a produced object but also as a producer, as having an effect upon the world even as it is affected by it. Certainly a doctrine such as Marxism which extols the "unity of theory and practice" cannot fault an effort to understand the theory's effects upon the social world. Yet the moment we begin to take Marxism seriously in this way, exploring its relation to political practice, we will be told by Marxists (and some academic "social historians" alike) that we cannot properly hold Marxism at fault for the political failures with which it has been associated. Most particularly, this will be the judgement of those who want to dissociate Marxism from the rise of Stalinism in the Soviet Union. Seeking to rescue Marxism and socialism from disgrace by association with those terrible events, some Marxists tell us that they were produced only because the Bolsheviks betrayed or misunderstood Marxism, rather than enacted it faithfully; or that these events were simply the outcome of the overriding special backwardness of Russian society, or of the "force of circumstances" there, thus assuring us that Marxism—the disembodied thing in "itself"—bears no share of the blame and should not be surrendered.

To explore the links between Marxism and Stalinism is, nonetheless, a litmus test of the capacity of Marxism to attain its emancipatory aims and of the problems encountered in achieving these in practice; it also provides an important perspective on the political vulnerabilities to which Marxist theory may be susceptible, that bear on its own basic reason for existence—its potential contribution to human liberation. Nowhere, however, will I argue that Marxism contained the seeds of its own inevitable undoing nor imply that Stalinism was an unavoidable outgrowth of the "inherent logic" of Marxism.

The Russian revolutions could be pursued only in clandestine forms under Czarist absolutism with its secret police, gallows, mass arrests, deportations and exiles, and these created conditions conducive to counter-terror and counter-repression. Lacking deep-rooted traditions of political freedom, either from their own national culture or from their rebellion against it, facing the resistance of powerful forces within and outside of their own society, isolated from European ideas and from assistance by socialists in the West, and bent on imposing themselves despite the resistance of the country's overwhelming majority—its peasantry—the Bolsheviks quickly adopted terror, total censorship, and absolute authoritarianism as a way of life.

Yet having said this, we cannot conclude that Marxist theory itself bears no responsibility at all for what happened. We cannot act as if Stalinism was simply a myth invented to slander Marxism. Marxists were and are historically unique political men in their emphasis on intellectuality and in their commitment to theory. More than any other political movement, Marxism insisted on taking its theory seriously. It will be totally incomprehensible as a political community unless an effort is made to understand how this theory was linked to the political catastrophes with which it is associated. In short, the examination of Marxist theory to follow is centrally inspired by the conviction that Marxist practice has in some substantial measure been shaped by its theory and that if we wish to understand this practice, and the Marxist societies under which a third of the world's population now lives, we cannot ignore the substantial role of Marxist theory, anymore than we can hold it alone responsible for events.

5. I began by saying that the project here was, "at one level," a critique of Marxism. The qualification indicated bears upon the fact that I am not interested in *Marxist* theory alone, for its own sake or even for understanding political events; I also wish to use the occasion to deepen an understanding of the life of theory more generally, of how any kind of social theory is produced and develops. This, however, means there is a moment of reflexivity in our undertaking, for among the social theories into which we seek insight—even as we wield it—is, of course, our own.

Let me add immediately, however, that unlike certain forms of theorizing, I am not primarily concerned to seize this occasion to exhibit my own concept of reason, and especially not to use my commitment to reflexivity to divert investigation from the topic at hand.[12] In contrast to "analytic" sociology, which can indifferently study Sherlock Holmes, Sigmund Freud, Woody Allen, Georg Simmel, or the Gospels, and somehow contrive to reach the same conclusion about them all, I am indeed committed to the topic at hand, to the study of Marxism, and to an attempt to grasp it in its uniqueness.

The project here, then, holds that a proper view of critique requires us to *respect the topic*. Analytic sociology is sometimes rather like an exotic carnivorous plant, flashing colorful "topics" only in order to attract edibles that it can assimilate into its own being and, in the end, it bores us because it transforms different topics into a single, uniform nutriment and excrement. My own different view of critique is as prepared to serve as be served and is as ready to answer as to ask questions; which means that it shall hew to its topic, even while striving for a reflexivity that knows it is always interpreting, reading, and constructing the Marxism of its critique.

Finally, the study of this very specific topic properly makes demands on us that another might not; most particularly, it requires us to speak candidly of the *political* perspective by which the following account is to be informed. Considering that the topic is Marxism, this demand is surely legitimate. Without using the occasion for extended political analysis, let what follows be thought of rather as a partial political summary of the conclusions at which I have arrived thus far, among which the following are most important.

In Western Europe a strange situation has developed. The dominant society, a bourgeois society that evolved into corporate, late capitalism succeeded in producing a revolutionary critique of itself in Marxism and socialism. I mean this rather precisely and rigorously, for Marxism was not just produced in *reaction against* bourgeois society and its elites but *by* them. The idea that Marxism was simply a critique of bourgeois society is, at best, only Marxism's limited self-understanding.

The Marxism that emerged in Western Europe, however, was never successful in winning state power in the territory of its birth, but only elsewhere in developing societies that, by its own standards, were "backward." The "socialist" solution to the contradictions and problems of capitalism turned out to be appealing only to societies in desperate straits and often not very capitalist. If the corruption, callousness, incompetence, and lassitude of the West are increasingly evident, so, too, are the pathologies and political monstrosities of capitalism's supposed antithesis, the "socialist" states intended to transcend the ills of capitalism.

Following the October Revolution, there was the extirpation of all socialist democracy in the first "socialist" state, the USSR, which subsequently laid the grounding of Stalinism that devastated Soviet society and leaves it still blighted. This Soviet State has exerted pressure on socialisms elsewhere and has widely reproduced in them its own "dinosaur" socialism, as far as it could. As other Marxist parties took power in Asia, this became the occasion not for a new internationalism but for a new internecine violence. The new Marxist states proved as mutually wary and self-aggrandizing as the old imperialisms. The Soviet State took it upon itself to invade "socialist" Hungary, Czechoslovakia, and East Germany. Socialist Cambodia, having produced a society whose authoritarianism was so primitive that it could not be properly called "totalitarian," engaged in depredations against socialist Vietnam which, in turn, and with the prior consent of the Soviet Union, launched a full-scale invasion of Cambodia and placed her under a puppet regime, which in turn caused China, Cambodia's patron, to launch its own massive punitive invasion of Vietnam. This, of course, causes profound gratification to those who supported France and the United States's earlier wars against Vietnam. Marxist socialism, in short, did not overturn the clash of empires but raised it to a new level.

The political uniqueness of our own era, then, is this: we have lived and still live through a desperate political and social malaise while, at the same time, we have also *outlived* the desperate revolutionary remedies that had once been thought to solve it. The old illnesses remain but the remedies once proposed for them, including Marxism, have not really improved the human prospect. We live, then, in a period when—except for those with millenarian talents—the West's political past and its political future have alike exhausted themselves. It is, therefore, time to begin a fundamental rethinking of our historical and our theoretical position. Our study, then, is informed by this political vision and it aims to make a contribution to the larger, ongoing discussion needed to transcend the unique contradictions of our era.

The Crisis Within Marxism

If this situation speaks to the existence of a crisis in the West, its unstanched wound, it speaks no less pointedly to a similar crisis for Marxists. Indeed, this has become so acute that many Marxists now openly acknowledge it.

The Swedish Marxist, Göran Therborn has thus observed that the lack of a Marxism of Marxism "is hardly warranted by the history of Marxism, which has in no sense been a success story free from blockages and reversals. Fundamental aspects of Marxist theory have been called into question both by its historic defeats, so far, in North America and Western Europe, and by the aftermath of its successes—Stalinism, the Sino-Soviet split, the present social and political condition of that third of the world claiming to be governed by Marxist theory. These and other contradictory and often unexpected developments of the union of Marxist theory and practice make it possible to speak also of a crisis of Marxism."[13]

Louis Althusser's appraisal of Marxism today is essentially similar in its implication. Although bland, his remarks are devastating in their import for Marx's expectations: "the revolution did not take place in nineteenth-century Britain nor in early twentieth-century Germany; it did not take place in the advanced countries at all, but elsewhere, in Russia, then later in China and Cuba, etc. . . . the revolutions which we know are either premature or miscarried."[14] This is nothing less than an acknowledgement that the most fundamental expectations of Marxism have been falsified by history.

It is particularly notable that Marxists' growing awareness of their internal crisis is not confined to one particular theoretical tendency; an essentially similar judgement is rendered not only by Scientific Marxists such as Althusser but by their ancient adversaries, Critical Marxists such as George Lukács. In his last interview with Franco Ferrarotti, while Lukács does not invoke "crisis" to characterize Marxism's condition, the substance of that idea is clearly conveyed:

> Marxism as a general theory of society has in fact undergone an interruption. It has stood still. One may say that Marxism, conceived as it should be conceived, as a general theory of society and of history, no longer exists, that it came to an end some time ago. . . . Our analysis stood still, but capitalism continued to evolve. We stopped with Lenin. After him there has been no Marxism.[15]

For Lukács, the source of these problems is essentially the incomplete and outmoded character of Marxism. In that vein,

Lukács notes that "Marx never studied seriously the economies of Asia, Africa, and Latin America" and adds that capitalism has so changed that "it is utterly useless to refurbish the idea of individual profit of the capitalistic type or to invoke the law of the market . . . the nineteenth-century market is dead!" Thus "there are new phenomena about which we have nothing to say," such as mass consumerism among the working class, which serves to limit economic crises.

Lucio Colletti, too, has added his own substantial authority as a Marxist scholar to the widening consensus concerning the crisis in Marxism. Colletti focuses on its manifestations in the avoidance by leading Marxist economists of the central Marxist categories of value and surplus value. "Baran and Sweezy [in their *Monopoly Capitalism*] decided they were unable to use the theory of value and of surplus value in their analysis of postwar US capitalism." But these concepts, observed Colletti, are the keystone of Marx's theory and, without them, "*Capital* crumbles." Colletti also notes with astonishment the reliance of Maurice Dobb and of young Italian Marxist economists on the work of Piero Sraffa. It is "absolutely absurd," says Colletti, to use him to shore up Marx's economics, since Sraffa's work "implies the demolition of the entire foundation of Marx's analysis" being a critique of neoclassical economics that involves a return, behind Marx, to Ricardo.

Noting that Marx's theory of the falling rate of profit has never been empirically verified; noting (like Althusser) that "the central test of *Capital*," namely, a socialist revolution in the industrially advanced West, has not yet come to pass; and observing the widening Sino-Soviet conflict, Colletti, too, concludes that "Marxism is in crisis today."[16] This, he adds, is a crisis which can be surmounted only on the condition that it first be acknowledged in its full extent, both theoretically and politically.

My own critique of Marxism is grounded in part in this growing recognition (among Marxists) of the contemporary crisis in Marxism. In my view however, to be developed below, this crisis was due not only to the fact that the world has outgrown a Marxism limited by its European-centered origins, or that Marxism was based on an intensive study of only one single case, the development of English capitalism. All these significant limits imputed to Marxism are correct, yet Marxism's problems go deeper still. The contemporary crisis of Marxism[17] derives also from the sharpening of a contradiction always inherent to it. In this respect, my view of Marxism differs from that shared by Lukács and Althusser, for both of them maintain a common silence about the internal contradictions that Marxism has and always had.

NOTES

1. Merle Fainsod, "Soviet Communism," in the *International Encyclopedia of Social Sciences*, vol. 3, ed. David L. Sills, 17 vols. (London: Macmillan & Co., 1968), p. 105.

2. V. I. Lenin, *What Is to Be Done?* (New York: International Publishers, 1929), cited on p. 27.

3. Ibid., pp. 27–28. Lenin's italics.

4. Cited in Lenin, ibid., p. 30.

5. Ibid., pp. 32–33.

6. Ibid., pp. 39–40.

7. Ibid., p. 118.

8. Perry Anderson, *Considerations on Western Marxism* (London: New Left Books, 1976), p. 1.

9. Louis Althusser, *Essays in Self-Criticism* (London: New Left Books, 1976), p. 110. It is notable that Althusser compares Marxism here with a formal discipline rather than an empirical science.

10. Moreover, in *macho* cultures, however "weak" women are defined as being, they are not usually defined as so weak as to be unable to "bear" or give birth to children or to offer no resistance to attacks on their "honor."

11. Indeed, in his *Critique of Hegel's "Philosophy of Right,"* Marx calls the proletariat a passive element and the "heart" of revolution whose virgin ignorance needs to be pierced by the lightning bolt of theory, the "head" of the revolution. "Revolutions require a passive element, a material basis . . . just as philosophy finds its material weapons in the proletariat, so the proletariat finds its spiritual weapons in philosophy; and once the lightning of thought has struck deeply into this naive soil of the people the emancipation of the Germans into men will be accomplished. . . . The head of this emancipation is philosophy, its heart is the proletariat." See Karl Marx, *Critique of Hegel's "Philosophy of Right,"* ed. Joseph O'Malley. (London and New York: Cambridge University Press, 1970), p. 138.

12. Thus Alan Blum holds that "every approach to a corpus is a re-view not of the corpus . . . but of our tradition of Rationality. We use Marx to once again put our tradition into view." But if that is *all* we do then we never have the opportunity to put *Marx's* tradition into view. There seems to be a certain confusion between reflexivity and narcissism here. Reflexivity means, among other things, that we are aware in scanning a text

that we do so within the limits of our own tradition and the perspective it affords; but narcissism views the other, the text, simply as a mirror in which to see our own image. Given what *he* calls his "violent" reading of Marx, Blum thus concludes that "theory and practice are metaphors for speech that is historically reflexive and speech that is forgetful . . . capitalism and socialism are respective code names for the typification of inquiry guided by interest, body, impulse, and situation, and for the ideal of inquiry guided by the standard of the Good." In the first instance, practice is reduced to speech and, in the second, socialism or capitalism to modes of inquiry. These are most imaginative readings. But one wonders why one should bother to bridle his imagination by confronting it with any text at all. See Alan Blum, "Reading Marx," *Sociological Inquiry*, Spring 1973, pp. 23, 30–31.

13. Göran Therborn, *Science, Class and Society* (London: New Left Books, 1976), p. 38. My own efforts differ from Therborn's in certain ways; among them that he commits himself to an Althusserian perspective which he does not appraise critically and thus launches himself upon a Marxism of Marxism in which "Marxism" has a taken-for-granted character. Indeed, we are *not* told how he understands the Marxism that he takes both as method and topic, and his work thus exhibits a lack of reflexivity inherently paradoxical in any effort at a "Marxism of Marxism." Most critically, Therborn's concept of Marxism, and his Marxism of Marxism, diverge from my own with respect to the different importance we each attribute to *contradiction*, I making it central to my conception of Marxism, while Therborn treats it as peripheral.

14. Althusser, *Essays in Self-Criticism*, p. 196.

15. "A Final Rethinking: Georg Lukács Talks with Franco Ferrarotti," *Social Policy*, July/August 1972, pp. 7, 57.

16. Quotations are from the interview with Lucio Colletti in *New Left Review*, July/August 1974.

17. No one has more deeply grasped, more comprehensively gauged, nor more concisely laid out "The Crisis in Marxist Sociology" than Norman Birnbaum (see *Social Research*, Summer 1968, pp. 348–80). Considering the brevity of his statement, it was definitive for that time. My own work here, not as acutely limited by spatial requirements as was his, differs from it in the following ways: (1) I stress the internal contradictions of Marxism which have been with it from the first. (2) Consequently, my own focus is on original Marxism, Marx and Engels's own work. (3) I focus on the genetic process through which this crisis develops over time during the founders' lifetimes, (4) seeing it as a result partly of the confrontation between their original paradigm and their own research-generated anomalies, (5) and partly as the product of history-generated anomalies, (6) which Marxism in both cases glossed and repressed for sociological reasons rather than systematically worked through and incorporated into a cumulatively developing theory. (7) I am concerned not

only with the theory's internal logic but additionally (as in chapter five, "The Social Origins of the Two Marxisms") I seek to explore some of the historical conditions for the original character and subsequent transformation of Marxism in millenarian movements, the development of natural science, the vagaries of the economic cycle, and the political dilemmas of the international socialist community. In a later volume on the social origins of Marxism, other historical moorings of Marxism will be systematically developed, including its technical antecedents. A recent discussion, "Some Reflections on the Crisis of Marxism," by the Spanish Marxist Fernando Claudin is interesting because it is not so much concerned with demonstrating the existence of the crisis in Marxism but, taking this for granted, dwells on the various reactions it has elicited among Marxists. See *Socialist Review*, May/June 1979, pp. 137–44.

2

MARXISM AS SCIENCE AND CRITIQUE

Marxism and theorists of the Marxist community have been divided, it has long been noticed,[1] into roughly two tendencies: one conceiving Marxism as "critique" and the other conceiving it to be some kind of social "science." Marxism has been divided then between Critical Marxists and Scientific Marxists, as I shall call them here.

Marx conceived of the emergence of socialism as depending on the prior maturation of certain "objective" conditions, especially the structures of an advanced industrialism, while also conceiving of capitalism as producing these conditions through the operation of its own blind, impersonal, and necessary laws. Thus viewed, capitalism is a stage in a social evolution *destined* to give rise to another, higher society—socialism.

At the same time, Marx did not think of his theory simply as a social science (the view of "clubby" academicians who want to "normalize" Marxism into something familiar). It was also a doctrine of violent revolution. Marxism is not attempting simply to understand society; it does not only predict the rise of a revolutionary proletariat that will overturn capitalism, but also actively mobilizes persons to do this. It intervenes to change the world. The problem is that if capitalism is indeed governed by lawful regularities that doom it to be supplanted by a new socialist society (when the requisite infrastructures have matured), why then stress that "the point is to change it"? Why go to great pains to arrange capitalism's funeral if its demise is guaranteed by science? Why must persons be mobilized and exhorted to discipline themselves to behave in conformity with necessary laws by which, it would seem, they would in any event be bound.

In his famous eleventh Thesis on Feuerbach Marx had held that "the philosophers have only interpreted the world in various ways; the point is to change it." This surely reads as if Marx was calling on people to put forth an effort to change their world in reality and not only in thought. Yet, the question is, what obliges them to do so? Marx does not reply by invoking some general ideal which he holds incumbent on persons, for he supposed such ideals are only the reflex of class interests. As Marx said, communism was the real movement that abolishes the present state of society, not just an ideal. But if communism is only a real social movement expressing laws of society, then Marx was just describing—and validating his description of—the social world, either predicting what will happen or stating what had already happened. Yet in the eleventh Thesis he is clearly doing more: he is *urging* persons to undertake action—i.e., "praxis."

That eleventh Thesis surely cannot be understood as saying that impersonal laws govern society; rather, that the purposive actions of men and women, to which Marx urges them, can shape human destiny. This implies that human effort and purpose, and the ideals shaping them, influence the outcome of human action. There is, then, a tension between Marx's dismissal of idealism and his call to change the world,[2] and it is a contradiction in Marx that existed almost from the beginning. Marx was a paradoxically idealistic materialist who suppressed his own idealism, declaring that he was not really pursuing an ideal but (like Socrates) was only a midwife delivering what had been prepared in the womb of history, and calling upon others to do likewise.

This ambiguity is reproduced in his conception of "praxis." Marx had two tacitly different conceptions of praxis or, as I will usually call it here, of practice: $Praxis_1$ is the unreflective labor on which capitalism rests, the wage labor imposed by necessity which operates within its confining property institutions and its stunting divisions of labor. While this labor inflicts an alienation upon workers, it also constitutes the foundation of that society, reproducing the very limits crippling workers. Here workers are constrained to contribute to the very system that alienates them. This conception of praxis is congenial to Scientific Marxism. In the second, more heroic concept of practice—$Praxis_2$, more congenial to Critical Marxism—emphasis is on a practice that is more freely chosen, most especially on political struggle. If $Praxis_1$ is the constrained labor that reproduces the status quo, $Praxis_2$ is the free labor contributing toward emancipation from it. In undertaking the first form of labor or practice, persons submit to necessity; in the second, however, they undertake a deliberate and Promethean struggle against it.

In one part, then, Marxism is a philosophy of praxis; in another it is a "science"—i.e., the political economy of the laws of capitalism. Marxism is thus a tensionful conjunction of science and politics, of theory and practice. Its topic is the objective socioeconomic conditions imputedly requisite for socialism. Its object in addressing this topic, however, is not only understanding but also a revolutionary practice aimed at changing the world. It must accomplish this, as all politics does, partly by appealing to and arguing with people, by attempting to persuade them through rational discourse and promises. For politics never assumes that since "history is on our side" we may wait for things and people to come our way; but it premises that outcomes depend upon the active mobilization of people. So Marxism is both: science and ideology; rational understanding and political practice; "reports" about the world and a "command" to do something to change it.

Yet there is also an irreducible tension between the call to do something now and the warning that those who do not wait for appropriate conditions or use scientific guidance are dangerous adventurers or mere "utopians." Marxism as science premises that some things will happen without men's rational foresight and whatever their efforts. As a *politics*, however, it also premises that events depend crucially on people's efforts, struggle, capacity for sacrifice, and self-discipline. Indeed, while all politics premises that men "must seize the time," science premises that things have their own nature and rhythms.

The two readings of Marxism briefly outlined here have, in part, grown up around the nuclear tension between voluntarism and determinism, between freedom and necessity. Both of these readings, let me hasten to insist, are a true part of Marxism. We are not faced with only a *seeming* contradiction that can be glibly resolved by claiming that one side is false, revisionist, opportunist, misguided, not really Marxist, while the other is the authentic, genuine, dyed-in-the-wool, true revolutionary article.

Our Two-Marxisms thesis maintains that both are in fact structural differentiations of a single originally undifferentiated Marxism; that over time the "two" emerge in *part* out of an effort to reduce the real internal tensions of original Marxism. Indeed, the Two Marxisms could not emerge as structurally distinct tendencies but for the fact that both are truly present in Marxism. Their conjunction in ordinary Marxism is recurrently productive of tensions and of a tension-reducing segregation of the inconsistent elements, by insulating them from one another into two (or more) distinct and boundaried systems of "elaborated" Marxisms, Critical and Scientific Marxism.

As I will document, Marxism did indeed *say* that capitalist society was governed by blind and necessary laws to which persons were inescapably subject; it is also true that Marxism *treats* persons as free agents who will not only do what they must, but who can respond to appeals and be won over *even against their own class interests*. There is thus both determinism and voluntarism in Marxism.

As the *Communist Manifesto* remarks, "a small section of the ruling class cuts itself adrift, and joins the revolutionary class. . . . Just as, therefore, in an earlier period, a section of the nobility went over to the bourgeoisie, so now a portion of the bourgeoisie goes over to the proletariat, and in particular, a portion of the bourgeois ideologists who have raised themselves to the level of comprehending *theoretically* the historical movement as a whole."[3]

If the blind laws of economics imprison people, it is also evident that Marx and Engels believed that *theoretical* enlightenment might cast the scales from their eyes and strike the shackles from their hands. Theory might make persons, or at least some persons, free. Indeed, they had made the same point earlier in *The German Ideology:* "the consciousness of a fundamental revolution, the communist consciousness . . . may, of course, arise among other classes than the impoverished working majority too, through the *contemplation* of the situation of this impoverished class."[4]

No one has better caught the impatient, voluntaristic spirit of a Critical Marxism—and the epistemological inclinations of that voluntarism—than the young Max Horkheimer:

> Present talk of inadequate conditions is a cover for tolerance of repression. For the revolutionary, conditions have always appeared right. What appears in retrospect as a preliminary state or a premature situation was once, for a revolutionary, a last chance to change. A revolutionary is with the desperate people for whom everything is on the line, not with those who have time. The invocation of a scheme of social stages which demonstrates *post festum* the importance of a past era was *at the time* an inversion of theory and politically bankrupt. . . . Critical theory . . . rejects the kind of knowledge that

one can bank on. It confronts history with that possibility
which is always concretely visible within it. . . . [Mankind is]
not betrayed by the untimely attempts of the revolutionaries
but by timely attempts by the realists.[5]

In distinguishing Critical and Scientific Marxisms, there is,
however, no intention of suggesting that the voluntarism/
determinism differentiation is the deepest "essence" or truest
meaning of that larger distinction. It is but one marker in a larger
set of elements constituting the two syndromes; the precise relationship of the elements and their relative importance for the
larger syndrome remain to be established empirically.[6]

Voluntarism/Determinism as Deep Structure

The tension between voluntarism and determinism within Marxism, and around which there clot the Two Marxisms, is not the
special plight of Marxism. It is, in fact, only the expression within
Marxism of a larger condition common to social theory, to
academic sociology no less than Marxism. It has thus been observed repeatedly that "sociological theories may be grouped
around two poles. The first presents us with a view of society as a
network of human meanings and as embodiments of human activity. The second . . . presents us with society conceived as a
thing-like facticity, standing over against its individual members
with coercive controls and moulding them in its socializing processes. . . . the first view presents us with man as the social being
and with society as being made by him, whereas the second view
sets society as an entity over and against man, and shows him
being made by it."[7]

The crucial problem of sociology is not to find clever ways in
which these two standpoints can be "harmonized" but, rather, to
accept that institutions made by men do somehow acquire a certain givenness opposed to their makers and to study the manner in
which this strange objectivity comes about: "One must take seriously the objectivity of social existence in its relatedness to human
subjectivity . . . and [ask how] is it possible that human activity
should produce a world of things . . ."[8]

But it would be intellectual parochialism to imagine that this
problem existed only for sociology or social science. Modern
philosophy itself reproduces some of these very limits and, in
particular, the tension between voluntarism and determinism.

The tension between existentialism and structuralism is a familiar case in point. "Existentialism focuses on the creating of meaning, structuralism focuses on structures of meaning as pre-given. . . . Existentialism assumes that social actors are moral agents who (in principle are able to) consciously intend their conduct. Structuralism assumes that intentions are *super*-intended by the deeper structures of the mind . . . laying behind or beneath the actors' conscious awareness."[9]

Nor is the dissonance between voluntarism and determinism peculiar only to modern secular thought as the tension between "free will" and "natural law" in Christian theology has long indicated. In fact, that centuries-long debate was but the theological scholasticism of an earlier encounter with the dilemma where, as in so many other spheres, religion's insight was preceded by myth in the earlier, imprinting culture of ancient Greece.

In the Greek view, there was a sacred law by which men were bound, there was a division of the cosmos by fate (or *Moira*) into distinct spheres by which even the gods themselves were bound. There was, in short, "necessity." Yet to pursue a course of conduct simply out of "necessity" was a slave's way and a free people insisted on going to their fate, even if this were death itself, out of their own free will. It was slavish for persons to be dragged to their fate; free people would face it unblinkingly. "Even if the fates have spun death for a man," said the poet, "he should always march straight forward carrying his spear."

When Oedipus sins, the land of Thebes suffers for it; yet Oedipus *could* sin. Law and destiny were imposed upon humanity, yet they were not robots and could conform to their destiny or might struggle against it. The Greek "necessity," then, did not contain the idea of the absolutely impossible. The boundaries around people, their destiny, could indeed be stretched or breached, at least momentarily; all that the law ensured was retribution for the breach, but could not prevent it from happening. The forbidden is not the same as the impossible; it is merely the costly, and men *can* do proscribed things if they are prepared to pay the price.

Such, at any rate, was something of the way in which the Greeks expressed the tension between (and sought to reconcile) freedom and necessity.[10] The tension between voluntarism and determinism in Marxism, then, is part of the deep structure of Western thought that it shares. Marxism did not invent this tension and it did not resolve it.

Critical and Scientific Marxism:
The Larger Paradigms

As different, elaborated paradigms of Marxism, Critical and Scientific Marxism emerge under different sociohistorical conditions and among different persons and in differentiated social networks and groups. It also seems clear that some who were Critical Marxists at one point in their lives may change and become Scientific Marxists at a later time, and vice versa.

The rolls of Critical Marxism include Georg Lukács, the early Karl Korsch, Antonio Gramsci, J-P. Sartre, Lucien Goldmann, Rudolph Bahro, Schlomo Avineri, Carmen Claudin-Urondo, the *Telos* circle in its more Lukácsian days, Victor Perez-Diaz, the "News and Letters" group in Detroit, and such members, or onetime members, of the "Frankfurt School" as Max Horkheimer, T. W. Adorno, Franz Neumann, Leo Lowenthal, Erich Fromm, Walter Benjamin, Herbert Marcuse, or its second generation, such as Albrecht Wellmer, Alfred Schmidt, and Jürgen Habermas.

Opposed to this distinguished group, there are other Marxists who eschew critical theory as mere ideology and who conceive Marxism as a true science. They include such men as Galvano della Volpe, and the Marxist mandarin of l'École Normale Supérieure, Louis Althusser, and those influenced by him, including (at one time) Nicos Poulantzas, Maurice Godelier, André Glucksmann, Charles Bettelheim; the intellectual leader of their Swedish outpost in Lund, Göran Therborn, and an editor of the British *New Left Review*, Robin Blackburn. The boundaried social networks of these Two Marxisms is the sociological shell of an intellectual skirmish that has manifested itself among Marxists for some fifty years now.[11]

Some part of this theoretical tension is organized as a conflict between those supporting (and those rejecting) the importance of Hegel for Marx, and between those using and those rejecting a more Hegelian conception of "ideology critique."

Both Scientific and Critical Marxism even tend to view ideology differently and their critique of ideology differs as well. Scientific Marxism views ideology as a distorted reflection of the world, indeed, as turned upside down by the distorting lens of self-interest but, nonetheless, as a reflection mirroring (albeit it weirdly) the world. Critical Marxism, however, believes that even as men go about fashioning ideological masks for class domination, they do so under the scrutiny of their own and others' critical reason, and must thus seek masks that will persuade themselves and others. What makes ideologies persuasive (and thereby capable of legitimating class domination) is precisely their elements of rationality and reasonableness. From the standpoint of Critical Marxism, then, reason even seeps into ideology itself and it must, therefore, contain something more than the false and mistaken; consequently, ideology cannot simply be shrugged aside as a mere tool of domination, or straightened out simply with a transformative criticism that turns it "right side up."

The difference between Critical and Scientific Marxism reflects a conflict between those viewing Marx as the culmination of German idealism and those emphasizing Marx's superiority to that tradition. It is, therefore, also a difference between those accepting the young (and consequently more Hegelian) Marx as authentically Marxist and others who regard the young Marx as still mired in ideology.

On each side of this division between Critical and Scientific Marxism there is a set of correlated commitments which is the mirror image of the syndrome of correlated commitments on the other side. Critical Marxists (or Hegelianizers) conceive of Marxism as critique rather than science; they stress the continuity of Marx with Hegel, the importance of the young Marx, the ongoing significance of the young Marx's emphasis on "alienation," and are more historicist. The Scientific Marxists, or anti-Hegelians, have (at times) stressed that Marx made a *coupure épistemologique* with Hegel after 1845. Marxism for them is science, not critique, entailing a "structuralist" methodology whose paradigm is the "mature" political economy of *Capital* rather than the "ideologized" anthropology of the 1844 Manuscripts. In one part, the controversy about the young *versus* the old Marx is a metaphor for the more analytic distinction between Critical and Scientific Marxism.

Critical Marxists, therefore, commonly stress the *continuity* between the young and old Marx because the young Marx was patently an Hegelian; they wish to establish Marxism's abiding link with the larger tradition of German philosophy of which Hegel was the culmination.[12] Correspondingly, Scientific Marxists may stress the quantum leap that the maturing Marx presumably made from ideology to science, as well as imputing sharp differences between ideology and science in general.

Critical and Scientific Marxisms differ, then, in their most basic background assumptions: in their epistemologies, especially with

respect to the role of science as against critique, and with respect
to their domain assumptions concerning the fundamental nature
of social reality (i.e., their social ontologies). Critical Marxists
stress an historicism that emphasizes social fluidity and change, a
kind of organicism calling for the contextual interpretation of
events; Scientific Marxists search out firm social structures that
recur and which are presumably intelligible in decontextualized
ways.

Cognitive Styles

The structuralist propensities of Scientific Marxism express themselves as a cognitive style that sees objects as having hard-edged
boundaries with little or no commingling of different objects; different objects are neatly assigned to different categories, and the
criteria of categorization stress the unambiguous assignment of an
object to one and only one category, generally devaluing the "ambiguous," rather than seeing it as valuable under certain conditions (as for example, in William Empson or Kenneth Burke).
Critical Marxism's cognitive style, however, does not view objects
as hard edged; deemphasizing dichotomous notions of infra- and
superstructures and invoking the "totality" within which boundaries among objects are blurred, it avoids carefully graded ranks
and hierarchies, each having a distinct Apollonian separation from
the other—which is the preference of Scientific Marxism—but has
a more mystical impulse toward oneness, communion, the Diony-
sian. Scientific Marxism's cognitive style, then, evidences the
presence of a low tolerance for ambiguity; Critical Marxism's style
rejects formal, hard-edged categorization as a vivisection that
mutilates and distorts living reality.

   The central problematic around which this distinction in cognitive styles expresses itself is Scientific Marxism's tendency to divide the sociocultural world of objects and events into two basic
structures:[13] the economic infrastructure, centering on the mode of
production, and the superstructure, involving the ideological and
the state, with the firm insistence that the former controls the latter
"in the long run."

   In contrast, Critical Marxism's tendency is to reject such a
dichotomous division of the social world as vulgar oversimplifica-
tion, to stress the "totality," and to argue that those using the
dichotomy have unduly narrow conceptions of the elements that
enter into either side of it. Thus, in this vein, Russell Jacoby re-

marks that "what needs to be avoided is, as it were, the vulgar critique of vulgar Marxism. The mere addition of a political-superstructure component to a political economy which has lost its politics may yield only a pluralist formula . . . the objection against vulgar Marxism is not that it overemphasized the role of the economy, but *conceived it too narrowly.*"[14] In a similar way, it has been claimed that the state has been too narrowly conceived by other Marxists: "the State is much more than its manifest apparatuses of coercion. . . . The State is *all* the activities employed by a ruling class to secure its collective conditions of production."[15] (What, then, is *not* the State?)

Evolutionism and Catastrophism

Scientific and Critical Marxisms, however, do not differ only in their epistemologies, styles of cognition, and modes of analysis and interpretation of the social world. They differ also in the ways they deliberately seek to change the world and in their conceptions of natural social change. Since it accents the density of social structure and the weight of history (to use Merleau-Ponty's phrase), Scientific Marxism sees the social world as difficult to deflect in its course and thus as unchangeable by "mere will." Indeed, Scientific Marxism sees the social world as imposing itself on persons, rather than being a fluid medium open to human intervention. Critical and Scientific Marxisms differ also, then, in their politics; in their conception of revolution and how it is made; and, vitally, in their vision of what is to be brought into existence, i.e., in their imagination of what socialism is, no less than in their conception of capitalism and its pathologies.

Marx employed two concepts of change: one gradualistic, evolutionary, and continuous; the second, more discontinuous, abrupt, catastrophic. The first is largely *Scientific* Marxism's conception of historical change and is coincident with Darwinianism; the second is more nearly how *Critical* Marxism focuses on historical change and is grounded in Hegel. The concepts of change held by both Scientific and Critical Marxism differ primarily in that the first (Darwinian) view is object-centered, addressing the changes in a series of natural forms, while the second partly involves the activity of the knowing subject and the corpus of his knowledge.

Hegel's notion of contradiction, involving an *Aufhebung* in which the later form incorporates parts of the earlier form which is synthesized in a new, more encompassing whole, embodies a specific concept of progress. This concept of progress is that all that is true, or still of value, in the past is carried forward and preserved in the new object, so that all that one needs is the most recent or modern form, since it embodies and transcends the truth of the past. In the Hegelian notion of *aufgehoben*, having the new object thus allows us to drop the old one, to cease honoring it, indeed, to forget it; a rupture with the past is inserted.

Critical and Scientific Marxists differ, also, in what they relate Marxism to in the surrounding culture. Those defining Marxism as science naturally link it to science and technology more broadly and to the institutions on which these depend. They are more disposed to assume that science and technology—"forces of production"—are central in defining the essential character of the modern world, are linked with efforts at "modernization," and define that as nucleated with science. Critical Marxists, however, connect Marxism to a very different layer of culture, a more humanistic culture that preceded modern science and technology, and which feels itself to be older and more fundamental than science and technology. Critical Marxism is linked to a humanistic culture—not without its own forms of arrogance—that may in fact feel itself to have been improperly displaced by parvenu, shallow science.

A basic difference between Scientific and Critical Marxism is to be found, then, in their relationship to what Robert Redfield once called the "great tradition," which he contrasted with the "little tradition," of folk and peasant culture. Both Critical and Scientific Marxism are bearers of the great tradition of European culture. Each is connected more closely, however, with a different aspect of it. Scientific Marxism, of course, is oriented to modern technology and science and accepts the great value placed upon them, while Critical Marxism is oriented to the older, more "humanistic," more literary and more philosophical aspects of Europe's great tradition. Stated differently, Scientific Marxism is grounded in a more "instrumental" culture, in that part of the great tradition which is valued not so much for itself, but for what it can bring about. Critical Marxism, however, is oriented more strongly toward the transcendental aspects of Europe's great tradition, the basic goals and values it has long prized. Put in other and older terms, Scientific Marxism is concerned with technical "civilization", while Critical Marxism is more concerned with the preservation of "culture." Scientific Marxism seeks technical "modernization"; Critical Marxism aims at a moral reinvigoration that may even be dissonant with technical modernization.

It is in part for this reason that Critical Marxism has a closer affinity with Hegelian views, for the latter (as I will suggest) is a kind of secular Protestantism that stresses the importance of "sectarian" internal conviction and authentic belief, contrasting this invidiously with the "positivity" of churchly reliance upon institutional forms, i.e., mere behavioral conformity. Significantly, no one has stressed Hegel's critique of "positivity" more emphatically than the Critical Marxist Georg Lukács, in his splendid study of *The Young Hegel*.

The Critique of Science

In the lexicon of the Scientific Marxist, "science" is both powerful and, for the most part, good. Science provides the lexical anchor for a devaluing context in which "philosophy" is perceived as a diminished figure that needs to be "abolished" or sublated, and in which the *evaluative* implications of critique are perceived as misplaced sentimentalities. Critical Marxism's judgement on science clearly differs, regarding it in general less benign or *good*, even if accepting Scientific Marxism's judgement of its great power.

In large measure, then, for Critical Marxism, science is part of the modern human problem, or too intimately associated with those producing it; for Scientific Marxism, however, science is more comfortably accepted as part of the solution. Critical Marxism's critique of contemporary society does not exempt science, and it does not see the limits of science as due only to the property system within which it operates. At the same time, a direct critique of science is dissonance-generating, partly because it violates the value so widely awarded it in the larger society. Since science is defined as the dominant form of rationality, any critique of it exposes the critic to condemnation as antiscientific, antiintellectual, and even as irrational and nihilistic.[16] Because of the intense pressure exerted against almost any generalized critique of science in industrial society, Critical Marxism pursues its critique obliquely, often focusing its attack on diffuse "positivism" rather than science itself. In this, however, what it is basically objecting to is that—unlike Scientific Marxism which retains a certain ambiguity about this—it rejects a *de*-contextualized notion of science, i.e., as self-contained. In short, critique rejects science as the ultimate form of rationality. For Critical Marxism, "positivism" is a dyslogism referring to any commitment to science mistakenly presenting itself as autonomous or self-grounded, or which fails systematically to raise questions about this grounding.

Scientific Marxism seeks to *re*-contextualize the topics and objects it studies and is thus drawn to versions of "systems analysis." Critical Marxism (as I will develop in a later volume) additionally seeks to *re*-contextualize the very intellectual *resources* with which it grapples with these topics. It is thus more capable of a reflexivity that can transform its own resources into topics, or its assumptions into problematics. Critical Marxism pursues its studies of social structure, of its development and of efforts to change it, as the doing, making, and commitment of persons, undertaking these studies with a critical effort to appropriate the traditions in which they had developed.

Critical Marxism thus generates a discourse oriented both to the social world *and* to the traditions in which that world had been discussed, whether the latter were extraordinary, technical languages such as "political economy," or the ordinary languages of the everyday life and its "common sense." Critical Marxism, like Scientific Marxism, of course has a politics. Rather than being positivistically obsessed with the certainty of its knowledge, however, as Scientific Marxism is, Critical Marxism is more fearful of the dangers of Hamletian procrastination. Its anxieties center on the threat of passivity. Critical Marxism thus refuses to wait indefinitely for "certain" (or "positive") knowledge about the social world before acting. Indeed, it may plunge into action at some point, in the expectation that action will resolve epistemological ambiguities. Indeed, Critical Marxism does at times even manifest an antiintellectual impulse, occasionally intimating that the very quest for knowledge is the mask of a cowardly avoidance of struggle.

Politics of the Two Marxisms

Beyond the intellectual differences separating Scientific and Critical Marxists there are also, as suggested earlier, *political* differences which are in themselves linked to Scientific Marxism's stress upon instrumental measures and to Critical Marxism's concern with ultimate values. The political expression of this is found in the Scientific Marxists' great commitment to their party and political organizations, in short, to the means as such, while Critical Marxists make their deepest commitment to a set of values, to a conception, a consciousness, to the inward "spirit" or *ends* of the revolution as such. Scientific Marxists risk losing touch with the emancipatory ends sought by socialism and the revolution in order to protect the *means*, the organizational instrument, the party "vanguard." The pathological potentiality of this tendency is a political "ritualism" in which what was initially regarded as an instrument, the party, comes in time to be redefined as an end in itself. In the language of Marxism itself, this is "revisionism." As the master revisionist, Eduard Bernstein, himself remarked: The end is nothing, the movement everything.

Critical Marxists, however, are not, as I will be at pains to indicate, immune to political pathologies; they merely have different vulnerabilities, rather than none. Their lunge toward the revolutionary goal is so dominating that they have only calculating instrumental ties to any specific organizational instrument, such as the "vanguard" party, *or even to any specific social class such as the proletariat.* Correspondingly, they are also less insistent on the prior presence of certain "objective" historical conditions as the requisite for the revolutionary plunge. (Critical Marxism is thus the Marxism toward which the less industrially developed countries of the Third World are disposed.) If the political pathology of the Scientific Marxists is ritualism and revisionism, that of the Critical Marxists is adventurism or (as Georg Lukács termed his early position) "revolutionary messianism." In one part, then, this tension between the Critical and Scientific Marxists is the theoretical counterpart of the fundamental sociological dilemma—the Scylla and Charybdis—of revolutionary politics: "sectarianism" and "opportunism."

If each side has characteristic political pathologies, each also has its own characteristic political strengths. For the Critical Marxists, this is in their refusal to submit to "what is," their reluctance to wait interminably, their expectation that the time is always right to change the world, that there is always some way to exert pressure against the status quo—in short, that there is always some path forward to the revolution. There is an echo of millenarianism here. They are constantly alert to the dangers of political exhaustion, apathy, and of undue reliance upon forces outside of their own control. Their political position insists that people count more than technology and weapons; that men can and should do something without waiting interminably for other "forces" to mature. They see the importance of courage and commitment in politics; of consciousness; of the here-and-now transformation of human relationships. In its *strengths* no less than its weaknesses, Critical Marxism is romantic. It sometimes borders on a *macho* utopianism aggressively ready to "seize the time."

Scientific Marxists, however, have different political talents: they stress the cultivation of political endurance and patience; the husbanding and developing of cadres until the time is right; the careful appraisal of historical conditions for what they are, not confusing them with what they would like them to be. Above all, Scientific Marxists seek to protect their future ability to act when objective conditions promise to better their chance of success. They place their greatest reliance on the development of the forces of production and on the opportunities and contradictions this will create.

Critical and Scientific Marxists are each committed to revolution, yet each views the revolution's future as protected in different ways. Critical Marxists see the future of revolution as depending on the clarity of awareness and the vigor of inner, conscious commitment, on a consciousness that can be imprinted on history like a kind of germ matter, by those with courage. Scientific Marxists, however, see the revolution's future as vouchsafed not by the revolutionary's clear-sighted heroism, but by history itself; by the inexorable contradictions of each society; by the scientific appraisal of these contradictions; and by exploiting the political crises created by these unfolding contradictions. The mission of Critical Marxism is to safeguard revolutionary purpose and élan; the mission of a Scientific Marxism is to protect the organizational instrument and its future options. It is thus easier for revolutionaries out of power—or whose power is still precarious—to be Critical Marxists. Revolutionaries are exposed to great pressure to be Scientific Marxists, however, once their power is institutionally stabilized. Mao's "cultural revolutions" had been a struggle against such tendencies, and they lost.

The stress on consciousness typical of Hegelian or Critical Marxists is intensified in the work of Lenin and matures in the theory of Karl Korsch and Georg Lukács in the early 1920s, after the defeat of the revolutions in Hungary and Germany, but also in the buoyant wake of the successful revolution in Russia. The defeat of the revolution in nations that were industrially *advanced,* and its paradoxical success in one that was *backward,* went far toward undermining the authority of a "scientific," materialistic Marxism and supporting a critical, dialectical Marxism.

Critical Marxism compensates with its emphasis on voluntarism for the deficiency of economic and technological conditions once deemed requisite (by Scientific Marxists) for socialism and is, therefore, a Marxism appropriate to revolutionary efforts in "underdeveloped" or Third World nations. This is in part why, before Lukács and Korsch, it was Lenin who launched the movement toward a Critical Marxism. (Launched, but did not pursue it.) Such a Marxism was an effort to compensate for deficient material socioeconomic conditions by stressing the significance and potency of the "human" agency and of his awareness, consciousness, sacrifice, and courage. Underlying the "consciousness-raising" of the Critical Marxist, then, is an inability to rely on material conditions to support his efforts; and more, he has a sense that the "natural" drift of things is inimical to the revolution. The call to consciousness, then, is the ideology of those who have come to suspect that neither time nor "history is on our side."

Scientific Marxism, however, confidently relies on social evolution and on the unfolding of certain "natural" tendencies to fulfill its socialist expectations. It feels itself allied with history and nature. Correspondingly, however, Scientific Marxism also views objectified social structures as those upon which it would rely *rather than* "men," and their will and consciousness. Scientific Marxism regards men as the *products* of such structures; Critical Marxism, however, sees men (some men) as the producers of social structures. In short, Scientific Marxism is sedimented with a tacitly dour judgement on human nature, as somehow falling short of history's requirements; it does not rely on people but on social structures to solve the historical problem. In contrast, Critical Marxism does not rely upon an objectified history, on social structures, or on nature, but on people's will and consciousness, to overcome the deficiencies of nature, history, and economic structures.

Critical Marxism relies upon and seeks to evoke the extraordinary potentialities of men. It holds that people make a great difference; it is capable of relying upon at least *some* persons, although sometimes only a few charismatic leaders, "great men." Critical Marxism's reliance upon persons, then, is not incompatible with a hierocratic elitism. It shares this potentiality for elitism and authoritarianism with Scientific Marxism, although the latter's elitism is more nearly the meritocratic hierarchy of technocrats, while Critical Marxism's elitism has a more charismatic tinge.

Pessimism and Optimism in the Two Marxisms

If Scientific Marxism is characterized by an insistence on the *limits* imposed by the world—by its historical density and weight—and thus conceives itself as a "materialism," Critical Marxism celebrates the "dialectic," and defines social situations in ways maximizing the importance of the "subjects" (or actors) and of their action in or interaction with the situation. Critical Marxism is thus precisely an activistic "theory of praxis" (in Gramsci's terms), focused on the shifting dialectic of subject and object. It is, in short, most definitely *not* a generalizing social science enunciating immutable "laws" of social evolution, or of the connections among abiding social structures that limit, channel, and constrain the action of persons. Critical Marxism thus defines social reality in ways maximizing the justification for intervening politically—at almost any time or place. By stressing the indeterminate openness of the situation and the uncertainty of its character or of its course, Critical Marxism thereby opens itself to the possible effectiveness and potential success of political initiatives.

But not all knowledge of social situations is equally inhibitive of political initiative and intervention. Knowledge inhibits action primarily when it alleges (or implies) that the natural, "lawful" drift of social life runs *counter* to goals which persons seek or to the hopes they hold. Only when knowledge stresses the weight, destiny, and strength of the status quo and, correspondingly, of the frailty of the forces opposing it must knowledge undermine radicals' political morale. Critical Marxism's disposition to oppose a generalizing social science is partly due to its tacit supposition that "history" is *not* on its side. Critical Marxism rejects a generalizing social science, then, not simply because of judicious qualms about its inherent epistemological difficulties but, rather, because of certain of social science's specific reports or implications—its "bad news" concerning the world in which revolutionary politics must be made. It was Eduard Bernstein's "bad news" about capitalism—that its "crash" was not inevitable—that was conducive to Georg Lukács's reconceptualization of Marxism as a "method" focused on the "totality," rather than on the sphere of the economic.

Critical Marxism contains a profound ambiguity. On one side, it limits reliance on any "objective" knowledge of society, grounded in a generalizing science of society. It stresses the limits of knowledge, doing so thereby to allow greater room for political action and will, and thus has an opening toward irrationality. On the other side, however, Critical Marxism tacitly predicates a certain concrete knowledge of the social world which, being dissonant with its revolutionary purpose, is a "bad news" which it then maneuvers to discredit on "methodological" grounds. Here, on this side, it is not just that Critical Marxism rejects the possibility of a science of society but, rather, it tacitly accepts as knowledge what it experiences politically as bad news. Critical Marxism's structure of sentiment thus has an undertow of pessimism.

Scientific Marxism's structure of sentiment, however, is more optimistic. Indeed, Scientific Marxism will be attractive and accepted in part because its specific generalizations about society and its development are consistent with hopes for the future. It will be attractive at least to those groups whose hopes for the future are consistent with its reports about the social world. History is here experienced objectivistically, as apart from us and our doing, as something with which one is "allied." When what is seen of history is viewed as legitimating and ensuring one's political project, the epistemological grounding of these reports is less apt to be made problematic; one does not then call for their critique from the standpoint of "method."

Correspondingly, this means that a Scientific Marxism would be dissonant with the politics of those for whom it did not bear glad tidings but, rather, bad news; of those, that is, whose revolutionary aspirations it did not support but who, nonetheless, *persist in their revolutionary project*. Scientific Marxism and revolution have been sundered because the will to revolution persisted in certain places and among some to whom it offered little hope. Rather than relinquish their politics they exerted pressure to redefine their theory, that is, to surrender Scientific Marxism and to substitute for it Critical Marxism. All of this was accomplished, however, not by openly opposing Marxism but, rather, by the "discovery" of *true* Marxism. This "true" Marxism is claimed to reside in hitherto unknown, only recently available works, the works of the younger, more Hegelian Marx, of the economic and philosophical manuscripts, the theses on Feurbach, or the *Grundrisse*, and which indeed Marx never sought to publish.

The problem was that Scientific Marxism was a theory about certain historically specific entities: about advanced industrial capitalism, about the proletariat, and about *its* socialist revolution. But revolution in our time betrayed the Marxist expectation that it would occur in advanced capitalist societies and be made by mature proletariats. Modern revolution has largely been an affair of industrially backward societies, of the peasantry, and of their agrarian revolutions under the tutelage of radicalized intellectuals.[17] Critical Marxism was a response to this unexpected development, serving to bridge the gap between the industrial backwardness of the Third World and the persisting vision of socialism. As I shall later show, however, this is not to say that Critical Marxism is *produced by* underdevelopment; rather, it was produced *for* undeveloped societies by highly advanced Europeanized intellectuals whose theories did not simply reflect the economic level in the Third World. Critical Marxism is thus not an expression of industrial backwardness but of the gap between the ambitions of an extremely advanced intelligentsia *and* the weakness of the industrial proletariat and of industry in their locality. Critical Marxism is the expression of Europeanized intellectuals' will to socialism, of their refusal to surrender this goal despite the prevalence of conditions which, from the standpoint of Scientific Marxism, were defined as unfavorable to it.

As the ideology of those who have few or no resources of power and control other than those they themselves can activate, the power of Critical Marxists depends on their effectiveness in mobilizing others. Being a Marxism that is less able to rely on forces already in being—whether an advanced industrial economy or a trade union movement—Critical Marxists must seek hegemonic authority, must be able to move persons by their *appeal*, and hence must be more open to their needs and suffering, at least during the initial period of political mobilization. Critical Marxism is, therefore, more populistic and less bureaucratic than Scientific Marxism. It is precisely this combination of populism and its need to rely on rational persuasion that now makes Critical Marxism particularly attractive to many young Western socialists and intellectuals. Yet these elements are in tension with Critical Marxism's impulse to antiintellectualism and its suspicion that the quest for knowledge may deter revolution. Moreover, since Critical Marxism has an underlying pessimism about its revolutionary prospect, it also has a readiness for violence and terror to produce the revolutionary "leap" as a substitute for Scientific Marxism's inevitable laws which, under advanced capitalism, presumably guarantee the victory of socialism. It is a central contradiction of Critical Marxism, then, that while it has a potential for rationality and populism, it is also vulnerable to an authoritarian voluntarism, irrationality, and elitist terror.

Cuban and Chinese Marxism as Critical Marxisms

Cuban and Chinese Marxism both converge more with an Hegelian, Critical Marxism than with a "scientific" socialism.[18] In both, the importance attributed to revolutionary will and voluntarism, so characteristic of Critical Marxism, is signaled by the crucial place each assigns to military initiative, to the guerrilla column, and by their common conviction that "power comes out of the barrel of a gun." Both believed that the revolution need not require the prior maturation of the objective conditions of an advanced industrial economy. If the limited Leninist movement toward voluntarism was exhibited in Lenin's emphasis on the initiative of the political instrument, the party "vanguard," then the full-blown voluntarism of Cuban and Chinese Marxism is indicated by the importance each attributes to the military instrument, the army, and to the latter's influence on (if not priority over) the vanguard party itself.[19]

Maoism, says Robert Jay Lifton, assumed two things: first, it views

> ... the human mind as infinitely malleable, capable of being reformed, transformed, and rectified without limit. The second is a related vision of the will as all-powerful, even to the extent that (in his own words) "The Subjective creates the Objective."[20]

Much the same may be and has been said of Castroism.

In a converging analysis, Richard R. Fagen stresses that the style of Cuban revolutionary politics was crystallized by the guerrilla experience in the Sierra Maestra during 1958–59, whose enduring legacy was "voluntarism, egalitarianism, and ruralism."[21] Voluntarism, Fagen indicates, refers to "the expansive sense of efficacy, competence, and personal power generated during the guerrilla period . . . [and denotes] a philosophy which conceives human will to be the dominant factor in experience and thus history."

Whether Cuba's voluntarism *derives* from (was "generated by") the guerrilla period or, as seems far more likely, whether it also preceded it and was the underlying consciousness that allowed Castro to launch guerrilla warfare, is a secondary point. The essential consideration here is that this voluntarism is surely a sa-

lient feature of Castroism and a central symptom of its convergence with Critical Marxism.

It is, however, a salient but *not distinctive* feature of Castroism.
I would also say the same about the two other components Fagen
deems distinctive of the Cuban style of revolutionary politics,
ruralism and egalitarianism. They are distinctive only in that they
set it apart from political models consistent with a "scientific"
socialism, but they are certainly *not* peculiar to *Cuba*. Exactly this
same triad of voluntarism, ruralism, and egalitarianism also
characterized Mao's Marxism.

Fagen's analysis suggests that the egalitarianism of Cuban
socialism was accentuated by the experience of shared danger and
shared struggle characteristic of a military brotherhood; this experience affected the participants' ideas about the character of a
good social order, which they subsequently sought to reproduce
in society at large, and their notion of political method. In short
(and to reverse Clausewitz), politics became a continuation of war
by other means. It may be that insofar as the military brotherhood
becomes a societal paradigm this helps explain how
egalitarianism can be associated with decision-making concentrated at the top and with strict control over dissent. "In Cuba, a
radical economic, social and cultural egalitarianism is married to
an authoritarian and hierarchical decisional structure."[22] The
stress of men in combat frequently generates informalities, mutual
reliance, and a sense of shared fate without, however, actually
changing the formal hierarchical social structure of the military
unit and the differential authority of officers and men. As battle
and danger recede with victory, the informal egalitarianism gives
way to the abiding formal hierarchy.[23]

Cuban (and, as I will indicate, Chinese) voluntarism was also
associated, in the manner characteristic of Critical Marxism, with a
stress of the importance of consciousness and awareness. In Castro's view, socialism is not simply socialization of the means of
production but the *transformation of men*, the creation of a new
revolutionary man, "a man devoid of *egoismo*, guided by *concien-
cia*, who puts service to society above service to self." "A communist society," in Castro's own words, "is one in which man will
have reached the highest degree of social awareness ever
achieved. . . . To live in a Communist society is to live without
selfishness."[24] Certainly this is far more reminiscent of *the young
Marx's* philosophical manuscripts than of his *Capital*.

Castro's model of development, like Mao's, does not give first place to the classical verities of *Scientific* Marxism: resources, capital, technology, efficiency or growth. Instead, it stresses "mass participation, determination, selflessness, enthusiasm, and faith." Again: "a profound general faith in achieving economic progress through the *formación* and utilization of revolutionary man certainly pervades the highest decisional circles." The leadership's commitment to development rests less on technological factors than on the transformation of human relations and consciousness. It rests, in Castro's own formulation, on "factors of a moral order, factors having to do with awareness."

Much the same portrait of Maoist development policies has been drawn by E. L. Wheelwright and B. MacFarlane who note that

> a fundamental axiom of Maoist thought is that public owner-
> ship is only a technical condition for solving the problems of
> Chinese society . . . the goal of Chinese socialism involves
> vast changes in human nature, in the way people relate to
> each other. . . . Once the basic essentials of food, clothing, and
> shelter for all have been achieved, it is not necessary to wait
> for higher productivity levels to be reached before attempting
> socialist ways of life.[25]

Michael Kosok expressly counterposes the Soviet view of development with the Maoist, indicating the economistic side of "scientific" socialism with incisive clarity. Kosok holds that the "economism" of Scientific Marxism implies that the "structure of society is essentially the development of *productivity* and the 'level of production'," and it regards man as an "efficiency machine serving the dictates of technology. . . . Communism and socialism are seen [by Scientific Marxism] as contingent upon the availability of a sufficient number of things," quantification and reification being characteristic of it. Again, Scientific Marxism stresses the importance of technical skills rather than will or motivation; in holding that expertise is more important than "redness," it ultimately delivers the economy to the control of specialists,[26] alienating the proletariat from the revolution.

The Unity of Critical and Scientific Marxism

Critical and Scientific Marxism each opens a space for the other by reason of its own characteristic limitations. Scientific Marxism typically focuses on the necessary internal contradictions of a capitalist economy that inevitably doom it. Since the transformation of capitalist society into socialism is seen as taking place via an inevitable economic catastrophe, Scientific Marxism fails to develop a political theory which explains how the working class would struggle for and seize power in the state. Politics is treated as an epiphenomenon, as falling automatically into line with changes in the mode of production, the mature development of which need only be capped by the capture of state power in order to establish socialism—in the vision of Scientific Marxism.

This, therefore, omits any clear indication of the rational preparation and political organization required to produce socialism. Scientific Marxism, then, is a kind of *political utopianism* which assumes that the political conditions and effort requisite for socialism will, somehow, arise from the maturation of capitalism's economy and contradictions. Thus an automatic evolution of the economy, rather than the determined struggle, discipline, effort, and will of people, suffice to produce socialism. If, however, this economic evolution will yield socialism inevitably there is no reason why anyone should exert, much less sacrifice, themselves for it. It is as if soldiers at the front had heard that the war was soon to end and the enemy was shortly to surrender. Under these conditions, few will be inclined to run risks. In short, a Scientific Marxism has ambiguous consequences: it leads adherents to wait for the unfolding of the inevitable, induces a certain passivity, and yields an evolutionary, parliamentary socialism, even as the guaranty of victory it provides sustains hope.

Scientific Marxism generates just those difficulties to which Critical Marxism, with its focus on voluntaristic struggle, is a precise response. It is Scientific Marxism's disregard of the political instrument—its *political* utopianism—that in part fosters Critical Marxism which minimizes the importance of prior economic development for socialism—its own *economic* utopianism—which, in turn, opens a space for a Scientific Marxism, etc. In short:

$$\text{Scientific Marxism} \dashrightarrow \text{Critical Marxism}$$

Thus though they are in tension, the Two Marxisms constitute a dialectical "unity of opposites," each contributing to the development of its adversary.

Critical Marxism, like critique in general, judges that a political and social system can be something other than it is now, and that an effort—involving struggle, discipline, courage, consciousness—ought to be made *to close the gap* between what the system is and what it could be. But to call for the closing of this gap is to invoke a morality, implying that what could be *should* be. To make a critique of something is thus to state its limits in terms of a set of *values;* a critique implies—if it does not state outright—that what is *ought* to be otherwise. Yet what are the grounds on which this morality, this "ought", is itself justified? Marx argued that moralities and ideals were disguises of the egoism of class interests, that ruling ideas were the ideas of the ruling class and the instruments of their hegemony. No reason, then, to consider them binding.

But what reason is there to believe that the ruling class's moralities are anymore egoistic than any other set of ideals and values? Are not all moralities instruments for pursuing *some* group's interests? Indeed, one of the Young Hegelians, Max Stirner, argued just that, relativizing all values, declaring them *all* lacking in validity, asserting that *all* were the camouflage of the will, disguising someone's egoism and self-interest under the banner of a universal morality. Socialism, then, simply becomes the egoism of the proletariat (or whichever class is behind it). The values underlying it are thus as specious as those underlying the hegemony of the ruling class, essentially disguising and reflecting class needs. In short, critique and the critic expose the limits of *others,* without being aware that they too share the same kind of limits. If this situation is allowed to stand, what has been generated is a relativization of all values and an onrushing nihilism in which all moral claims are seen as equally selfish, as possessing no intrinsic merit justifying the choice of one rather than the other. Critique and Critical Marxism, then, require a value grounding for choice and for the criticism of what is, *but they do not actually have one.*

Correspondingly, if Scientific Marxism only says what is going to happen, pronouncing the inexorable laws of economic evolution, it presents no intrinsic grounds for *accommodating* to the future they portray. For although death too is inevitable it is commonly resisted and put off. Scientific Marxism thus does not embody *grounds* for *accepting* what it holds to be economically ordained; its enemies will continue to oppose it, while friends who believe its predictions may wait complacently for the happy event to come about. Correspondingly, Critical Marxism provides no justified grounds for rejecting the present. Thus neither Critical

Marxism nor Scientific Marxism justify the commitments they seek.

Scientific Marxism sought other, *non*-moral grounds, grounds in the *necessity* of certain developments, to justify the commitments it sought, premising that *unnecessary* poverty deserved to be opposed and that changes which were historically *necessary* deserved to be made. Necessity became its morality substitute. Yet the question remains: *why* should anyone accept, let alone actively support, what is necessary; why oppose unnecessary poverty? People do not accept death despite its necessity. One response is that it does not matter whether persons actually accept (and hence work for) what is necessary, since, being necessary, it will in any event occur. That is precisely the implicit logic by which Scientific Marxism is conducive to a passivity which triggers critical Marxism's activistic voluntarism, which, lacking a foundation for its morality, in its turn triggers a search for an amoral grounding, which Scientific Marxism claims to find in the inexorable necessity of its economic laws. The cycle is thus complete, each Marxism generating its adversary.

Yet why was it assumed by Max Stirner and others that persons' collective arrangements, made by men in society or in their smaller groups, did not suffice to form a morality that might bind them? If men are the source of values, why can they not make values that bind and lay effective claim to allegiance? On what assumption was this ruled out?

It was assumed that the decisive interests that persons have are always *partisan* interests. If the decisive interests are egoistic, then men can change their ideals as their circumstances change, revoking or de-authorizing tomorrow what they had invoked and authorized today. Again, if emphasis is placed on a mind-as-mirror epistemology, in which mind simply reflects what is, then the focus shifts from the moral to the cognitive; attention is given over not to the question of how *men* made their commitments, but to the social forces that shaped them. Justification is supplanted by the sociology of knowledge. Scientific Marxism's mirror epistemology tends to divert attention from what ought to be to the question of what is.

On the further assumption that "the people" alone can and should decide what is good, that they alone are sovereign *and that there ought to be nothing limiting their choice,* any existing set of ideals is continually open to challenge in the name of "the people." Being the sole and exclusive governor of their destiny, the people have the sole and exclusive right to determine what limits them and to change their commitments as they see fit. A radical doctrine of popular sovereignty is conducive to the radical de-authorization of morality. For since any morality limits persons, it can be defined as restricting their proper sovereignty. Neither god nor church, neither tradition nor past, can now authorize what should be, but only "the people."

But since it is here supposed that the decisions and moralities which the people make are grounded only in their conditions, and that the former mirror the latter, then people who have been subjected to the corrupting influence of past institutions cannot be trusted to make the right decisions. Thus neither they, the "sovereign people," nor certainly old regime traditional authorities, may say what is good. Where can any standard, value, ideal, or morality then find justification? Stirner had concluded there was none. Indeed, Marx too had also said there was only "the clash of right against right."

We are then left with several possibilities. One is that an educated elite appoints itself as the trustee of the people's interests. This, in fact, is precisely the logic that led Lenin to the conclusion that the working class could not itself generate a socialist consciousness (that this had to derive from the bourgeois intelligentsia); this is precisely what underlies Lenin's conception of the Bolshevik Party as a "vanguard." Yet insofar as members of the vanguard accept a radical popular sovereignty in principle, they certainly cannot acknowledge they are usurping the people's sovereignty. Thus one possibility for overcoming the radical crisis of values that had been generated was for an intellectual elite to usurp, and conceal their usurpment of, popular sovereignty by proclaiming themselves the mere servant of that sovereignty. But how can they justify this?

Their common justification, and again Lenin's theory of the vanguard exemplifies this clearly, is their self-imputed possession of a superior knowledge or theory. But how does it happen that their knowledge is not distorted—as everyone else's is—by their social conditions? How is it that they escape the general ideological corruption of the status quo?

One answer given is that theirs is not just ordinary theory, and certainly not another mere "ideology," but an extraordinary and very superior knowledge, having some special quality immunizing it from the corrupting social conditions in which it was born. In short, they claim their knowledge is "science" and they further assume that science somehow rises above its social origins. Yet this special immunization from the common corruption of circumstances is never demonstrated but merely asserted.[27] The whole point of calling this new theory, "science," is to claim that it has escaped distortion by social circumstances. Scientific Marxism was thus grounded in a crisis of *morality*. In effect, its tactic is to *obviate* the question of how—in a world where "social consciousness is determined by social being"—*our* knowledge escapes the common fate, by surrounding itself with the aura of the new, highest secular authority: science. As Merleau-Ponty notes, given its own assumptions, it was a kind of miracle that was being proclaimed.

Scientific Marxism sought to provide a grounding for revolutionary transcendence of the status quo in essentially the same way that Auguste Comte's "posivitism" sought to mend the rift in the status quo. Being "certain" (or "positive"), science—according to Comte—would induce consent and produce consensus, relieving "rational" men of the problem of moral choice. Marxism's own effort to find a ground for decision, however, ends in the conclusion that moralities are unnecessary sentimentalities. For it, the question of how to criticize the world without a grounded value position is answered by replying that *one is not criticizing the world*; one is simply relying on the impersonal laws of history, not on morality or ideals, to bring about the social change desired. That is how Scientific Marxism comes to cut itself off from critique. In Scientific Marxism, this is the posture taken by "historical materialism." Historical materialism expresses the renunciation of critique in Marxism on behalf of necessity. Once committed to necessity, however, it needs to know, and know with *certainty*, what is becoming, otherwise there is no *necessity* to which it can consent. It must therefore insist that what it sees in the world, it knows with certainty (i.e., it too must be "positive" about it).

The Two Marxisms: A Preliminary Recapitulation

To summarize some of the differences between Critical and Scientific Marxism: Critical Marxism leans toward a perspective in which human decisions can make an important difference, toward a voluntarism in which human courage and determination count, while Scientific Marxism stresses the lawful regularities that inhere in things and set limits on human will, counterposing determinism to voluntarism. Critical Marxism pursues a policy of active interventionism, organizing instruments such as the Party "vanguard" or military forces that facilitate intervention; Scientific Marxism leans toward an evolutionism in which the requisites of change have their own rates of maturation and, believing history to be on "their side," is prepared to wait until things come their way. The cognitive focus of Critical Marxism is therefore "critique," while that of Scientific Marxism is "science." Critique goes beyond science toward "epistemology" and philosophy which serve as an effort to probe the limits of science, to find a basis in which science itself might be appraised as an intellectual enterprise and cultural product. Scientific Marxism, however, tends to view science as self-justifying and regards philosophy as suspect and démodé; like Marx, it sometimes speaks of "abolishing" philosophy.

In part, for that reason, Critical Marxism is more favorably disposed toward Hegel and accents Marxism's continuity with Hegel, while Scientific Marxism focuses on the discontinuity between Hegel and Marx, stressing the leap forward or *coupure* that Marxism supposedly involved. In consequence, and since the young Marx was the more Hegelian, Critical Marxism is also prepared to accept the continuity between the young and older Marx and see the young Marx as authentically Marxist, while Scientific Marxism is disposed to view the young Marx as still mired in ideology, as not yet "Marxist," thus accenting the differences between him and the older one.

If Critical Marxism accepts Hegel and the young Marx, it is often disposed to suspect Engels, defining him as the source of the "positivistic" distortion of Marxism, as the "first vulgar Marxist." Scientific Marxists are more inclined to appreciate Engels, giving him his due as one of the founders of Marxism.

Critical Marxism is more disposed to an historicism in which each different social phase of society is seen as operating according to unique and different requirements, and it stresses society's organic character as a special totality. Scientific Marxism is more disposed to a structuralism in which the social totality is viewed as a conjunction of abiding elements, which transcend its boundaries in time and space, and thus has an atomistic and mechanistic character. For the Scientific Marxist life is a game always played with essentially the same pieces, although these are arranged differently in different societies and form different structures; the enduring unit-structures, however, limit the possible games that can be played. The Critical Marxist, in contrast, accents the emergent novelties possible under new historical circumstances. For the Scientific Marxist it is these socioeconomic institutions that shape, pattern, and limit social action; it is these impersonal structures that are (for him) the true "actors." Scientific Marxism is thus "decentered." Its focus is no longer on the central role of persons but on the encompassing structures and roles within which persons play their part, and it thus tends to deemphasize the importance of "alienation" insofar as this is understood as grounded in human nature. Contrariwise, Critical Marxism views "alienation" as grounded in human nature which resists crippling by historical circumstances.

For the Scientific Marxist, exploitation grounded in the structures of capitalism replaces alienation as the source of resistance to the present, while for the Critical Marxist alienation remains the more encompassing limitation on human life. The fundamental goals of Critical Marxism are to preserve human culture and certain transcendental values, to reinvigorate human morality, and to restore men to a life in an integral community. This is socialist "emancipation" for them. The socialization of the means of production is, for them, only the first requisite of socialism. For the Scientific Marxist, however, socialism means emancipation from "necessity" by developing the forces of production, by intensifying industrial development and science, by modernizing. Critical Marxism, by contrast, seeks to foster a New Man and a new consciousness and is as much concerned about the kinds of social relations of production to which persons are exposed, as the intensification of the forces of production.

Both Scientific and Critical Marxism are *analytic* distinctions, or ideal types, rather than concrete historical groups and persons. Thus it is fundamentally not correct to say, for example, that Louis Althusser *is* a Scientific Marxist or Georg Lukács a Critical Marxist, or that Maoism *is* a Critical Marxism. The ideal types facilitate our examination of concrete groups and specific persons, but the latter are not identical with or reducible to the former. A specific Marxist (or group of Marxists) may be *more* Scientific Marxist than others, but to speak of him as a Scientific Marxist is only an elliptical, shorthand expression for referring to his relatively greater Scientific Marxism-ness.

NOTES

1. See Werner Sombart, *Le Socialisme et le mouvement social au XIX Siècle* (Paris: Giard et Brière, 1898), pp. 108–10.

2. See the pithy discussion by N. Lobkowicz, *Theory and Practice: History of a Concept from Aristotle to Marx* (South Bend, Ind.: University of Notre Dame Press, 1967), pp. 412ff.

3. *Communist Manifesto* by Karl Marx and Friedrich Engels, authorized English edition of 1888, supervised by Engels, published by Charles H. Kerr, Chicago.

4. K. Marx and F. Engels, *The German Ideology*, trans. W. Lough and C. P. Magill, ed. R. Pascal (New York: International Publishers, n.d.), p. 69.

5. Max Horkheimer, "The Authoritarian State," *Telos*, Spring 1973, p. 11.

6. In short, we do not know where in, say, a Gutman scale the voluntarism/determinism alternative would figure in relation to the other "items," or how "popular" or "difficult" an item it would be; we do not know how large a "factor loading" voluntarism/determinism would have on any dimension of Critical or Scientific Marxism yielded by a factor analysis, although we hypothesize that either a Gutman scale or factor analysis would yield valid dimensions of Critical and Scientific Marxism. We may conceive of the various proposed differentia of Critical and Scientific Marxism to be discussed as "items" for an instrument measuring theoretical and ideological differences among Marxists.

7. Peter Berger and Stanley Pullberg, "Reification and the Sociological Critique of Consciousness," *New Left Review*, January/February 1966, p. 56. See my own discussion of this dualism in sociology in *The Coming Crisis of Western Sociology* (New York: Basic Books, 1970), pp. 51ff.

8. Berger and Pullberg, "Reification and Sociological Critique," p. 56.

9. This admirably succinct formulation is found in an interesting paper by Richard H. Brown, unpublished at the time of this writing.

10. For further discussion see Alvin W. Gouldner, *Enter Plato: Classical Greece and the Origins of Social Theory* (New York: Basic Books, 1965), pp. 121–22.

11. That it still continues vigorously is evident from Gareth Stedman-Jones's Althusserian critique of Lukács as the "first irruption of Romanticism within Marxism" (*New Left Review*, November/December 1971, p. 44). While too sanguine by far, this compares favorably with George Lichtheim's long-standing effort to weigh the effect of Romanticism on Marxism—an effort somewhat vitiated by Lichtheim's Goethean inclination to view Romanticism as *Krankheit*.

12. George Lichtheim's well-titled *From Marx to Hegel* (New York: Herder & Herder, 1971), deals directly with the conflict between Hegel-

ian and anti-Hegelian Marxisms, as well as with the development of the former into the Critical or Frankfurt School in the work of Adorno, Marcuse, and Habermas. Lichtheim always knew who the players were and situated them deftly. The very breadth of Lichtheim's scholarship, his even-handed treatment of conflicting standpoints, his insistence on clarity even from Germans, and his feeling for the historically concrete—all these are substantial virtues which make this book, with the exception of its last and very dated essay, useful reading for students of Marxism.

13. "This basis-superstructure metaphor," we are reminded by Hal Draper, "sometimes treated as a late invention by Engels, was first set down in [their 1846] *The German Ideology:* 'The social organization, evolving directly out of production and commerce . . . in all ages forms the basis of the state and of the rest of the ideological superstructure. . . .' " Hal Draper, *Karl Marx's Theory of Revolution, Part I: The State and Bureaucracy* (New York: (Monthly Review Press, 1977), vol. 1, p. 252.

14. Russell Jacoby, "Politics of the Crisis Theory," *Telos,* Spring 1975, p. 48. Italics added.

15. Philip Corrigan, Harvey Ramsay, and Derek Sayer, *Socialist Construction and Marxist Theory: Bolshevism and Its Critique* (New York: Monthly Review Press, 1978), p. 10. Italics in the original. A very able study written with great economy.

16. It has seemed to me that precisely this attitude prompted the denunciation of Thomas Kuhn's careful critique of "normal" science, even though the critical facet of Kuhn's view of science is greatly muted. See the volume edited by I. Lakatos and A. Musgrave, *Criticism and the Growth of Knowledge* (London and New York: Cambridge University Press, 1970).

17. For details see Alvin W. Gouldner, *The Future of Intellectuals and the Rise of the New Class* (New York: Seabury Press, 1979), pp. 53ff.

18. As I will clarify in a later methodological appendix, Critical-Scientific Marxisms are on a different, more analytic level than Cuban or Chinese Marxisms which, being concrete, are admixtures.

19. In this respect, Maoism represented the *extension* of Lenin's emphasis on the initiatives of the political organization to a voluntarism stressing the initiatives and importance of the military. While Lenin had "regarded the use of armed force for revolutionary purposes as legitimate at all times and as crucial in the hour of decision, he never viewed it as means of gaining mass influence or of *bringing about* the revolutionary crisis" (Richard Lowenthal, "Soviet and Chinese Communist World Views," in Donald W. Treadgold, ed., *Soviet and Chinese Communism: Similarities and Differences* , Seattle: University of Seattle Press, 1967], p. 383). Mao's political strategy aimed at using "protracted armed struggle . . . as a means for reversing an originally unfavorable relation of forces between a revolutionary minority and an apparently strong regime" (Ibid., p. 385).

20. Robert Jay Lifton, *America and the Asian Revolution* (Chicago: Aldine Publishing, 1970), p. 153.

21. Richard R. Fagen, "Cuban Revolutionary Politics," *Monthly Review*, April 1972, p. 27.

22. Ibid., p. 30.

23. This seems to have been the experience of the Yugoslavian Partisan fighters, and it may be a source of the disillusionment of those, such as Djilas, who retained a vivid image of the older military brotherhood and therefore keenly resented the emergence of new, socioeconomic distinctions—the "New Class."

24. Fagen, "Cuban Revolutionary Politics," p. 46.

25. E. L. Wheelwright and B. MacFarlane, *The Chinese Road to Socialism* (New York: Monthly Review Press, 1970), p. 221.

26. Michael Kosok, "Review of Wheelwright and MacFarlane," *Telos*, Spring 1971, pp. 127–43.

27. In this vital respect, academic social "science" makes exactly the same claim and for much the same reason. See Alvin W. Gouldner, *The Dialectic of Ideology and Technology* (New York: Seabury Press, 1976), pp. 3–6, 8–13, 16–19, 34–35, 55, 57, 112–17, 216.

3

PHILOSOPHY, SCIENCE
AND THE TWO MARXISMS

Among the most ingrained ambiguities of Marxism are its relationship both to philosophy and to science. The ambiguity with which each one is viewed is amplified in part because Marx had a commitment to both. As an intellectual system with an interest in knowledge, Marxism vacillates concerning its most fundamental "paradigm"—in Thomas Kuhn's sense of that term.[1] At times Marx looks to science as his paradigm of knowledge, but at other times he looks to "critique" born of philosophy.

Long before he wrote *Capital,* but especially in that work, Marx had begun to think of himself as a scientist. Indeed, even before that great work begins, the very first page of Marx's preface to the first German edition places him in the camp of science. He reminds his readers that "the saying that all beginnings are difficult applies to every science,"[2] and hence they may, he warns, experience their chief difficulties in the very first chapter to follow. In short, Marx's opening assertion is that *Capital* is a work of "science." He then immediately goes on, at some length, to explain that the analysis of economic "value" has no microscope or chemical reagents to help and, substituting for these, "the power of abstraction has to take the place of both these expedients."[3] He adds that if this sometimes seems like hairsplitting, the uninitiated reader should remember that we are no less concerned "with minutiae when we study histology, the microscopic study of the tissues."[4] Note, "when *we* study histology. . ." A few lines later, Marx is no longer the histologist but is now the physicist who, he explains, "pursues his investigations either by studying natural process . . . in the most pregnant forms . . . or else, whenever he can, he performs experiments." He himself, says Marx, shall pursue the first option, studying capitalism in England, where it is most fully developed. In one case histologist, in another physicist, in a third case Marx is a chemist, comparing his analysis of commodities to a chemical analysis which reveals that different substances are sometimes "made up of the same chemical elements."[5]

As a scientist, Marx explains his object is the study of "the natural laws of capitalist production, . . . these laws in themselves, the tendencies which work out with an *iron necessity* towards an *inevitable* goal."[6] Marx refers to his laws as "tendencies." Does this mean, as it usually does, an (inherent or acquired) inclination to move in a certain direction which can, however, be *opposed* but (unlike the notion of a "trend") only with *great difficulty*? In short, does "tendency" mean, for Marx, some inclination close to but still less than "inevitable"? Marx himself answers, insisting that "tendencies" are inclinations which "work out with an *iron* necessity toward an inevitable goal."

When Marx speaks of natural law and of tendency he clearly means, here and in other *but not in all cases*, inclinations that are *un*opposable, inexorable, and "inevitable." We have no choice but to believe that Marx meant what he said. No invocation of "tendency" can escape the conclusion that Marx—at any rate, *this* Marx—was a "determinist" who, in the plain meaning of that term, refers to someone who adheres to the doctrine that occurrences in nature are determined by antecedent causes and take place in accordance with natural laws, and who, further, holds that acts of the will are also the result of causes that determine them.

For Marx, knowing the natural laws governing capitalist society does not permit us either to "overleap the natural phases of evolution, nor shuffle out of the world by decrees." Such knowledge, said Marx, does not permit any change in the *direction* of social evolution; all it can do is "shorten and lessen the birth-pangs."[7] But the movement remains one of "iron necessity toward an inevitable goal."

I take some care to fasten down the determinist implications of Marx the scientist, for it has lately become fashionable to deny this outright, to gloss over it, or to soften it by saying that all Marx meant by laws were "tendencies"—as if there was more than a difference of degree. Inclinations to deny that Marx often conceived himself a scientist searching for inexorable laws are, in part, rationalizations seeking to modernize and salvage Marx; but, in part, they are also efforts grounded in ambiguities resident in Marx himself, but eagerly seized upon by those embarrassed by Marx's determinism and anxious to blot it out rather than to confront the meaning of his determinism and of his ambivalences about it.

As early as 1847, Marx had declared that the proletariat could not "overleap the natural phases of evolution," and that its political victory depended upon the prior development of an advanced industrial economy. If a proletariat forgets this, he warned, any victory it achieves will be only temporary and it will suffer a retribution:

> If the proletariat destroys the political rule of the bourgeoisie, that will only be a temporary victory, only an element in the service of the bourgeois revolution itself, as in 1789, *so long as in the course of history, in its "movement," the material conditions are not yet created which make necessary* the abolition of the bourgeois mode of production. Men do not build themselves a new world out of the fruits of the earth, as vulgar superstition believes, but out of the historical accomplishments of declining civilization. They must, in the course of their development, begin by themselves producing the material conditions of a new society, and *no effort of mind or will can relieve them from this destiny.*[8] [Note: this is Marx, *not Engels*, and was written a full twenty years before his remarks quoted above.]

In this, Marx gave voice to a cardinal political doctrine of Scientific Marxism, namely, that a successful socialist revolution requires, as its indispensable requisite, a prior high level of industrial development. This early determinism, later echoed in *Capital*, forbidding any "overleap [of] the natural phases of evolution" is clearly not Engels's corruption of Marx, and the former was thus utterly faithful when he wrote: "only at a certain level of development of the productive forces, an even very high level of our modern condition, does it become possible to raise production to such an extent that the abolition of class distinctions can be a real progress—can be lasting without bringing about stagnation."[9] There was, then, no point in a classless society if this meant an equality of poverty and a stagnant economy. For Marx and Engels, socialism *also* means development and modernization.

In *Capital* itself, Marx wrote that the accumulation of capital is one of the basic laws of capitalism and that "in proportion as capital accumulates, the condition of the worker, be his wages high or low, necessarily grows worse; . . . poverty grows as the accumulation of capital grows. The accumulation of wealth at one pole of society involves a simultaneous accumulation of poverty, labour ferment, slavery, ignorance, brutalisation, and moral degradation, at the opposite pole—where dwells the class that produces its own product in the form of capital."[10] In short, there is a mathematical proportionality as well as necessity in this law, which, by the way, Marx had already enunciated twenty years earlier in his polemic against Proudhon, *The Misery of Philosophy*.

The entire process comes to its necessary and catastrophic culmination when "the monopoly of capital itself becomes a fetter upon the mode of production, which has sprung up and flourished along with, and under it. Centralization of the means of production and socialization of labour at last reach a point where they become incompatible with their capitalist integument. The integument is burst asunder. The knell of capitalist expropriation sounds. The expropriators are expropriated."[11]

That there can be no doubt that Marx thought himself a scientist who had discovered the laws guarantying the doom of capitalism is, finally, discernible in his familiar "preface to the second German edition" of *Capital*, where he quotes approvingly—calling it "apt" and generous—from a laudatory Russian review of the first edition. The Russian reviewer (Illarion Kaufman) had written:

> For Marx, only one thing is important: to discover laws of the phenomena he is investigating. . . . As soon as he has discovered this law he proceeds to work out in detail the effects as manifested in social life. . . . Marx troubles himself only about one thing: to demonstrate by means of *exact scientific investigation*, the *necessity of definite and orderly successions* in social relations. . . . Marx regards the social movement as a natural process, *guided by laws which are not merely independent of the will, the consciousness, and the purposes of men, but, conversely, determine their will, their consciousness, and their purposes.*[12]

Like scientists of that period, Marx understood science as encompassing laws that governed human consciousness and will as they did any other natural object. In that specific sense, he was as polemically determinist as Robert Chambers and others of the scientific avant-guard of his time. Marx thus continually counterposes morality and "will" to the conditions and power of persons and classes, and he frequently comments on this in the most admonitory manner. "What you think just or equitable is out of the question," replies Marx to those calling for equal wages. "The question is: what is necessary and unavoidable with a given system of production?"[13] And again, "the will of the capitalist is certainly to take as much as possible. What we have to do is not to talk about his will, but to enquire into his power, the limits of that power, and the character of those limits."[14]

In 1872, during the course of a polemic against Bakunin, Marx denounces him because he "does not understand a thing about social revolution, only the political phrases about it; its economic conditions do not exist for him. Now since all hitherto existing forms, developed or undeveloped, include the servitude of the worker (be it in the form of the wage worker, peasant, etc.) he believes that in all of them a radical revolution is equally possible. But even more! He wants the European social revolution, founded on the economic basis of capitalist production, to take place at the level of the Russian or Slav agricultural and pastoral people." Marx concludes in disgust, "Will, not economic conditions, is the foundation of his social revolution."[15] Notice: Marx does not say *both* are necessary in some admixture. He himself treats each as mutually exclusive of the other; in short, he treats the two as contradictory.

This is one of the key doctrines usually separating Scientific from Critical Marxists, as suggested in the following comment by the arch Scientific Marxist, Karl Kautsky, in his review of *Marxism and Philosophy* by the sometime Critical Marxist, Karl Korsch: "In reality the conviction that social revolution is possible only under determinate conditions, and thus only in particular countries, belongs to the most important features of Marxism. The communist sect to which Korsch belongs has totally forgotten this. In its view, social revolution is possible and under all conditions."[16]

Marx's discussion of the role of "will" is more balanced yet unmistakable in its thrust in his *Eighteenth Brumaire of Louis Bonaparte:* "Men make their own history, but they do not make it just as they please; they do not make it under circumstances chosen by themselves, but under circumstances directly encountered, given, and transmitted from the past." Engels was to repeat this more than once. Here it seems as if Marx leaves room for the voluntaristic element—for "will"—as, indeed, he formally does. Yet the thrust of his argument is in the opposite direction, stressing not the freedom of the will but the limits on it. Thus in the very next sentence Marx invokes the constraint of tradition: "the tradition of all dead generations weighs like a nightmare on the brain of the living."[17]

There is, then, a *scientific* Marx and Marxism in which there are laws governing the evolution and inner dynamics of capitalism, dooming it inexorably; and, likewise, imposing a necessity no less severe upon revolutionaries; requiring that they, too, surrender to necessity, and remember that before a socialist revolution can succeed there must first have been established, by capitalism, an advanced industrial economy, whether in the state undergoing the revolution or at least in one able and willing to render aid to it. It is not "will" that is the foundation of revolution, Marx told Bakunin, but economic conditions. It is precisely this insistence, upon a prior advanced economic development for socialism, that Marx used to distinguish his own socialism from utopian socialism.

Marx generalized the point by formulating a sociology in which the focus is not on what persons wish or on their moralities, but on what their situations prevent or enable them to do. His focus, then, is on the *constraints* of social structure; it is this that is an authentic mark of scientific socialism. Here, the central emphasis is that all persons are *limited* by the roles they play, the classes of which they are members, the times and places in which, and the traditions and institutions under which, they live. Marx is especially concerned with the manner in which persons are limited by the level of the forces of production in their *economy* and, above all, by the direct social relationships into which owner and worker enter. For Marx the scientist, the center from which constraint emanates out into society is the mode of production, while the public sphere of the "will" is the realm of *politics*. Note, for example, how in his polemic against Bakunin, Marx counterposed the two. Bakunin, he says scornfully, "does not understand a thing about social revolution," only the political phrases about it; its economic conditions do not exist for him. Marx the scientist thereby created a political lacuna in his theory that called for a remedy.

Marxism as Critique and Art

If at times Marx thinks himself a scientist among scientists, there are also other times when he thinks himself something different, when he regards himself as a *critic* and his work as *critique*. Thus *Das Kapital*'s subtitle is, of course, *A Critique of Political Economy*. Critique is the realm of philosophy and of the *art* of interpretation. I have noted how, in the pages of *Capital,* Marx portrays himself as a scientist. Yet there was another self-portrait that he also drew: "when Marx was working on his first volume, he wrote Engels (July 31, 1865) that whatever the shortcomings of his writings might be, they had the 'merit of making an artistic whole'; and in his next letter to Engels (August 5) he speaks of his book as a 'work of art' and mentions 'artistic considerations' in connection with his delay in getting it finished."[18] Edmund Wilson is surely correct in adding that, "certainly there went into the creation of *Das Kapital* as much of art as of science"; but it should not be missed that the art was vaunted only privately and the science publicly. In the public presentation of his scholarship, Marx offered it as science and suppressed a definition of it as art, thereby telling us about the *hierarchy of values* to which his work submitted. Indeed, the three main texts used to portray Marxism as critique rather than science—the *Grundrisse,* the Paris manuscripts of 1844, and the theses on Feuerbach—were never published by Marx himself. They were in effect suppressed by him, self-censored.

Scientific and Critical Marxism are divergent paradigms because Marx's "science" is especially concerned to discover laws independent of human will and which cannot be suspended by science itself, while his "critique" is concerned to exhibit the manner in which outcomes depend on human efforts. His science's standpoint, then, is deterministic and structural; his critiques's standpoint is voluntaristic. Science is generally concerned with the internal cultivation of technical knowledge. It does not make focal the "command" implications of what it "reports," and (in August Comte's words), neither "praises nor blames" events. Critique, however, is concerned with interpreting events in terms of values that are not merely technical and it thus works at the interface between a technical speciality and the larger, encompassing culture.

Unlike the "laws" of Scientific Marxism, which exhibit the inexorable working of events, critique is not determinist. It does not show what must be but only what may be, or what can or could be. The standpoint of critique and its special reading of Marx is well exhibited by the young Max Horkheimer.

> The illusion that the advent of the socialist order is of the same order of necessity is hardly less of a danger to correct action than is skeptical disbelief. If Marx did not prove social-

ism, he did show that capitalism harbors developmental tendencies which make it possible.... The socialist order of
society is not prevented by world history; it is historically
possible. But it will not be realized by a logic that is immanent
in history.[19]

Critique, then, only shows what may be, not what must be. It
may examine emerging trends and their relative strength as one
element in establishing what may be. It is open to the truly new
and emergent. Critique especially throws light on the hidden,
repressed, unspoken possibilities, the possibilities that may be
hostile to "what is," indicating what they are, why they have been
hidden, and by whom. It is thus not "what is" or even what is
becoming on which critique is grounded. For it cannot opt for all
that is possible, but must select among possibilities on the basis of
some set of values to which it has committed itself.

To make a critique of something—to criticize it—inevitably
premises things might be otherwise. There is a tacit Kantianism in
critique which assumes, "ought implies can." Thus a knowledge
of what is (or is becoming) may indicate what is *possible* and is the
empirical part of critique; but there is no way of choosing among
various possibilities without grounding choice in some value system. Critique, then, is inevitably a fusion of the empirical and the
moral. It implies that human history is the outcome not of structural constraints or "necessity" but of human striving, of persons'
efforts and powers, even if these are hidden. The basic conclusion
of the Left Hegelians' critique of religion—the concrete paradigm
of the more general critique used by Marx—thus stressed that
God's being was entirely a projection of people's own alienated
being.

Critique, therefore, aims at making human potency manifest; it
is grounded in a humanism optimistically convinced that humanity can make and remake the world. To that extent critique shares
the antitragic perspective common to all ideological discourse (as
discussed in Chapter Three of my *Dialectic of Ideology*).

Marx as Darwin, Marx as Hegel

The polymorphous diversity of Marx's thought, continually vacillating between science and critique, had a very personal and indeed biographical grounding expressed in Marx's own shifting
identifications, first with Hegel, then with Darwin; the two are his

greatest models. There is an archeology here: Marx starts by taking Hegel's role but then moves toward an identification with
Darwin, which in part replaces and in part suppresses that earlier
identification. Marx is soon happy to be compared with Darwin
and wants to dedicate an edition of *Capital* to him.

On 19 December 1860, Marx writes Engels that, in the last four
weeks, "I have read all sorts of things. Among others Darwin's
book on Natural Selection. Although it is developed in the crude
English style, this is the book which contains the basis in natural
history for our view."[20] A year later he writes Lassalle (16 January
1861) that "Darwin's book is very important and serves me as a
basis in natural science for the class struggle in history; . . . the
death blow is dealt here for the first time to 'teleology' in the
natural sciences but their rational meaning is empirically explained."[21] At Marx's funeral, then, it was not Engels's vulgarizing
distortion that led him, in his final eulogy at the Highgate Ceme-
tery, to compare Marx to Darwin: "Just as Darwin discovered the
laws of development of organic nature, so Marx discovered the
law of development of human history." Similar comparisons later
made by Karl Kautsky are, again, no evidence at all of a corruption
of originary Marxism.

For Marx, Darwin is Hegel scientized and modernized while
Hegel is the philosophic depth of Darwin—without the English
"crudity." Both saw development as blind and unconscious; and
both saw it as occurring through struggle. For Hegel, there is the
metaphysics of "contradiction" and the sociological archetypal
contest between master and bondsman, eventuating in the latter's
paradoxical triumph; while for Darwin, struggle inheres in the
natural processes producing survival of the fittest. Both theorists
also work with nonpredictive "interpretations"; for both, the Owl
of Minerva flew late. As George Herbert Mead clearly saw, in his
much neglected but very valuable work,[22] the convergence between Darwin and Hegel was profound. Indeed, it was in part that
very convergence that enabled Marx to move from critique to science, to sublate and escape from philosophy.

Though convergent, Darwin and Hegel were scarcely identical.
Each permitted Marx a different perspective on himself and expressed different sides of his ambitions. Marx had been Hegel but
was for a while tempted to "become" Darwin. Matters were not
made simpler, however, when Darwin politely declined Marx's
offer to dedicate the English translation of *Capital* to him. But if
Marx recognized the convergence between Darwin and himself,

he clearly saw certain ideological limits in Darwin. In a letter to Engels of 18 June 1862, he observed that "Darwin recognizes among beasts and plants his English society with its division of labour, competition, opening up of new markets, 'invention,' and the Malthusian 'struggle for existence'." To which Engels (in a letter to P.L. Lavrov, 17 November 1875) added ironically that, after having projected society's characteristics on nature, "the same theories are transferred back again from organic nature into history and their validity as eternal laws of human society has been proved."

To surrender Hegel and dwell only on Darwin, then, was to surrender to a shallow natural history, which was devoid of sociological insight and which would extinguish subjectivity as an element in human history, transforming human conflict into a blind species struggle for existence. Marx thus retained an abiding ambivalence toward both these different paradigms, and they remained two worlds uneasily juxtaposed within him, *even as he edged ever closer to science.* While Marx was respectfully ambivalent toward science, his critique of philosophy is far sharper and less evenly balanced. Marx thus creates an opening toward positivism[23] to which some among the next generation of Marxists, lacking his philosophical heritage and depth, would be susceptible.

The Ambiguity of Hegel

Marxism's potentiality for a positivistic segregation of philosophy and science, with its corresponding devaluation of philosophy, was clearly signaled in Engels's analysis of the development of German philosophy from Hegel to Ludwig Feurbach. With Hegel, Engels assumes, "there is an end of all philosophy in the hitherto accepted sense of the word, . . . instead, one pursues attainable, relative truth along the path of the positive sciences, and the summation of their results by means of dialectical philosophy. At any rate, with Hegel philosophy comes to an end; . . . he showed us the way out of the labyrinth of 'systems' to real positive knowledge of the world."[24]

In this judgement, Engels treats philosophy as a passive "summation" of the sciences, as science's bookkeeper, rather than as the independent auditor appraising its intellectual solvency. He clearly intimates the obsolescence of philosophy and its supersession by the sciences. Unlike science, philosophy remains in his view linked intrinsically to ideology and even to religion: "Still higher ideologies . . . take the form of philosophy and religion."[25] In a later passage, Engels also holds that the Marxist conception of history . . . puts an end to philosophy in the realm of history," maintaining that now "philosophy has been expelled from nature and history."[26]

The above remarks, having been written by Engels, will quickly be seized upon by those who believe that weaknesses in Marxism were all produced by Engels and the strengths by Marx. But this crude view of the matter is soon dispelled if we look at *The German Ideology* which was written by *both* of them in 1846. There it may be seen that both invidiously counterposed positive science to philosophy—and not just once: "When reality is depicted, philosophy as an independent branch of activity loses its medium of existence." And then expressly foreshadowing Engels's remarks above—about philosophy serving as a "summation" of the sciences—they immediately add: "At the best its [philosophy's] place can only be taken by a summing-up of the most general results, abstractions which arise from the observation of the historical development of men."[27] The invidious contrast between philosophy and empirical science is again formulated in the following manner: "when we conceive things thus, as they really are and happened, every profound philosophical problem is resolved, as will be seen even more clearly later, quite simply into an empirical fact."[28] These comments mark the transition in both Marx and Engels from philosophy to science and, indeed, to a view of science which stressed the decisive role of empirical observation.

It is in this sense that Louis Althusser is correct in noting that Marx's critique of "ideology" entailed a transition to a focal affirmation of a social "science" (*historical* materialism), along with a simultaneous (but *de*-focalized) philosophical innovation, *dialectical* materialism. In Althusser's words: "as the new philosophy was only implicit in the new science it might be tempted *to confuse itself with it. The German Ideology* sanctions this confusion as it reduces philosophy . . . to a faint shadow of science, if not to the empty generality of positivism."[29]

Althusser, however, ignores the *reason* that Marx's dialectical philosophy remained de-focalized or "only implicit." He fails to understand Marx's silence properly, treating it as a kind of passive lacuna or mere oversight, rather than as the symptom of an active *repression* grounded in a real struggle within Marxism. The point is that philosophy is not simply ignored but comes to be *devalued* in Marx and Engels. This devaluation is expressed in a conception of philosophy as ideological, as idealistic, even religious. In Marx's experience, the dominant, paradigmatic philosophies of his time were in fact idealistic; his critique of idealism and ideology therefore becomes identified with and colors his critique of philosophy as such. Marx's critique of philosophy, then, has the same structure as his critique of ideology and idealism; both entail the affirmation of the *contrary*. In his critique of philosophy there is an affirmation of "positive science"[30] that presents science as an *alternative* to philosophy. In that framework, to favor science is to *oppose* or at least suspect, philosophy and to treat it repressively rather than to complement and complete it with a social science.

The tendency invidiously to contrast philosophy and science within Marxism is not recent then, but is faithfully grounded in Marx's own intellectual transition from Hegel's philosophy to what he takes to be the *scientific* scholarship of empirically grounded political economy. This transition should be thought of as a shift in *languages* occasioned by moving from one intellectual territory (or problematic) to another. It does not necessarily mean that the mover comes to hold his first language in contempt or reject it; indeed, he may even feel a certain warm nostalgia when he thinks about it; certainly it has a lingering influence on his thinking; but he begins to forget and to lose competence in it and, in time, he begins to think and even dream in the new language.

While Marx stressed that political economy needed to be subjected to a purifying critique before he appropriated it to his own purposes, this was a process of stripping it of its ideological impurities so that what remained for his use would be *authentic* science. Increasingly, Marx developed a sense of the kinship between his own views and those of the sciences then burgeoning and (as we saw) most especially with Darwinianism.

When Marx spoke of abolishing (*aufgehoben*) philosophy, many take this as mere hyperbole, as if this greatly learned man could not have contemplated a "sin against philosophy" or harbored truly destructive impulses toward this capstone of culture. Others, however, seem to think that Marx renounced philosophy and became antiintellectual. Both views vulgarize the matter, missing the complexities; missing, above all, Marx's and Marxism's real *ambivalence* toward philosophy. Karl Korsch captured this when he remarked, "I described the dialectical materialist, critical revolutionary theory of Marx and Engels in the 1840's as an '*anti-philosophy*' which yet in itself remained philosophical. On the one hand, socialist 'science' became positive and gradually turned away from philosophy altogether. On the other hand, philosophical development occurred, apparently in conflict with the former but in fact complementary to it."[31]

Marx's judgement on philosophy is complex and ambivalent: suspecting that philosophy is rooted in the past, regarding it as world-avoiding and academic, as interpreting but never achieving. He viewed philosophy's very paradigm as idealism, believing that idealism was a secret secularisation of religion, and that all critique begins with the critique of religion. Marx's reaction to philosophy embodied a certain warm contempt as well as cool critique. Other Marxists heard this contempt correctly. Franz Mehring thus once allowed himself to speak of the importance of rejecting "all philosophical fantasies," while Karl Kautsky could blandly confess, "philosophy was never my strong point." In this very articulate group, it is easy to miss the silences in Marx and Marxism. Therefore one notes: while there was much talk about "philosophical" fantasies there was no corresponding curt dismissal of the fantasies of *science*; while there was heady talk about the importance of "subsuming" and transcending philosophy there was never any corresponding passionate plea with regard to science.

This multi-layered critique of philosophy—whose full passion is revealed in Marx's mocking work, *The Holy Family*—spills out in two different directions. One is toward positivism, where he drops the mantle of critical philosopher and attempts to squeeze into the garb of scientist. At the same time, however, and even as he slowly stops thinking in the language of philosophy, he senses that the new science has been left without intellectual depth. Seeing the political crudities of scientists, the ease with which they are snared in ideological traps,[32] and recognizing that the new sciences are used by and fused with capitalist industry, Marx silently revisits the old haunted house of philosophy—as in 1857 when he takes up Hegel's *Logic*, the year he starts the *Grundrisse*. The first, the scientific culture in which he (and Engels still more) immersed himself, eventuated in an articulate scientific theory of society—"historical materialism"—while the second was a critical standpoint, a philosophy, Althusser's unborn "dialectical materialism," present only in embryo. Around these different archeological layers there grew the tendrils of the subsequent differentiation between Scientific and Critical Marxism.

It is in this light that we can perhaps reinterpret the relationship of the two Marxisms to Hegel. For it is not so much that only

Critical Marxists return to Hegel, and that Scientific Marxists forgo that pilgrimage. There are tendencies in this direction, but only that; a more accurate formulation would suggest that both sometimes return to Hegel, *but for different reasons*. Scientific Marxism goes back to restore its sense of a comprehensive system, to prevent itself from drowning in the narrowness of the new scientific specializations, to refurbish its feeling for wholeness. In *this* return to Hegel, as Merleau-Ponty suggests, it is not a question of the dialectic but of Hegel's logic, with its promise that order is embedded in the universe. In its most extreme manifestations, Scientific Marxism centers on "materialism"—in which mind is thought of as mirroring an out-there reality—while Critical Marxism becomes the guardian of mind-as-lamp. Critical Marxism returns to Hegel precisely for his dialectic: i.e., for his sense of the subject-object interaction, therefore of the subjective side of boundaried things, of the inserted character of boundaries, and, above all, because of the dialectic's power of negativity—its ability to draw a line and to say, No. When Critical Marxism returns to Hegel and when it invokes philosophy more generally, it strives to establish the grounds for a standpoint outside science that will allow a critique even of vaunted science which will not allow science to become a law to itself and will not take science's fusion with technology for granted. Critical Marxism returns to philosophy and to Hegel, then, in part because it does not altogether trust science and certainly does not believe (as George Lundberg once said) "science can save us."

The return to Hegel, then, is not simply the impulse of the Critical Marxist alone; this is quite plain in Engels's own admiration for Hegel which, he acknowledges,[33] was his and Marx's "point of departure." Engels, too, stressed the ambiguity of Hegel, distinguishing between Hegel's "system" which he felt was of conservative import and his "method" which maintained a revolutionary ethos. Engels held that when Hegel claimed that "all that is real is rational; and all that is rational is real," that this was "tangibly a sanctification of things that be, a philosophical benediction bestowed upon despotism, police-government, star chamber proceedings and censorship."[34] Yet, at the same time, Hegel also

> dealt the deathblow to the finality of all products of human thought and action; . . . all successive historical situations are only transitory stages in the endless course of development of human society from the lower to the higher. Each stage is

necessary, therefore, justified for the time and conditions to
which it owes its origins. But in the newer and higher conditions which gradually develop in its own bosom, each loses its
validity and justification. It must give way to the higher form
which will also in its turn decay and perish; . . . so this dialectical philosophy dissolved all conceptions of final absolute
truth and of a final absolute state of humanity corresponding
to it. For it, nothing is final, absolute, sacred. It reveals the
transitory character of everything.[35]

Whether Engels finally judged Hegel as primarily conservative or
primarily revolutionary is far from certain. On one side, he held
Hegel's conservatism was only "relative," declaring that his
philosophy's "revolutionary character is absolute."[36] On the other
side, however, Engels also declared that "Hegel, himself, despite
the fairly frequent outbursts of revolutionary wrath in his works,
seemed on the whole to be more inclined to the conservative
side."[37] Thus Engels seems to have been tempted to accept a
contradiction between Hegel the man and the Hegelian
philosophy, as well as an inner tension between the philosophy's
system and its method.

Clearly, however, no interpretation of Hegel's philosophy as an
unequivocal critique of the present can be sustained. There is a
powerful element of conservative positivity in the Hegel who
claimed that his own *Philosophy of Right* "must be poles apart
from an attempt to construct a state as it ought to be. . . . To com-
prehend what is, this is the task of philosophy, because what is, is
reason." Again, in his introduction to *The German Constitution*
Hegel wrote that "the thoughts contained in this essay cannot
have any other aim or effect upon publication than the understanding of that which is and thus promote calmer contemplation
as well as the ability to endure it."[38]

Rejecting the separation of reality and morality, Hegel identified the task of his philosophy as understanding the "present and
actual, not the construction of an ideal world." It is not farfetched
to hear Marx's rejection of utopianism, of sentimentality, and of
morality as echoing this. In short, it is not just Marx's turn toward
science that is the grounding for the emergence of "scientific"
Marxism; so, too, are elements in Hegel's philosophy. Hegel, like
Marx, also believed that he had turned philosophy toward science: "To help bring philosophy near to the form of science; . . .
that is what I have set before me."[39] It would be difficult to state
Marx's own ambition more aptly. The essential point, then, is that

Marx was exposed to positivism and, indeed, readied for positive science, not simply by his studies of science but, well before that, by his own most basic grounding in a philosophy whose own aspirations were scientific. Marxism's own tendency to differentiate itself into Scientific and Critical Marxism is thus partly rooted in its very Hegelian legacy which had, even earlier, already sought to transform itself into science.

Marx was Hegelian in seeking to ground communism in what was, and in what was becoming, in the "present and actual." He was edged toward positivism as much by his Hegelian heritage as by his involvement with the empirical sciences themselves. At the same time, and like Hegel, Marx does not take "what is" as final; he does not simply describe it or accept it. He opposes the present with a critique which, in turn, requires the standpoint of a philosophy and not just a science; in particular, he requires a philosophy that can provide a grounding for political choice and action. Essentially, then, Marx is caught in a tunnel connecting science and philosophy, and he shuttles back and forth between them. He cannot relinquish science without capitulating to a moralistic view of socialism and he cannot renounce philosophy and the grounding it provides critique without surrendering to the present. For Marx's double-pronged project—to know *and* to change the world—philosophy was insufficient to know the world, science insufficient to criticize it. Marx cannot therefore embrace critique without science and science without critique.

NOTES

1. For further discussion of Kuhn, see Alvin W. Gouldner, *The Dialectic of Ideology and Technology* (New York: Seabury Press, 1976).

2. Karl Marx, *Capital: A Critique of Political Economy* Vol. I, translated from the 4th German ed. by Eden and Cedar Paul, published in 2 vols., with an introduction by G. D. H. Cole (London and Toronto: J. M. Dent & Sons, 1930), vol. 2, p. 861.

3. *Capital* I, Dent ed., 2:862.

4. Ibid.

5. *Capital* I, Dent ed., 1:20.

6. *Capital* I, Dent ed., 2:863. Italics added.

7. *Capital* I, Dent ed., 2:864.

8. Karl Marx, *Selected Writings in Sociology and Social Philosophy*, ed. T. Bottomore and M. Rubel (London: Watts, 1956), p. 240. Italics added.

9. Robert C. Tucker, ed., *The Marx-Engels Reader* (New York: W. W. Norton & Co., 1972), p. 590.

10. *Capital* I, Dent ed., 2:714.

11. *Capital* I, Dent ed., 2:763.

12. *Capital* I, Dent ed., 2:871. Italics added. That Marxism was construed by Kaufman as a scientific Marxism bent on identifying the governing laws of capitalism was not, therefore, as is sometimes supposed by certain critical Marxists, a late misinterpretation that sprang up only under the impress of social democracy or was inserted by Engels after Marx's death. There is no question at all but that Marxism was widely defined as a "scientific Marxism" during Marx's lifetime and, indeed, under his auspices. This can be seen in the interpretations given of his work *immediately* upon his death in 1883, and in the eulogies and obituaries whose spontaneiety suggests that this was a definition of Marx's work already in being. The definitive source for such materials is the very useful collection of materials edited by Philip S. Foner, *When Karl Marx Died: Comments in 1883* (N.Y.: International Publishers, 1973). Here we may plainly see that, for example, it was not only in Engels's funeral address that Marx is eulogized as having "discovered the special law of motion govering the present-day capitalist method of production" (p. 39) but in others as well. Thus the Paris Brotherhood of the French Workers' Party sent a telegram emphasizing that Marx's contribution had been the creation of "scientific socialism" (p. 41). Wilhelm Liebknecht's funeral oration, "as representative of German social democracy," also extols Marx as having created the scientific basis of socialism, defining Marxism as centered in and characterized by its scientific character, and going on to eulogize science itself (p. 42.) As many of the contemporary obituaries make plain, Marxism was then widely understood as distinguished from other socialisms in large part by reason of its discovery of capitalism's laws.

13. Karl Marx, *Value, Price and Profit*, ed. Eleanor Marx Aveling (New York: International Publishers, 1935), p. 39.

14. Ibid., p. 11.

15. Karl Marx, *Selected Writings*, ed. David McLellan (New York: Oxford University Press, 1977), p. 562. Italics added.

16. From *Die Gesellschaft*, (1924), Vol. 1, pp. 306–14; cited by Paul Breines "Praxis and Its Theorists," *Telos*, Spring 1972, p. 74.

17. Karl Marx, *The Eighteenth Brumaire of Louis Bonaparte* (New York: International Publishers, 1964), p. 27.

18. Edmund Wilson, *To the Finland Station* (Garden City, N.Y.: Doubleday & Co., 1940), p. 287. This is a magisterial work of passionate scholarship that remains the best standard by which to measure the achievements of the post–World War II generation of Hegelian interpretations of Marxism. Set against Wilson's lucid synthesis, my generation's self-celebrations seem somewhat intoxicated.

19. Max Horkheimer, *Dawn and Decline: Notes 1926–1931 and 1950–1969*, trans. Michael Shaw (New York: Seabury Press, 1978), p. 37. Originally published by Horkheimer under the pseudonym Heinrich Regius in *Dammerung, Notizen in Deutschland* (1926–1931).

20. Karl Marx and Friedrick Engels, *Selected Correspondence 1846–1895*, trans. Dona Torr (New York: International Publishers, 1942), p. 126.

21. Ibid., p. 125.

22. G. H. Mead, *Movements of Thought in the Nineteenth Century* (Chicago: University of Chicago Press, 1936).

23. Positivism is a mode of consciousness in which science is taken as a given and is not concerned to justify itself and the basic criteria it applies. Its sociological premise is the segregation of science from philosophy, partly through an institutionalized academic division of labor and partly through bourgeois culture's contempt for philosophy as impractical, useless, and powerless.

24. F. Engels, *Ludwig Feuerbach and the Outcome of Classical German Philosophy* (New York: International Publishers, 1941), p. 15.

25. Ibid., p. 55.

26. Ibid., p. 59.

27. K. Marx and F. Engels, *The German Ideology*, trans. W. Lough and C. P. Magill, ed. R. Pascal (New York: International Publishers, n.d.), p. 15.

28. Ibid., p. 35. On p. 13 empirical observation is contrasted invidiously not only with mystification but also with "speculation."

29. Louis Althusser, *For Marx* (London: Allen Lane, 1969), pp. 33–34.

30. This positivistic dimension of Marxism and Marx has been brilliantly explored in the work of Jürgen Habermas and Albrecht Wellmer.

31. Karl Korsch, *Marxism and Philosophy* (London: New Left Books, 1970), p. 95.

32. Marx most especially scored the ahistorical abstractness of science: "The abstract materialism of a natural science that excludes the historical process is defective; we can see in a moment where we glance at the abstract and ideological conceptions voiced by its advocates whenever they venture beyond the boundary of their own specialty." But, still, this is said only in a footnote. *Capital* I, Dent ed. 1:393.

33. Engels, *Ludwig Feuerbach*, p. 8.

34. Ibid., p. 10.

35. Ibid., pp. 11–12.

36. Ibid., p. 12.

37. Ibid., p. 16.

38. Cited in Walter Kaufmann, *Hegel: A Reinterpretation* (Garden City, N.Y.: Doubleday & Co., 1966), p. 86.

39. G. W. F. Hegel, *The Phenomenology of Mind*, trans. J. B. Baillie (New York: Harper & Row Pubs., 1967), p. 70.

APPENDIX
Conflating the Contrary and Negation[1]

At the center of Marxism's conception of itself is the view that it is a "materialism." This materialism emerged in the course of Marx's determined opposition to two different types of "theories." On the one hand, he opposed and sought to differentiate his views from other forms of *materialism*, e.g., from "vulgar," mechanical, or bourgeois materialisms. This, however, was only a *secondary* opposition. The overshadowing context in which Marx's materialism arose was his opposition to everyday *idealism*, expressed in a critique of traditional religion, that was extended into an opposition to the dominant German philosophical *idealism*, and especially Hegelianism. This critique of *idealism* is essentially a critique of the idea that mind or consciousness determines or is independent of the other spheres of life; it is also a critique of the Enlightenment premise that social changes proceed from prior changes in understanding or consciousness. The Marxist critique of ideology, which is also part of its rejection of idealism, entailed the transformation of Destutt de Tracy's positive appreciation of "ideology" into a negative symbol. This inversion derived from the fact that de Tracy's concept of ideology[2] rested on the idealistic assumption that changes in ideology were the key to social transformations; it premised that if one changed the present belief system, eliminating its errors, and educating the populace into the newly purified ideologies, a better society and state would result. Marx, who recurrently mentioned de Tracy's work polemically, had picked up de Tracy's word, "ideology," fully explicated its idealistic assumptions, but then evaluated these negatively rather than positively. Marx thus inverted de Tracy's notion of ideology and then used it as a way to generalize the Left Hegelians' critique of religion. The focus now moved from the critique of *religion* to a more general ideology critique. This allowed a critique of secular belief systems, including rational philosophies and metaphysics, even of those defining themselves as "sciences." It is via Marx's devaluation of ideology that he moves from an explicit critique of religion to a critique of rational secular philosophy and of the social *science* of political economy. These, he holds, are also ideological because they believe themselves autonomous when, in fact, they are dependent on other social conditions.

An essential *beginning* for Marx, what he faced as a *given*, was an entrenched idealism that existed on different levels: on the level of everyday Christianity with its stress on the godly, sacred, spiritual; on the level of German culture with its concepts of *Geist* and *Kultur*; and on the level of the continuous tournament of technical German philosophical idealisms that became entrenched institutionally as the everyday subculture of German universities of the time, and which made a certain affirmation: *ideas (spirit, mind, consciousness) are all-powerful, independent, and self-controlling.*

Marxism first defined itself by drawing a line between itself and idealism. Affirming itself as a "materialism," it opposed idealism in two ways; first, by asserting the *contrary* of idealism and, secondly, by *negating* idealism. For example, one may say of a political party, "It is *good* for the people." Opposition to this statement can take, at least, two different forms: one can reply, "No, that party is *bad* for the people." Here opposition takes the form of asserting the contrary. In the contrary, two alternative attributes are set forth as tacitly encompassing all the alternatives, each of which has been asserted explicitly and with equal clarity, and an object cannot be both but must be one or the other.

The second form of opposition, *negation,* rather than holding that the political party is "bad," simply says that it is *not*-good. Note, this does not say *what* the party *is,* but only what it is *not.* This may seem to be a trivial distinction, but it isn't; for while negation *may* entail the contrary, it need not. That is, if we say X, a political party is *not*-good, we may or we may *not* hold that it is *bad,* for we may be *tacitly* making a different type of affirmation altogether. For instance, to hold that X is "powerful" or "active" are cases of the negation that X is good; but they do not necessarily affirm that X is *bad.* Indeed, a negation may imply that an affirmation (good) and its contrary (bad) are both irrelevant, and that X is *neither*; it may focus X on an altogether different dimension, say, on a "potency" rather than an "evaluative" dimension. A negation, then, leaves open the question of *what* is being *affirmed* and thus has an inherent ambiguity.

In negation one *might* affirm the contrary, thereby accepting that the object must be characterized on the dimension tacitly implicated in the initial affirmation; or negation may imply the rejection of this dimension and focus on another dimension, and a specific point on this second dimension. Negation, then, includes the *possibility* of a contrary, but does not limit itself to it.[3] A familiar instance of this in current discourse is the relationship between "reason" and "violence." In liberal discourse, reason and violence are commonly treated as contraries, implying that they are at opposite poles of one dimension. This further implies that if you settle a dispute by violence you cannot settle it with reason, or if you choose reason you cannot choose violence. A different contention, however, would be that (made, for instance, by Roy Edgely)[4] violence does not exclude the rational; that violence may or may not be rational; and hence the contention is that the negation of the rational, the nonrational, is not *necessarily* the violent but may include the *non*-violent. That is, certain settlements of disputes may be neither rational *nor* violent; for instance, throwing dice to see who wins; and certain settlements may be both rational and violent.

Marx's opposition to German idealism, with the latter's affirmation that ideas (spirit, mind, consciousness) are all-powerful, independent, and controlling vis-a-vis other things, sometimes proceeds by negating idealism and sometimes by affirming its contrary. In short, Marx conflated the contrary and the negation. In affirming idealism's contrary—the less ambiguous and the more limiting response—Marx is led to affirm that ideas are weak, dependent, and controlled (epiphenomenal) elements. Instead of causing something, ideas are caused. The affirmation of the contrary, then, is the distinctive method of critique; it is the "transformative criticism" or "inversion" common to the Young Hegelians from whom Marx emerged. Thus in rejecting "Consciousness determines social being," Marx often affirms the contrary, namely, "Social being determines consciousness."

This is quite different from an alternative mode of opposition to idealism also used by Marx, that of *negation*, in which he would simply hold: rather than being all-powerful, ideas are *not* all-powerful; rather than being independent, ideas are *not*-independent; rather than being controllers, ideas are *not*-controllers. Marx's conflation of these two forms of opposition, of the negation with the contrary, was a consequential confusion. For to say ideas are *not*—all-powerful is not necessarily to say they are *weak*; and to say ideas are *not*-autonomous is not necessarily to say they are dependent.

Marx's opposition to idealism thus opened in two different directions, sometimes toward negation and sometimes to an affirmation of the contrary, an *inversion*. Many of the problems of Marxist materialism are grounded in serious ambiguities born of his conflation of the contrary and the negative.

In the following there are alternating concrete examples of the differences between Marx's use of the negation and the contrary to oppose German idealism; they are taken from a single source, one of Marx and Engels's early critiques of idealism, *The German Ideology*.[5] The juxtaposition of contrary and of negation, often only a few pages apart, documents that there was indeed a confusion of the two.

> *Materialism as Negation:* "Morality, religion, metaphysics, all the rest of ideology and their corresponding forms of consciousness thus no longer retain the semblance of independence." (p. 14)

Materialism as Contrary: "Life is not determined by consciousness but consciousness by life." (p. 15)

Materialism as Negation: "When reality is depicted, philosophy as an independent branch of activity loses its medium of existence." (p. 15)

Materialism as Contrary: "Our conception of history does not explain practice from the idea but explains the formation of ideas from material practice; and accordingly it comes to the conclusion that all forms and products of consciousness cannot be dissolved by mental criticism, . . . but only by the practical overthrow of actual social relations which gave rise to this idealistic humbug." (pp. 28–29) ". . .the removal of these notions from the consciousness of men, will as we have already said, be affected by altered circumstances, not by theoretical deductions." (p. 32)

To oppose idealism only by negating it is commendable from a standpoint concerned to be prudent and seeking to avoid insupportable overstatement. But negation is dramaturgically weak since it leaves open the question of what it is *for* and hedges on the issue of *what is.* Negation is a weaker, seemingly empty form of opposition, that presents no positive alternative to what it opposes but simply rejects it. It is "negative," in the sense of incomplete. The contrary, however, opposes the adversary and, at the same time, exhibits the alternative to his position; it does not simply seek to put him down but to raise up something and someone else. It is "positive." The contrary not only holds the opponent to be wrong but adds under its breath that he could not have been more wrong, and that the truth was the very opposite of what he had held. The contrary, then, has vividness and metaphysical overkill that gives it a dramaturgical edge.

To constitute itself as a positive alternative to idealism, Marxism was often led to affirm idealism's contrary which, on the *sociological* level, meant affirming that it was not ideologies but the forces and relations of production—the material, economic, and property institutions—that determine outcomes in society, "in the final instance." The only alternative to this, in opposing idealism, was to speak of the *mutual* interaction and *reciprocal* influence of infra- and superstructures, i.e., a version of holistic analysis, which in effect denies that there is any *infra-* or *super*structure at all. The first formulation, stressing the dominance of "material" forces and organizing itself as the contrary of idealism, constitutes Marxism as a "factor model" counterposing its own single factor against other competing single factors. Holistic analysis, however, derives from an opposition to idealism grounded in its negation, and is open toward a version of systems or totality analysis.

The Marxist use of the contrary to oppose idealism had the effect of *focalizing* material conditions—certain relations and forces of production—as the *necessary* condition of socialist revolution.

Materialism-as-contrary (of idealism) asserts something *positive* as a politics. Its strategy of revolution focused on the more advanced industrial nations and led to an expectation that they comprised the best investment for political struggle and the best arena for socialist transformation. Materialism-as-contrary became the basis for a decision by socialists concerning which societies they should invest themselves in and which they should not. In effect, then, the Marxism that came to be called "scientific" Marxism, epitomized by the Second International and Karl Kautsky, grounded itself in a positivistic Marxism that opposed idealism by affirming its contrary. Not only did this imply a conception of revolutionary strategy, but it also entailed a conception of the essence of socialism itself, seeing this as grounded in the construction of a new technology, new forces of production, the growth of science, and other "material" forces. Materialism-as-contrary, then, was what became "scientific" Marxism, particularly when combined with a determinist and wooden conception of social evolution stressing the inevitability of socialism. This conception had ambiguous political consequences. On the one side, it sustained political opposition by those in a weak minority, allowing them to carry on despite this weakness, feeling that history would ultimately send reinforcements if they could only hang on. But if such an "historical materialism" gave socialists the courage to endure, it also fostered their passivity and quiescence, leading them to expect that deliverance was in the historical works, quite apart from anything that they might have to do or to suffer.

A socialist politics grounded in a materialism-as-negation, however, is ambiguous with respect to what is essential to socialist strategy and tactics, as well as what defines a socialist economy or society. Such negation-grounded Marxism remains flexible about political strategy or tactics or, for that matter, about the nature of socialism itself. Such a Marxism can acknowledge that the transformation of "material" conditions is an element, or beginning, that is indeed necessary for socialism and socialist revolution. This acknowledgement permits it continued membership in the Marxist community and asserts a "Marxist" identity, without, however, accepting the limits commonly imposed on the politics of Scientific Marxism. This materialism-as-negation can now attribute heightened importance to voluntaristic, theoretical, and ideological dimensions—to "consciousness"—and is less bound to define its enemies only in terms of their economies and technologies. Above all, it need not restrict its political ambitions to those societies that already have an advanced industrial basis. A negation-grounded Marxism, then, can seek revolution anywhere and at any time, without being limited by the presence of an advanced material base.

The most important historical case of a negation-grounded Marxism, *Maoism*, continually exhibited its own grounding in the negating dialectic by repeatedly emphasizing, as Mao himself did, that "It is *always* right to rebel." Here the "always" signaled that the right to rebel need not wait for the emergence of "appropriate" material conditions, or for prior industrial development. Mao's remark, "Power comes out of the barrel of a gun," similarly implied that it is struggle and combat, rather than science, technology, and other forces of production, that are the essential conditions for revolution and socialism. But if materialism-as-contrary Marxism inhibits and limits revolutionary militancy, and may thus become a kind of ritualistic socialism, materialism-as-negation Marxism escalates revolutionary militancy but runs the danger of losing sight of the goal, blurring the distinguishing essence of the socialism it seeks; for it now premises that socialism can be built anywhere, on any technological, material basis. In the Maoist case of a negation-grounded Marxism, the essence of socialism came to be defined in terms of new egalitarian *relations* of production, the struggle against the division of labor between mental and manual work and between the city and countryside, rather than in terms of the material *forces* of production.

The evolution of Marxist parties since the nineteenth century has been from a contrary-focusing to a negation-grounded socialism. The latter is *context-freeing* for Marxism and for socialist politics, allowing them to operate in less developed economies; at the same time, it is a context-freeing which threatens Marxism's identity with boundary dissolution. Materialism-as-negation Marxism was what came to be called Critical Marxism, Western Marxism, or Hegelian Marxism. Its essential characteristic is that it *also* stresses the importance of theory, of ideology, or consciousness, of militant struggle as necessary agencies of revolutionary change, *no less than of* material forces. In short, Critical Marxism focalizes exactly what had been repressed by Scientific Marxism, i.e., the "subjective" factor, just as Scientific Marxism focalized what idealism had been silent about, the "materialist" elements. The dialectic and oscillation between Scientific and Critical Marxism, is grounded then partly in Marx's original conflation of "negation" and "contrary," in his polemic against idealism.

NOTES

1. I shall suggest, rather audaciously, that Marxism involved a fundamental logical confusion. Marx, I shall argue, confused two modes of opposition to idealism, conflating the "negation" with the "contrary" of idealism. As to the meaning of these terms, I intend to commit myself to no more than I explicitly state below. Moreover, in characterizing this conflation as a mistake, I mean only to suggest that the negation and the contrary are quite different forms of opposition with different conse-

quences. Finally, if the mistake takes a logical form, it does not necessarily have its roots only in a logical miscalculation.

2. For further discussion of de Tracy's views see Gouldner, *The Dialectic of Ideology and Technology,* pp. 11–14.

3. See, for instance, A. J. Greimas and François Rastier, "Les Jeux des Constraintes semiotiques," *Du Sens* (Paris, 1970), pp. 135–55. See also the discussion by Fredric Jameson, *Prison House of Language* (Princeton: Princeton University Press, 1973), pp. 163–68, and Jameson's subsequent application of Greimas's model to the analysis of Max Weber, surely one of the more original discussions of Weber in a decade, in F. Jameson, "The Vanishing Mediator: Narrative Structure in Max Weber," *New German Critique,* Winter 1973, pp. 52–89.

4. See R. Edgely, "Reason and Violence," in Stephan Korner, ed., *Practical Reason* (Oxford: Basil Blackwell, 1974), p. 113ff.

5. Marx and Engels, *German Ideology,* p. 69.

4

SOCIAL STRUCTURE AND THE VOLUNTARISM OF SUFFERING

Scientific Marxism came to center on a concept of social *structure* which holds that persons are *constrained*, often against their will, to act in patterned ways. The familiar paradigm, of course, is Marx's concept of a "capitalist system" within which even the capitalists themselves, quite apart from their own personal wishes, are *constrained* to economize, to exploit labor, and continually to heighten productivity in order to keep abreast of competition: "capitalism subjects every individual capitalist to the immanent laws of capitalist production as external coercive laws. Competition forces him continually to extend his capital for the sake of maintaining it, and he can only extend it by means of progressive accumulation."[1]

Marx's structural perspective sees bourgeoisie and proletariat alike as doing what they *must* rather than what they *will;* men are under constraint to pursue their typically different courses of action by reason of the different positions they occupy within the social structure. For Marx and Engels, structure centers on constraint and constraint is understood as an impersonal property of a spacelike locus, i.e., a social "position."

In a later chapter, I will show that a structural perspective is assuredly that of the mature Marx at the height of his intellectual powers. But are these structural views of Marx's mature scientific socialism a belated development that manifests itself only after his supposed *rupture épistemologique* with his "ideological" youth? Are they symptomatic that Marx had now reached his scientific maturity and, in Louis Althusser's conception, had put his prescientific, ideological youth behind him? There seems no evidence of this, for *Marx's youthful views were not one whit less struc-*

tural. Thus as early as 1843, the young Marx's "defense of the Moselle Correspondent" observed that

> in the investigation of *political* conditions one is too easily tempted to overlook *the objective nature of the relationships* and to explain everything from the will of the persons acting. There are *relationships,* however, which determine the actions of private persons as well as those of individual authorities, and which are as independent as are the movements in breathing. Taking this objective standpoint from the outset, one will not presuppose an exclusively good or bad will on either side. Rather, one will observe relationships in which only individuals appear to act at first. As soon as it was demonstrated that something was *necessitated* by conditions, it will not be difficult to figure out under which *external* circumstances this thing actually had to come into being, and under which other circumstances it could not have come about although a need for it was present. One can determine this with almost the same certainty as a chemist determines under which external conditions some substances will form a compound.[2]

This, in 1843.

As a preliminary indication of the implications of this "structuralism," fully characteristic of *Capital* although written when Marx was only 26, we may note: (a) his counterposing of objective conditions and of the will; (b) the stress on the potency of the former; (c) the bracketing or setting aside of good or bad intentions; (d) the view of individual behavior as an illusion masking or expressing underlying conditions; (e) the view that these underlying conditions act with the force of necessity; (f) finally, the claim that they are understandable with scientific rigor.

The genealogy of this structural necessitarianism is traceable to an even younger Marx, and may be found even in a kind of "life aims" paper that he wrote at age 17 for his graduation from the Trier Gymnasium and in which he held regretfully that "we cannot always choose the vocation in which we believe we are called. Our social relations, to some extent, have already begun to form before we are in a position to determine them."[3] In the same paper it is altogether evident that, while Marx clearly saw the *power* of social constraint, he also judged it negatively. Constraint was powerful, but not good. He condemned constraint for debasing persons to "servile tools," a fate incompatible with human dignity.[4]

In this, Marxism exemplifies the more general circumstance that a significant part of all social theorizing is a symbolic effort to overcome "unpermitted social worlds"[5]—that is, worlds where either the good is seen as weak or the evil as strong. Struck by the sheer power of constraint, Marx sometimes obscures the fact that he detests it. Like the medical researcher proud of the new virus he has discovered, he wants others to know about it, goes about lecturing on it, and, after a while, the fact that he hates it is mentioned less than the fact that he discovered it. The tension between determinism and voluntarism was thus already visible in Marx's *adolescent writings.* Marx was indeed right: there are some structures—cognitive no less than social—that we acquire "before we are in a position to determine them." The idea of a necessitarian structure was one of them. The continuities in Marx's work and the implications of his Hegelian heritage are often seen in a one-sided way, focusing only on the importance that the young Marx attributed to the role of the subject-actor. Nonetheless, there is also the clearest foreshadowing of Marx's determinism in his earliest writings, a determinism which, as I mention below, is scarcely incompatible with Hegel.

Structuralism as De-centering

In structural analysis, the analyst (Marx or any other) shows that human actions are patterned without having been designed by the will or policy of any person or group. Actions are not only shaped by intended influences, but there are also unintended outcomes. The real "genius" of the capitalist "system" was that it produced a patterning (de-randomization) of gratifications and costs without these having been necessarily intended by the advantaged or consented to (and even recognized) by the disadvantaged. In that vein, Marx quotes Hegel on the cunning of reason.[6]

Marx's reaction to this is ambivalent, on the one side rejecting its idealism, but, on the other, accepting its determinism. The *dis*-continuity is a familiar point; the remnant *continuity* is less commonly recognized. Marx's structuralism only rejected Hegel's idealistic assumption that the directive force was reason. For Marx, the influence is not some demiurge above the actors but a blind, unwitting force of nature *within society.* Structural analysis profoundly redefined human affairs, ejecting providential design and relocating social order within blind nature. Persons and society are now the sphere of a natural order.

As a natural order, a society's patterns are not to be understood as conforming to *anyone's* plans or policies, even powerful authorities governing the group. The conception of (group life and) society as a *natural* order—this very sociological conception—was thus always *potentially* subversive of established authority and power, for it sees these as blind and subject to the natural order. Groups and societies are now no longer thought intelligible simply if the policies of their leaders are known, and there is now little point in appealing to leaders, for they themselves are controlled by other forces. Authority and rationality are now split; relations to authority are not to be guided by rational appeal or persuasion, since authority (no more than anyone else) is not an agent free to follow the urgings of reason; force, power, and struggle, rather than reason, now become the instruments through which authority is moved. The policies of a group's leadership also lose their grounding in rationality; instead, they are seen not as initiating action but as only *mediating* other unintended and often unrecognized natural forces. To justify a policy, one must now show that it is born of necessity and, conversely, to deauthorize it requires that it be shown as *no* longer historically necessary.

If Marx rejects the idealism of Hegel's reason he does not, therefore, reject her cunning *control* over other objects, i.e., her capacity to "guide things to her own ends." Hegel's transcendent reason was the expression of an *objective idealism* that was no less deterministic than it was idealistic. For Hegel, persons did not choose to conform to the spirit of the times or the *Volksgeist*, but this spirit constituted persons and their identity. In Hegel's terms, "individual personalities disappear from our point of view, and the only ones that are relevant are those that posit in reality the will of the *Volksgeist*." Hegel's objective idealism thus postulates the very depersonalized structures and determinism that Marx *retained*, even while rejecting Hegel's idealism.

In constituting societies as natural *systems*, structural analysis involves a paradigm shared by both Marxism and normal, academic sociology, as well as by political economy or economics. In the first lecture on sociology given in France (1888), Emile Durkheim observed that while reflection on society was as old as Plato's *Republic*, "until the beginning of this century, most of this work was dominated by an idea which radically prevented the establishment of sociology. . . . nearly all of these theorists saw society as a human creation, a product of art and reflection. . . . in this view, a nation is not a natural product, like organisms or plants, which grow and develop through some natural necessity." With August Comte, said Durkheim, sociology emerges and centers itself on that idea that "societies, like everything else, are subject to laws" and constituted "a natural realm to observe."[7] Marx and Comte are thus members of the same naturalistic cohort.

The conception of society as a naturally developing entity has two facets, one liberative and critical, the other, conservative and dehumanizing. In the former, to view societies as natural systems is a tacit critique of authority which undermines irrational views concerning the importance of political leadership and their self-serving claims to special privilege. The natural-systems view of society denies the aura of potency which political leadership commonly prefers to draw around itself; it dispels the mystique of authority and says, in effect, that outcomes do not depend as much upon them as they like to pretend, but on forces over which even they have no control. In this view, leaders can be legitimated only as *mediators* open to and transmitting the requirements of natural processes. In the second (conservative and dehumanizing) implication of the natural-systems view, however, ordinary persons may come to be viewed as mere objects—"like organisms or plants"—shaped by natural forces, rather than as subjects capable of influencing their own lives. If even leaders and "great men" are, in the natural-systems view, simply "midwives," then ordinary persons are likely to be judged even more passive and impotent to effect their social world.

At this point, however, the structuralism of Marxism and academic sociology *diverge*. To normal academic sociology, the autonomy of groups from control by their members—the fact that groups develop requirements and a direction of their own independent of the will of group members—is accepted as a *normal* condition. In contrast to academic sociology, however, Marxism viewed this same condition as *ab*normal, as a pathological alienation, as the very reason to overthrow capitalism and replace it with socialism: i.e., with production by a "free association of producers under their conscious and purposeful control."[8]

The central *interest* (or value grounding) on which Marx's structuralism rests, is the revolutionary overthrow of the present *because* it transforms persons into passive objects, rather than treats them as autonomous subjects. Thus Marx's structuralism focuses on persons as controlled by impersonal conditions precisely *because* he deplores this. Marx's structuralism, then, is sociological description made from the perspective of a critique of society grounded in the value of human autonomy, and aiming to *emancipate* persons from autonomy-impairing structures. Marx's structuralism was grounded in the supposition that human autonomy had, in fact, been undermined and in a *value* judgement that rejected this condition. For Marx as proponent of critique, structuralism is fetishism. To that extent, his is not an antihumanism but a humanistic imperialism, aiming at the unlimited dominion of the human species over all things. It is both structural sociology and critique and, indeed, a sociology *founded* on a critique, where description and analysis are guided by the specific value interests in human autonomy.

Some Formal Aspects of Structure

The concept of structure as constraint is, as indicated, an element that Scientific Marxism shares with normal, academic, scientifically committed sociology. This is plainly evident, for example, in Robert K. Merton's formidable essay, "Manifest and Latent Functions." Merton first makes systematic use of "structural context" to indicate how social outcomes are generated and *limited:* "The interdependence of the elements of a social structure limits the effective possibility of change or functional alternatives. The concept of structural constraint corresponds, in the area of social structure, to Goldenweiser's 'principle of limited possibilities', in a broader sphere."[9]

The analytic function of this *concept* of structure, then, is to account for certain patterns by citing the inhibition of some (not all) of the possible alternatives in a situation. It treats the situation as a kind of ecology affecting the growth of its inhabitants by discouraging certain species. Most importantly, "structure" accounts for the survival of some and the elimination of other alternatives, *not* by examining the interrelationship among the alternatives themselves, and specifically not by examining the survival of some as the result of their mutual competition or direct struggle against their adversaries. This conflict is omitted in the concept of structure. It is not the interrelationship of alternatives, nor their struggle *against one another* that is invoked, but the effect of something *outside* of them all: structure is an external environment. Thus the structuralism congenial to Scientific Marxism is dissonant with an emphasis on class struggle, the latter being more congenial to Critical Marxism.

The notion of structure also entails a treatment of some element as an independent variable within the context of a tacit discourse about system, where every variable is formally held to be both independent and dependent. Structure is thus a way of singling out some elements and assigning special causal potency to them, and thus has a certain dissonance with general systems analysis which focuses on any element as both cause and effect.

On the most general level, structure refers to any enduring arrangement of interconnected elements. As "interconnected," structure constitutes a system. That some interconnections "endure" refers to the persistence of the system (of the ongoing interconnections of elements) relative to aspects of the surrounding "environment." "Structures" are stable arrangements of elements seen from the standpoint of their effect upon their environment; they are seen as producers rather than as produced.[10]

Most generally, the effect of any structure upon its environment is to *de-randomize* certain aspects of it. Given a structure, certain aspects of the environment hitherto randomly distributed are now differentiated in patterned ways: they are "sorted out." A physical structure, for example, a flour sifter, takes a hitherto unsorted batch of flour and de-randomizes it; it sorts it out with respect to size, only allowing flour particles smaller than a certain size to pass through, and retaining the larger ones, thus creating two different piles of flour where before there had only been one. The de-randomization produced by a structure thus occurs only with respect to a certain, limited criterion, here size; the color of the flour particles as well as other attributes may continue to be randomly distributed.

A structure is thus treated as if it were relatively unchanging, like a rock in a river deflecting a waterflow in different directions. *Social* structures are deemed to operate in essentially similar ways, de-randomizing persons impersonally, for example, in terms of attributes such as wealth, power, prestige, skin color. Given a capitalist structure, some will be constrained to sell their labor power for wages; those owning the means of production will control the production process; and, according to Marx, wealth will accumulate at one pole while poverty and misery will accumulate at the other, and the units of production will continually get larger and more centralized.

Structures, however, are not ontologically given; things are not "structures" simply because reality has dictated that they should be. But to treat things as producers rather than as produced is not inherent in *them;* it is a selective perception expressing the viewer's interest and decision, rather than the structure's inherent nature. Structures are thus constituted by the interest and perspectives in terms of which they are viewed, no less than by the "things-in-themselves." It is not that structures and nonstructures refer to different concrete *things.* The structuralist decentering of the world is always grounded in interests centered in a selective subject.

Constraint as Costs That Can Be Met

The normal, unexamined notion of structure looks upon a given arrangement of parts as producing its effects in certain specific ways, namely, via the constraining effects of its "properties." Structures are imputed to produce effects through the mediation of properties attributed to, and seen as inhering in, them. In the view of structure held by Scientific Marxists, a "constraint" is *in* the constrainer; *it* has a certain "necessity"; this cannot be escaped by the object constrained, precisely because the constrainer is in no way dependent on *it*. This objectivistic view is the everyday concept of "constraint" for which Scientific Marxism has an elective affinity.

From the standpoint of Critical Marxism, however, the effects of some constraining property are always partly dependent on its interaction with the "constrained" object, and the outcome varies with the latter's ideology, culture, and definition of the situation. Here constraint refers to the *costs* of producing any outcome, which are potentially *variable* under different circumstances. The notion of structure held by Scientific Marxism also operates with an unexamined and common-sense assumption of "normal" persons that, given a certain structure, persons are "unable" to do, to accomplish, or to bring something about. (As noted earlier, from the standpoint of Scientific Marxism, it is supposed that without a maturely developed capitalism and its advanced productive forces, socialism cannot be brought into existence.) From the more voluntaristic standpoint of Critical Marxism, however, "constraint" makes reference to the variable *costs* of pursuing a certain line of action, not to its intrinsic impossibility. The "impossible," from this standpoint, is the limiting case of a goal that cannot be achieved whatever the costs invested in achieving it.

To view certain conditions as *constraints* is to treat them as "givens," or as unalterable. To view certain conditions as entailing *costs* of action, however, is to treat conditions as capable of being overcome with sufficient struggle, sacrifice, or exertion, rather than taking them as naturally given. The same events can be treated from either standpoint; the events themselves do not impose the standpoint. From the standpoint of Critical Marxism, many circumstances defined as unalterable "conditions" of action may indeed be altered, if only given enough *effort* by those who want to. Sometimes, at certain moments, conditions may conceivably be unalterable but, often enough, intimates the Critical Marxist, they are unchangeable only because people *define them as naturally given;* have not thought of changing them; would not want to, even if they could; or are unwilling to invest the time, resources, and energy that it would require. The faintheartedness of persons and the unyieldingness of structures are simply different sides of one coin.

The "unalterability" of patterns is *in part* always a function of persons' *commitments,* and not *only* of the character inherent in the structural conditions themselves. If persons are committed to maintaining a life style that would need to be changed, or to husbanding resources that would need to be expended to achieve a goal, or if they prefer to spend them on something else, then the structural "condition" persists as much because of these *commitments,* as because of properties inhering in the structure. "Conditions" are simply ways of defining circumstances naturalistically, as if persons' actions and commitments did not matter and as if the conditions existed apart from commitments.

From the standpoint of a Critical Marxism, it is not that different structures do not contribute differently to the shaping of outcomes, *but only that they never do so in isolation and apart from the actions or understandings of persons willing to pay the costs of changing their world.* From this perspective, structures and their constraints are commitments which were once made but which persons now take as givens, and in which, therefore, they persist. To Critical Marxists, "structures" are produced by *persons' alienation from their own actions and commitments,* and history is not made by social structures but by groups of persons who—having "nothing to lose but their chains"—are ready to pay costs. From the standpoint of a Scientific Marxism, however, the real actors are the structures, and persons are the objects on (or through) which they act. Here structure is *Geist.* The structuralism of a Scientific Marxism premises that persons are *not* significantly different from other objects and is thus *anti-humanistic.*

Different Accounting Systems

It is not, then, that Critical Marxists do not see structures or that Scientific Marxists do not understand that historical outcomes will differ depending on the sacrifices or costs persons are willing to pay. Rather, they are using different "accounting systems," different rules of accounting for social events. The differences in them are related to their different value commitments and interests—values and interests, not surrendered lightly, are constitutive of commitments—and these, over time, are generative of different structural conditions.

The accounting system of Critical Marxism proceeds by holding structure constant, while varying (and making problematic) the commitment, will, or energy of persons devoted to some goal. Scientific Marxists do the opposite, varying the structural conditions (which requires that *they* be made problematic), while tacitly taking commitments as given. Critical Marxists want to know (and show) how much historical outcomes will differ when persons' commitments vary; Scientific Marxists want to know (and show) how outcomes will differ if there is variation of the structures within which action is situated.

Underneath their accounting systems, the two Marxisms differ on another level. At this deeper reach, their difference devolves around value differences, particularly the value and potency attributed to "normal" *persons.* Scientific Marxism wants to eliminate persons, personhood, personality, and other person attributes (e.g., "ideas") from its accounting scheme, regarding them as things to be accounted *for,* as dependent or mediating variables, rather than as things with which to account for others. Scientific Marxism is, as will be shown in the next chapter, manifestly identified with nineteenth-century science, most especially with evolutionary Darwinism. Critical Marxism, however, is grounded in an older "humanism" precisely because it wishes to utilize person (or "subject") attributes as among the loci of power accounting for events, thereby systematically distinguishing persons from all other "things." (It would not, however, be correct to say that Critical Marxism's humanism alone reflects subterranean links to Christianity. Rather, what happened is that Christianity's "natural law" and its "free will" were split, the former fusing with the uniformitarian science paradigm of impersonal regularities and assimilated into Scientific Marxism, the latter, "free will," becoming part of the tacit grounding for Critical Marxism.)

As differing accounting systems, Scientific and Critical Marxism also entail different action systems, i.e., different command, therapeutic, engineering, or political systems. Each looks to a different site for its leverage. To change the world, Critical Marxism focalizes the way in which change is contingent on changes in and of persons—in their consciousness, ideologies, theories, values, knowledge, energies. Critical Marxism is thus closely linked with (what Scientific Marxism denigrates as) "utopian socialism." Scientific Marxism, conversely, views the true actors as the social structures themselves and regards persons as the "supports" bearing the structures or as "actors" playing constraining roles they did not write. From this standpoint, the appropriate political tactic is to change the structures in which people act without addressing (or appealing to) the goodwill, or reasoned understanding of persons. In short, Scientific Marxism is grounded in an extension of nineteenth-century science to human behavior, which entails that it be viewed as a *thing* like any other thing studied by science; Critical Marxism, however, is grounded in a view that stresses that change requires an *inner change of the person*, along with other things, and is thus tacitly grounded in a certain "spiritual" view of persons.

Scientific Marxism's structural accounting method is also to be understood as arising out of its opposition to two other ideological movements: (1) liberalism as an historically recent ideology of the bourgeoisie, and (2) the agent centeredness of the mass consciousness of everyday life in Christian society. Marxism's structuralism can, from this standpoint, be effectively appraised only in the context of the theoretical traditions and everyday culture which it opposed.

Both Christianity and liberal political economy portrayed men as "free to choose," the former because of their divinely provided "free will," the latter because the market provided them with free choices. Liberalism contended that the market system enabled men to make rational decisions free of coercion. The contention here is that *both* liberalism and Marxism are *in part* "systems of social accounting," rules partly tacit and partly explicit, for explaining human behavior. The liberal system accounts for outcomes in terms of the inner traits of persons; the structural model, however, refuses to treat individuals in isolation or to understand them by their inward characteristics. Marx's structuralism entails a de-atomization (or recontextualization) in which persons are seen as related to one another within arrangements which exist prior to their actions and which limit these actions. This structure is seen as accounting for the behavior of persons; what happens to them is held to depend less on their innards than on their *location* in the ongoing arrangement. The liberal model accounts for behavior by imputing intentions and motives; the structural model accounts by locating persons in social regions that would constrain them quite apart from what they might want.

Liberalism's accounting system thus centered on the motives, appraisals, and knowledge of persons whom it saw as the fount of actions and events: i.e., principals. Marxism, however, replied that liberals were operating with a very *limited* notion of coercion, of coercion as originating with persons and their intentioned action. Marxism certainly recognized that persons could be sources of coercion, but its polemical emphasis was directed against the omissions entailed by liberalism, which focused it on the *variety* of other *unintended* coercions to which persons are subjected—in short, it focused theoretically on coercion via *structure*. Correspondingly, Marxism understands social structures as making reference to and *recovering* those unintended but patterned coercions systematically ignored in the liberal accounting system.

Harold Draper has made the relevant point here with singular clarity:

> Marx was concerned to point out more than once that the course of social development was historically accompanied by a change in the forms of coercion. . . . "the totality of the process appears as an objective interconnection arising directly from nature; . . . it emerges out of the interaction of conscious individuals, but it does not reside in their consciousness. . . . Their own mutual collisions produce an *alien* force that stands above them. . . . Under capital, the association of workers is not compelled by direct physical force or by forced labor, *corvée* labor, slave labor; it is compelled by the fact that the conditions of production are another's property."[11]

Structure as Critique of Liberalism

Structure, then, pertains to that impersonal "force of circumstances" that patterns human events and actions, in contrast to that force and violence inflicted knowingly upon persons by others. It operates through the impersonal constraints of the price, the wage, and the property systems, whether or not any intend it. *Structure, then, is a critique of the liberal concept of the "free market" and, more generally, a critique of the liberal accounting system that was centered in the actions and intentions of individual persons.* It says that it is not the person but the "system" that counts.

The liberal accounting system was also a command system: it said, if you want persons to do something then they may be appealed to, shown that it is in their "interest" to do something; persuaded, that is, by material incentives or rhetoric, persons will do as desired. Responses to such persuasion are seen as free acts. Marx, however, replies that despite the absence of deliberate force or violence, coercion may yet exist. Submitting to or concurring with an appeal is one thing when there is no cost inflicted for refusal, or no rearguard availability of force; it is quite another, however, to reject an offered incentive and to know the alternative is privation or starvation. Much of persuasion, therefore, is *"coercive persuasion."* Every property system is a structure producing a patterned allocation of differential advantages and costs for different classes that cumulatively strengthens the position of the advantage and weakens that of the disadvantaged.

Although Marx never theoretizes it with any reflexivity, the idea of a structure is fundamental to Scientific Marxism and is one of the most important of his theoretical contributions. The notion of structure enables Marx to bring into view and recover certain aspects of social causation which liberalism had obscured. Like any contribution, its worth can be judged only within some tradition of discourse. This contribution by Marx must be measured against a liberal accounting system which failed to register that coercion may not necessarily entail either an act of commission, or an act of force and violence, and its results may not be intended or even recognized. Christian liberals had overemphasized the extent to which what happened to persons was the result of their own or others' intentions. They tended to untie persuasion and rationality from other features of the social situation, never noting that, quite apart from the arguments adduced, some features of the *situation* furthered conformity. For Marx, the worker accepts his wage because he is constrained to, not because he is persuaded that it is a fair price for his labor. The absence of alternatives for workers may not be intended by employers; nonetheless it structures their relationship. Structure, then, relative to liberal discourse, is all

those ways of patterning outcomes other than by deliberate force
or by a rational appeal to self-interest. Structure focuses on
"blind" constraints, nonforceful and nonrational institutional arrangements, commonly treated as natural or taken for granted,
which de-randomize costs and benefits, allocating them systematically, differentially, and cumulatively among different classes,
thereby yielding stratified hierarchies.

Now, though Marx's view of structure constitutes a substantial
advance over the liberal system of social accounting, it imposes its
own costs, tending as it does toward a generalized fetishism. It
"fetishizes" precisely in the Marxist sense of stripping persons
from the social scene, when, in fact, structures are only persons
doing structure. In the situation where the worker is portrayed as
constrained to accept his wages, it is not just physical starvation or
the threat of it that constrains him. The worker who rejects an
offered wage is threatened by starvation only if there are no welfare provisions or no unemployment insurance in his community;
this, in turn, depends in part on what he and others have brought
about through their political efforts. It depends also on the solidarity of his fellow workers and on whether they will scab on
him, or stand by him should he refuse the wage offer. It depends
as well on what his own family is willing to suffer.

The constraints of the wage system, then, are the collective
actions of a large number of persons, giving or withholding their
collaborative efforts, and thus upholding or cancelling the threat
"in" the wage structure. Structure, then, is people doing
things—or not. Social "situations," then, are not regions *in* which
persons act; they *are* the recurrent and collective actions of persons. These do indeed impose costs and benefits on actors,
thereby "structuring" them. But the resultant constraint is not
merely "in" the actions with which persons are confronted but
depends on the relationship between the situation and those interacting with it. Partially but inescapably, the structuring costs
depend on *how the situation is defined.* However false or incorrect the "definition of a situation," as Antonio Gramsci and W. I.
Thomas have both noted, it is real and its consequences vary with
its character. In that sense: "a situation defined as real is real in its
consequences." Costs which pattern actions are thus not imposed
mechanically, apart from human understandings and intentions.

If Marx's structuralism must be understood as a critique of
liberalism, structuralism is obviously not limited to Marx and has
other roots. One is the very nature of language itself, with its

distinction between subjects who do the acting and objects on which they act; Jerome Bruner speaks of "the presence in *all* languages of categories of agent, action, object of action, recipient of action, location, possession, etc."[12] To the extent that language premises that some beings are intrinsically acting agents and others intrinsically acted-upon objects, it provides a cultural grounding for notions of structure. That certain kinds of things, especially persons, should intrinsically be regarded as the origins of actions, the source of effects, is the common-sense wisdom of some ordinary languages; *structure*, however, is the secularized, nonprovidential *but* impersonal unmoved mover. There is thus a further *liberative* element in structure: it opposes the traditional spiritual hierarchy of mind *over* body; structure's determinative element is not a form of "minded" *steering* that controls the body from the outside but a property of the "body" itself. Structuralism is thus intrinsically a critique of idealism, and "materialism" is but the explication of that critique. Structure, in short is the secularization of pantheism. It continues to reflect its linguistic grounding, however, to the extent that it assumes that some things are intrinsically producers, while others are intrinsically produced, without asking how structure itself is produced and reproduced. The whole concept of a structure is modeled on and hence grounded in the kind of one-way influences and potencies linguistically imputed to persons. The linguistic paradigm embedded in the notion of structure resists assimilating the full reciprocity of a more radical *system* view in which each thing is both producer *and* produced, for in language the subject is not and cannot also be the object.

The notion of structure is also a contextualizing one, saying that peoples' actions are constrained by their *location* in a situation. In its contextualizing, structure thus reaches out toward *holistic* analysis, focusing on the ways in which outcomes depend on locations within some larger whole, on the one side and, on the other, on the ways in which these locations are interconnected with others. Structural analysis always involves the exhibition of the interconnection of constituent elements which are positioned by the specification of their interconnections. "Structure," then, is a tacit *spatial* metaphor; or as Louis Althusser has noted, infra- and superstructure in Marx are *topographical* metaphors. Structures tacitly liken social action to edifices or buildings, treating it as an "environment" and thus viewing action as a thing capable of being *made* once for all; as a product separable from the process of action that produced it, rather than an *ongoing, continuing perfor-mance* which, like a musical performance, ceases once the actions and doings constituting it stop. Structure thus conflates doing and making.

If structure is a recontextualizing system of accounting, the cir-cumference of the context it encompasses is limited; the context into which it recontextualizes events is arbitrarily narrowed to *exclude* systematically the ways in which persons' understandings and definitions of their situation are part of the meaning-bestowing, action-shaping context. Structures are, therefore, seen as *producing* meanings rather than as *incorporating* them, and as not varying in their effects with such incorporated meanings. The "structure" of Scientific Marxism, then, is an abortive, incomplete recontextualization.

The view that persons are affected by their positions in social structures does not, of itself, entail a rule establishing the amount of power that structures exercise over persons' actions. This can be a varying influence, ranging from a very tight control to a loose boundary within which there is room for considerable variability. A social position (or role) need not be a destiny imposed on per-sons, and persons need not be viewed (as Althusser does) as mere vehicles for social roles. A role is one thing; a role *performance,* quite another, for obviously all persons do not play the same role in the same way. Indeed, there is no known role system or social structure impervious to subversion and rebellion. The twentieth century has been a century of revolutions, some successful and some not, against brutal social systems and imperialisms. This, then, is how Mao may be understood when he held that "im-perialism is a paper tiger": there is no social structure, however brutal, callous, vicious, and powerful, that can forever confine a resistant people. Under special circumstances established struc-tures may be destroyed or overthrown; and even under ordinary, everyday circumstances they allow considerable variability in the behavior and events they "constrain."

Structure and the "Normal" Person

Structures do not eliminate variability in the actions of those playing roles in them because role "requirements" must *always* be *interpreted* in the light of the tacit, background, common-sense understandings of the role players. There is also always consider-able variability in how these understandings are applied because there is variability in the "interests" and past history of the persons applying them. When structures are defined as successfully constraining persons there is, as suggested earlier, a tacit, common-sense assumption about "normal" persons. It is premised that "most people," of a certain (usually unspecified) variability would on the average capitulate to the "pressures" of the structure, i.e., be unwilling to pay the costs of resisting it. Under unspecified commonsensically understood normal conditions, normal individuals do what people with guns tell them to do. Normally, *but not always;* because persons vary in their conceptions of who they are and what they will tolerate. Even "normally" conforming, submissive, and passive persons have limits that can be overstepped and will not submit to certain situations. There *are* mutinies, revolutions, hi-jackings, strikes, riots, uprisings, sabotage, bombs planted—resistance. Structural analysis which fails to make problematic the idea of the normal with which it tacitly operates is, therefore, commonly taken by surprise when change erupts. It forgets that there are always conditions under which some will *not* behave "normally" and will opt for conflict rather than resign themselves to pressure.

How compatible, then, can structuralism be with revolution? A revolutionary theory such as Marxism is, indeed, caught in internal contradiction when it interprets itself as a Scientific Marxism and opts for a structural analysis. Here, again, and from a deeper perspective, we note the fundamental contradiction within Marxism itself, around which its diverging polarities of Critical and Scientific Marxism are differentiated.

Critical Marxism rejects the passivity-generating aphorism of Scientific Marxism that "freedom is the recognition of necessity," holding instead that *freedom is the willingness to pay the price to achieve one's values,* to the extent that these indeed *are* one's own values; that is, to the extent our values are critically sifted and are not the result either of an external mechanical programming or of internal obsessions and compulsions. *Persons are free, then, to the extent that they struggle for what is their own and to the degree that they can eject from the self what is not theirs.*

The capacity to endure and struggle against odds (i.e., against structures) is, after all, the meaning of "heroism"; the ability to absorb punishment is the power of the weak. A dominant group with power routinely available to it, but which loses the will to combat, may be defeated by a dominated, bondsmen group without institutional power, if it has the stomach to absorb punishment and to make sacrifices; these are the bondsmen's substitute for the power of the master group. It is this capacity and this alone that enables a bondsmen group to play an historical role. When the master group loses its taste for struggle, then the days when it can play an historical role are numbered, no matter how advantaged by the structure. The paradox of every master group is this: as a master group it has, of course, structured the situation to advantage itself and it therefore comes in time to rely on that structure, rather than on its own personal qualities, so these in time deteriorate, leaving the masters vulnerable to structurally weaker but more vigorous bondsmen.

Yet, there is also a necessary interaction between the bondgroups' willingness to pay costs and the size of the costs involved. There will be limits, even if these vary, on the bill "normal" persons are willing to pay. If there is no outcome that is inevitable because of the way a situation is structured, still the more costs inflicted by a structure on those resisting it, the more precarious and short-lived their will to resist. Ideology and consciousness held equal, increased punishments and costs deter resistance. In *part*, the will to resist is a function of the costs of resistance that are experienced and anticipated. In what is or is imputed to be an overpowering situation, the will may flag; faced with what is defined as a manageable situation, the will may exert itself. But clearly, situations will be overpowering or manageable, not in themselves, but in some relation to the energies and commitments that are ignited by ideologies. Ideologies and consciousness are never "held equal"—especially by Critical Marxists.

In human society, there is no inevitable law and no structuring that automatically brings anything into existence; there is also no voluntaristic freedom that ensures the success of heroic efforts. We had best assume that there are limits on what may be achieved in any situation. Yet these do not depend only on what is "in" that situation but vary also with how persons define it and what they bring to it. The indeterminancy of this condition is acute. We really do not and cannot *know* just how limiting a structure is, or how strong the will to overcome it is, without pitting each against the other. There is an irreducible indeterminacy here. Neither strength of will nor of structure may be known apart from grappling with one another.

This does not mean that one is not obliged to bend every effort to gauge each occasion with the most painstaking rigor in advance of launching action. For without such intellectual effort the call to test a situation in action is a foolhardy adventurism that gambles with human lives. What it does mean is that such efforts at prior intellectual assessment have an irreducible (if changing) measure of uncertainty, with the result that they may often be judged true or false only *after* the issue has been joined in action. It is in that sense, too, that Hegel was right in holding that the Owl of Minerva extends its wings only when dusk falls.

NOTES

1. Karl Marx, *Capital: A Critique of Political Economy*, vol. I, translated from the 4th German ed. by Eden and Cedar Paul, published in 2 vols. with an introduction by G. D. H. Cole (London and Toronto: J. M. Dent & Sons, 1930), vol. 2, p. 651.

2. L. D. Easton and K. H. Guddat, eds., *Writings of the Young Marx on Philosophy and Society* (New York: Doubleday & Co., 1976), pp. 144–45.

3. Ibid., p. 37.

4. Ibid., p. 38.

5. For full development of the distinction between permitted and unpermitted social world, see Alvin W. Gouldner, *The Coming Crisis of Western Sociology* (New York: Basic Books, 1970), pp. 484–88.

6. "Reason is as cunning as she is powerful. The cunning of reason is mainly shown by the indirect activity through which, making objects act and react against the other in accordance with their own nature, she is able without direct interference in this process, nevertheless, to guide things toward her ends." Cited in *Capital* I, Dent ed., 1: 171.

7. Emile Durkheim, *On Institutional Analysis*, ed. Mark Traugott (Chicago: University of Chicago Press, 1978), pp. 44, 47, 50.

8. *Capital* I, Dent ed., 1: 54.

9. Robert K. Merton, *Social Theory and Social Structures*, rev. ed. (Glencoe, Ill.: Free Press, 1957), pp. 52–53.

10. It is thus revealing that references to "social structure" in Merton have more citations to its role in "generating behavior" than any other subcategory. Ibid., p. 644.

11. Hal Draper, *Karl Marx's Theory of Revolution, Part 1: The State and Bureaucracy* (New York: Monthly Review Press, 1977), vol. 1, pp. 241–42. Quotations from Marx are from *Grundrisse: Der Kritik der politischen Ökonomie*, 2nd ed. (Berlin: Dietz Verlag, 1953), pp. 111, 484.

12. Peter Collett, ed., *Social Rules and Social Behavior* (Totowa, N.J.: Rowman and Littlefield, 1977), p. 92.

5

SOCIAL ORIGINS
OF THE TWO MARXISMS

Marxism emerged in a social world in which the sense of an integrated culture made coherent by a sovereign and united Christianity was deteriorating among the educated and well-off, as
among the poor and uneducated. It deteriorated increasingly
among the educated with the appearance and spread of Mal-
thusianism in 1798 which called into question "the benevolence
of both God and man." "God would not provide food for all the
mouths but more than enough mouths for all the food." The expectation of a benign, natural harmony superintended by God was
thus upset. Similarly, Charles Lyell's *Principles of Geology*
(1830–33) challenged "the belief in divine interference in
nature—in miraculous catastrophic intervention in the course of
the history of life and the history of the earth." Thus miracles and
scientific law were held to be inconsistent. Soon afterward, Robert
Chambers would emphasize that it was inconsistent to apply the
concept of uniform natural laws to the history of the earth but not
to the history of life; all of nature, he insisted—including man and
his mind—were governed by natural law.

Robert Young thus emphasizes that the debate over
evolutionism was only an extension of an earlier and broader debate; they "were not merely reports of scientific discoveries. They
were concerned with the principles of reasoning, the assumptions
of science," from which they concluded "that the interests of both
science and theology required that their foundations be considered separately. Each . . . could only suffer from intermingling."[1]

Science and Religion: Tensions and Accommodation

There was, then, a growing tension between science and religion based not merely on the different views each had about specific bits of history but on broader issues, including the resultant image of man and perhaps, even more, on their basic conceptions of rationality and the place of rationality in life. This dissonance between science and religion affected the consciousness of the educated and the uneducated, among both of whom it lent support for emerging forms of "free thinking" and even of atheism. With the rise of the new rationality of science, and with its stress upon the self-groundedness of its own thinking, the "hypothesis" of a Supreme Being became superfluous to working scientists. There began the waning of belief in an afterworld and that long "death of god" in which established religion was no longer the single over-arching center of European culture.

Western religion's monotheism had been the symbol of the unity of the world—of society and nature alike—and its church had once bridged different levels of existence by affirming their common origins in and continuing governance by a single Supreme Being. The Supreme Being was now, however, promoted to a lofty irrelevance for everyday life; rather than being seen as a continuing presence, deity came increasingly to be regarded as launching the course of the general laws governing the world, which, once set in motion, were not again intruded upon by their remote Author. While the new sciences might be only too glad to surrender everyday life to the church[2] in return for acceptance as a part of respectable society and for autonomy in their own intellectual sphere, the church to whom they surrendered was hardly in a position to resume its once central role.

In any event, the tacit terms science offered religion were a new ecumenicism of the double truth. The truth of science and that of religion were to coexist without "intermingling," and each was to be supreme within its own sphere. If the church could reign supreme in the everyday life, it is clear, however, that the new sciences were not about to surrender the ground they had won in high culture. Moreover, the emerging tendencies toward scientific specialization were fast closing off the sciences to one another, making each a sovereign terrain to which those without special credentials were not admitted. Scientific specialization and technical development, then, contributed to cultural dispersion. Science could thus neither revive religion as the keystone to culture, even if it had a mind to do so, nor could it itself reintegrate culture, although it was often tempted to do so under the banner of a common "method."

Marxism: The Interface with Religion and Science

Marxism emerges, then, when neither science, religion, nor yet again the still remote state, could reintegrate a society and culture that was reeling under the impact of the eruption of a great new technology and a vast new world market. Marxism was thus invisibly drawn into providing a new cultural unification to fill the vacuum that the fragmented sciences, waning established church, and distant state could not meet, most particularly for the impoverished and marginal working classes. Borrowing visibly from science, Marxism borrowed if less visibly from religion, while at the same time it planned a new empowering of the state, to achieve the effort at cultural reunification into which it had been thrust.

In one part, then, it is clear that the emergence of "scientific" Marxism was simply a part of the development of science, and especially of the culture of science, and most especially of the gradual extension of science and scientific laws to the study of mankind that Chambers in England and Comte in France had insisted was implicit in Lyell's uniformitarian geology. Indeed, as we have seen, Marx himself fully acknowledged that his own work was kin to this development and especially to Darwin's *Origin of Species*.

While stressing that the development of evolutionism had largely accommodated to a theistic framework, Robert Young also shows that "when the advocates of an evolutionary view did encroach on the domain of theism, they provided an alternative view of man and society which was as sanguine and utopian in its belief in progress as were the views of the afterlife advocated by the most evangelical, antiscientific, scriptural literalist." Young concludes that in "promising inevitable social progress," Marxism was simply one of the more striking examples of an optimistic, Victorian, this-worldly philosophy.[3]

In effect, the *culture* of science had introjected theism's optimistic structure of sentiments, quietly offering inevitable social progress as a substitute for a dwindling belief in the soul's afterlife, and thus seeking that integration of the good with the powerful which Christian religion had accomplished through its notion of God. The new culture of science avowed that what happened in the world was not only governed by scientific law and necessity but was, additionally, benign and progressive in its outcome. In short, insofar as Marxism embodied a residue of religion, *one* reason it did so was precisely because it adhered to the contemporary culture of *science which also did so,* and because science and religion were not then as radically segregated as some subsequently thought them.

Working Class Religion and Politics

Marxism had emerged out of the occluded relationship between a highly secular intellectual elite alert to science and a raw industrial working class whose religious sentiments had been intensified by their newly uprooted and anxiety-inducing exposure to a mushrooming urbanism. Steven Marcus's probing reexamination of Engels's study of the condition of the English working class accents the industrial revolution's disorganizing impact, its disruptive unemployment and depressions, and the resulting "insecurity" among the working class which, in Engels's words, was "far more demoralizing than poverty."[4] Marcus also cites Asa Brigg's *Victorian Cities* which observed that "insecurity was at the heart of the industrial and consequently urban system."

The Communist Manifesto itself had similarly noted, as *Capital* would later, that the new capitalist order did not simply mean poverty and unemployment but also increasing "misery" and uncertainty: "Constant revolutionizing of production, uninterrupted disturbance of all social conditions, everlasting uncertainty and agitations distinguish the bourgeois epoch from all earlier ones."[5]

Marcus notes the special impact of these disruptive conditions on the working class's religious behavior, remarking on "the large-scale loss of active religious faith among the English working class, and the equally large-scale retention of some kind of religious commitment among them, largely in the form of allegiance to some dissenting sect. . . . the extreme conditions of urban working-class existence were likely either to severely damage the possibility of continued religious belief, or to stimulate an intense and relatively aberrant experience of belief."[6]

In some part, the working class's religious faith had been damaged by the visible alliance of the Established Church with the ruling class and ruling order, and by the callous indifference of both to the squalor and terrible suffering of workers' lives. "The

period 1750 to 1850 is a distinctive one in the history of the Established Church," writes Alan Smith: "It is an age when the Church
accepted total identification with the existing social fabric; an age
of the most complete Erastianism and of entire subservience to
the purposes of government."[7] According to a contemporary, William Cowper, greater than the church's parson or clerk was the
Squire: the service must not begin "until the Squire has strutted
up the aisle to the great pew in the chancel" and it ended when
the Squire lurched up from his nap. Reporting on public worship
in metropolitan London, the agricultural publicist Arthur Young
remarked in 1798 that "it afforded a subject of melancholy reflection to see nearly their whole space occupied by pews to which
the poor have no admittance. . . . In some churches few or no
benches to sit on and no mats to kneel on. A stranger would think
that our churches were built, as indeed they are, only for the
rich."[8]

In 1849, E. Miall wrote in his *British Churches in Relations to
the British People:*

> . . . religious profession, and respect for the public means of
> grace, are far more common amongst, and characteristic of, the
> middle, than the labouring classes, in Great Britain. The bulk
> of our manufacturing population stand aloof from our Chris-
> tian institutions . . . they generally pass through the prime of
> life, and too frequently reach its appointed term, without
> being even momentarily attracted, and without being in the
> slightest degree interested, by what the Churches of Christ
> are doing in their respective neighborhoods. The Churches
> are, to all practical purposes, as little known, as little cared for,
> as little trusted in, by this numerous body, as if they had no
> existence.[9]

But if this bears upon the damage to workers' faith, and the
rupture between them and the Established Church, the other side
of workers' religious conditions—an often desperate intensity of
faith—may be seen in the proliferating growth of dissenting sects,
in the spread of Methodism and in the lingering pulsations of
millenarian movements. Indeed, the millenarian impulse was not
confined to the poor and working class; as late as 1832, some as
respectable and educated as the headmaster of Rugby might give
voice to it: "My sense of the evil of the times, and to what prospects I am bringing up my children, is overwhelmingly bitter. All
the moral and physical world appears so exactly to announce the

coming of 'the great day of the Lord'—that is a period of fearful visitation, to terminate the existing state of things—whether to terminate the whole existence of the human race, neither man nor angel knows."[10]

Prophet after prophet arose, remarks E. P. Thompson. In 1832 there was the prophecy of John Nicols Thom who appeared as Count Moses Rothschild, "King of the Jews." Earlier, there had been the prophecy of the peasant's daughter, Joanna Southcutt whose movement had two periods of frenzy, the first in 1801–1804 and a second in 1814. The "emotional disequilibrium of the times is revealed," notes Thompson, "not only in the enthusiasm of the 'Joannas' but also in the corresponding violence of feelings of the mobs. . . . [Southcuttianism's] apocalyptic fervour was closely akin to the fervours of Methodism—it brought to a point of hysterical intensity the desire for *personal* salvation. But it was certainly a cult of the poor,"[11] which, in Joanna's words, condemned those who "starve the poor in the midst of plenty."

The Methodists, too, were of the poor, strong in working class communities of miners, weavers, factory workers, seamen, potters, and rural laborers. At the same time—and like other nonconforming sects—Methodism also became the religion of the emerging industrial bourgeoisie. As "a 'religion of the heart' rather than of the intellect, the simplest and least educated might hope to attain towards grace."[12] Methodism provided the *inner* discipline sought in the emerging labor force to overcome the idleness, profligacy, and improvidence of which the middle class constantly complained. Clearly, however, Methodism also taught workers things that might stand them in good stead and were not only serviceable to the authority of employers and the church. The same dedication and discipline, observes Thompson, "will be seen in the men who officered trade unions and Hampden Clubs, educated themselves far into the night, and had the responsibility to conduct working-class organizations."[13] Moreover, with its open Chapel doors, Methodism offered the poor and uprooted "some kind of community to replace the older community patterns which were being displaced."[14] Starting in 1789 with a membership of about 60,000, Methodist numbers grew to 90,000 in 1795, to 107,000 in 1805, to 154,000 in 1811, and to 237,000 in 1827. And even as orthodox Wesleyanism flourished, all manner of breakaway sects sprang up, Ranters, Jumpers, Tent Methodists, Bible Christians, Independents.

Eric Hobsbawm[15] has noted a certain correspondence between religious movements and those of a political character. Thompson, also, sees the relationship between religious and political movements as "intimate" but obscure and somewhat complicated. In part, both religious and political movements of the time may be regarded as different responses to the same soaring insecurity and terrible suffering; in some measure they were functionally alternative responses that workers might make to their grinding condition. But there are also differences that Thompson notes, namely, that there were periods, for example 1819, when there was great political activity but little religious revivalism. The two movements were thus not entirely parallel and not fully interchangeable. Political movements were efforts at practical, this-worldly reform which might be buoyed during periods of hope and optimism, while religious revivalism might be a response both to the suffering of the everyday life *and* to the failures of practical political efforts. The point, then, is that we must neither overstate the correlation between religious and political movements, nor ignore their frequent concurrence. If both religious and political movements were responses to the same suffering, the former were, additionally, sometimes responding to the failures of practical earthly politics.

Marxism and Religion

Marxism performed both functions: offering or allying itself with short-term political reforms—seeking footholds for an overturn of the entire system—and through the promise of a long-term but inevitable universal revolution, it simultaneously offers hope for a salvific transcendence of the present. Marxism also contains elements both of uniformitarianism and of catastrophism which, in its broader meaning, simply refers to any view that holds that the millennium (or some great social transformation) will be ushered in by an abrupt catastrophe. Marxism was antiuniformitarian in insisting that vulgar political economy was ideological in assuming that the laws of capitalism's political economy were eternal; at the same time, however, Marxism also held that the historical laws of a capitalist economy worked with an inevitable necessity to bring that system down. The latter is incipient with a utopian catastrophism, for the mechanism to surmount the present and to make the transition to a vastly superior future world is held inherent in the blind laws of the capitalist economy, and these, it is said, will surely bring it to ruin. The *Zussamenbruch* or crash theory in

Marxism, or at least as Marxism was commonly understood by Scientific Marxists, resonates a latent millenarian catastrophism. Indeed, Perry Anderson has suggested that "the very absence of any political theory proper in the late Marx may thus be logically related to a latent catastrophism in his economic theory, which rendered the development of the former redundant; . . . a tacit economic catastrophism thus functioned to dispense socialist militants from the difficult work of developing a political theory of the state structures with which they had to contend in the West."[16]

Marxism also exhibited precisely that radical ambiguity, so characteristic of the period, between damaged religious faith and an intense need to believe, to which Marcus refers, all the more so as it developed into Scientific Marxism. On one side, Scientific Marxism expressed a critique of religion from the standpoint of a modernizing culture of science and militant atheism. On the other, however, it also constituted itself as a new certainty that might control the burgeoning insecurities let loose by the industrial revolution. It counterbalanced the ruling class's alliance with the church by implying its own alliance with the newly prestigious science whose allegedly iron laws guaranteed the fulfillment of its earthly hopes.

Christianity and its church had conceived the "soul" and had provided comforting assurances of its continuity in an afterlife, as well as developing a community of believers, all of which—soul, afterlife, and church—provided mechanisms for a meaningful sense of posterity. As these and other identities that transcended the single generation—family, neighborhood, parish, guild— underwent severe disruption, they provided less or no assurance of a future in which workers' present sufferings might be meaningfully compensated.

The pub in which so much of the working class's time came to be spent was not theirs but the publicans, and this only at the pleasure of the licensing authorities. The Established Church largely belonged to the ruling class, and even the Methodist Churches were often under the hegemony of the mill owners and other new men of business. New temperance, adult education, and cooperative groups had little historical perspective and continuity, and were under the hegemony of the upwardly mobile, who left their class behind. The emerging nation-state became one compensating identity for older waning solidarities, but this was at first much more important and real to the middle than to the working classes.

Scientific Marxism was relevant to this development. It not only served as an anxiety-binding prospect of future redemption, no less certain for being this-worldly, but also produced new corporate identities—most notably the proletariat and the Party—to which it gave a newly heightened pathos (as Socrates had assigned a new pathos to the "soul") and which were promised a historical mission and continuity that might help them serve as a substitute for the waning of older cross-generational identities, or of a religious faith in the soul. Scientific Marxism's rhetoric of scientific certainty and its emphasis on the inevitable victory of socialism buoyed a sense of posterity, served as a mode of handling the disintegration of cross-generational identities, as a substitute for a faith that was declining and as a counterbalance to a church that was yet intact. Marxism's evolution toward a Scientific Marxism, then, does not simply exhibit the pressures and temptations of the working class's "economism" but also of the working class's spiritual crisis and psychic anguish under the impact of industrialism.

Scientific Marxism is thus a classical "symptom," being a compromise of conflicting tendencies: on the one hand, a tendency to supplant old religion with science (which had, in any event, subterranean links to theism) and, on the other, a tendency to perform functions similar to the religion being abandoned. But that there is a tension here is important, making it difficult for Scientific Marxism fully to satisfy the special requirements either of religion or of science, but at the same time providing a quasi-synthesis of both.

The link between Marxism and religion thus cannot be expressed simply by saying, "It is just another religion." It is not that Marxism cannot be thought a religion because it denies a Supreme Deity—for its belief in the iron laws of history converge on such a sacred being. The more important point is not the formal similarities of Marxism and religion but that religion and Marxism, and especially Scientific Marxism, perform *some* similar functions. Marxism maintained, and was certainly understood by its nineteenth-century adherents as maintaining—that the future it promised was a certainty, that socialism was not simply a vastly better society than capitalism but an historical *necessity* that did not depend on the will of any class, let alone on their good will, but was vouchsafed by the inexorable laws of capitalism's development. As Rosa Luxemburg stated, "the secret [sic] of Marx's theory of value . . . is to be found in the transitory character of capitalist economy, the *inevitability* of its collapse, leading—and this is only another aspect of the same phenomenon—to socialism."[17]

The point, then, is not that religion is the secret "essence" of Marxism but that it, and especially Scientific Marxism, was a response to some of the same forces that then constituted the grounding of religion; to anxieties newly intensified by the disruption of traditional institutions and groups, by industrialism and the world market. Its "hidden essence" is not religion per se but some of the *functions* that religion performed, its provision of an anxiety-relieving certainty—the same certainty that Comte's "positivism" provided his own "religion of humanity"—partly by establishing new pathos-infused cross-generational identities, and partly by the guarantees its science offered for a better future life. Scientific Marxism's determinism and materialism served as functional substitutes for the shelter and security once offered persons by traditional religion, while its cooptation of science functioned as a counterweight to the ruling class's alliance with the Church.

More particularly, Scientific Marxism's definition of the proletariat as the center of modern suffering expresses an elective affinity with that part of Christianity which is a religion of the lowly and the oppressed, the religion of a suffering god, and which embodies the promise of an end to suffering. Here Marxism converges with what Max Weber called "religions of salvation" whose central theme is the restoration of human unity through brotherhood. *Scientific Marxism is thus a syncretism, fusing science with Christianity's millennial promise to overcome all suffering and to enact brotherhood. It is thus the great modern synthesis of religion and science.*

But Marxism did this in a special, blindfolded way; it produced its cultural synthesis in the dark. Marxism is thus neither religion nor science as conventionally known, but a new hybrid with a special inner archeology: underneath its salient commitment to science was a latent link to religion. What Marxism did was to split off the manifestly theological superstructure of religion from religion's concern with suffering. In then linking itself to suffering, Marxism made contact with and drew upon religion's principal source of power, now making it available for its own development. It is precisely because of Marxism's link to suffering that it, like any religion, cannot be permanently refuted; it always arises from the ashes of criticism insofar as it continues to join its own fate with that of the suffering. Whatever the defects of its intellectual edifice, its human roots go deep.

At the same time, Marxism limits its concern for suffering by inserting "scientific" qualifications: by asserting that certain socioeconomic conditions must have first developed before suffering can be relieved; that one need be concerned only for unnecessary suffering because only it can be relieved; above all, that suffering cannot be alleviated by sheer will alone. Marx was continually admonishing those whom he thought granted the "will" undue power, condemning them as sentimentalists and utopians. He counterposed science and its laws as a humbling and chastening of the will in a manner reminiscent of the Methodists who believed "it would be presumptuous to suppose that a man might save *himself* by an act of his will. The saving was a prerogative of God and all that a man could do was to prepare himself, by utter abasement, for redemption."[18]

Marxism's opposition to voluntarism is kin also to Puritanism's opposition to magic and ritual. Magic involves the assumption that goals can be achieved by will mediated by sacred means, i.e., ritual. Here ritual is an instrument in principle capable of achieving any goal set by will; it is open to any ambition, regardless of earthly conditions. A religious hostility to ritual, such as Puritanism's, requires that there be methodical conformity to ethical principles that set limits on the will, bending it, disciplining it, not permitting it just any ambition, and requiring at all times a conscientious conformity to these principles in the everyday life. Marxism's contempt for voluntarism, like Puritanism's opposition to magic and ritual, means that persons must take a stand, must openly commit themselves to a course of action before the witness of a community of believers, and actively discipline their selves to conform to a set of principles, rather than indulge the fantasy that they can achieve whatever they wish whenever they wish, by appeal to supernatural powers. Scientific Marxism's polemic against voluntarism converges with Puritanism's opposition to ritual and magic and with its preference for disciplined work as a way of coping with anxiety. Insofar as Marxism is deliberately aimed at a select group of the lowly and suffering, stressing the redeeming character of their labor as the source of *all* value and of self-and-world transformation, and offering political struggle conceived as a methodical form of work, Marxism appears as another working class Protestant sect.

If Marxism introjected elements of religion in its effort to make the world coherent in an age of fragmenting sciences, shaken religious faith, and a remote state; if it was responsive to working class anxieties born of the industrial revolution's deterioration of the social fabric, this still does not explain how these religious elements came to be built into it, especially if we remember that it was the doctrine of secularising intellectuals of middle class origin. Can we suppose that these elements were built into Marxism because, sympathizing with working class suffering, its founders gave expression to religious sensibilities excited elsewhere? Actually, to say (as I have) that Marxism was grounded in the suffering of the working class of that time is quite different from holding that Marx, himself, exhibited great *personal* sympathy with their suffering. I know of little evidence for this. How, then, in the absence of such expressed sympathy, did Marx come to build into his theory elements that resonate religious sensibilities? How do these penetrate Marxism? To explore this we need to look at some of the religious attitudes of educated intellectuals in general and of the particular subculture among them in which Marx himself was first formed, the Young Hegelians.

Millenarianism and the Young Hegelians

Perhaps the first point in orienting ourselves to the Young Hegelians is to remember the difference between ourselves, or intellectuals in *our* time, and intellectuals of Marx's time. Generally, they were more involved with religion than we are, even if only as militant atheists. Today, however, there are fewer intellectuals, even among radicals, who care enough about religion to be militant atheists. It also needs to be remembered that a larger proportion of those then going to the university received formal training and degrees in religion and theology than we find today among the college educated. Nicholas Lobkowicz sums it up well: "Most of the men about whom we are speaking were originally theologians, and all of them were perfectly familiar with the Bible . . . they view their time in terms of this prophecy, whether they are believing Christians or not."[19]

The men Lobkowicz refers to are Herder, Schiller, Fichte, Humboldt, Arndt, the young Hegel, Holderlin, Novalis, Schelling, Eichendorf, and Heine, "to mention only the most important." Lobkowicz observes that far into the nineteenth century a "distinctly eschatological mentality was a common theme . . . of numerous German poets and thinkers." The expectation was that the "consummation of history was imminent . . . which is often accompanied by overtones unmistakably religious."[20]

Lobkowicz is at pains to differentiate Hegel's millenarianism from the tradition that preceded him, even as he connects him to it. Hegel's own millenarianism, like that of the utopian socialists including Saint-Simon and his disciples, is this-worldly while the preceding Catholic tradition had been other-worldly. Both the utopian socialists and Hegel, two of the main ingredients out of which Marx formulates Marxism, exhibit the movement from other-worldly to this-worldly millenarianism. Marx's historical perspective (like Hegel's) no longer dwells on the future, although having its culmination in it. Marx's whole theory points to the transformed future but never expatiates on it, having astonishingly little to say about the shape of the new society, primarily emphasizing that it will be based on the expropriation of the expropriators and the nationalization of the economy. Marx thus remains within Hegel's this-worldly millenarian time structure. Normally, this is viewed as an aspect of Marx's worldliness, or his having effected the transition from religion to secular and rational ideology/theory. But this is not quite what one sees in viewing the matter from the perspective that Lobkowicz exhibits. For plainly the shift to the new "realistic" time perspective had already been consolidated by Hegel who had developed his philosophy as "the ultimate expansion and fruit of Christian faith,"[21] providing a rational sublimation of the underground current of German millenarianism.

It is in that vein that Lobkowicz accounts for certain peculiarities of Hegel's followers: for example, their conviction that "as far as theory went, everything was essentially achieved." Therefore "they no longer considered themselves as men who had to fathom reality by way of trial and error."[22] Lobkowicz cites a letter written by a young student of Hegel which states, "I behold God face to face . . . the other world has become this world."[23]

When the nineteen-year-old Marx went to the University of Berlin in 1837, to continue his studies at its faculty of law, he was soon taken under the wing of the Doktorsklub, whose members, mostly older than himself, served to interpret and transmit Hegelianism to him. It was largely through their influence that Marx himself, despite an initial unease with Hegel's "craggy, grotesque melody," came to contribute to the development of Young Hegelianism. In particular, it was there that Marx came under the powerful influence of the Young Hegelian, Bruno

Bauer, with whom, as is well known, he later hoped to teach at Bonn.

Bauer believed that the present period was the great turning point of history, that all history up to then was merely a preparation for a total liberation of mankind that he believed imminent. In 1840, Bauer describes the mood of the Young Hegelians nine years after Hegel's death: "Like the blessed gods, the disciples dwelled with patriachical peace in the Empire of the Idea which their master had bequeathed them for contemplation. All the dreams of millenarianism concerning the fullness of time seemed to have come true."[24]

In a letter to Marx, Bauer (who was trained as a theologian) wrote that the final battle against mankind's enemy was looming: the "catastrophe will be frightful, it will of necessity be a great one, and I would almost go as far as to say that it will be greater and more monstrous than that which accompanied Christianity's entrance on the world scene."[25] David McLellan observes that "Bauer's influence was . . . not something that Marx passed through and left behind: it was permanently incorporated into his way of thinking."[26] McLellan notes the parallel between "Bauer's 'catastrophic' view of the history of ideas and Marx's catastrophic view of the history of classes. The plot is the same though the characters are very different."[27] Again, McLellan observes that as Bauer had described self-consciousness as the "solution of all riddles," Marx had spoken similarly of communism: "Communism is the true solution of the conflict between existence and essence, between objectification and self-affirmation, between freedom and necessity, between the individual and species. It is the solution of the riddle of history and knows itself to be this solution."[28]

McLellan also demonstrates that Moses Hess, who initially won Engels over to communism, had also spoken of the impending "catastrophe" in England, while in 1842 and 1844, Edgar Bauer, Bruno's brother, like Marx himself, also spoke of the imminence of catastrophe: "In the inmost part of the state a chasm will open which, with an earthquake that will shake to ruins our aristocratic framework, will send forth the hordes of the oppressed against law-protected egoism." Again: "criticism does not any longer merely send idea against idea, it sends into the field men against men. . . . It is the propertyless whose vocation it is to put an end to the pride of privilege. We find the practical beginning of the practical force for change in those who have suffered most under the old regime—the propertyless." History would then culminate in

communism: "Where everything is to be held in common, where
the goods of the spirit are to be divided equally, property must
also be in common."[29]

Edgar Bauer's comments above make plain the imperceptible
elision from a religiously resonant catastrophism to the revolutionary politics of the *self*-emancipation of the propertyless: "It is
the propertyless whose vocation it is to put an end to privilege."
Moses Hess was thus quite correct in observing that here, at least,
"religion and politics stand and fall with each other."[30]

The millenarian impulse was an intimate part of the social setting within which Marxism emerged, manifesting itself in Marx's
closest social circle. The most fully messianic expression of this
impulse, however, was not so much among the middle class
Young Hegelians but among authentically working class radicals,
such as Wilhelm Weitling, who were connected with Marx's circle, with whom Marx wanted to maintain contact, but with whom
he in time broke. The illegitimate son of a working class girl and a
French officer, and himself a tailor, Weitling was an indigenous
working class militant and a revolutionary equalitarian who opposed utopian socialism's favoritism toward men of property, had
a pronounced Babeuvian suspicion of culture as a mark of class
privilege, and was reputedly a "professor-eater" hostile to men of
learning.

As Hans Mühlestein observes, "seeing the forces arrayed
against him, he is possessed by a fury of destruction. . . . In this
state he takes himself to be the Messiah, saying once more, 'I am
not come to bring peace, but the sword. . . . I am come to cast a fire
on this land, and what more can I seek that it burn?' The religious
Messianism is seen in his third book, *The Gospel of a Poor Sin-
ner*. . . . His Messianism increased during his stay in Switzerland. It reached the point of pure mystical madness—or
megalomania—where he believed himself to be the Messiah and
wrote a new religious doctrine of salvation."[31]

My conclusion, then, concerning Marxism's link to religion
converges with Alisdair MacIntyre's, that Marx's thought was both
"continuous with and successive to the development of the
philosophies of Hegel and Feurbach; and one cannot understand
these adequately unless one understands them as at least partially
secular versions, or attempted secular versions, of the Christian
religion. Thus Marxism shares in good measure both the content
and the functions of Christianity as an interpretation of human
existence."[32]

In having noted the religious elements in Marxism, I must repeat what I once said in making a similar analysis of sociological functionalism.[33] I have always found it odd that people who profess to a respect for religion should act so triumphantly when they find a religious side of Marxism, and that they should brandish this as if it were a conclusive argument against it. It is of course no argument at all against Marxist ideas. Although not "religiously musical," I experience such exercises in righteousness as repellent; I cannot share in the sport of baiting the "false religion" because I have too keen a sense of the close connection between religion, any religion, and human suffering, and thus experience contempt for religion as callousness toward suffering.

Evolutionism and Catastrophism as Transitions to Socialism

It is precisely Marxism's ambiguous grounding, its manifest mooring both in the culture of science *and* its subterranean ties to millenarianism, that uncovers some of the deepest roots of the differentiation between Scientific and Critical Marxism. Each of these reflects and generates very different conceptions of social change in general and, more particularly, of the transition to socialism. In one, Scientific Marxism, change is seen as organic, a slow growth of the embryo of the new society within the womb of the old, epitomized by the rise of the bourgeoisie within the urban framework of feudal society and subsequently the old regimes. In Frank Parkin's pithy summary:

> [This] organic interpretation of change, associated above all with the works of Kautsky, picked out those various and many strands running through Marx's writings which portrayed the demise of capitalism as following inexorably from the social and political ascendency of the working class. In this view of things, the assumption of state power is not regarded as especially problematic; it is seen as the final act of a lengthy drama whose dénouement has been clearly signalled by preceding events in the shape of social and economic victories notched up by the newly emergent class. Political power simply follows from and makes manifest, the power already contained in emergent socio-economic forces. The interpretation of Marxism as an organic theory of change thrived abundantly upon Marx's curious fondness for gynaecological imagery when discussing the process of transition. His frequent allusions to

embryos, wombs and midwives did much to bolster the view
that societies move through a sequence of phases—from infancy to maturity, and to eventual senility and decline—in
which the notion of gradual evolution has far more place than
that of sudden and violent alterations of condition.[34]

This is the more gradualistic imagery of scientific socialism
congenial to a Marxism that viewed itself as kin to Darwinian
evolutionism. There is, however, another conception of social
transformation also to be found in Marxism, which is more characteristic of Critical Marxism, and this is that of the abrupt and
violent transformation that cleaves the normal social world like a
bolt of lightning, "it is humanity's leap from the realm of necessity
to the realm of freedom" (Engels), an abrupt overturn of the old
social order whose forces of production had been stifled by the
dominant relations of production and property, leaving behind the
"prehistory of mankind," and for which nothing less will satisfy
than a forcible overthrow leading to universal emancipation,
where there will be heard the resounding great "crash" with
which the old economy will be toppled, an impending struggle in
which everything, the entire world, hangs in the balance. *The
Communist Manifesto* remains the inspired source of that heady
vision of the revolutionary leap:

> The Communists disdain to conceal their views and aims.
> They openly declare that their ends can be attained only by
> the forcible overthrow of all existing conditions. Let the ruling
> classes tremble at a Communistic revolution. The proletarians
> have nothing to lose but their chains. They have a world to
> win.

And in Marx's *Critique of Hegel's Philosophy of Right* of 1844,
he declares: "When all of the intrinsic conditions are fulfilled, the
day of German resurrection will be announced by the crowing of
the Gallic cock."[35]

There are thus two views of social change and of the transition
to socialism incipient in Marxism. One, characteristic of Scientific
Marxism, is uniformitarian, tends toward gradualism and even
parliamentarianism, and is, we might say, more secularised. The
other, congenial to Critical Marxism, is infused with the more
catastrophic imagery of abrupt and violent revolution. If the first is
grounded in the emerging science of the late eighteenth and early
nineteenth centuries, the second resonates to the fading tremors
of millenarianism.

At this point we need to be very careful, however, not to intimate that the first is therefore unambiguously the more advanced, modern, and rational or that the second is linked only to nonrationality and backwardness. Nothing of the sort is intended here. As already indicated, early science had an interface with theism, was anxious to work out an accommodation to it, and was itself ready to sublimate millenarianism into a "secular" utopianism. Moreover, as science became increasingly fused with industrial and military technology—a complaint made, by the way, as early as the utopian socialism of Saint-Simonianism—how could one celebrate science's contribution to human depersonalization and mass destruction as epitomizing a pure rationality?

Further, millenarianism itself is not simply to be viewed as a fantastic form of escapism or as the basis of wild political adventurism. It can be that, but it can also be a way in which people who have been subjected to grinding suffering, multiple catastrophes, and repeated political disappointment hold themselves together as a community and as persons rather than sink into a disoriented apathy and hopeless atomized passivity. Millenarianism's fantasy, like magic's ritual, enables persons to insulate themselves from hopelessness born of the failure of normal, routine solutions. And in any event, nineteenth-century science's uniformitarian rejection of catastrophes was quite probably an overstatement, born of polemic against purveyors of religious miracles, and inspired by more than a reading of the evidence. If it is arguable that abrupt catastrophic changes occur in nature,[36] it is certain that they do occur in society and history.

Science and Scientific Marxism

Although observing the continuity between certain aspects of Marxism and millenarianism, my principal emphasis has not been that Marxism was simply an echo of religion but a *synthesis of religion and the emerging sciences*. In noting this conjunction I am not, however, saying that Marxism improperly bent science to its own purposes, did not understand it properly, or distorted it. If anything, Marx's understanding of science was often more sophisticated than that of some contemporary scientists themselves. Yet Marxism, and especially Scientific Marxism, became what it did in important part because it accepted the premises of the new sciences. Thus, for example, Scientific Marxism's insistence that the laws governing capitalism's development were not only independent of the human will but in fact shaped that will and consciousness—this didactic antivoluntarism of Marx's preface to the second edition of *Capital*—was at one with Robert Chambers's interpretation of Lyell's uniformitarian geology. "Chambers argued that all of nature was under the domain of natural law. He particularly scandalized his readers by saying that man and his mind are governed by natural laws."[37] Being lawful, said Chambers, mental action must now be viewed in a natural rather than a metaphysical light, "and the distinction usually taken between physical and moral is annulled." Marxism developed by incorporating this self-understanding of the emerging natural sciences. What it thought a social science was—i.e., what it thought *it* was—reflected the new sciences' premises that will and consciousness were derivative *things*. At worst, Marxism stated simply and baldly what the new sciences implied, but sometimes also said outright. Marxism thus involved, first, what was largely an uncritical acceptance of much of the new sciences and, secondly, an uncritical transfer of their premises—which *were* understood correctly—to the social sciences. Marxism thus entailed an impulse to assimilate and reduce social relations to the natural sciences, an impulse to which Scientific Marxism surrendered. This, of course, meant that the future of Scientific Marxism would be bound up with the paradigm of early natural science it had incorporated. It meant that the science it had incorporated was an historically *transient* achievement and that when, after the middle of the nineteenth century, the old paradigm of science buckled, Scientific Marxism itself would be under pressure to change.

The basic paradigm of science on which Marx had relied consisted of the following elements:

1. "The basic assumption of the scientists of 1851 was that there was lying before them a world of material objects, moving about in space and time. . . . There was, in fact, a fundamental dichotomy between the material world on the one hand, and, on the other, human minds with their hopes and fears, despairs and aspirations, . . . [which] did not exist in the sense in which the material world existed."[38] Marx's own philosophical "materialism" is grounded in exactly that view; most especially this is the grounding of its own conception that human consciousness constituted a derivative sphere subordinate to the material. The parallel thus involves both the dichotomous division of the world and the specific hierarchy of the two elements.

2. The fundamental notion of "matter" in Marx's "materialism" was also essentially similar to that of the science of the period.

This "implied that any particular piece of matter—say a stone—though it was made evident to us by its qualities—its hardness, colour and so on—was nevertheless not compounded of those qualities but was some underlying entity of which they were merely accidents, . . . 'that there is, besides the external characters of things, something *of which* they are the characters. . . . Behind the appearances we conceive something of which we think.' "[39] Marx's materialism like the early scientific paradigm premised an out-there world consisting of a kind of "substance" anterior to any attributes assigned to it.

3. "The world was . . . regarded as exhibiting with the passage of time, a succession of states, each connected with its predecessor and successor by what were regarded as unbreakable links of absolute necessity."[40] This assumption parallels Marxism's determinism.

4. "The scientific quest may be summed up as the search for the universal, inviolable, causal laws that governed the course of events in the real world." In short, uniformitarianism. While Marx rejected the premise that political economy's laws were universal, he focused on the specific laws of capitalism and assumed these were a special case of a more general set of laws governing class exploitative societies.

5. If the world of physical science formulated "laws of heat, of light, of sound, of magnetism and electricity, . . . all of these had either been reduced, or were believed reducible, to the fundamental mechanical laws."[41] In like manner, Marxism held that the evolution and movement of the state or of ideological systems were "in the last instance" derived from the laws of the system of production.

This was, as mentioned, the perspective of science up to about the middle of the nineteenth century. Thereafter, however, things began to change slowly until Maxwell's field theory, and they came to a radical transition in Einstein's special theory of relativity, published in 1905. Unlike the older views, Maxwell's field theory did not attempt to reduce events to forces acting between material particles. "In Maxwell's field there are no material actors. The mathematical equations of this theory express the laws governing the electromagnetic field . . . they do not connect the happenings *here* with the conditions *there*."[42] Einstein's theory of relativity added the premise that observations were always made from some frame of reference, from the standpoint of some coordinate system (CS), and what could be observed would vary there-

fore with the CS chosen as a frame of reference, and thus with the
position taken up by the observer. If a moving body moves uniformly, for example, it does so only relative to some chosen CS.
The CS, or frame of reference, then, is not imposed by *what* is
observed but depends on a choice of the observer. To say someone is walking three miles per hour, for example, premises that we
assume that he is walking on an "unmoving" object, but which for
other purposes may be taken to be moving, thus changing the
aggregate speed. How fast the man is moving, then, depends on
the frame of reference; it is relative to the CS from whose
standpoint he is observed. Two events can thus be simultaneous
for one observer, but not necessarily for another located
elsewhere or using a different CS. And not only may the position
of an event vary for two observers but so, too, may the time at
which it occurs; "as motion is relative and any frame of reference
can be used, there seems to be no reason for favoring one CS
rather than the other."[43] In the special theory of relativity, "mass,"
which was once the very paradigm of "substance" became interchangeable with energy. Thus with the emergence of the field
perspective on the importance attributed to the motion of particles,
of relativity's emphasis on the dependence of observations on
frame of reference, and of the interchangeability of mass with
energy, science was no longer grounded in a metaphysics of "substance." What was observed was now seen to depend on the location of the observer or the standpoint he chose to adopt, so that any
lawful or inevitable sequence of states were true only relative to
some limited frame of reference and were thus "necessary" only
within it, but not in others.

The view of science on which Marx's "materialism" had rested
was thus radically changed. Observations were no longer seen simply as reflecting an immanently unfolding order but as depending
on the frame of reference and this, in turn, was seen as something
that might be chosen. It is noteworthy that the culminating development that overthrew the mechanical paradigm of science,
Einstein's special theory of relativity, was being developed about
the same time as the publication of Lenin's voluntaristic *What Is
to Be Done?* and only slightly later than Sorel's critique of
evolutionary Scientific Marxism. At this point, of course, and as
science could no longer be a source of certainty, those occupying
the ground of Scientific Marxism were beginning to feel the
shocks. It is thus in association with developments internal to
science—as well as in science's social position—that there begins

the movement away from a Scientific toward a Critical Marxism which affirms the importance of the voluntaristic, of choice, consciousness, ideology, the actor's decisions, initiatives, and frame of reference.

As science came increasingly to be associated with capitalist industry and military technology and with their elites, there were growing tendencies to associate the critique of capitalism with the critique of science. As capitalism, technology, industrialism, the military, and science all became institutionally fused, the critique of capitalism began slowly to incorporate a critique of science and technology themselves.

The growing internal critique of the old paradigm of science also provided one basic source for the resurgence of Romanticism in early nineteenth-century Western Europe. This Romanticism had always had a profound political ambiguity, holding in precarious suspension elements of both a left and a right critique of modernism. Its political ambiguity was epitomized by George Sorel's doctrine, notably its opening toward both socialism *and* Italian fascism. Romanticism—resurgent and politically ambitious—might now develop in two directions: (i) toward a critique of the Enlightenment, that celebrated irrationality and antiintellectualism and which would ultimately eventuate in Naziism and fascism. Or (ii) as a politically committed doctrine, it could also develop into a Critical Marxism with Lukácsian undertones of "revolutionary messianism." In a more academic key, Critical Marxism evolves into the critique of science and of instrumental rationality made by the Frankfurt School of critical theory.

It is thus clearly not supposed here that it was only developments internal to science, and relevant only to professional scientists, that created the crisis for nineteenth-century science. Science's public prestige was then also being impaired; growing specialization in the sciences meant a growth of narrow technical forms of rationality; each science became increasingly cut off from the other and, also, from the larger society, as each refused responsibility for its impact on society and the public interest. This had the consequence of alienating sectors of older, humanistic intellectuals who were open to the need for new movements of cultural revitalization and who sought a new unifying vision to rebind their cultures.

As science came to be identified with industry and technology, and technology with unemployment and the callous depersonali-

zation of the everyday life in factories; as science and technology
also came to be associated with disruptive social change and gross
materialism, there slowly diffused a broader public uneasiness
about science that went well beyond the educated humanist. Far
from remaining the symbol of a benign universalism as it had
earlier been, science in the late nineteenth century became increasingly associated with the power elites of industry and the
state. They came to be seen as privileged servants of power
("mere technicians"), or as academically aloof from the rest of
society and unwilling to assume responsibility for the social impact of scientific innovations. These forces converged to amplify
the crisis within science itself and they generated a more public
crisis of confidence concerning the sheer rationality of science, as
suggested by the growing critiques of conventional science offered by Jules Henri Poincaré and Henri Bergson. The new
philosophy of science quickly caught the drift of the new science
or perhaps, better still, was itself caught up in the same drift that
was also transforming science. It took a romantic turn away from a
mirror image epistemology toward a mind-as-lamp epistemology;
mechanical models came under attack; the law of entropy inflated
the pessimism of the intelligentsia; Bergson was writing a
metaphysics in which the old science was condemned for artifi-
cially freezing the flow of reality.

Clearly, science and the view of science were undergoing a
multi-faceted change and with this the intellectual grounding of
Scientific Marxism was undermined. Again, however, we must be
careful not to oversimplify. For while the critique of Scientific
Marxism was indeed associated with these important changes in
science itself, nonetheless, the former was already evident in
France and Italy even before publication of Einstein's special
theory of relativity in 1905. In point of fact, the emerging critique
of Scientific Marxism, the new philosophy (e.g., Bergson), and the
internal shift in science's paradigm may all be viewed as interdependent parts of a larger historical shift, rather than as one causing
the other. The crisis of science and of Scientific Marxism seem to
be different symptoms of a larger shift toward a voluntarism that
had a variety of expressions.

The Political Economy of the Rise
of Critical Marxism

The fortunes of Scientific and Critical Marxism, however, were by
no means linked only to developments within science, to chang-

ing public attitudes toward it, or to philosophical developments. There were important economic and political shifts—in the Marxist community and in the larger society—that also contributed to the deteriorating position of Scientific Marxism and to the rise of Critical Marxism.

It is paradoxical that so little has been done to understand Marxism's development in relationship to its environing economy and to economic cycles. Without in the least supposing that Marxism's character can be understood as the reflex of economic conditions, nonetheless it would seem that historical materialists especially should have had some curiosity about the link between their own theory's development and changing economic conditions at the time it was written. Yet the latter are surely *one* factor, if not ultimately determining "in the last instance." In what follows I shall suggest that there was indeed a connection between changing economic conditions and developments in Marxism, especially for its evolution from Scientific to Critical Marxism. The key period on which attention is centered will be the last half of the nineteenth and the beginning of the twentieth century, where there is the emergence of Bernstein's revisionism and a broader voluntaristic critique of Scientific Marxism. I shall begin with an overview of the economic cycles during that period.

Shepard Clough and Charles Cole's *Economic History of Europe* is helpful and I quote them at length:

> Studies of the business cycle indicate that there was from the depression of 1848 a revival of activity . . . [but] confidence was broken by bank failures (1857), by a drop in stocks, by unemployment and failing prices. A recession and contraction set in over a wide area—in fact this crisis is usually considered to be the first of a purely capitalist creation. . . . The revival was not slow in appearing . . . the failure in 1866 . . . marked a new downward movement of business. By 1868 the revival had set in with business being aided by railway construction. . . . Prices rose by 1873 to a point higher than they had been in fifty years; wages and the standard of living went up; and profits were large. The period of recession and contraction began in 1873. . . . This time revival was slow in asserting itself. . . . There came, however, a revival and a short period of mild expansion that lasted from about 1879 to 1882. . . . These beneficient conditions did not last for long, for prices began to decline in 1882; profits were small . . . the upswing was slow but revival conditions began to be manifested in 1886 and there was some prosperity to 1890. . . . In 1889 . . . a new re-

cession set in that lasted until about 1895. By the latter date
new supplies of gold were pushing prices upward. . . . In fact,
the future of business looked bright and there was after the
long period from 1873 to 1896 another long period of generally increasing prices. Nevertheless a mild depression took
place in 1900–1901. . . . Recovery began in 1902 and in the
usual fashion led to the crisis of 1907. Signs of revival appeared in 1909 and the swing of the cycle was upward until
1913–1914 when another depression threatened . . . there
were those in 1914 who feared that the world was in for another lengthy siege of bad times . . . but the First World War
certainly postponed their predicted long depression.[44]

To recapitulate:

> From 1850 to 1873 and again from 1896 to 1914 the long-term
> trend of prices was upward and cycles tended to have long
> periods of prosperity (about six years) and short periods of
> depression (about two years). For this reason some historians
> have referred to the time span from 1873 to 1896 as the 'long
> depression'—a term that is not absolutely accurate unless a
> special meaning is given to it.[45]

As for real wages of workers: in Germany they declined about
10 percent from 1830 to 1859 but thereupon rose steadily until
1909, going up about 50 percent, but then manifested a sharp
decline around 1920. More generally, "real wages in the United
Kingdom went up roughly some 20 percent per worker from 1876
to 1914."[46] "In spite of hardships, it appears probable that the real
wages of workers in Western Europe improved from 1850–1914,
although they did not increase in proportion to the wealth of the
capitalist class."[47] Between 1880 and 1913 the industrial production index in Europe rose about 270 percent, from 27 to 71.[48]

Although real wages were increasing, they were not however
increasing equally in all occupations and trades, and Jurgen
Kucyzinski has argued that the wages of the skilled, "labour aris-
tocracy" in England (and elsewhere) rose much more than the
great mass of workers' wages.[49] Kucyzinski also demonstrates that
there was a fairly steady, although uneven, decline in the number
of hours worked from about 1860 onwards, descending for example from (among English engineers) about 57–63 hours per week
in 1851 to about 54 in 1879. Thus as the gross real wage was
increasing in this period, the rate of increase in the hourly real
wage was probably somewhat higher.

It is interesting to relate certain key works by Marx and Engels to the above outline of business cycles. The work of the "early Marx" clearly coincides with the declining wages and pre-1848 depression in Germany. Marx worked on his doctoral dissertation between 1839–1840; began studying the French utopians about October 1842; wrote "On the Jewish Question" and his *Critique of Hegel's Philosophy of Right* in the summer of 1843; from April to August of 1844 he worked on *The Economic Philosophical Manuscripts;* in 1845 he and Engels published *The Holy Family;* in the spring of that year he wrote his so-called "Theses on Feurbach" and in September started working on what will be *The German Ideology,* which, with Engels, he completed in the summer of 1846. In 1847, Marx worked on *The Poverty of Philosophy* and lectured on "Wage Labour and Capital." These were published in the *Neue Rheinische Zeitung* in 1849 but greatly rewritten by Engels (in the edition most usually translated) "as Marx would have written it in 1891."[50] Marx wrote and published with Engels *The Communist Manifesto* in 1848. In large measure, this body of work may be regarded as the core of "young Marxism." It is what I shall later call Marxism's period of paradigm coalescence. It is this work that is most clearly infused with catastrophism—the sense of imminent, universal revolution. And it is this work that was written during that period of economic contraction, mass privation, and depression in Germany which contributed to the political coalition of forces that made the revolution of 1848.

After that revolution there was a brief literary hiatus. Until about 1850, Marx published no major intellectual work: he edited the *Neue Rheinische Zeitung,* he was placed on trial in Cologne, expelled from Germany, and went to Paris and London. In 1850 he published the *Class Struggles in France, 1848–1850* and in 1851 settled into the British Museum for his studies, working on *The Eighteenth Brumaire of Louis Bonaparte* which was published in 1852. These may be regarded as transitional works, yet of great symptomatic significance.

As Marx and Engels settled in England the depression through which they had lived prior to 1848 came to an end. There then followed the key years of Marx's mature intellectual productivity centered on political economy and which occurred during the long-range economic upturn in Europe from 1850 to 1873. During this period, Marx curbed his catastrophism and evidenced his increasing transition toward the structuralist perspectives of economism with its sense of the massiveness of evolving socioeconomic formations.

"After the defeat of the workers' insurrection in Paris, in July 1850, Marx and Engels advanced the thesis that revolution had become impossible in the immediately foreseeable future, that a rapid return could not be counted upon, and that the tasks of the League of Communists must be reset accordingly to give first priority to the work of education, study, and development of revolutionary theory. It fell like cold water on the flames of exile fantasy . . . the great majority of the exiles stood against them, even the workers. 'I want at most twelve people in our circle, as few as possible,' Marx stated, and under taunts of being counter-revolutionaries, anti-proletarians, and impractical literati . . . Marx and Engels withdrew from organizational and practical political activity; Engels to Manchester to earn a living, Marx to the British Museum to begin his economic studies anew from the beginning."[51]

In 1857 Marx commenced a preliminary synthesis of these studies in a series of seven notebooks, the so-called *Grundrisse*, the preparation for his *Capital*. While 1857's first purely capitalist crisis was a year of widespread economic crisis and increased deprivation for the Marx family, it is also true that it came after a period of substantial economic growth, and that following this, as Cole and Clough hold, "the revival was not slow in appearing." On 8 October 1858 Marx wrote Engels from London, speaking of "the favourable turn of world trade at this moment." In that same year Marx began writing his *Critique of Political Economy*, the first part of which was published the next year, and in 1860 worked on a second part which was never completed. In that year, too, Marx read Darwin and in a letter of 19 December wrote Engels: "it is a book that contains the natural-history basis of our philosophy." In 1862, Marx worked on *Theories of Surplus Value;* in 1865 wrote and lectured on "Wages, Price and Profit" and a year later began preparing volume one of *Capital* for the publisher which appeared in September of 1867.

The next year he began work on volume two. Eduard Bernstein states that certain of the passages of volume two must also have been written in 1870 and about 1878, while some passages of volume three were written even earlier than that, in 1864 to 1865.[52] In short, much and perhaps most of the materials for *Capital*'s several volumes appear to have been written *prior* to the onset of the "long depression" (that starts in 1873), during the long upturn trend of 1850 to 1873. Indeed, his *Civil War in France* is published in 1871, about the uprising of the Paris Commune that year, an uprising Marx had energetically opposed. Engels's *Anti-Dühring* (to which Marx wrote the first part of Chapter Ten) was written in 1877 well after the "long depression" had begun, but there is little doubt that the main environment of this work by Engels was Marx and his last twenty-seven years of economic studies and publications under Marx's guidance.

Only one year after the massacre of the Communards, Marx appeared, in 1872, at the Hague for the First International's last congress during which—in his formal remarks as well as in later press statements—he repeated that:

> You know that the institutions, mores, and traditions of various countries must be taken into consideration, and we do not deny that there are countries—such as America, England, and if I were more familiar with your institutions, I would perhaps also add Holland—where the workers can attain their goal by peaceful means.[53]

The subsequent evolutionary socialism of the Second International, then, is essentially continuous with certain earlier development in Marx himself; following Marx's death in 1883 and Engels's subsequent influence over Bernstein and Kautsky, this evolutionary socialism germinates during the "long depression" of 1873 to 1896. It is during this period that the growing expectation takes hold among German socialists that capitalism is doomed by its own necessary internal contradictions. A few years after the long depression ends, however, in 1898 to 1899, Bernstein takes the offensive against catastrophism:

> I have set myself against the notion that we have to expect shortly a collapse of the bourgeois economy, and that social democracy should be induced by the prospect of such an imminent, great, social catastrophe to adapt its tactics to such an assumption.[54]

Bernstein adds that Engels himself, who had died several years earlier in 1895, was "thoroughly convinced that the tactics based on the presumption of a catastrophe have had their day."[55] Bernstein's culminating remarks, developing his theme that it was not socialism but the socialist *movement* that was everything, were clearly of an antimillenarian cast: "I have at no time had an excessive interest in the future. . . . My thoughts and efforts are concerned with the duties of the present."

In noting that Bernstein's anticatastrophic revisionism appears soon after the end of the great depression, I do not mean to suggest that it represents a sharp break with earlier developments in the German socialist party. From at least 1887 onwards, the net real wages or net money wages of German workers had—despite the long depression—increased until about 1909, while the German gross product and the per capita physical volume of production were up substantially. At the same time, German socialists' parliamentarian commitments grew as they became a legal political party and acquired an increasing electoral following. Thus by the time of their Erfurt Congress in 1891 a large group of socialists were attracted to parliamentary reform and gradualism.

Bernstein was thus only the most open expression of an earlier development. In particular, Bernstein drew the theoretical conclusions of this economic and political development in his open critique of Marx. Noting that the class struggle had not reached anything like the pitch predicted in *The Communist Manifesto*, Bernstein forcefully rejected catastrophism with its theory of an automatic economic crash that would usher socialism in. While many socialists agreed with him, he was outvoted largely because they could not then bring themselves to an open rupture with Marx.

The essential point, then, is that socialists all over Europe had by then seen several economic depressions come and go without having produced a general economic collapse. Rather than the increased misery of the working classes, they saw that the latter were experiencing increased real wages and lower working hours as capitalist economy expanded. In short, the economy had not polarized as Marx had predicted. The rich were indeed growing richer and there was a great concentration of wealth, but the working class *was not growing poorer but was steadily improving its living conditions*. It was against this background that there emerged the sense among many European socialists that, as George Sorel reported, something had gone profoundly wrong with Marxism. It was out of this context, political and economic, in the larger society and in the debates of the Marxist community, that left socialists such as Lukács began their voluntaristic rereading of Marxism which saw it as the study of the "totality" and prepared to jettison the priority of the "economic."

Voluntarism, Genteel and Revolutionary

After the long depression ended in 1895, largely with the extension of colonialism, the capitalist economy seemed to have taken on new life. The old catastrophe theory then fit everyday life even less than it had during the long depression. As capitalism grew and was stabilized, some Marxists began to wonder whether revolution was now necessary, while others wondered whether it was now possible. The development and stabilization of capitalism evoked a crisis within the Marxist community, the central symptom of which was Bernstein's challenge to scientific socialists' assumption that capitalism's internal economic contradictions would lead inexorably to the proletariat's increasing misery, to the crash of the economy, and to a socialist revolution. Rosa Luxemburg went to the root of the problem Bernstein had created in the Marxist community with her usual incisiveness, noting that he "began his revision of social Democracy by abandoning the theory of capitalist collapse." The trouble was that "the latter . . . is the corner-stone of scientific socialism."[56] She amplified:

> The greatest conquest of the developing proletarian movement had been the discovery of grounds of support for realisation of socialism in the *economic conditions* of capitalist society. As a result of this discovery, socialism was changed from an "ideal" dreamt by humanity for thousands of years to a thing of *historic necessity* . . . the secret of Marx's theory of value . . . is found in the transitory character of capitalist economy, the inevitability of its collapse, leading—and this is only another aspect of the same phenomenon—to socialism.[57]

Above all, at least according to Luxemburg, what Bernstein had done was to attack the grounds for believing in the *inevitability* of socialism, particularly as these had been grounded by Marx in a necessity that was *economic*. Bernstein had asked, "Why represent socialism as the consequence of economic compulsion? Why degrade man's understanding, his feeling for justice, his will?"[58] Bernstein's revisionism, then, was grounded in a genteel *voluntarism*.

As our discussion of Leninism will show (in a later volume), what happened in consequence of the revisionist challenge, and the left's struggle against it, cannot properly be described as a successful defense of the old Scientific Marxism or as its restoration. To have vanquished Bernstein was one thing; to restore the old orthodoxy, quite another. The left only succeeded in the first, but not the second.

On the contrary, for under the Scientific Marxism he had salvaged, Lenin inserted a stress on the political initiative of the vanguard party that was no less voluntarist. What happened following Bernstein's challenge to Scientific Marxism, then, was the splitting off of *two* voluntarisms; the genteel voluntarism of revisionist social democracy and the Promethean voluntarism of revolutionary Leninism. If Bernstein openly said that socialism need not be necessary but may still be *chosen* because it is better, the Leninists in effect replied, so, too, may revolution be chosen. While rejecting Bernstein's critique of the inevitability of the capitalist crash and the rise of socialism, the Leninists took steps—i.e., organized the Bolshevik Party—to ensure that they need not wait for that crash, being mindful that their own economy was still immature and therefore still a long way from the lethal contradictions of a ripe capitalism.

Lenin, then, was no less a revisionist than Bernstein, and Bernstein no less a voluntarist than Lenin. Indeed, both had taken the turn toward voluntarism for much the same reasons. Bernstein, because he no longer saw capitalism as leading inexorably to "increased misery" for the working class and thus inevitably to revolution; and Lenin, because he did not believe capitalism necessarily led the working class to a socialist consciousness and thus to revolution. *Neither any longer saw revolution as grounded in economic necessity.* Both shared the assumption—and Critical Marxism with them—that social conditions were not evolving spontaneously toward desired socialist outcomes, in contrast to the optimistic metaphysical pathos of Scientific Marxism that "history is on our side." Suspecting that waiting only made them weaker and their enemies stronger, Critical Marxists would not defer their drive toward socialism until economic conditions had matured—as Scientific Marxism had counseled—and they were thus attractive to radicals in developing areas where industrialism was backward.

Retrospectively then, as Marxism was drawn into the orbit of a powerful and organized working class, its millenarian and utopian elements were blunted. As organizational instruments for achieving the working class's goals were created, Marxism's utopian-millenarian impulses gave way to more economistic concerns with working class melioration within the framework of capitalism, precisely because this was what the working class demanded. The working class's initial attraction to Marxism, then, had been the attraction of the weak for whatever buoys its hopes and promises that its future will be better, and thus, at the beginning, the working class had an affinity for Scientific Marxism with its determinism.

As its own forms of organization develop within an expanding economy, and as these allow it some experience of success in improving its own condition, the working class became less dependent on betterment by impersonal mechanisms outside of itself. They learned to depend on themselves and were then drawn to a theory affirming the importance of their own efforts, to a temperate voluntarism reflecting the modest success of their own efforts and their own growing self-confidence. Such a temperate voluntarism was also congenial to their allies among the intelligentsia who could increasingly pursue public careers in movement journalism, parliamentary politics, and in party and trade union organizations.

When Marxism spread to less developed regions where there was no powerful working class and only a small trade union movement, the millenarian-utopian elements encysted within it were reawakened. The less developed countries were attracted to a different kind of Marxism, one accenting the power and initiative of consciousness and of determined struggle—not merely moral choice—guided by it. This Marxism reflects the voluntaristic ideology to which the intelligentsia is natively disposed, an ideology stressing the power of ideas. This is revitalized where the intelligentsia is limited neither by a mature and organized proletariat, nor by a developed bourgeoisie, nor by a viable land-based elite. In this situation, if the intelligentsia seek to pursue a revolutionary project they must and can come out more fully into the open. Here intellectuals define themselves in Leninist fashion as "professional revolutionaries," as more central to the revolutionary process, as the veritable source of a socialist consciousness, developing a more agonic and authoritarian voluntarism. This stresses the importance of choice based not so much on an overt morality—which as such is open to all—but of cognitive clarity, knowledge, or "theory," achievements primarily available to an intellectual elite.

"Pessimism" and Critical Marxism

At the nucleus of Scientific Marxism there had been a tacit and very optimistic analogy between the history of the French Revolution and bourgeoisie, on the one side, and the socialist revolution and the proletariat, on the other. One of the views shared by Sorel, Lukács, and Lenin is that this analogy was suspect. They all stressed the differences rather than similarities between the two revolutions. As Lukács remarked, "capitalism already developed within feudalism . . . [but] even the most highly developed capitalist concentration will still be qualitatively different, even economically, from a socialist system."[59]

Lenin himself had reached much the same conclusion:

> One of the basic differences between the bourgeois and the socialist revolutions is that, in the case of the bourgeois revolution, which grows out of feudalism, the new economic organizations are gradually created within the womb of the old order, and by degrees modify all the aspects of feudal society. The bourgeois revolution had but one task to perform . . . to destroy all the fetters of the previous society. . . . But the socialist revolution is in an altogether different position. The more backward the country in which . . . the socialist revolution has to be begun, the more difficult for it is the transition . . . to socialist relations . . . the difference between the socialist revolution and the bourgeois revolution is precisely that, in the latter case, finished forms of capitalist relationships already exist, whereas the Soviet power, the proletarian power, does not get these relationships.

Above all, what was lacking for the Russian Revolution was that it had not inherited the advanced technology that Scientific Marxism saw as the decisive requisite of socialism. Even the most advanced forms of Russian capitalism (continues Lenin) "embraced only a few peaks of industry and affected agriculture only to a very slight extent. The organization of accounting, the control over large-scale enterprises, the transformation of the whole state economic mechanism into a single great machine, into an economic organism which shall work in such a way that hundreds of millions of people shall be directed by a single plan, such is the tremendous organizational task which lay on our shoulders."[60]

Starting as a Scientific Marxist, Lenin at first regarded Russian economic underdevelopment as a weakness of Russian socialism;

as a weakness that could be overcome only with help from revolutions abroad, or else and at best, coped with temporarily by the most exceptional exertions and desperate measures. Viewing economic underdevelopment from the standpoint of a scientific socialism it necessarily comes to be defined as "backwardness." Faced with the "backward" economic development of Czarist Russia, Scientific Marxism began to be transformed into a Critical Marxism that could protect it from emerging pessimism by stressing that men are not limited by objective conditions.

Gradually, then, Critical Marxism began to redefine economic underdevelopment so that rather than seeing it as a weakness that limits, it slowly redefined "backwardness" as providing opportunities for revolutionaries. This reassessment of backwardness—the transvaluation of it—which had already been begun by Lenin and his contemporaries before the November Revolution was later culminated in Mao and the Cultural Revolutions in China. As Edward Friedman has observed, Mao argued that backwardness meant poverty and poverty meant revolutionary readiness. Mao had remarked:

> Lenin said: "The more backward a nation the harder its transition from capitalism to socialism." In fact, the more backward the economy, the easier, not the harder a transition from capitalism to socialism. The poorer people are, the more they want a revolution.[61]

Lenin *began* the shift in communist strategy in which increasing reliance was placed on a temporary alliance with the peasantry. The climax of this realignment will occur when Mao places the peasantry at the very center of the Chinese Revolution and in his use of "backward," *lumpen* (uprooted and declassed) elements in Chinese society as cadres for the Chinese People's Army.

The fundamental dilemma of Marxist revolutionary strategy, then, was this: the stronger and more maturely developed a capitalist society, the more powerful its bourgeoisie, the greater their hegemony over the consciousness of other classes, and the more difficult it is to seize power from them. Correspondingly, the weaker and less developed a capitalist class, the less influence they have over the working and other classes, and the easier they are to overthrow. The more readily any capitalist system can be overthrown, therefore, the less developed are the economic and industrial requisites for the transition to socialism, as these had been conceived by Scientific Marxists: the easier the revolution, the harder the road to socialism.

An immature capitalist society presents revolutionary socialists with a greater political opportunity to seize power, but once power is won it is more difficult to build (a scientific) socialism. This dilemma could be resolved either by opting for the seizure of power at once in a backward economy, risking the consequences of its backwardness, or one could defer power and await the development of the kind of economic infrastructure typically required by Scientific Marxism.

It was this very dilemma that split the Russian Social Democratic Party into two factions, the Bolsheviks and Mensheviks. The Bolsheviks compromised their Scientific Marxism and, spurred by Lenin, leaned toward a more voluntaristic Critical Marxism, opting for revolution-now. The Mensheviks maintained the purity of their Scientific Marxism and deferred their revolution. The Mensheviks were destroyed by the Bolsheviks when the latter seized power, while the Bolsheviks themselves were destroyed by the Stalinist system into which their effort to cope with this dilemma had plunged them. Neither side escaped it.

Suspecting that the maturation of capitalism meant a powerful capitalist class with increasing hegemony over the working class, that this meant trouble rather than opportunities for revolutionaries, premising that the historical drift might *not* bring them to power, Lenin determined to seize power in Russia despite its backwardness and, indeed, to rely upon the backward peasants in his move toward power, although not believing them a truly reliable ally in the socialist project. The political prospect here is grim and forbidding. The Bolsheviks were caught between Scylla and Charybdis: (i) either they defer the launching of their socialist revolution (as the Mensheviks had wanted) but then risk confronting a greatly strengthened capitalist class, or (ii) pursue it as soon as a target of opportunity presented itself, but without a developed industrial economy and proletariat on which to build. Either course was obviously ominous to Marxists.

It is essentially the surfacing of this dilemma that is a major source of the emerging pessimism that Perry Anderson correctly sees as fundamental to Western Marxism. Anderson, however, offers no explanation of this pessimism and dubiously assumes that the tendency begins with Gramsci. Anderson is correct: "The confidence and optimism of the founders of historical materialism and of their successors, progressively disappeared."[62] What he fails to note is that it disappeared well before Gramsci, whom Anderson treats as a demarcation point and first indication of that pessimism (because of the former's expectation that socialism was in for a long war of attrition in the West). This pessimism does not emerge abruptly and unheralded only after 1920, but is of course fully visible in Sorel's veritable celebration of pessimism. It is also visible in Lenin's (as in Eduard Bernstein's) turn toward voluntarism, a turn both made precisely because they were no longer optimistic about the immanent drift of history.

Rosa Luxemburg had differed with Lenin in her suspicion of the elitism of the Bolshevik organization and its usurpation of working class's prerogatives. Yet she herself was scarcely less voluntaristic than he, insisting on the importance of both objective conditions and ideological commitment for socialism, although placing greater reliance on the ability of the former to generate the latter. She was particularly voluntaristic, however, in her insistence that Bernstein was wrong in warning against a premature lunge toward socialism: "there can be no time when the proletariat, placed in power by the force of events, is not in the condition, or is not morally obliged, to take certain measures in the direction of socialism."[63] However, in insisting that "the conquest of political power by the working class cannot materialize too 'early'," Luxemburg had essentially concurred in Lenin's ambition to seize power in Russia, despite its backwardness, with all the fateful consequences that would subsequently materialize in Stalinism.

After the successful capture of power in Russia by the October Revolution and the failure of the revolutions in central Europe, the dilemmas of Scientific Marxism sharpened. It now faced a double anomaly: (i) the failure of the revolutions that had been predicted for industrially advanced capitalisms, and (ii) their victory in societies that had not been predicted by Scientific Marxism.

The advent of Critical Marxism represents a specific conjunction: the pursuit of revolutionary socialism in industrially backward societies led by a very culturally advanced elite. Theirs was a specific generation of Marxists: those to whom it had become increasingly clear that something had gone wrong in the old paradigm of scientific socialism. The more culturally secure and self-confident—those in the West—openly concluded that it was Marxism itself that was misguided—e.g., Bernstein. Left Marxists in the East, however, concluded that it was only the social democratic reading of Marxism that had gone wrong. The Leninist effort

to reformulate Marxism thus understood itself as an effort to rescue true Marxism from distortion and simply to adapt it to a new
era in history. The Leninist reformulation of Marxism thus proceeded with a dimmed self-consciousness. Emphasizing the importance of an intellectual elite operating through a centralized
and disciplined organization, they stressed the importance of their
own initiatives and the danger of waiting for economic conditions
spontaneously to produce a socialist consciousness. If they no
longer relied on the automatic economic crash, they also tacitly
relied on the random catastrophism of war. They thus offered a
reformulation of Marxism appealing to those in industrially backward areas by stressing ideological initiatives that compensated
for economic backwardness, and allowing an escape from the passivity into which Scientific Marxism would have thrust local radical elites.

The subsequent era of *embourgeoisement* of the working class
in the most industrially advanced nations, and its accommodation
to capitalist society as material standards of living improved, still
further undermined the claims of scientific socialism. For the latter had supposed that it would be the economic contradictions of
advanced capitalism that would make their societies vulnerable to
socialism. When it was the proletariat's militancy rather than
capitalist hegemony that succumbed, Scientific Marxism came
into continuous dissonance with the experience of everyday life in
Western capitalism, no less than in developing countries. This
was all the more sharpened as some of the most manifestly militant groups, such as college students, were far from impoverished.

The experience of everyday life was now read as supporting the
importance that Critical Marxists attributed to consciousness and
to the flawed quality of everyday life in modern society. In moving from a Scientific to a Critical Marxism, the socialist critique of
modern society moved from the condemnation of capitalism's
economic exploitation to a denunciation of its sociological dehumanization, i.e., of alienation and reification. The resurgent
emphasis on alienation and reification in Marxism—found princi-
pally in the industrially advanced West—was rooted in
capitalism's growing control over the economic cycle, its growing
welfare system for the poor, and its improving living standard for
the working class. The movement toward a Critical Marxism in
the sixties and seventies resulted in part from an effort to reformulate Marxism so that it would be consistent with experience
under late capitalism.

In partial summary: Marxism's catastrophism was formed prior to 1848, influenced by the mass suffering of that period's economic depression, by the revitalization of a waning this-wordly millenarianism—among the working and the "educated" classes—as well as by the gathering of political forces discharged in the 1848 revolution. So powerful is Marxism's early catastrophism that, in some expressions, it is conceived as a total, universal revolution.

This expectation of imminent revolution waned as Marx settled into London and as Marxism was exposed to the basic upturn of 1850-1873. Marx's subsequent studies of political economy must now accomodate his earlier catastrophism with the new economic growth and prosperity, for the latter are dissonant with the expectation of imminent revolution. The new sense of capitalism's growing strength is reflected in *Das Kapital's* structuralism, and the pathos it conveys of the power of economic formations. At the same time, *Das Kapital* also provides a new "scientific" grounding for the earlier catastrophism. Thus, if the prosperity of 1850-1873 was bad news for revolutionaries, *Das Kapital* can be read as comforting them, helping to ward off apathy:

> This prosperity, says *Das Kapital* in effect, need not overwhelm revolutionaries because it is only temporary. Revolutionaries need not lose hope in their revolution, but must bide their time and prepare for it, because the basic economic structures of capitalism and their contradictions ensure a new and great crash. Prosperity has thus derailed the revolution only temporarily. The true essence of capitalism's structural contradictions will lead inevitably to the increased misery of the working class and to the suffocation of the forces of production by capitalism's relations of production. The stability of the moment, then, is the stability of a volcano only momentarily dormant.

Scientific Marxism, then, was this: it was an effort to overcome the threat to revolutionary morale that had been born of the defeat of the revolution of 1848 and which was intensified by the prosperity of 1850-1873. It did this by offering a rational basis for believing that stabilization of the economy was only temporary and that the inexorable drift of things favored revolution. In this new framework, however, the catastrophe began to be deferred to an indefinite future. By emphasizing the inevitability of the coming crash, *Das Kapital's* dramaturgy diverted attention from the fact that it was no longer imminent. This is the familiar adaptive mechanism of a millenarianism whose predictions about the "coming" have failed to materialize. In short, while Scientific Marxism embodies catastrophism, it also gelds it.

Scientific Marxism's emasculation of catastrophism was continued on the political level by German social democracy. Giving lip service to the theory of the automatic crash, it no longer expected this was imminent, and began accommodating to opportunities within the framework of the *status quo*. While the long depression might temporarily revitalize the hope of revolution, it thoroughly undermined catastrophism when it became plain that this was not to happen, finally dashing catastrophism on the rocks of revisionism. After the long depression had ended without revolution in sight, the revisionists could renounce catastrophism openly while other socialists, still loyal to Marx, would think the same thing to themselves.

During the long depression, the western working classes had learned to organize trade unions and political parties and to mobilize electoral followings. Such working classes no longer needed millenarian hopes but could now rely on their own practical efforts. The automatic crash and scientific Marxism's determinism could thus give way to a surge of genteel voluntarism in middle Europe. In Eastern Europe, however, Scientific Marxism had long been a source of apathy rather than an antidote to it. Lenin's version of voluntarism, his revolutionary vanguardism, premising that the working class would not develop a socialist consciousness of its own, comes to embody a new opening to catastrophism.

In this less developed area, however, catastrophism is no longer deemed inevitable due to the contradictions of capitalism's economic structures, but now comes to be grounded in the leverage exerted by political and military organization. Lenin thus exults when World War I erupts. Mao subsequently announces that power comes out of the barrel of a gun, and Castro organizes his military column. War now becomes the functional equivalent of crises grounded in capitalism's economic structures and serves as a new basis of Critical Marxism's catastrophism.

NOTES

1. Robert M. Young, "The Impact of Darwin on Conventional Thought," in *The Victorian Crisis in Faith,* ed. Anthony Symondson (London: S.P.C.K., 1970), p. 25. I have drawn from this excellent study at various points in this paragraph, and all quotations in it are from Young.

2. Robert Young has argued that even the debate about evolution "produced an adjustment within a basically theistic view of nature rather than a rejection of theism." Ibid., p. 27. In that vein, Young notes that Herbert Spencer's version of evolution never allowed that the great problems of philosophy were solved. "Only such as know not the scope and limits of science can fall into so grave an error," observed Spencer, piously adding, "The ultimate mystery of things remains just as it was." Ibid., p. 28.

3. Ibid. p. 31.

4. Steven Marcus, *Engels, Manchester and the Working Class* (New York: Random House, 1974), p. 202.

5. *Communist Manifesto* by Karl Marx and Friedrich Engels, authorized English edition of 1888, supervised by Engels, published by Charles H. Kerr, Chicago, p. 16.

6. Ibid., pp. 203–204.

7. Alan Smith, *The Established Church and Popular Religion, 1750–1850* (Bristol: Longmans, 1971), p. 3.

8. Document published ibid., p. 101.

9. John Briggs and Ian Sellers, eds., *Victorian Nonconformity: Documents of Modern History* (London: Edward Arnold, 1973), cited on pp. 79–80.

10. Smith, *Established Church*, p. 106.

11. E. P. Thompson, *The Making of the English Working Class* (New York: Pantheon Books, 1963), pp. 385–86.

12. Ibid., p. 363.

13. Ibid., p. 380.

14. Ibid., p. 379.

15. E. J. Hobsbawm, "Methodism and the Threat of Revolution," *History Today* 7 (1957).

16. Perry Anderson, *Considerations on Western Marxism* (London: New Left Books, 1976), pp. 116–17.

17. Rosa Luxemburg, *Reform or Revolution* (New York: Three Arrows Press, 1932), p. 34. Italics added.

18. Thompson, *English Working Class*, p. 364.

19. Nicholas Lobkowicz, *Theory and Practice: History of a Concept from Aristotle to Marx* (South Bend, Ind.: University of Notre Dame Press, 1967), p. 163.

20. Ibid., pp. 161, 162.

21. Ibid., p. 177.

22. Ibid., p. 185.

23. Ibid.

24. Cited by Lobkowicz, ibid., p. 187.

25. David McLellan, *The Young Hegelians and Karl Marx* (London: Macmillan Publishers, 1969), p. 66.

26. Ibid., p. 80.

27. Ibid., pp. 80–81.

28. Karl Marx, *Frühe Schriften* (Stuttgart, 1962), vol. 1, p. 599.

29. The quotations here are cited in McLellan, *The Young Hegelians*, pp. 83–84.

30. Ibid., p. 148.

31. Hans Mühlestein, "Marx and the Utopian Wilhelm Weitling," *Science and Society*, Winter 1948, p. 118. For the most part this is a doctrinaire apologia for Marx's rough treatment of Weitling. Weitling's hostility toward culture and men of learning (pointedly directed against Marx and Engels), his radical egalitarianism, his impulse to gather up the "lumpen proletariat" for militant action, are an interesting (if urban) anticipation of Maoism. It brought a furious break with Marx who finally condemned him for his lack of scientific theory, while Weitling, for his part, suggested that Marx's influence in their social circles rested in part on his support by rich men who gave Marx access to the communication media. See also the discussion of Weitling in Saul K. Padover, *Karl Marx: An Intimate Biography* (New York: McGraw-Hill Book Co., 1978), pp. 227ff. Padover notes that when Weitling was jailed in 1843 in Switzerland, the charge was blasphemy, because "he hinted at a resemblance between himself and Jesus Christ—and for preaching communism" (p. 227).

32. Alisdair MacIntyre, *Marxism and Christianity* (New York: Schocken Books, 1968), p. 6. Compare Richard Bernstein's remark that "the more one penetrates to the quintessence of Marx's thought, the more one can see the presence of themes (in a secularized form) that have preoccupied religious thinkers throughout the ages—the severity of human alienation, the apocalyptic sense of the imminence of the coming revolution, and the messianic aspiration that infuses much of Marx's thinking. Even the temperament and outlook of Marx are in the direct vein of the Biblical prophets." Richard Bernstein, *Praxis and Action: Contemporary Philosophies of Human Action* (Philadelphia: University of Pennsylvania Press), p. 77. On Marx's biblical character compare Edmund Wilson: "Marx is of the tradition of the Old Testament, not of that of the New." Cited in his *To the Finland Station* (Garden City, N.Y.: Doubleday & Co., 1940), p. 308.

33. Alvin W. Gouldner, *The Coming Crisis of Western Sociology* (New York: Basic Books, 1970), p. 264.

34. Frank Parkin, "The Transition to Socialism" (unpublished manuscript).

35. Karl Marx, *Critique of Hegel's Philosophy of Right*, ed. Joseph

O'Malley (London and New York: Cambridge University Press, 1970), p. 142.

36. See Robert McAulay, "Velikovsky and the Infrastructure of Science," *Theory and Society*, November 1978, for further discussion.

37. Young, "Impact of Darwin," p. 16.

38. Herbert Dingle, "The Scientific Outlook in 1851 and 1951," in *European Intellectual History Since Darwin and Marx*, ed. W. Warren Wagar (New York: Harper & Row Pubs., 1966) pp. 161–62.

39. Ibid., p. 162. Here Dingle cites Whewell's *Philosophy of the Inductive Sciences*.

40. Ibid., p. 165.

41. Ibid.

42. Albert Einstein and Leopold Infield, *The Evolution of Physics* (New York: Simon & Schuster, 1951), p. 152. All other formulations in this paragraph are either quotations or paraphrasings from this volume.

43. Ibid., p. 223.

44. Shepard Bancroft Clough and Charles Wesley Cole, *Economic History of Europe* (Boston: D. C. Heath & Co., 1952) pp. 663ff.

45. Ibid., p. 665.

46. S. B. Clough, *Economic Development of Western Civilization* (New York: McGraw-Hill Book Co., 1959), p. 375.

47. Clough and Cole, *Economic History*, p. 677.

48. Clough, *Economic Development*, p. 420.

49. Jurgen Kucyzinski, *Labor Conditions in Great Britain, 1750 to the Present* (New York: International Publishers, 1946), p. 69. See also Kucyzinski, *Labour Conditions in Western Europe, 1820 to 1935* (London: Lawrence & Wishart, 1937).

50. In other words, the original lecture was a work of transition to economic studies and analysis; but the Engels version of 1891 is a later work and a "joint product."

51. Karl Marx, *Grundrisse: Introduction to the Critique of Political Economy*, trans. Martin Nicolaus (Harmondsworth: Penguin Books, 1973), from the foreword by Martin Nicolaus, pp. 8–9. Compare Engels's account of that period: "When, after the defeat of the Revolution of 1848, a period began in which it became more and more impossible to influence Germany from without, our party surrendered the field of emigrational quarrels—for they remained the only possible activity—to vulgar democracy. While the latter indulged in intrigues to its heart's content, and squabbled today in order to make up the day after, and the day after that again washed all its dirty linen in view of everyone—while vulgar democracy went begging through the whole of America in order immediately afterwards to stage new scandals over the division of the few pence secured—our party was glad once again to have some leisure for study. It had the great advantage of having a new scientific outlook as its theoretical basis, the working out of which kept it fully occupied." *Ludwig*

Feuerbach and the Outcome of Classical German Philosophy (New York: International Publishers, 1941), p. 74.

52. Eduard Bernstein, *Evolutionary Socialism* (New York: Schocken Books, 1961), pp. 75–76.

53. From Karl Marx, *On Revolution* (New York: McGraw-Hill Book Co., 1972), vol. 1, p. 239 in the galleys. This two-volume work is a splendid effort to establish what Marx really wrote and when, and much of the preceding chronology is taken from it.

54. Bernstein, *Evolutionary Socialism*, p. xxiv.

55. Ibid., p. xxviii.

56. Luxemburg, *Reform or Revolution*, p. 48.

57. Ibid., pp. 29, 34. Luxemburg's italics.

58. *Vorwaerts*, 26 March 1899. Cited in Luxemburg, p. 38.

59. Georg Lukács, *History and Class Consciousness*, trans. Rodney Livingstone (Cambridge: MIT Press, 1971), pp. 243, 282, 283.

60. V. I. Lenin, *Report on War and Peace to the Seventh Congress of the R.C. P. (B.)*, Mar. 6–8, 1918.

61. Mao Tse-tung, *Mao Tse-tung ssu-hsiang wah sui* (Hong Kong: Po Wen Book Co., 1969), pp. 333–34. Cited by Edward Friedman, *Mao Tse-tung, Backwardness and Revolution* (unpublished manuscript, June 1978).

62. Anderson, *Considerations on Western Marxism*, p. 89.

63. Luxemburg, *Reform or Revolution*, p. 47. Luxemburg had tacitly assumed, however, that there would be a lengthy contest for power, under the conditions of an advanced industrialism such as that in Germany, during which the workers would educate themselves for power. In short, she had assumed a "definite degree of maturity of economic and political relations."

APPENDIX
Mannheim, Coser and Lasswell on the Origins of Critical Marxism

Just as I have not been the first to distinguish between Scientific and Critical Marxisms, neither does the analysis of their social origins begin here. There is an established intellectual tradition that in effect (and sometimes expressly) links Critical Marxism to backwardness and Scientific Marxism to the historically progressive. In outlining these other analyses of the origins of Critical Marxism I shall use the occasion to sharpen my own perspective. For all practical purposes, the discussion begins with a brief paragraph in Karl Mannheim which states rather cryptically:

> Marxist thought appears as the attempt to rationalize the irrational. The correctness of this analysis is vouched for by the fact that to the extent that Marxian proletarian groups rise to power, they shake off the dialectical elements of their theory and begin to think in the generalising methods of liberalism and democracy, which seeks to arrive at universal laws, whilst those who, because of their position, still have to resort to revolution, cling to the dialectical element (Leninism).[1]

One can sympathize with Mannheim's judgement on the dialectic, considering that some Marxists tend to invoke it, like the idea of a miracle, to explain events when no logical explanation is available. In that vein there is Sorel's tongue-in-cheek remark, "There is no agreement on the meaning of the term 'dialectic' but it seems that the dialectic is a very important thing."

I do not agree, however, that the dialectic is to be equated with irrationalism. This illusion occurs only from the singular perspective of those who equate rationality with the Enlightenment outlook and fail to understand—as I shall show in a later volume—that the dialectic is an attempt to overcome the *limits* of Enlightenment rationality. Mannheim's view is that this "dialectical" Marxism is somehow associated with the lack of power and irrationalism; like the other perspectives on Critical Marxism considered below, the premise is that Critical Marxism is symptomatic of a kind of "backwardness." While I shall return to that issue, I can say at this point that Mannheim seems correct in implying that Critical Marxism has an elective affinity for those with weaker, and Scientific Marxism for those with stronger, power bases. But to go beyond that, and associate weakness with backwardness/irrationality, would imply that the forces of the status quo already in power, ought always to represent the most rational elements in society.

In 1967, Harold D. Lasswell's comparative analysis of "Russia and China in a Modernizing World"[2] argued that the "voluntarism" of some of these societies (which I associate with Critical Marxism) stems from their development in traditionalistic, *prescientific* societies. Here, again, Critical Marxism is linked with backwardness.

Lasswell views technology and science as disciplining fantasy, inhibiting persons from believing in the power of will, and curbing the subjective factor. Indeed, he tends to equate reliance on the subjective factor with magic, thus altogether ignoring the latter's invocation of the sacred through meticulous conformity to ritual. His general implication, then, is that Scientific Marxism is the product of a culture's scientific and technological development, while Critical Marxism is *produced in and by* backward societies.

Several things need to be said, perhaps the first being that his view is grounded on a certain anthropological insensitivity; for example, the reduction of magic to a "subjective factor." Moreover, his view implicitly overstates the voluntarism even of traditional societies. After all, people in traditionalist societies do not simply practice magic to feed their families or defeat their enemies. They also work and fight. Indeed, even in tribal societies, work and magic *coexist;* the existence of magic never implies the absence of work. The great Polish anthropologist Bronislaw Malinowski long ago observed that magic is more likely when work outcomes are less certain; i.e., when persons pursue goals for which routine, technologically adequate means do not exist, magic enables them to control their anxieties and carry on with their project.

Lasswell's thesis, that a voluntaristic political ideology is the product of a *pre*-industrial society, ignores the modern experience with Naziism and fascism. Clearly, these were among the most extremely voluntaristic and irrational politics produced anywhere in the contemporary world. Yet it is equally obvious that the societies in which they emerged were not backward but among the world's most scientifically and technologically advanced and whose populations, according to Lasswell's thesis, should therefore have been immune to voluntarism.

Lewis Coser's analysis of "Marxist Thought in the First Quarter of the Twentieth Century"[3] is a most illuminating work but, much like Mannheim and Lasswell, associates Critical Marxism with backwardness and has the same difficulties as Lasswell's views. Essentially Coser sees Scientific Marxism as grounded in the industrially advanced parts of Europe, particularly Germany, thus missing the way in which Scientific Marxism serves to counterbalance the decline of religion as a source of security among workers. At the same time, Coser holds that a voluntaristic Marxism is the product of the industrially backward parts of Europe. Tom Bottomore has noted that Coser can hold this thesis only by ignoring the fact that Karl Korsch, a left voluntarist for a while, was a product of the heartland of German industry and only by ignoring Sorel's Paris-fostered voluntarism. As Bottomore asks, "why emphasize so strongly the formative influence of Gramsci's Sardinian childhood and not his student years in the industrial city of Turin?"[4] One should add that Lukács, the arch apostle of a Critical Marxism was, though Hungarian by birth, greatly under the influence of German culture and education, including the strong influence of Max Weber and Georg Simmel.

All of the leaders of the critique of Scientific Marxism—Lukács (1885), Korsch (1886), Gramsci (1891), and Horkheimer (1895)—are a generation cohort born after the stabilization of capitalism at the end of the nineteenth century. Sorel, who was born in 1847, did not start writing as a socialist until he was 45 in 1892, and published his *Reflections on Violence* in 1908. It was their generation that grew up with the conviction that Marxism had been proved wrong or was irrelevant; but they had sought a remedy from the left, as Bernstein had sought it from the right.

A basic difficulty with both Lasswell's and Coser's view is that it makes inferences about the ideology of this intellectual elite from larger conditions in certain types of "backward" societies, "traditionalist" according to Lasswell, and the rimland economies beyond the industrial center in Europe, according to Coser. This supposes that this elite was actually formed by the same backward conditions as were the masses of people in these societies. Such an assumption, however, is unfounded. Critical Marxism was the product of an intellectual elite with *advanced education and considerable familiarity with science and technology,* either through their studies or from first hand travels in industrial societies. Their development thus does not reflect the magical premises or backwardness of traditionalist, preindustrial economies but of cultures as advanced as any of their time. Indeed, Critical Marxism was the product of an advanced elite who knew that modern science was undergoing a major transformation. Theirs was not an ignorance of science but a critique of it; their position about science did not reflect a naive traditionalism but the most advanced philosophy of science of their time (e.g., Sorel) and other very sophisticated and sociological traditions (Lukács and Gramsci). This elite was impelled toward Critical Marxism because, unlike Bernstein, they persisted in their revolutionary ambitions in the face of the collapse of the "automatic crash." That their doctrines were subsequently attractive to people in less developed areas of the world does not imply that those people had been primed for them by immersal in a culture of magical traditionalism, but rather that they, too, were bent on an activistic radicalism while a Scientific Marxism seemed to counsel passivity. For them, therefore, Critical Marxism allowed continued revolutionary activism despite their own economic backwardness, and substituted a politico-military catastrophism for Scientific Marxism's economic catastrophism.

NOTES

1. Karl Mannheim, *Ideology and Utopia: An Introduction to the Sociology of Knowledge,* trans. Louis Wirth and Edward Shils (New York: Harcourt, Brace & Co., 1946), p. 118.

2. In Donald W. Treadgold, ed., *Soviet and Chinese Communism: Similarities and Differences* (Seattle: University of Washington Press, 1967).

3. Lewis Coser, "Marxist Thought in the First Quarter of the Twentieth Century," *American Journal of Sociology,* vol. 78, no. 1 (July, 1972).

4. Ibid., introduction to issue.

Appendices to Part I

APPENDIX ONE
Other Formulations of the Two Marxisms

As I have already noted, the thesis that there are diverse and dissonant dimensions of Marxism, that there are Two Marxisms (or more), is scarcely original to this writer. It began emerging most articulately after the Bolshevik revolution had failed to be accompanied by a successful revolution in central, industrially advanced Europe, and as part of a critique of the parliamentarism, the revisionism, and the deterministic evolutionism of the Second International. The thesis of the "Two Marxisms," was fully articulated by Karl Korsch in 1923:

> I described the dialectical materialist, critical revolutionary theory of Marx and Engels in the 1840's as an *"anti-philosophy"* which yet in itself remained philosophical . . . "anti-philosophy" developed in two separate directions. On the one hand, socialist "science" became positive and gradually turned away from philosophy altogether. On the other hand, a philosophical development occurred, apparently in conflict with the former but in fact complementary to it. This is first to be found in the late 1850's, in the writings of Marx and Engels themselves, and then later in those of their best disciples—Labriola in Italy and Plekhanov in Russia. Its theoretical character may be defined as a kind of return to Hegel's philosophy and not just a return to the essentially critical and revolutionary "anti-philosophy" of the Left Hegelians in the *Sturm and Drang* period of the 1840's. . . . Labriola and Plekhanov developed this Hegelian philosophical trend, which is to be found in every line of their writings. It also persisted in Plekhanov's pupil, Lenin.[1]

Clearly, then, Korsch saw one of the Two Marxisms—Scientific Marxism—as a scientizing, positivistic impulse hostile to philosophy in general and to Hegel in particular. He saw the other Marxism as a reaffirmation of the critical philosophical and Hegelian grounding of Marxism. Korsch's own work "aimed to re-emphasize this philosophical side of Marxism." It also cautiously rejected the "fundamentally dogmatic and therefore unscientific procedure of the 'orthodox' who make it a completely self-evident and unshakeable article of faith that the 'doctrine' produced by the two Church Fathers was absolutely consistent," while rejecting any view of the ideas of Marx and Engels that one-sidedly treated them as "completely at variance."[2]

The Italian Marxist Lucio Colletti also develops his own version of the thesis of the Two Marxisms, focusing on a convergent distinction between Marxism as science and as critique:

> There are two possible lines of development in Marx's own discourse, expressed respectively in the title and subtitle of *Capital*. The first is that which Marx himself advances in his preface to the first edition, the postscript to the second edition, in which he presents himself simply as a scientist. Marx, according to his own account here, is performing in the field of the historical and social sciences a task that had already been performed in the natural sciences. . . . The title of *Capital* spells this direction out. It promises that political economy, which started with the works of Smith and Ricardo but remained incomplete and contradictory in them, will now become a true science in the full sense of the term. The sub-title of the book, however, suggests another direction: a "critique of political economy.". . . Lenin would certainly have rejected the idea that Marxism was a critique of political economy; for him it was the critique of *bourgeois* political economy only, which finally transformed political economy into a real science. But the sub-title of *Capital* indicates . . . that political economy as such is bourgeois and must be criticized *tout court*. This second dimension of Marx's work is precisely that which culminates in his theory of alienation, and fetishism.[3]

The French phenomenological Marxist, Maurice Merleau-Ponty in his 1955 analysis of *Les Aventures de la dialectique,* also formulated a distinction between what he calls "Western Marxism" and "Leninism" convergent with our own distinction between Critical and Scientific Marxisms. Holding that this "is already found in Marx as a conflict between dialectical thought and naturalism," he speaks of a "communist eclecticism" which is

> "thought without candor . . . that unstable mixture of Hegelianism and scientism which allows the orthodoxy to reject, in the name of "philosophical" principles, all that the social sciences have tried to say since Engels, and yet allows it to reply with "scientific socialism" when philosophical objections are raised. . . . On the theoretical plane, it means closing off any attempt at "comprehension" as, on the plane of action, it means replacing total praxis by a technician-made action, replacing the proletariat by the professional revolutionary.[4]

Raymond Aron has also stressed the essential instability and oscillatory quality of the two Marxisms:

> La mode Parisienne oscille entre les Manuscrits *économico-philosophiques* et la protostructuralisme de *l'Introduction à la Critique de l'économie politique* et du *Capital:* d'une part la version hégéliano-existentialiste, l'odyssée de l'humanité entre la chute dans la lutte de classes, l'aliénation et le salut révolutionnaire, la réconciliation de l'homme et de la nature, de l'essence et de l'existence, d'autre part, la version scientifique des lois naturelles selon lesquelles fonctionne et se transforme le mode de production capitaliste abandonné à lui-même. Cette oscillation trouve son explication, sinon sa justification, dans les incertitudes de la synthèse marxiste elle-même.[5]

Again, the Yugoslavian philosopher, Mihailo Marković in an essay of 1969, stressed a similar distinction between Scientific and Critical Marxism:

> Marx developed a theory which is both scientific and critical. However, in most interpretations and further developments of his thought either one or the other of these two essential characteristics has invariably been overlooked. . . . To the latter group (who stress criticism) belong . . . various apologists of post-capitalist society who develop Marxism as an ideology and . . . those romantic humanists who consider positive knowledge a form of intellectual subordination to the given social framework. . . . To the former group belong all those scientists who appreciate Marx's enormous contribution to modern social science, but who fail to realize what fundamentally distinguishes Marx's views from those of Comte, Mill, Ricardo and other classical social scientists, as well as from those of modern positivists, in his constant criticism of both existing theory and existing forms of social reality.[6]

The American philosophers, Dick Howard and Karl Klare, also note the existence of Two Marxisms, of a split between Scientific and Critical Marxism, holding, however, that the latter, Critical Marxism is the true Marxism, and that it has been repressed by the former, untrue Scientific Marxism. For them, then, Critical Marxism is the "hidden and unknown dimension." "Marxism, in short, is other than what we know it as," writes Karl Klare, and "the theoretical currents that make this clear have had, for reasons of political history, an underground existence within Marxism."[7]

I should reiterate here that, in my own view, "real" or "true" Marxism is no more "critical" than "scientific." *Both* are equally real in Marxism and both are authentic to it. The contradiction within Marxism is not that of an *incorrect* versus a *correct* reading of Marxism. The contradiction is made up of alternatives which are both truly Marxist. Finally, I would add that the contradictions of Marxism are internal and essential to it, rather than artifacts of an external, contingent "political history."

Critical Marxism, stresses Klare, is concerned with aspects of what once were deprecated in Scientific Marxism as the ideological superstructure. Wilhelm Reich, for example, stresses the significance of the authoritarian structure of the patriarchical family and of the character structure it produces, as well as the ideological implications of its repression of sexuality. Again, Antonio Gramsci focuses on the importance of morality, regional differentiations in culture, differences in types of intelligentsia, the importance of the bourgeoisie's ideological hegemony for its domination of society. The Frankfurt School's further studies of the authoritarian character structure, of its stress on ideology critique, and of its recent emphasis on communication and language, are of a similar import.

The main feature of the unknown Marxism, for Klare, is that it restores "human consciousness, human subjectivity, to the heart of Marxism and rejects as a 'vulgar' Marxism the view that 'consciousness' is strictly determined by the economic realm."[8]

A Critical Marxism that rejects all forms of economic determinism and reductionism, is seen as an essentially Lukácsian theory of the "totality," as opposed to positivism, allying itself with continuing efforts to develop Marxism in the light of modern social science developments, particularly those having an opening to philosophy. Thus Lukács is the pupil of Max Weber and George Simmel; Sartre bases himself on Freud and Husserl; Marcuse on Heidegger and Freud; and Gramsci has roots in Croce. Critical Marxism, then, is seen as open to other theoretical communities and not as having dogmatic closure.

What has long been called "vulgar" Marxism also entailed an *incipient* distinction between the Two Marxisms. This involved a focal and negative critique of Scientific Marxism—which is what is termed "vulgar," from the standpoint of a Critical Marxism that was still only tacit and untheoretized. The idea of a "vulgar" Marxism is a rejection of Scientific Marxism that leaves the grounding of this rejection tacit, so that the other, Critical Marxism remains "hidden" or only residual.

The convergence between vulgar Marxism and Scientific Marxism can be seen in the formulation of vulgar Marxism made by the English Marxist historian, Eric Hobsbawm:

> vulgar Marxism embraced in the main the following elements:
> 1. The "economic interpretation of history," i.e., the belief that "the economic factor is the fundamental factor on which the others are dependent" ... on which phenomena hitherto not regarded as having much connection with economic matters depended. ...
> 2. The model of "basis and superstructure" (used most widely to explain the history of ideas) ... this model was usually interpreted as a simple relation of dominance and dependence ... mediated at most by

3. "Class interest and class struggle."
4. Historical laws and historical inevitability" downgrading accidents and the role of the individual in history.[9]

In that sense, then, a Scientific Marxism, is structuralistic, a Critical
Marxism, voluntarist. To put it another way, Scientific Marxism conceives
of men as *other*-grounded, i.e., as produced objects, as products of society,
or of society's structured contradictions and of the blind laws expressing
these. Scientific Marxism is fused with the technological pathos characteristic of modernism. Critical Marxism, however, stresses that men are
doers and producers. In accenting the *self*-groundedness of men, it fuses
with recurrent social movements toward a cultural revitalization that is a
"romanticized" opposition to the "mechanization" of the modern world,
resonating inhibited "spiritual" sentiments.

The last case to be discussed here is Perry Anderson's *Considerations
on Western Marxism.*[10] Having chosen to use Merleau-Ponty's terminol-
ogy (i.e., "Western" Marxism), Anderson might have been expected to,
but does *not*, refer to Scientific Marxism and Critical Marxism in the
sense used here and, indeed, in the whole tradition of discourse outlined
above. Anderson's is a negative case that conflates Scientific and Critical
Marxists and plainly exhibits the corresponding intellectual loss of not
making some such distinction. Anderson's method is that of an informal
generation (or cohort) study in which the generations are treated primarily
in relationship to each other, but are not linked systematically to their
differing political and economic environments comprehensively conceived. The different historical character of each Marxist generation's
social milieu remains unclarified with the singular exception that, under-
standably, much is made of the effects of the October Revolution. The
study is thus in the tradition of the old history of ideas, where one idea is
related to others but not to the surrounding historical situation except that
here, instead of ideas, the unit examined is the generation.

Anderson's attention is essentially focused on Western Marxist
theorists whose work appeared from about 1920 to the present. This, of
course, has the effect of locating such otherwise diverse theorists as
Gramsci and Althusser, or Della Volpe and Horkheimer, in the same
school. For Anderson, they are all Western Marxists. Having asserted that
they are members of the same generation and category, Anderson then
seeks common attributes they may be said to have, thus diverting analysis
from the substantial differences they also have. The very title of the study
starts by promising to focus on Marxists distinguished by their common
origins or cultural orientations—i.e., Western—and then makes a 180 degree turn and sorts them out by *generation*. Anderson's method of the
intergenerational study of isolated generations thus focuses on the similarities of the post-1920 generation, as these become visible when contrasted with pre-1920 generations. Most especially, Anderson holds that
one of the main, common themes of Western Marxism is its pessimism.

A first problem is whether this conclusion is correct. Is it really true that Marxist pessimism begins *only after 1920* with those he calls Western Marxists? It does not seem so. Such pessimism is already fully manifest even before World War I in Georges Sorel, who was clearly the first and foremost pessimist among Critical Marxists, having condemned the very doctrine of "progress," which he viewed as an ideology of a privileged elite who justified their advantages by promising that everyone else would, in time, enjoy the privileges now enjoyed only by themselves. Anderson is able to define pessimism as post-October Revolution only because he ignores Sorel, whom he mentions only once and in passing.

Anderson wants to account for this pessimism as due to the failure of the revolutions in central Europe and their inability to rescue the October Revolution from subsequent bureaucratization and deformation by Stalinism. In effect, Anderson wants to account for pessimism among Western Marxists as due to the political defeat of Marxism, that is, *as due to events extrinsic and only contingently related to Marxism itself.* If pessimism is to be explained by the failure of the October Revolution, it must therefore be allowed to make its appearance only after that Revolution. Actually, however, Marxist pessimism precedes that failure and contributes as much to it as it receives from it. *Marxist pessimism is central to Bolshevism.* Lenin's fundamental doctrine of the external origins of socialist consciousness—that it must be brought to the proletariat by bourgeois intellectuals, and that it is not a consciousness *natural* to the working class—is a profoundly pessimistic doctrine for a Marxist. Certainly it is every bit as pessimistic as those other doctrines Anderson regards as pessimistic: e.g., Althusser's belief that socialism does not overcome ideology and its false consciousness, or Marcuse's doctrine of the uni-dimensional society which can coopt all resistance to it.

Anderson is twice mistaken: first, about the timing of Marxist pessimism and, second, about its origins. In Chapter Five, I related part of this *pre*-revolutionary pessimism to the "long depression" of the last quarter of the nineteenth century, to its failure to result in an economic crash that brought down capitalist society, to the growing strength of the capitalist class, and to the growing parliamentarianism of social democracy. As an outgrowth of these developments, Bernstein's revisionism flatly held that Marx's political economy was wrong, and that there would be no crash produced by the internal and necessary laws of the capitalist economy. It is this that is the grounding of prerevolutionary, Marxist pessimism. This, too, is part of what leads Lukács to assert that the essence of Marxism is not the priority of the economic factor but the primacy of the "totality," and which intensifies the development of a voluntaristic Critical Marxism, where "will" and political determination are to substitute for the results Scientific Marxists once expected from capitalism's internal contradictions. This, too, is one of the main sources of other common characteristics Anderson attributes to Western Marxists, that is, their rejection of theoretical work in economics, their focus on aesthetics and ideological superstructures, and their "methodism."

Anderson's difficulties are essentially grounded in his impulse to salvage Marxism. He wants to be loyal to Marxism, but does not say what this requires. Although he clearly sees that Marxism's difficulties are not simply due to its lacunae but also involve "mistakes," he thinks that Marxism's basic structure provides a suitable corpus for a surgery which will permit amputation of the mistakes, allow new transplants, and suture sundered parts. Yet it is not helpful to be told that Marxism made mistakes but is fundamentally adequate, if we are never told what Marxism's fundament is. Above all, the idea that Marxism has its own *internal contradictions* is a thought that Anderson will not contemplate.

But if, as Anderson relates in a candid "Afterword," Marxist theory, politics, and economics have gained surprisingly little from extensive recent developments in Marxist historiography; if Marx never produced a coherent account of the bourgeois state and political structures; if he manifested "an incomprehension of much of the nature of the later epoch through which he lived," never registering the new international state system and underestimating the continued vitality of nationalism; and if Anderson also has doubts about Marx's very theory of value, the lynchpin of his economic theory; and if Marxism was also born lacking a political theory; if all this is wrong, it is difficult to understand what is the sound fundament of Marxism to which Anderson wishes to remain loyal. Indeed, given this blossoming of a hundred doubts about the most basic aspects of Marxism, it is understandable that Anderson wants to proceed with his fundamental critique of Marxism in a manner that is full of "courage and calm" but it is astonishing, that he wishes to remain "resolutely revolutionary in political position" (p. 118). It is altogether perplexing why anyone should want to remain a resolute revolutionary if his whole theory of history admittedly has the most profound defects, except on the premise that theory and practice no longer have much to do with one another. Indeed this is just what Anderson says in declaring that there is an "inherent scissiparity between knowledge and action, theory and practice." (p. 110).

For Anderson, then, there are no inner contradictions of Marxism itself; only contradictions between generations of Marxists. In short, Anderson tries to solve the problem of the internal contradictions of Marxism in much the same manner as those who want to split Marx and Engels, or split the young and old Marx, assigning acceptable elements to one side and rejected elements to another, only this time the split is made between different generations of Marxists. With this strategy, the problem is soluble by writing off Engels in one case, the young Marx in another, or, in Anderson's case, writing off Western Marxism. For linking it as he does with the failure of the October Revolution, tarring all Western Marxists with the brush of pessimism, and never asking which parts of their work retain validity and should be preserved, Anderson must end with the liquidation of modern Marxism and the return to a critically reappropriated earlier generation. Most notably to Trotsky's reading—although this, too, is seen as defective. At bottom, although he wants to return to an updated, critically purified Trotskyism, as a pure unbureaucratized Leninism, Anderson's solution is intellectually regressive and, what is worse, manifests a failure of nerve. What he fails to understand is that Trotskyism is the defeated underside of Leninism, a close kin of Stalinism itself—playing Yin to its Yang—and that all three share a common elitism.[11]

Looked at closely, however, Anderson does admit tacitly the distinction between Scientific and Critical Marxism, so central here, when he acknowledges that Louis Althusser's writings do have features distinguishing them from other schools (whose description converges with our Critical Marxism). Anderson thus remarks of the Della Volpean and Althusserian schools, "Their hostility towards Hegel . . . demarcates them most obviously in a tradition otherwise predominantly drawn towards Hegel. Together with this, they shared an aggressive re-emphasis on the scientific character of Marxism."[12]

Yet, insists Anderson, such differences do not allow us to divide post-1920 European Marxism into two "antithetical camps nor even warrant speaking of a more subtle or continuous spectrum . . . For the attitudes of individual theorists have often coincided or overlapped in disconcerting ways." This is the authentic but archaic voice of "public school," British empiricism and comes with the porridge. The intellectual Ulysses has wandered home from his adventures abroad, settling snugly into his old hearth after wenching with foreign theories, and returns to the sound ways of his fathers, his old dog Empiricism at his feet. What Anderson has not got clearly is that Scientific and Critical Marxism are *analytical* distinctions, like "bureaucracy," the "state," even "class," and thus concrete persons or specific groups will inevitably have "scores" on *both* dimensions. (Thus even "bald" persons may have some hair or the hirsute may have "high foreheads.") There will always be some, however, who score so high on one dimension and so low on the other that that it will be reasonable, as a kind of shorthand, to speak of them as "Scientific Marxists" or "Critical Marxists," even though we know perfectly well that each has some of the other in him. Notice, too, that the same is true of those Anderson terms "Western Marxists," and those he distinguishes from them, their predecessors. If they are all not so much distinguished by when they were born (and even here there is a "subtle, continuous spectrum") but by *what* they believe, there is much overlapping among them. The point, then, is that Anderson has confused analytic categories with concrete things, having gotten the flea of his old dog on him.

NOTES

1. K. Korsch, *Marxism and Philosophy* (London: New Left Books, 1970), p. 95.

2. Ibid., p. 108.

3. Interview with Lucio Colletti in the *New Left Review*, July/August 1974, p. 18.

4. Maurice Merleau-Ponty, *Adventures of the Dialectic* (Evanston, Ill.: Northwestern University Press, 1973), p. 64. In Merleau-Ponty's version of a Critical Marxism, however, there is not, as in Lukács's, a Hegelian tendency to assimilate the Other or to have the "subject" annihilate and ingest the object. Merleau-Ponty had a more Durkheimian sensitivity to the real constraints imposed by the Other; he views the Other as evidencing its own reality by the external constraints it imposes—the "heaviness" of history. Merleau-Ponty holds that "it is this feeling of the objective world's weight, which is acquired only in contact with things."

5. Raymond Aron, "Equivoque et inépuisable," in *Marx and Contemporary Scientific Thought*, Social Science Research Council (The Hague: Mouton, 1969), p. 37.

6. Mihailo Marković, "Marx and Critical Scientific Thought," in *Marx and Contemporary Scientific Thought*, pp. 155–67.

7. Dick Howard and Karl E. Klare, *The Unknown Dimension: European Marxism Since Lenin* (New York: Basic Books, 1973), p. 4.

8. Ibid., p. 7.

9. Eric Hobsbawm, "Karl Marx's Contribution to Historiography," in *Marx and Contemporary Scientific Thought*, p. 197–211.

10. Perry Anderson, *Considerations on Western Marxism* (London: New Left Books, 1976).

11. That is a theme I have developed elsewhere. See Alvin W. Gouldner, "Stalinism: A Study of Internal Colonialism," *Telos*, Winter 1977–78, esp. pp. 20–26. See also the pointed and succinct argument by Philip Corrigan, Harvey Ramsay, and Derek Sayer, *Socialist Construction and Marxist Theory* (New York: Monthly Review Press, 1978).

12. Anderson, p. 71.

APPENDIX TWO
The Two Marxisms as an Analytic Distinction

The Two Marxisms are clearly not concrete objects but analytic distinctions, ideal types, or imputed latent dimensions. Each may be thought of as a kind of factor (or scale) produced by a (qualitative) factor analysis. Or each may be viewed as an hypothesis about which dimensions would appear if we made a "factor analysis" (in the precise sense of that mathematical term) of our information about specific and concrete Marxists. Correspondingly, then, a specific Marxist should *not* be spoken of as "a" Critical or Scientific Marxist. Rather, each specific theorist should be thought of as always containing an admixture of both dimensions; as always having a "score" on each of the dimensions. Nonetheless, some theorist's score on the Scientific Marxist or Critical Marxist dimension can be consistently higher (or lower) than others, during certain periods of time.

For us, then, both Scientific and Critical Marxism are underlying, latent factors, discriminable from a set of observables (which are attributes) of a number of concrete, social theorists, with personal names. In short, the concepts of Critical and Scientific Marxisms are hypotheses for a factor analysis of concrete Marxist theorists. Thus viewed, the critique of Lukács or of Engels or Althusser, or of the young or old Marx, unduly particularizes and *over*-concretizes the issue. The important issue, in our framework, is not what were the theories of Georg Lukács or Louis Althusser. By that route, one gets involved in the exegesis—the critique or apologia—of an individual's theoretical system, forgetting that it has many merely personal idiosyncracies.

Certainly, Critical and Scientific Marxisms are dimensions that may be inferred from a matrix of ongoing observables simultaneously copresent. We, however, will also look upon them as quasi-archeological data, in the sense that, though copresent, they are also *differently dated*. The dimensions, moreover, are not just copresent but, also, mutually interactive; and not just mutually interactive synchronically, but also diachronically. Each affects the other over *time*, and at specific times; each becomes what it is at a certain historical period and because of what the other was *then*. And, to put the matter in Fernand Braudel's terms, each may also have a different *durée*,[1] so that two objects copresent may have emerged at different times, have different developmental rhythms, be at different stages of their development—one perhaps waning, the other waxing.

Critical Marxism emerged following World War I, the October Revolution's success, and the German revolution's failure. Its character is partly an effect of a prior dominance of Scientific Marxism in the Second International. Critical Marxism is thus in part a *reaction* against that prior Scientific Marxism and a polemical critique of it. In our view, then, Critical Marxism is *not* to be understood as the ideology generated *by* (however serviceable it is *in*) the industrially backward areas of the world; it is, rather, the newer Marxism of a younger generation of Marxists, whose cohort developed in opposition to the Marxist establishment-in-being around the turn of the century. Each, then, is a time-dated object, and each plays a different historical role. Critical Marxism faces two ways: it is a tool of ideological struggle within Marxism itself, at first most especially directed against the determinism and wooden evolutionism of the Second International, as well as a distinct critique of capitalist society.

But if Critical Marxism is a later dimension, if it is responding to the prior failures of Scientific Marxism, there is, *also,* in Scientific Marxism itself, an earlier and prior rejection of objective philosophical idealism and of utopian socialism. This is exhibited by the work of Marx and Engels themselves, whose polemic against idealism moved their theoretical structure into the orbit of modern science—at first, most especially, Darwinism—and under its influence. Marxism crystallized into a political movement, under the tutelage of Engels and Kautsky after Marx's death. It was then dominated by a Scientific Marxism opposed polemically to idealism, characterized by an antiidealistic naturalism alertly focused on the *limits* of voluntarism, and affirming the power of economic structural constraints over human action and reason. Critical Marxism, however, emerges in reaction to *that* reading of Marxism, counter-affirming the role of a voluntaristic consciousness against Scientific Marxism's naturalism, determinism, and its focus on the constraining character of economic structures. If Scientific Marxism emerges as the negation of academic philosophical idealism and of "utopianism," Critical Marxism is the "negation of that negation."

This means that Critical Marxism is susceptible to a certain ambiguity. On the one hand, it has the potentiality of becoming a merely negative dialectic that would make it regressive—i.e., another form of German idealism. On the other hand, Critical Marxism might not simply react against Scientific Marxism but, selectively assimilating the latter's contribution, it might transcend the originating structural dichotomy of idealism and materialism. Such a transcending Critical Marxism, then, need be neither a regression to philosophical idealism, nor simply the mirror-image of Scientific Marxism.

Our study, then, rejects any idea that Marxism is a reified "thing"-in-being, an intellectual sword that lays waiting in its scabbard. To study Marxism, from our standpoint, is not simply to *point* to it as an object-topic, but to raise a *question* about *what* it is and how to conceptualize it.

There is, moreover, no reason to suppose that Marxism is an intellectual island unconnected with other modes of critical discourse or other reflexive speech variants. Nor need we suppose that our view of Marxism—either as topic or resource—must be limited only to the unique characteristics distinguishing it from other social theories and movements. Again, there is no reason to limit our view of Marxism to the *self*-understanding of Marxists (or of those defining themselves as such). Certainly, our rejection of this is consistent with Marxism itself which has never believed that consciousness determined being.

In insisting that Marxism be viewed as an historical product, I am not suggesting in the slightest, however, that this obviates the need for separate rational-empirical evaluation. Thus, I veer from Karl Korsch's formulation, when (among the very first) he raised the question of a reflexive, auto-critique of Marxism: "dogmatic calculations of how far different versions of Marxist theory correspond to some abstract canon of 'pure and unfalsified' theory should be abandoned. All these earlier and later Marxist ideologies must, on the contrary, be seen in a historical materialist and dialectical perspective as products of a historical evolution." This formulation seems to open the door to a radical relativism and an inevitable nihilism. For how could one view Marxist ideologies as "products of a historical evolution" without first saying what Marxism is; which then, seemingly, plunges us back into that very "dogmatic calculation" of Marxism against which Korsch warns. A reasoned provisional statement of what Marxism is, a tentative analytic characterization of it, is necessary for and prior to its historical examination.

When indicating which aspects of Marxism we are willing to use as our resource (to understand Marxism as a topic), we are thereby committing ourselves, tentatively, to a judgement of the *truth* in Marxism—not to "all" its truth, but, at least, to that part on which we necessarily rely when using it as a resource.

This is really the essential question with which I am concerned, but which I cannot address directly until a later volume. For if concerned to understand Marxism, it is not simply so that, once having discovered what it is, we may then contemplate it passively. We seek to know what Marxism is *from the standpoint of its defensibility in the light of critical reason,* no less than as an historical object. We want a knowledge of Marxism that distinguishes its true or rational part from its untrue, mystified, and false consciousness. And we want it so that we may use the former, and transcend, avoid, and discard the latter.

There is, however, one difficulty with this view of the matter. The standards of critical rationality, with which we judge Marxism, are not themselves eternal objects autonomous from the critique that Marxism makes of the world. To say it differently: the value of Marxism is not limited to middle-range sociological truths about economy and society, but also entails Marxism's critique of critical rationality itself. Marxism's value derives in part—or, at least, so I shall argue in later volumes—from its ability to help us transcend certain limits of our historically evolved rationality: i.e., the culture of critical discourse's reflexive speech. Clearly, then, Marxism implicates our most fundamental intellectual resources, and reflects not only on our sociological or economic *topics*.

NOTE

1. See J. H. Hexter, "Fernand Braudel and the *Monde Braudellien*," *Journal of Modern History*, December 1972, pp. 480–539.

APPENDIX THREE
On Social "Contradictions"

In speaking as I have of the contradictions of Marxism, how do I conceive the *objects* having or experiencing these contradictions? Most generally, I think of Marx*ists* as a common-language-speaking community; as the historically evolving community of those speaking the sociolect, "Marxism," of those submitting to its rules—its grammar—and its practice. Marxism is the community of those performing a practice whose standards are those rules of the Marxist life that we may term its grammar or culture.

Marxism, therefore, is not at all only a theory or grammar. It is also an historically evolving culture and social structure, having several distinct *concrete* aspects:

(1) There is Marxism as a technical theory-ideology-social science; in short, as an extraordinary and "artificial," elaborated speech variant, spoken with considerable reflexivity by some (relatively small number of) intellectual specialists;

(2) There is also the "living" or "plain" Marxism of those for whom Marxism is part of an everyday life and practice, who submit to its grammar, obey its rules, using them to define or pursue political projects, and to organize their own personal identities. This is Marxism as an everday culture, as a *less* reflexive language, i.e., a "Weltanschauung."

(3) There is Marxism as a structured network of associations and social relations instrumental to the achievement of its political projects, and actively enforcing its grammar in evaluating its community's projects or its members' performances. Here we deal with Marxism as a "social movement," which may include one of the highly-boundaried, risk-taking, combat parties the movement has developed, i.e., the "vanguard" organization.

(4) Finally, there are Marxist "societies"—e.g., specific nation-states—in which children are socialized routinely into a Marxist grammar, and

in which people's diverse needs can be satisfied by various community institutions whose legitimacy is defended on the grounds of their imputed conformity to the grammar of Marxism.

As for my use of "contradiction": I use contradictions to refer to a situation in which persons pursuing projects encounter alternatives, such that the choice of one alternative necessarily entails some loss of, or places some limit on, the use of the other. Contradictions are thus *constraint*-generating, inhibitory situations; they provide satisfaction of one alternative only at the cost of losing the alternative or some part of it. Thus, while all courses of action entail costs, those undertaken in the face of contradictions entail further costs implicated in alternatives foregone—however successful the pursuit of the chosen alternative.

Contradictions are thus courses of action that limit compromises between several courses. They entail the inhibition of one course as the price of opting for another.

The "external" ambiguity of such a social situation is likely to be matched by an ambivalence *internal* to the actor involved in it. The strategy and tactics of dealing with ambivalences and ambiguities constitute the special problems of the psychology and sociology of contradiction. For example, a long familiar response to *ambivalence* is to "over-react," i.e., to choose one alternative with an emphatic commitment to it, and with polemical (as against, say, reluctant) rejection of the other. Or, again, a paralysis of choice may result, such that neither alternative may be given any commitment, with resulting Hamletian inaction. Finally, there may be an erratic oscillation back and forth between the alternatives, first rejecting one and opting for the other and then reversing course.

Contradictions thus assume importance since they imply impending change precisely because they proliferate pathologies of action and communication, multiply the costs, and hence diminish the advantages of pursuing *any* course of action. Thus, the desirability of any outcome is always reduced in a contradictory situation. At the extreme, one may find himself in a "no-win" situation, such that the net costs of foregoing one alternative equal the net gains of the one undertaken. In short, a contradiction is a "bind"; one cannot escape one horn without impaling oneself on the other.

I shall not consider here all the familiar varieties of contradictions, for instance, dilemmas, paradoxes, or antinomies. I will limit myself here to one analytic distinction that exists at any and all of the concrete levels of Marxism. This is a distinction between "internal" contradictions and others. (Clearly, the "others" are a residual category, that can be tolerated only in a preliminary formulation such as this.)

An *internal* contradiction is one in which a system, at any concrete level, is blocked/inhibited from conforming with one system *rule* because (or to the extent that) it *is* performing in conformity with another system *rule.* It is, in short, a "double bind." Here, each rule is an accepted part of the code, grammar, or culture, that governs the system and defines its identity. A concrete case of such an *internal* contradiction arises where the specific goals, projects, or social identities generated by conformity with one rule are thwarted (or inhibited) by reason of efforts to *conform* to another rule of that *same* code-culture-grammar. In the case of the internal contradictions, then, a grammar is generating a zero-sum game against itself, and one of its parts achieves conformity only at the cost of deviance from another, equally authentic part of itself.

Several important implications of this deserve statement. One is that an internal contradiction or double bind derives ultimately not from avoidance of the system's grammar but from efforts to *conform* with it. "Deviance" from *one* of the rules is produced by *commitment* to another. Thus, the system is producing *anomie* in one area, deteriorating the normative structure in one zone, precisely as a result of its members' faithful conformity in another. An internal contradiction, then, *does not result from anomie, but produces it.*

A solution to an internal contradiction, then, cannot be brought about by holding to the status quo. For here there is a conflict of "right against right" (as Marx described the relationship between labor and capital). Given a situation in which each alternative is rule sanctioned, thus legitimating its support, the solution to the dilemma cannot come from undermining the moral authority of any one side. Appeals to morality fail here, not because moral considerations are rejected as empty sentimentalities but because each side feels its moral position *unshakeable,* is convinced of its own rightness and the other side's wrongness.

There are essentially two ways in which such an internal contradiction can be resolved. One is to search for a higher rule that subsumes, or is prior to, those lower rules inducing the opposed actions; for example, the higher "good" or "survival" of the group, or "order," or "justice." A second common mode of resolving an internal contradiction is social conflict among the forces supporting each of the alternatives; here each side mobilizes and deploys power, force, and violence against the other. Internal contradictions, then, may in one case be resolved by redefining the cultural alternatives in conflict. They may be composed by redefining the situation so that, instead of being given conflicting definitions, it is given one common definition. Again, an existing contradiction may be "transcended" not by reverting to an already existing hierarchy of rules but by a cultural innovation, such as launching a new movement for cultural revitalization that successfully imposes a *re*-ordering of cultural imperatives, thus restructuring the code itself.

But composing contradictory rules by appeal to a higher level, or their "transcendence" by reorganizing the grammar, has limits placed upon it by another, fundamental consideration: by *interests.* Conformity to a rule is always generated by at least two conditions; by interest and by morality. In believing a rule to be right, conforming performances provide performers with that specific moral gratification we may call "righteousness," confirming them—in their own and others' judgements—as normal, reputable persons. This, in turn, gives them preferred access to the resources with which persons defined as trustworthy or estimable are normally rewarded. Persons thus usually have an *interest* in conforming with the rules, for this produces an advantageous allocation of gratifications quite apart from bestowing a sense of righteousness.

But this is viewing the situation in a post factum way, and without a condition of internal contradiction. Given a double bind or internal contradiction, where persons' conformity with one rule results in their crimping another, persons will *not* receive the rewards normal to conformity. One of two things may then happen. For one, some persons may continue to adhere to this rule but may resent those withholding the rightful reward. In this case, contradiction heightens conflicts among those supporting different rules. Or, secondly, persons may simply stop supporting the unrewarded rule. They may become "deviants," coming into opposition with those still supporting the rule. In both cases, however, social conflict has intensified.

Clearly, conformity with a rule is not reinforced solely by a resulting righteous feeling or social prestige. For this premises that any rule is interchangeable with any other. In any grammar, conformity with different rules produces different *consequences*. Actors will then support different rules, depending on the consequences. The rule, "a fair day's wage for a fair day's work," may be accepted by all; but it will be more salient to, and be given greater commitment by, a wage worker than a *rentier*. In short, alongside the grammar or code of rules, there is, also, a structure of differential *interests*. These interests structure the manner in which different groups relate to the grammar, leading some to place priority on rules different from those accented by others. Differential support is given different rules by different groups because rules produce different consequences, satisfying different groups' interests. Differential *interpretations* are also given to "one" rule, for the same reason.

Interests, then, set limits on the choice of, the emphasis on, the queueing of, the priority assigned to, or the interpretation of rules. An internal contradiction thus involves a choice of consequences and generates different outcomes for different groups. It implies and fosters social conflict among groups, strata, persons. Since they introduce rigidities and inflexibilities in commitments, interests limit the possibility of resolving internal contradictions by composing or transcending differences through changes in the moral code. The imposition of a solution through power struggles therefore becomes increasingly probable, under conditions of internal contradictions.

Of course, not all contradictions need be *internal* contradictions, and other contradictions have less likelihood of generating power conflicts. In short, some internal contradictions are "antagonistic" contradictions; others, however, need not be so, even though they increase the costs and problems of action. A system may impose some rule upon a community which may have difficulty in conforming with it, but not because this would entail nonconformity with some other rule of the system. A grammar may, for example, confront persons with the choice of either refusing conformity to one of its rules or of using up some scarce resource; say, for example, a choice between relinquishing personal automobiles or paying an ever higher price for gasoline. Here one is facing a choice between living in a style defined as desirable—i.e., in conformity with a code—and protecting another *interest* which may be compelling, but is prescribed (not by the code but) simply by a wish to economize resources and avoid costs. Such a situation confronts actors with an unpleasant choice between alternatives; a contradiction, to be sure, but not necessarily an *internal* contradiction in our terms. Only if automobile use and economizing resources are both *code* imposed, would we then speak of an internal contradiction, or double bind.

The existence of scarcity generally imposes economizing considerations. These, in turn, mean that persons often cannot have both things they wanted, and are faced with choosing one and renouncing the other. An economy of scarcity, then, is a basic and familiar grounding of social contradictions.

But conversely, resources are scarce, in *some part,* the more that persons value, want, and use them. The more things persons want, the greater the strain on their resources and the sharper the economic problem. A general limitation of wants, however, reduces the economizing problem; so does focusing wants on things not scarce, such as "goodness," "justice," "temperance"—the "quiet" values. Hence religious codes emphasizing asceticism or "spiritual" (nonscarce) values, have long been modes of reducing contradictions, for they reduce pressure on scarce resources.

There is thus an interaction between economic scarcities and moral codes. Scarcity concerns the resources available to achieve the imperatives of a moral code, imposes choices, and thus fosters contradictions. But whether resources are scarce (or the extent to which they are scarce) depends, in turn, on the extent to which they are in demand, and thus depends also on the moral code. That is, demand depends partly (1) on the extent to which resources are valued by a moral code, and (2) on the kind of goods the code values. A system thus always has two strategies for dealing with contradictions engendered by scarce resources: (1) *reducing scarcity,* either (a) by changing the moral code and the demand-schedules it generates or (b) by increasing the production of these resources; (2)

accepting the reality of scarce resources and allocating them on the basis of conflict.

There are then two kinds of contradictions of Marxism: (1) internal contradictions, derivative of efforts to conform to its own grammar which embodies mutually inhibiting alternatives;, and (2) contradiction generated by conditions external to the grammar. The first converges with what I have termed the nuclear contradiction between Scientific and Critical Marxisms and the second, with what I have termed "anomalies" born either of the theoretical scheme's research applications or dissonant information generated by events in the world.

PART II

The Dialectic of the Final Instance
Considerations on Marx's Political Economy

. . . . any possible future belongs to the realm of necessity not that of freedom and . . . every political theory and practice—including that of socialists—is confronted not with the problem of abundance but with that of survival.

Hans Magnus Enzensberger

Thou wouldst go into the world, and Thou art going into the world with empty hands, with some promise of freedom which men in their simplicity and their natural unruliness cannot even understand, which they fear and dread—for nothing has ever been more insupportable for a man and a human society than freedom.

Fyodor Mikhailovich Dostoevski

6

ALIENATION
FROM HEGEL TO MARX

One of the pivotal issues between Critical and Scientific Marxists is the importance of "alienation" in the work of the mature Marx, and whether or not, as Scientific Marxists often believe, it was an Hegelian vestige that lost significance in his later work. Within Marx's own tradition, the notion of alienation derives most immediately from Feuerbach and Hegel. The roots of Marx's critique of alienation may be found, as Georg Lukács found them, in Hegel's Protestantizing critique of "positivity."[1] In this critique, Hegel rejects as "dead" those human relationships or institutions in which persons give only an outward and constrained conformity, but concerning which they lack a freely given inward conviction. The roots of the theory of alienation, then, reach down into the rejection of "constraint," into the disjunction in which constraint is experienced as powerful-but-wrong; it is a response to the perception of this violation of the grammar of societal rationality and an effort to overcome such an "unpermitted social world."

In his early Berne period, Hegel invidiously contrasted the positive faith of Christianity with that of antiquity, which he regarded as a religion of dignity and freedom. In that connection, he remarks:

> A positive faith is a system of religious propositions which are true for us because they have been presented to us by an authority which we cannot fault . . . the concept implies a system of religious propositions or truths which must be held to be truths independently of our own opinions, and which even if no man has ever perceived them, and even if no man has ever considered them to be truths, nevertheless remain truths.[2]

Here positivity entails the authoritatively imposed, rather than
the voluntarily accepted. It is that which is accepted out of defer-
ence to the *position* of another, rather than for the *reasons* given
on its behalf. It is that which is supported by the powers that be.
To that extent, the critique of positivity in Hegel becomes the
potential basis for the critique of any status quo. It is this early
critique of positivity in Hegel, then, which is one of the ground-
ings of his philosophy's potential radicalism, just as Hegel's
vaunting of a kind of scientific positivity later disposes him to conservatism.

In his critique of Christianity, Hegel observed that "the objectivity of the deity increased in direct proportion to the increase in
the corruption and slavery of man, and this objectivity is in reality
no more than a revelation, a manifestation of this spirit of the
age. . . . The spirit of the age was revealed in the objectivity of its
God when . . . it was introduced into a world alien to us, in a realm
in which we had no share, where we would not acquire a place
through our activity, but at most by begging or conjuring our way
in; it was an age in which man was a Non-ego and his God another
Non-ego. . . . In such an age the Deity sheds all its subjectivity
and becomes nothing but an object."[3]

Hegel here indicates a foundation for the *materialist* critique of
religion subsequently developed by Feuerbach, Strauss, and
Marx, which views deity as a projection formulated by people; and
specifically by persons living in a world "alien" to them, i.e., by
alienated men. Hegel objects to Christianity because its deity can
be reached only by supplication, pleas, and prayers but remains "a
divinity beyond the reach of our power and our will." Men are
thus impotent, "reduced to the level of passive onlook-
ers . . . content to wait for a revolution at the end of the world."
What men now seek is a response to their supplications or a voluntary gift, but is not the result of their own potency: "we wait to
receive it without our own intervention."[4] Here Hegel's critical
platform appears to be a version of the "gospel of labor," a this-
worldly activism that overlays and sublimates a passive millenarianism.

In viewing the "objectivity" of Christian deity as the projection
of an alienated people, Hegel's concept of alienation is not only a
psychological estrangement, not simply a *feeling* of distance from
the object, but entails a practical, everyday absence of *control* in a
world where persons have become spectators, "passive onlook-
ers," incapable of themselves achieving their own values by their

own efforts—in effect, waiting for the revolution. In this critique of Christianity, Hegel is grounding himself in some tacit alternative conception of what is appropriate to humanity; or of what kind of persons are "normal" proper "subjects"; or, what "subject-hood" means to him. To be a subject, for Hegel, means to have power and control, not simply psychological union or closeness; it means the capacity to achieve one's goals against resistance and without supplication.

Hegel's critique of positivity is already a critique of alienation at the level of cultural criticism. What Marx adds to the theory of alienation, then, is *not* accomplished merely by transposing a psychology into a sociology. Hegel had clearly begun to understand that institutions such as religion, even the positive religions, were the products of the kind of life that people lived together, the "spirit of the age," and that thus persons were involved not only when they opposed these "dead" forms but, also, in the dead forms themselves. People were thus alienated by their practical ongoing activities—the things persons presently continued to do or make—and not simply by the lifeless residues of the past. In Lukács's formulation, "the independent existence of objects apart from human reason could be conceived as the product of the development and activity of that very same reason. . . . It contains the idea that the entire development of society together with all the ideological formations which it creates in the course of history are the product of human activity itself, a manifestation of the self-production and reproduction of society."[5]

Gradually, says Lukács, Hegel began to distinguish between the *process* by which objects are brought into "positive" being, which he calls objectification or externalization (*Entausserung* or *Entfremdung*), and the social institutions thereby created and which have an objectivistic character as alienated things. Out of his own studies of classical political economy, Hegel came to conclude that "work not only makes men human . . . it not only causes the vast and complex array of social processes to come into being, it also makes the world of man into an 'alienated', 'externalized' world. . . . In the concept of 'externalization', . . . we find enshrined Hegel's conviction that the world of economics which dominates man and which utterly controls the life of the individual is nevertheless the product of man himself,"[6] even if it has this dead, alien character.

For Hegel, then, the everyday world in which persons live consists, at one and the same time, of objects which are necessary to, and express human life, but from which they are alienated; and which, in both cases, are the products of people's activity, without which neither objects nor persons would be. For Hegel, alienation is the inescapable fate of humanity and its object world. Alienation is thus inherent in human life which necessarily and everywhere creates the social world by making and using objects, while making and transforming itself in that very process. At some point, however, these objects no longer coincide with human purposes, the object world and the inner world are no longer in gear, and men cease to recognize the object world as having been brought into existence by their own human activity.

Marx: The Alienation of Labor

Hegel's philosophy is both the fundamental source of Marx's own analyses of alienation and (along with Feuerbach's) a central polemical target that Marx uses to formulate his own distinct position. Most basically, Marx changes the site in which alienation is seen to manifest itself, as well as the conditions conducive to it. For Marx, the central locus of alienation is no longer in the making of *all* human objects; it has been narrowed to *work* products. Unlike Hegel, who stressed one-sidedly the *valuable functions* that labor performed for humanity, Marx stressed the "negative" side of labor that Hegel (as Marx recognized) had neglected, and he viewed labor as the major site of human alienation. Marx no longer regards alienation as a universal human phenomenon, but links it to the mode of production, in general, and to the property system of capitalism, in particular.

For Marx, the question is no longer that of the alienation of man in general but becomes increasingly that of persons as producers; Hegel's *externalization* of objects becomes, for Marx, the economic *production* of use values and commodities. The alienation of Hegel's philosophy is translated by Marx into English political economy and its special system of categories. But this was no violation of Hegel for, as Lukács indicates, Hegel was the most economically literate of the German philosophical idealists. Unlike Kant who had focused on play, or Schelling on aesthetic activities, Hegel had dwelt extensively on the importance of labor—although he had not dwelt on labor as a site of alienation and had instead stressed its *liberating* character. Marx accepts the fundamental value grounding of the Hegelian critique of alienation, namely, that humanity's proper estate is that of an autonomous "subject," the locus and agency of action; but he rejects the Hegelian analysis of alienation's sources. Marx moves the analysis of alienation down from its location in a grand theory at the anthropological species level where the universal dilemmas of man as actor are explored, to a more concrete societal level.

For Marx, the critical locus of alienation comes to be situated in the work place. The decisive form of alienation is now not that of man but the worker's alienation from objects he produces and from the means of production with which he produces. This alienation, Marx came to hold, was a result of property institutions essential to capitalism, centering on that division of labor in which some—capitalists—own and direct the means of production and purchase the labor power of others—the proletariat—who are subject to their domination. For by reason of their ownership of the means of production, the capitalist can direct their use and also own the products they produce.

Much of what Marx did here, then, was to historicize and relativize Hegel's theory of alienation. Alienation is now no longer man's eternal condition but the product of an historical, special division of labor that had a beginning and which, it is predicted, will also have an end when capitalism is supplanted by socialism. Marx thereby removes the problem of alienation from the tragic discourse in which it was still located in Hegel's formulation, and in which it was insoluble. He now places alienation in the framework of the historically newer discourse of ideology,[7] transforming it into a politics, in which it has a solution. It is this that makes Marx's reconceptualization of the problem of alienation more powerful, if not deeper and truer.

Alienation and the Division of Labor

In part, Marx's distinctive contribution to the analysis of alienation is to join it with another of Hegel's central concerns, labor, reconceptualizing the entire analysis within the analytic framework of English political economy. In their discussion of the division of labor in *The German Ideology,* Marx and Engels had held that "as long, therefore, as activity is not voluntary, but, naturally divided, man's own deed becomes an alien power opposed to him, which enslaves him instead of being controlled by him. For as soon as labor is distributed, each man has a particular, exclusive sphere of activity which is forced upon him and from which he cannot escape."

Marx and Engels conclude this formulation by observing that "this crystallization of social activity, this consolidation of what we ourselves produce into an objective power above us, growing out of our control, thwarting our expectations, bringing to naught our calculations, is one of the chief factors in historical development up till now."

Except for citing the division of labor as the source of alienation, the sweeping passages above might have been written by Hegel. Indeed, insofar as they stress the role of the division of labor in inducing alienation and, insofar as this is a "natural," universal division of labor, then this is still a half-Hegelian, transitional formulation, rather than a characteristically "Marxist" critique of alienation; it is as much a philosophical anthropology as a political economy.

It is useful as a corrective for any glib conception of Marx's theory that stresses the importance he attributes to property systems, but which leaves the notion of property unexamined, to see just how closely Marx linked property with the division of labor. Indeed, at a certain point, Marx saw the division of labor as the grounding of the property system. He remarks that "the various stages of the division of labor are just so many different forms of ownership."[8] "Division of labor and private property are, moreover, identical expressions," Marx held, "in the one the same thing is affirmed with reference to activity as is affirmed in the other with reference to the product of activity."[9]

This association of the class system with the division of labor, and, indeed, the conception of it as grounded in the division of labor is not simply the romanticism of the young Marx and it is not confined to early works such as *The German Ideology*. Indeed, in one of the most "scientific" works of their maturity, in Engels's *Anti-Dühring*, precisely the same analysis is offered:

> So long as the total social labour only yields a produce which but slightly exceeds that barely necessary for the existence of all . . . so long as, of necessity, this society is divided into classes. Side by side with the great majority, exclusively bond slaves to labour, arises a class freed from directly productive labour, which looks after the general affairs of society, the direction of labour, state business, law, science, art, etc. *It is, therefore, the law of the division of labour that lies at the basis of the division into classes.*

What Engels is saying is that the division of labor is a need of the society as a whole; it does not result from the class system but from the needs of society; it is not produced by class division but produces it. Engels adds, however, that "this does not prevent this division into classes from being carried out by means of violence and robbery, trickery and fraud. It does not prevent the ruling class, once having the upper hand, from consolidating its power at the expense of the working class, from turning their social leadership into an intensified exploitation of the masses."

In short, the function of the division of labor and of the class system organized around it is *not* simply to serve as a framework for the exploitation of one class by another; rather, it performs a service to the society as a whole. "But if, upon this showing, division into classes has a certain historical justification, it has this only for a given period. . . . It was based upon the *insufficiency of production*. It will be swept away by the complete development of modern productive forces."[10]

These pithy remarks indicate the importance that Marx and Engels attributed to *scarcity* as the grounding of the class system. They hold that scarcity generates a class system through an intervening variable, the division of labor. "Classes" were groups differentiated on the basis of their role in the division of labor. To this extent, class is simply the way of talking about how the product resulting from the division of labor is distributed, while the division of labor deals with the manner in which the goods controlled and distributed by the class system are in the first place produced.

As a division of labor, the class system, then, contributes to needs of the society as a whole, and thus cannot be abandoned, except with "the complete development of modern productive forces." The very class system itself, then, serves the entire society and not only the ruling class; although it yields special privileges for the ruling class, and special liabilities and alienation for the oppressed. It produces both social order and class privilege, a privileged order, an order of privilege. *The ruling class, then, is both: an agent of the productive system necessary for the society as a whole, for a certain period, and, also, a self-interested, self-satisfying, and self-reproducing group that turns its "social leadership into an intensified exploitation of the masses."* The ruling class extracts from society special privileges, advantages, and incomes for solving the problem of "order" and other collective problems.

There is, then, a certain ambiguity in the central idea of a ruling class. From one perspective (that of the division of labor), a ruling class is any group whose function in the division of labor is to direct production, to control the means of production. Wherever there is any institutionalized arrangement allowing one group to exercise control over the means and process of production, that group constitutes a ruling class. *This means that without the total elimination of division of labor, where some direct and others obey, there must always be a ruling class.* (It is precisely on this reading of the crucial role of the division of labor that Maoism had grounded itself.)

From another perspective, which stresses the legal aspect of property, a ruling class is one which *owns* the means of production, and whose ownership is recognized in law and protected by the state. Here a split between ownership and control of the means of production is possible and here socialism means the real and legal expropriation of private owners; but since this permits a split between ownership and control such an expropriation need not eliminate the rise of a new *controlling*, hence ruling, class.

Alienated Labor and Creative Labor

As mentioned, Marx centers his own analysis of alienation on the labor process. The alienation or *Entausserung* of labor consisted, according to Marx, in this: "First that the work is *external* to the worker, that it is not part of his nature; and that, consequently, he does not fulfill himself in his work, but denies himself, has a feeling of misery rather than well-being, does not develop freely his mental and physical energies but is physically exhausted and mentally debased. The worker, therefore, feels himself at home only during his leisure time, whereas at work he feels homeless. His work is not voluntary but imposed, forced labor."[11]

Alienation of the labor process is crucial to Marx because it is the labor process that, for him, defines the human species:

> Labor is in the first place, a process in which both man and nature participate, and in which man of his own accord starts, regulates, and controls the material reactions between himself and Nature . . . in order to appropriate Nature's productions in a form adapted to his own wants. By thus acting on the external world and changing it, he at the same time changes his own nature. . . . a bee puts to shame many an architect in the construction of her cells. But what distinguishes the worst architect from the best of bees is this, that the architect raises his structure in his imagination before he erects it in reality.

At the end of every labor process we get a result that already existed in the imagination of the laborer at its commencement.[12]

Marx's critique of alienated labor rests and must rest on a set of tacit standards concerning good, desirable, *non*-alienated, creative labor. The theory of labor alienation entails a tacit theory of the *ideal* labor situation. The Swedish social psychologist, Joachim Israel has seen this plainly and holds that, for Marx, "work is creative (1) if man makes 'his life activity itself an object of his will and consciousness', (2) if man through work can express his capabilities in a comprehensive way, (3) if through this work he can express his social nature, (4) if work is not simply a means for maintaining man's subsistence, i.e., if it is not purely instrumental."[13]

In order to achieve this and eliminate alienation of the labor process, conditions conducive to alienation would have to be removed. What were these conditions? One, as we have seen, was the *division of labor* which, in parcelling men into specialized roles, alienated them from their own unutilized human potentialities and produced a resultant dehumanization; the second was the *market* system, under which producers were constrained to disregard the human needs that their products satisfied or neglected—their use value—and to focus exclusively on the market or exchange value, and saleability of their products; and the third was the *property* system under which producers lost control over the work process and product to those owning the means of production. Together, the market and property systems constrained producers to sell their own labor power competitively, as a commodity like any other.

Marx and Engels's solution, the mechanism by which these several alienation-inducing conditions were to be abolished, was the expropriation of the private owners of the means of production and their transference to "collective" ownership. This would remove the market and the property systems as sources of alienation in work. But how the collectivization of production would avoid the alienation grounded in the division of labor is not at all clear in Marx. The reason for this lacuna is that the division of labor is viewed ambivalently. If, on the one side, specialization dehumanizes men, on the other, the increased productivity which it produces was also believed necessary for eliminating want and thus class domination.

Scarcity and Class Domination

A fundamental level in Marx's analysis of the sources of alienation is reached when he links it with a theory of class domination. Essentially, alienation of the working class is the other side of the domination of the ruling, capitalist class. The most fundamental implication of the working class's alienation is that it entails the loss of their autonomy and capacity for self-realization. The self control of any class is, by definition, at variance with its being dominated by any other class, or any other force. A class system, in general, and the capitalist—working class relationship in particular, necessarily implies a domination by the ruling class that undermines the lower class's capacity for autonomy.

Alienation, then, is grounded in class domination, is, in part, intrinsic to class domination. A strategy for removing alienation, then, must from this standpoint depend upon an understanding of the sources of class domination. In their formulation of a direct solution to the problem of alienation, Marx and Engels go directly to this question, in a powerful, compact account of the requisites for eliminating alienation:

> ... estrangement [*Entfremdung*] ... can, of course, only
> be abolished given two *practical* premises. For it to become
> an "intolerable" power, i.e., a power against which men make
> a revolution, it must necessarily have rendered the great mass
> of humanity "propertyless," and produced, at the same time,
> the contradiction of an existing world of wealth and culture,
> both of which conditions presuppose a *great increase in
> productive power, a high degree of its development.*[14]

Note that in this, the *first* premise of the abolition of alienation, nothing is yet said about the expropriation of private property or the removal of the market, or the division of labor. The fundamental presupposition was held to be increased productivity. Why? "This development of productive forces ... is absolutely necessary as a practical premise: first, for the reason that without it, only want is made general and with want the struggle for necessities and all the old filthy business would necessarily be reproduced."[15]

Here, then, is the grounding of Marx's cryptic theory of class struggle: classes seek control over scarce goods; class domination is a way of making control of these more secure; the maintenance of that class domination necessarily entails a loss of autonomy to the subordinated class, hence its alienation. Thus the first premise of the elimination of alienation, says Marx, is "a great increase in productive power." Without this, men will continue struggling for privileged access to scarce goods, will institute systems of class domination with resultant alienation of the dominated class. But with increased productivity, men need no longer struggle against and dominate one another, and impose an alienation on the defeated. Logically, then, the first task in removing alienation is to remove the cause of class domination, scarcity, by increasing productivity. For as Engels put it succinctly above, "The separation of society into an exploiting and exploited class, a ruling and an oppressed class, was the necessary consequence of the deficient and restricted development of production in former times."[16]

This solution to the problem of alienation, then, turns out to be nothing less than the "economistic" program of scientific socialism.

The second reason why an increase in productive forces is necessary for the abolition of alienation is that "only with this universal development of productive forces is a universal *intercourse* between men established, which produces in all nations simultaneously the phenomenon of the 'propertyless' mass, . . . makes each nation dependent on the revolution of others, and finally has put world-historical, empirically universal individuals in place of local ones."[17]

Plainly, the "practical premises" for abolishing alienation and establishing socialism have here become the *anti-*voluntaristic premises of Scientific Marxism. More exactly: *Scientific Marxism emerges when the contradictions inherent in a commitment to increasing productivity intensify; that is, when an increasing division of labor is seen as both the source of a hateful alienation and, at the same time, of an increased productivity that is prized precisely because it will supposedly remedy that very alienation.* Scientific Marxism thus arises when what was originally only a means or instrument increasing productivity, comes to override Marxism's goal, abolishing alienation. Put in another language, Scientific Marxism thus constitutes a kind of *anomie,* a pathology in which the means are ritualistically pursued and the ends forgotten.

The sheer existence of alienation (or any other pathology of capitalism, fetishism, reification, exploitation) does not by itself determine Marxism's attitude toward it. Under *some* circumstances, Marxism holds, all one can do is deplore the pathology, but under others, it can and should be opposed actively. What makes the difference? Marxism replies (with the tacit Kantianism) that "ought implies can." That is, it holds that one can (and should) take action against alienation (and capitalism more generally) when and only when there is some chance of success, and that it is foolish to launch a campaign that is doomed from the beginning. For Marxism, "evil" is not simply suffering—e.g., alienation, scarcity, etc.—but *unnecessary* suffering.

But this does not distinguish the Two Marxisms; both Critical and Scientific Marxism alike accept this. Where they differ is in their conception of what socialism's success or failure depends upon, or of what constitutes the signs of its possible success or failure. To the Scientific Marxist, revolutionary success and socialism are dependent on the *prior* development of thinglike *conditions;* on "natural," spontaneous developments which are independent of "mere will." For the Scientific Marxist, the decisive condition for the de-alienating *emergence* of socialism is the maturation of the productive forces which, spontaneously developing as part of capitalism, depends primarily on *bourgeois* rather than proletarian or socialist initiatives.

That socialism depends upon just such a prior development of the forces of production is insistently reiterated in *Capital* itself. For Marx, socialism meant that society's life process, the productive process itself, has lost its "veil of mystery" and is now "carried out by a free association of producers under their conscious and purposeful control." But before this can come about, adds Marx, there is an indispensable requisite, i.e., "a specific material groundwork (or series of material conditions of existence) which can only come into being as the spontaneous outcome of a long and painful process of evolution."[18] More precisely, the specific function of these material preconditions is to *heighten productivity* and, with this, to reduce material scarcity, so that social life will not be a Hobbesian struggle of each against all, expressing itself as a perpetual class struggle to obtain and then to secure material advantage by the domination of one class over another. What makes the capitalist of positive historical value and worth, says Marx in *Capital*, is that "frantically bent upon the expansion of value, he relentlessly drives human beings to production for production's sake, thus bringing about a development of social productivity and *the creation of those material conditions of production which can alone form the real basis of a higher type of society,* whose fundamental principle is the full and free development of every individual."[19]

Repeatedly, then, Marx manifests his "economistic" conviction that socialism requires a prior improvement in economic productivity and that this is its indispensable prerequisite, rather than any prior internal change in men's character, consciousness, or sentiments. Indeed, it is this that Marx affirms as the *distinctive* insight of his own socialism and which, he and Engels insisted, made it a *scientific* rather than a merely wish-fulfilling "utopian" socialism.

Critical Marxists, however, in contrast to Scientific Marxists, stress that it is usually far from clear just how independent of men's efforts the conditions truly requisite for socialism are; that this cannot always be determined by a contemplative assessment but may be better judged by attempting remedial action: *on s'engage et puis . . . on voit.*

The Persistence of Alienation

If man is such a marvel that even his alienation is of his own making, how is it that he does not stop inflicting this mutilation upon himself? Part of the answer makes visible the distance between the young and the old Marx's vision of alienation, a distance between man conceived anthropologically as a *species* and thus as a *unified* actor, and men and women conceived as workers implicated in a class-riven society. Here the ruling class visits an exploitation upon the working producers and thereby *imposes* an alienation upon them which it is in the ruling class's interest, and (mostly) in their power to *maintain*.

It is only in the species focus of an anthropological formulation innocent of class division that "man" inflicts his alienation upon "himself." In the more sociological vision of a stratified capitalist society riven between privileged and dominated classes, the alienation of the latter is imposed by the former who, far from wishing to remove it, accommodate to it; for ruling class advantages and powers are simply the other side of the same social order from which alienation ensues.

What the capitalist himself does, his very exploitation and extraction of surplus value from the worker, is not (as Marx sees it) simply a matter of free choice but a constraint imposed upon the capitalist by his role in the system as a whole. If he did not behave in this way toward the worker he would soon cease to be a capitalist, notes Marx. Just as the worker is constrained to sell his labor power, and could not do so otherwise, so the capitalist is constrained to buy it at the lowest rate possible otherwise he would fall prey to competing capitalists. Marx thus views even the capitalist not as a free agent, but as the agent of a system by which he, too, is constrained.

In this and other ways, the capitalist himself is alienated by the very system within which he is powerful and privileged. It is not only, then, that alienation is imposed by stronger groups upon weaker, but that both are instruments of a social system, of a stratified system of social roles which have a certain independence of their occupants, and by whose imperatives they are controlled. "To be a capitalist, is not only a purely personal, but a social status in production," Marx and Engels insisted. "Capital is a collective product, and only by the united action of many members, nay, in the last resort, only by the united action of all members of society, can it be set in motion. Capital is therefore not a personal, it is a social power."[20]

Alienation, then, is not just "deviant" behavior at variance with the system's prized properties but is produced by *conformity* with the system, when each dutifully performs his role obligations and secures conformity with his role rights. "I depict the capitalist as a necessary functionary of capitalist production," Marx maintained. "I simply show that in the very exchange of commodities only equivalents are exchanged, and that the capitalist—as soon as he has paid the worker the actual value of his labor power—expropriates the surplus value with full right, i.e., with right corresponding to this mode of production."[21]

In this view, human beings are limited by received systems of social relations—i.e., social "structures"—that exist before they do and are the conditions of whatever social action they undertake: "In the social production of their lives men enter into definite, necessary, relations that are independent of their will." In this, the point is that, at any given time, a social world precedes men and that, like actors in a play, men receive a script specifying parts that were written before them; if they are constrained by parts they did not write, in time, however, they rewrite the play with which they began and pass on a new script confining the next generation of actors in new ways. "History is nothing but the succession of separate generations, each of which," wrote Marx and Engels, "continues the traditional activity in completely changed circumstances and . . . modifies the old circumstances with a completely changed activity."[22]

In part, then, alienation persists because persons receive the conditions under which they live from an earlier generation as an historical legacy at first experienced as part of their natural environment—i.e., as a "traditional activity"—which they simply live, rather than reflect upon or question. Here, the unity of the species is differentiated across *time*, rather than across class lines; instead of being exploited by a ruling class, men are here dominated by previous generations, who impose forms of life that, in time, are out of keeping with the needs and experiences of the new period. In some part, then, social systems generate and sustain alienation because they confront men as a presented givenness; and they do this because they are the products of a history, of a past that lives in the present.

Relations of Production and Forces of Production

For Marx and Engels, the decisive social structure received from the past was the *relationships* of production, including most crucially, the property institutions. At some point these come to block the continuing development of the *forces* of production, which are nucleated by the technology. When this conflict between the relations and forces of production occurs, it signifies that the present society has exhausted the possibilities for developing productivity and that the time for revolution is drawing near.

As Marx and Engels wrote in *The German Ideology,* "all collisions in history have their origin, according to our view, in the contradiction between the productive forces and the forms of intercourse."[23] This was as true for the feudal society from which capitalism emerged as for capitalism itself. "At a certain stage in the development of these means of production and of exchange," observes the *Communist Manifesto,* "the feudal relations of property become no longer compatible with the already developed productive forces; they become so many fetters. They had to burst asunder, they were burst asunder. . . . A similar movement is going on before our own eyes. Modern bourgeois society with its relations of production, of exchange and of property, a society that has conjured up such gigantic means of production and of exchange, is like the sorcerer, who is no longer able to control the powers of the nether world whom he has called up by his spells. For many a decade past the history of industry and commerce is but the history of the revolt of modern productive forces against modern conditions of production, against the property relations that are the conditions for the existence of the bourgeoisie and of its rule."[24]

That the grounding of this basic structuralist perspective of Sci-

entific Marxism was a romantic one[25] could not be made more
obvious than by Marx and Engels's metaphor above of the sorcerer's apprentice: the hellish force that the sorcerer has summoned up but was unable to control. The image is a richly complex one, partly suggesting the eerie, *grotesqueness* so intriguing
to nineteenth-century Romanticism, the "unnatural" conjunction
of elements of a dead past (property relationships) and the living
present (forces of production), in which the present is thwarted
and dominated by the past. (The image also resonates the ancient
Greek view of men as destroying *themselves*, of being undone by
their own creations.)

Paradoxically, then, one grounding of the naturalism of Scientific Marxism was the *super*naturalism of a nineteenth-century
Romanticism that saw persons as dominated by "unnatural," demonic forces. (Here once again, we may note that science and
religion were not necessarily incompatible.) An emphasis on overriding depersonalized social structures, characteristic of Scientific
Marxism, partly originates (with an irony that a romantic would
appreciate) in the romantic ideology that was attempting to rescue
religion and accommodate it to the modern era. At the same time,
however, Romanticism also used religion as a standpoint to *condemn* the thingification and alienation of people in modern society. Romanticism is thus not simply a grounding of the alienating
structuralist ontology of Scientific Marxism, but is, also, one cultural source of Marxism's effort to *transcend* alienation.

Nothing is more central to Marxism than this structural image of
the living forces of production being blocked by dead or dying
property relationships. The fundamental contradiction of
capitalism to which Marxism points is, then, simply a special case
of an *Entausserung*, an externalization that was once living but
has died and now weighs upon the living present "like the Alps."
As we saw, Marx and Engels observed:

> This consolidation of what we ourselves produce, into an ob-
> jective power above us, growing out of our control, thwarting
> our expectations, bringing to naught our calculations, is one of
> the chief factors in historical development up till now.

The image of the past as independent and dominating the present is central to Marx's view of capitalist society as the domination
of *capital*, which is the "dead labor" accumulated through appropriating the workers' surplus value. "In bourgeois society,

therefore," insisted the *Communist Manifesto*, "the past dominates the present; in communist society, the present dominates
the past. In bourgeois society capital is independent and has individuality, while the living person is dependent and has no individuality."[26]

Utopianism and the Two Marxisms

Marx, then, has several accountings for the *persistence* of alienation. One centers on the class division in society, so that this
persistence is due in part to the domination of the ruling class, to
its interest in preserving its privileges and its control over communication media, so that its ideas dominate even the consciousness of those who are most alienated. A second answer is that both
are commonly dependent on and constrained by the social system
within which each has his social position and identity. A third
consideration relates to the fact that, as historically received from
the past, society and culture are, at first, the unreflected-upon
medium of existence and do not usually come into focus as either
problematic or potentially changeable.

The persistence of alienation, however, is grounded in something more fundamental than these several, special conditions. To
ask why alienation persists is something like asking why is it that
sickness or disease persists, and here it is evident that the very
condition itself sometimes generates an enfeeblement that im-
pedes its own remedy. The "sick" either get well because their
"illness," countered by the body's defenses, runs its course and/or
because others, not sick, help them recover. Can those leading an
alienated existence even know of their condition? or, if knowing,
believe in its overthrow? and, if believing, have the will and for-
titude to gird themselves for the long struggle required?

Marx thought so. He held that the working class had the capacity for *self*-emancipation, since the very radical character of their
suffering under capitalism left them with "nothing to lose but
their chains," so that they would unite and, in the course of their
long struggle, transform themselves from alienated objects into
human subjects capable of ruling themselves. Once alienation had
been shifted from the discourse of philosophy to that of the political economy of a class-riven society the rich and powerful were
ruled out as the historical agents of the struggle against alienation.
The proletariat becomes the historical agent of human self-
emancipation partly because there is no other *within the vision of*

*a class analysis that made class central and all other social differ-
entia peripheral.*

Yet the liabilities of the proletariat were also plain enough to
Marx who saw them as vulnerable to a "false consciousness" by
reason of the bourgeoisie's control of culture and the communication media. It would therefore take a long period of struggle for
them to fit themselves for rule: "Both for the production on a mass
scale of this communist consciousness, and for the success of the
cause itself, the alteration of men on a mass scale is necessary, an
alteration that can only take place in a practical movement, a *revolution;* this revolution is necessary, therefore, not only because
the ruling class cannot be overthrown in any other way, but also
because the class overthrowing it can only in a revolution succeed
in ridding itself of all the muck of ages and become fitted to found
society anew."[27]

But given a proletariat subjected to a long and debilitating
alienation, to a servitude not only of the body but also of the mind,
and given the premise that it is not only oppressed but in addition
backward—splattered with the "muck of ages"—how could Marx
expect that workers could see and do all that was needed by *themselves.* The answer, of course, is that he does not.

The theme of self-emancipation, so important to Marxism, is
joined with another, contradictory theme, namely, that the revolution will be born of a union of philosophy and the working class,
the former providing the theoretical consciousness or mind, the
latter the heart. There is, moreover, another force hovering around
the class struggle which is related to, but not quite of the proletariat, the communists themselves, who are not a class but
somehow lead and represent the interests, immediate and long
term, of the proletariat. The communists are held to be "the most
advanced and resolute section of the working class,"[28] even
though they may not themselves be working class in social origin
or present employment.

It is a basic paradox of Marxism that the class-centered analysis
so central to it constrains it to a reliance upon an historical agent
that is crippled and debilitated; which is to say, to a reliance upon
an agent not altogether reliable. At the same time, it is inherent in
Marxism's class focus that it has no systematic way of dealing with
those very forces that provide the proletariat with "outside leverage" in its effort at emancipation; these, therefore, remain only
implicit, untheoretized, in Marxism's reference to the revolu-

tionary stimulus of "philosophy" and of the communists themselves.

For Marx, the decisive "material" requisite for an emancipatory socialism is the proletariat. It was the maturation of this new class that made the critical difference between this socialism, that Engels called "scientific," and that earlier socialism of Saint-Simon, Fourier, and Owen that was stigmatized as "utopian." Utopian socialism was held to have been "utopian" because it was historically "premature," having advanced its critique of capitalism before the mature development of the capitalist mode of production and the proletariat.

> The first great attempts of the proletariat to attain its own ends . . . necessarily failed, owing to the then undeveloped state of the proletariat, as well as to the absence of the economic conditions for its emancipation, conditions that were yet to be produced and could be produced by the impending bourgeois epoch alone. . . . St. Simon, Fourier, Owen . . . see, indeed, the class antagonisms, as well as the action of the decomposing elements in the prevailing society. But the proletariat, as yet in its infancy, offers to them the spectacle of a class without any historical initiative or any independent political movement.[29]

It is noteworthy here that Marxism very early defines its own character by drawing a line between itself and other, competing socialisms, especially utopian socialism. Its critique of utopian socialism is essentially a critique of a *voluntaristic* socialism that believed that what was decisive was a correct theoretical understanding of the historical situation and an intervention in that situation on the basis of that understanding. Utopian socialism, complained Engels, assumed that a theory could rise above the conditions in which it found itself and that it did not depend upon material conditions. But the truth, insisted Engels, was that their historical situation also dominated the utopian founders of socialism. "To the crude conditions of capitalistic production and the crude class conditions, corresponded crude theories."[30]

In part, then, Marxism grew out of and defined itself in the course of struggles against utopian socialism. It thereby established itself upon an *anti*-voluntaristic grounding and affirmed the importance of the prior development of objective, material conditions for an emancipatory socialism. Indeed, Engels's antivoluntaristic formulation here is plainly anti-Leninist, condemning utopian socialism as an ideology of a passive working class "quite incapable of independent political action . . . to whom, in its incapacity to help itself, help could, at best be brought in from without or from above."[31] (It is just such help, from "without," that Lenin holds is the highest function of the communist vanguard.)

But if, on this side, Marxism's deepest character is grounded in an *anti*-voluntarism, at the same time, Marxism is also constrained *toward* a voluntarism. Marxism's own logic constrains it toward a voluntarism precisely because it is committed to a proletariat which suffers from a debilitating alienation and is crippled by its own servitude and cultural backwardness. Thus despite the fact that, for Marx and Engels, the proletariat is the hinge of history, its very oppressed and deprived position requires that it be subject to a reeducation; partly a self-education in the course of revolutionary action, but also, partly to a tutelage coming from outside itself, from philosophy and from the communist vanguard.

It is thus not the "infancy" but the maturity of the proletariat, not the weakness but the growth of capitalism that induces Marxism to retain an opening toward "utopianism," that leads not to its extirpation but only to its repression. Being repressed, this more voluntaristic level can never be fully confronted and dealt with systematically in originary Marxism. It remains a theoretically underdeveloped but consequential dark region. It is essentially the mission of Critical Marxism to protect, express, and develop that repressed side of Marxism.

NOTES

1. A different relationship to "positivity" underlies, defines, and differentiates both academic, normal, "positive" sociology and its adversary, Marxism. Both define themselves in relation to the "positive," but evaluate it differently. Academic sociology treats the positive as the good, as the ground of speech which is secured by reason of its being "outside" the speaker. It is precisely this conception of objectivity that is central to academic sociology. It is its "outsideness" that makes it good. For Marx, as for Hegel, as we will see, that outsideness is pathological, an "alienation," entailing a failure to bring things under control. Marx and Hegel both premise that what is not under human control is not good.

2. Cited in Georg Lukács, *The Young Hegel* (London: Merlin Press, 1975), p. 18.

3. Ibid., p. 69.

4. Ibid., p. 68.

5. Ibid., p. 75.

6. Ibid., p. 333. "In themselves there is nothing novel about the terms *Entausserung* and *Entfremdung*. They are simply German translations of the English word 'alienation.' This was used in works on economic theory to betoken the sale of a commodity, and in works on natural law to betoken the loss of an aboriginal freedom." Ibid., p. 538.

7. For fuller discussion of the differences between tragic and ideologic discourse see Alvin W. Gouldner, *The Dialectic of Ideology and Technology* (New York: Seabury Press, 1976), chap. 3, "Surmounting the Tragic Vision."

8. K. Marx and F. Engels, *The German Ideology*, trans. W. Lough and C. P. Magill, ed. R. Pascal (New York: International Publishers, n.d.), p. 9.

9. Ibid., p. 22.

10. The quotations in this paragraph are all from F. Engels, *Socialism: Utopian and Scientific* (New York: International Publishers, 1935), pp. 70–71. Italics added. These are chapters from *Anti-Dühring*.

11. Marx and Engels, *Historisch-kritische Gesamtausgabe* (Frankfurt; Marx-Engels Institut, 1927–1935), vol. 1, p. 85.

12. Karl Marx, *Capital: A Critique of Political Economy*, vol. I, translated from the 4th German ed. by Eden and Cedar Paul, published in 2 vols., with an introduction by G. D. H. Cole (London and Toronto: J. M. Dent & Sons, 1930), vol. 1, p. 78.

13. J. Israel, *Alienation: From Marx to Modern Sociology* (Boston: Allyn & Bacon, 1971), p. 39.

14. Marx and Engels, *German Ideology*, p. 24. Italics added.

15. Ibid.

16. Engels, *Socialism: Utopian and Scientific*, p. 70.

17. Marx and Engels, *German Ideology*, pp. 24–25. Italics added.

18. *Capital* I, Dent ed., 1:54.

19. *Capital* I, Dent ed., 2:650. Italics added.

20. *Communist Manifesto* by Karl Marx and Friedrich Engels, authorized English edition of 1888, supervised by Engels, published by Charles H. Kerr, Chicago, p. 32.

21. Karl Marx, "Randglossen zur Adolph Wagner's 'Lehrbuch der politischen Ökonomie,'" in Marx-Engels, *Werke*, Institut für Marxismus-Leninismus (Berlin: Dietz Verlag, 1956–58), vol. 19, pp. 370–71.

22. Marx and Engels, *German Ideology*, p. 38.

23. Ibid., p. 73.

24. *Communist Manifesto*, pp. 19–20. The decisive importance of the contradiction between the forces and relations of production was reiter-

ated in Marx's *Contribution to the Critique of Political Economy:* "At a certain stage of their development, the material forces of production in society come into conflict with the existing relations of production—what is but a legal expression for the same thing—with the property relations within which they have been at work before. From forms of development of the forces of production these relations turn into fetters. Then begins the epoch of *social revolution.* With the change of the economic foundation the entire immense superstructure is more or less rapidly transformed. . . . The bourgeois relations of production are the last antagonistic form of the social process of production—antagonistic not in the sense of individual antagonism, but of one arising from the social conditions of life of the individuals; at the same time the productive forces developing in the womb of bourgeois society create the material conditions for the solution of this antagonism." K. Marx, *Contribution to the Critique of Political Economy* (Chicago: Chas. H. Kerr & Co.,), pp. 12-13.

25. My analysis of the romantic, along with a systematic view of it as a deep structure implicated in both "normal" and Marxist sociologies is developed in chap. 11, "Romanticism and Classicism," in Alvin W. Gouldner, *For Sociology* (Harmondsworth: Penguin Books, 1975) pp. 323–68. Note especially my discussion of the grotesque as a theory of dissonance in relation to Kenneth Burke's cognate concept of "perspective by incongruity."

26. *Communist Manifesto,* p. 33.

27. Marx and Engels, *German Ideology,* p. 69.

28. *Communist Manifesto,* p. 30.

29. Ibid., p. 53.

30. Engels, *Socialism: Utopian and Scientific,* p. 36.

31. Ibid.

7

POLITICAL ECONOMY
Toward Sociologism and Economism

At no point in its evolution did Marxism ever surrender a concern with alienation or cease struggling against it. Yet there was also a shift in the salience of alienation within Marxism due, in part, to the shift in its theoretic languages. As Marx encountered it, alienation was part of the lexicon of philosophy. Going from Hegel's conceptual system to that of political economy meant a transition from a *language* within which "alienation" could be spoken at the most general level to one in which it could not.

Yet while alienation is spoken of less frequently as Marxism develops its political economy, it was expressed in other ways. One is in terms of Marx's concept of generalized "surplus value" that is produced by the worker but appropriated by the capitalist. At another more general level, Marx's analysis of the "blind laws" of capitalism refers to a condition in which the economy itself has become the actor, the potent "subject," and has deprived persons of their autonomy. The very autonomy of the system's economic laws, then, generates an alienation of persons and is capitalism's basic pathology. From a standpoint congenial to a Critical Marxism, therefore, socialism means destroying the *autonomy* of the economy and bringing it under the control of society. Marx's formulation is not, therefore, simply a bland description of capitalism but the simultaneous critique of it as a monstrous system whose very systemness usurped humanity's prerogatives. Alienation and the critique of alienation thus continue from the young to the old Marx.

Nonetheless, within this continuity there is also discontinuity. While Marx remains committed to the critique of alienation, his understanding of it shifts as he moves from the language of German philosophical idealism to that of political economy, and from a focus on "man" as a species to the more concrete study of the specific social roles "workers" and "capitalists" play within historically limited capitalist societies. As Marx situates his studies within an historical analysis of capitalism, and views its social structures as a constraining social system, the focus on alienation narrows to the alienation of *labor* through the capitalist's appropriation of the worker's unpaid labor. Other forms of alienation are ignored as it comes to be supposed that the remedy of this labor-centered alienation will more or less automatically repair all the others. Revolution, then, no longer has the character of the "universal human emancipation" sought by the young Marx but becomes the historically specific and sociologically limited revolution against capitalism on behalf of socialism.

As Marxism developed, then, it manifested a growing movement toward a "sociologism" or "economism." Having begun with the diagnosis that humanity's central problem was alienation—i.e., dependence or the loss of potent subjecthood—Marx moved toward a focus in which alienation and exploitation are seen as grounded ultimately in scarcity. It is not, however, that scarcity ever replaces alienation but overlays, partly refocuses and redefines it. The ancient enemy, scarcity, assumes a more salient place as Marx shifts his theoretical languages, moving from philosophy to political economy. A commitment to political economy inevitably implies a commitment to its main problematic: scarcity. As Marx formulated it: "Just as the savage must wrestle with Nature to satisfy his wants, to maintain and reproduce life, so must civilised man, and he must do so in all social formations and under all possible modes of production."[1]

In short, scarcity is a universal problem with which all economies—including socialism—must contend. Indeed, he adds that "with his [man's] development this realm of physical necessity expands as a result of his wants," adding, however, that "at the same time, the forces of production which satisfy these wants also increase." Scarcity, then, is in part physical and in part socially induced, the latter continually increasing human wants. Note, however, that wants are in part induced socially but, oddly, never *restrained* socially. There is an undertow here of a conception of human insatiability, for men's wants, growing ever greater, would appear incapable of achieving any final satisfaction. Satisfaction recedes even as production increases.

In noting Marx's push into political economy's central problematic, I do not mean that Marx, like the classical political economists, centered his analysis on supply and demand or on the price consequences of scarcity. Marx, rather, centered his own political economy on production, productivity, and the forces and relations of production. Jean Baudrillard observes[2] that Marx's critique of capitalism is grounded in his judgement that capitalism, especially its *relations* of production, sabotages productivity, that is, the *forces* of production. Although capitalism was originally a revolutionary force whose vast development of productivity lay the groundwork for socialism and an ultimate escape from scarcity, at some point, capitalism also inhibits, restrains, "contradicts" this very productivity; the forces of production must, therefore, be liberated from capitalist property.

Paradoxically, Marx's paean to productivity is the "scientific" *sublimation* of the early nineteenth-century romantic adulation of Promethean "creativity." It was the romantics who had counterposed *living* creativity to "dead" mechanization; their exaltation of creativity is expressed in Marx's own emphasis on the "creative" power of labor and the working class. Rather than invidiously counterposing creativity to modern mechanization and science, however, Marx defines creativity as essentially a process of *labor* epitomized by the working class's *exclusive* capacity to generate economic value and "surplus value." Labor becomes the political economy of the life force. Creativity is thus no longer "romanticized" as the exclusive possession of "genius" (another romantic enthrallment) and is defined not only in terms of imagination but in terms of energy and methodical bodily work. Creativity is thus both democratized and Protestantized. Rescued from the romantics' effusions, it is brought to the interface with the gospel of work, on the one side, and on the other, with scientific and technological modernity. Marx is attempting both to demystify creativity and to make it the center of his world view.

While installing labor and productivity as the uniquely human form of creativity, in contrast to the romantics' accent on the *symbolic* aspects of creativity, Marx, correspondingly, diminishes the significance of symbolic activity in its everyday, prosaic forms as language, speech, symbolic interaction, and culture. Humanity is thus largely viewed as *self-produced* and defined by labor, rather than its symbolic talents and linguistic heritage. The human "essence" is now work, not language, not the symbolic, not culture. In Marx, then, the economic and instrumental side of human and social activity comes to overshadow the symbolic and cultural, which is what the subsequent crystallization of Critical Marxism, in some part, attempts to repair.

Yet even after Marx entrenched his work in political economy, there are always two layers in his concern with labor and production. In one, there is an implication of the struggle against scarcity; at a deeper and now more obscure level, however, the labor emphasis still resonates the older struggle against alienation to restore man's Promethean subjecthood through labor. The first level, labor as antiscarcity, is preserved in Scientific Marxism; the second, labor as antialienation and as human "creativity," is situated in Critical Marxism.

As Marx's theoretical labors penetrate the technical complexities of classical political economy, the very structure of these new theoretical commitments embed his analysis in a more purely economistic conception of scarcity. At the same time, however, his older, alienation-grounded focus also led to a reciprocal change in the way he interprets political economy itself, moving it from a distribution, supply-and-demand, price-centered economics to a production-centered economic sociology. Here, the struggle against alienation's crippling of man's subjecthood is never extinguished, although it is now edged onto the periphery.

How production proceeds, with what instruments and forces, within what system of social and property relationships, with what intention, now becomes Marx's central concern. "Capitalism" is now defined as a system of *commodity* production where goods are predominantly produced, not with the aim of satisfying human needs, not, in short, because of their "use value," but because of their "exchange value" on the market. This very distinction between use value and exchange value implies a critique of capitalism's subordination of the former to the latter; there is an intimation that, in this, there is something intrinsically perverse about capitalism.

Capitalism is judged here from the standpoint of an *abiding* conception of what is *normal* and proper to human beings, of a philosophical anthropology within which the critique of alienation condemns the violation of people's inherent nature as a potent subject. In that vein, it is noted that under capitalism even people's capacity to labor, their labor power, has become a commodity, so that the human life force itself becomes something sold in the market place. The very production system established to serve people's needs now alienates them, subjugates and makes them its instruments; people are now controlled by blind forces. It is characteristic of capital, said Marx, that man's own products and creativity subjugate him, become a power over and independent of him. It is essential to capitalism's nature, he said, that it is "an independent social power . . . the dominion of past accumulated labour over immediate living labour. . . . It consists in the fact that living labour serves accumulated labour."[3] The present thus becomes subservient to the past, the living to the dead, the creative to the parasitic.

The problem, however, is this: There is nothing in the analysis of the blind laws of capitalism which grounds and justifies the *evaluative* standard in terms of which Marx tacitly views, judges, and rejects these laws. Why, after all, should one assume that people ought *not* be treated as cogs in the machinery of capitalism? What *justifies* the assumption that people should be treated with dignity and not transformed into insignificant ciphers? From the standpoint of a *Scientific* Marxism, however, it is not the task of political economy to do anything more than determine the laws of capitalism, to study how this economy operates, and what will happen as it evolves. From the standpoint of a scientific socialism and its political economy, the critical posture of the philosophical anthropology implicated in Critical Marxism entails a certain soft sentimentality, an arbitrary moralizing; it is an embarrassment that tends to be repressed. There is inherent in such a political economy a tendency to segregate itself from Critical Marxism and to become a "value-free" scientific socialism or an academic Scientific Marxism. It is essentially out of a similar difficulty that nineteenth-century sociological positivism—which for Comte and Saint-Simon entailed a religion of humanity and also sought a social reconstruction—itself evolved into modern "value-free" normal academic sociology. The problem was that if Marxism (or, for that matter, academic sociology) could not justify the values in which it was grounded neither could it free itself of dependence on such values. What actually happens is not the achievement of a value-free condition but the repression and masking of the values on which both disciplines actually rest. There then develops a compensatory *ideology* of value freeness, a merely dramaturgical affirmation of the principle of value freeness, that occludes the reality of value unfreeness in practice.

As Marx pushed deeper into political economy his focus on the analysis of production intensifies. One expression of this is the central importance he attributes to social "classes" as defined by their common relationship to the means of production. The capitalist class is characterized by its control and ownership of the means of production and its purchase of the proletariat's labor time while the proletariat, constrained by its propertylessness, must sell its labor power on the market for a wage. In time and in the course of struggle, a class may develop a common consciousness of its own condition—a class consciousness—thus becoming a class "for itself" instead of only a class "in itself."

Marx's very conception of class struggle reveals the characteristic ambivalences between his structural scientific socialism, on the one side, and his voluntaristic Critical Marxism, on the other. On the voluntaristic side, Marx argues that while capitalism's development will make ever greater encroachments on the working class, pushing the value of labor power down to a minimum, nonetheless, the workers have a duty to keep on struggling, even for improvements that can only be temporary. There is something very classically Greek in Marx's insistence that the workers owe it to themselves, to their human nature, not to stop struggling, for "if they did, they would be degraded to one level mass of broken down wretches past salvation." Their struggle must persist, says Marx, even though they are for the most part on a treadmill, i.e., are "only efforts at maintaining the given value of labour." Workers who stopped struggling would be cowards who had failed in their historical duty: "By cowardly giving way in their everyday conflict with capital, they would certainly disqualify themselves for the initiating of any larger movement." In this voluntaristic mood, then, Marx held that workers had a *duty* to struggle against capital, which they owed to their own manhood and to history. But where is it written that men must *fulfill* their duty to anyone? In the last analysis, that judgement is grounded in Marx on the unsupported conception of human nature which underlies the entire theory of alienation, namely, that it is *inherent* in human nature for persons to be potent, active beings, subjects' rather than passive cogs.

In contrast to this voluntaristic view on class struggle, there is also a deterministic side in which Marx stresses that there are limits on the improvements that struggle can achieve under capitalism, so long as the wage system remains. For "the very development of modern industry must progressively turn the scale in favour of the capitalist against the working man . . . the working class ought not to exaggerate to themselves the ultimate working of these everyday struggles. They ought not to forget they are fighting the effects, but not the causes of these effects; they are retarding the downward movement, but not changing its direction." In general, Marx held that in its "merely economic action capital is the stronger side" and hence workers must move beyond wage demands to "general political action," and they ought to understand that, "with all the miseries it imposes upon them, the present system simultaneously engenders the material conditions and the social forms necessary for an economic reconstruction of society."[4]

Given its basic structure, there was little workers could do to improve their condition in any fundamental way under capitalism and its wage system. Yet, they were to continue struggling, partly as a duty to themselves and history, partly to educate and to transform themselves (another duty?) in preparation for their overthrow of capitalism and its limits. But if the structure of capitalism offered little room for significant improvement, what would keep workers struggling against it? Little, it would seem, except a *theoretical* understanding whose vision transcended the boundaries of the present. But how can ordinary workers acquire such a transcending vision? Indeed, Marx recognizes there is a danger that workers might confine themselves simply to an effort to improve their economic condition and, indeed, he warns them that they ought "not be exclusively absorbed in these unavoidable guerilla fights incessantly springing up."[5]

Why is it, however, that classes enter into struggle? They are essentially seeking to improve their share of the economic surplus. It is the routine production of the economic surplus and the struggle over its appropriation that is at the core of mature Marxism: "The specific economic form in which unpaid surplus-labour is pumped out of direct producers determines the relationship of rulers to ruled, as it grows directly out of production itself and in turn reacts upon it as a determining element. . . . It is always the direct relationship of the owners of the conditions of production to the direct producers . . . which reveals the innermost secret, the hidden basis of the entire social structure, and with it the political form of the relation of sovereignty and dependence, in short, the corresponding specific form of the state."[6]

In Marx's view, the "surplus" is everything produced by labor over and above the cost of the labor power for which the worker was paid wages. It is this surplus that is central to the class struggle and the spoils of victory in it. Where the forces of production are well developed, the surplus can be greater than where they are immature. There are, however, two fundamentally different but conflated conceptions of how the surplus is *constituted*. In one, a view congenial to *scientific* socialism, the surplus exists as a product of the forces of production, prior to and distinct from its capture through class struggle. In this view, the surplus is only *allocated* by the class struggle, being a thing apart from it that will be the victor's prize. Here, the forces of production create the surplus; the class struggle only allocates it.

In a second conception, however, more congenial to *Critical Marxism*, it is not only the forces of production but the very class struggle itself that generates the surplus. The sheer size of the surplus is, in this view, not dependent only on the level of productivity but also on the power of the dominant class to exploit the working class, *and* on the latter's power to *resist* that effort. The size (hence, existence) of the surplus, then, will vary with the ruthlessness and power of the ruling class and with the courage or determination of the workers. The surplus, here, then, is not simply constituted *structurally* by the mode of production but is constituted *voluntaristically* by struggle.

Under some historical conditions it is perfectly plain, says Marx, which class is appropriating which class's work product. Under feudalism, for example, serfs worked a certain number of days for themselves while setting aside a definite number of days to work for their feudal lord. Under capitalism, however, there is no direct political-military domination, all goods and services appear to be exchanged freely and voluntarily and, therefore, presumably in accord with their true value. How, then, can there be the accumulation of a surplus in the form of profits, interest, rents?

Marx replies that there is one unusual commodity—and one alone—which produces *more* than its value, which produces a *surplus* value systematically appropriated by the capitalist; this, of course, is the proletariat's labor power. Since the worker's surplus value is not extracted from them under threat or violence, but is freely exchanged on the market, then the very existence of the surplus, and of its origin in the worker's activity, is concealed under capitalism. This concealment is a special factor in protecting the hegemony of the ruling class. It is clearly suggested that it is not simply the workers' exploitation but, additionally, their *knowledge* of that exploitation (or lack of it) which is a distinct factor in generating resistance to it. This voluntaristic side of the matter, while indicated clearly enough, is, however, never allowed to assume anything like the importance that Marx attributed to the sheer production of surplus value and its appropriation by the capitalist. Here, then, "critique" is subordinated to structural analysis.

Since the problem of the surplus is central to Marx's political economy, its production and distribution (as Marx viewed it) deserves to be described in greater detail. Marx himself[7] saw his main contributions to the study of capitalism as twofold: first, his distinction between labor as a use value, actually employed in the productive process, and labor *power* as exchange value, that is, as a commodity bought and sold on the labor market; second, his systematic, generalized analysis of the production of surplus value (grounded in the above distinction) which focuses on the fact that what capital buys from the worker, indeed paying its *true* value, is only the *capacity* to do work, (which Marx terms) labor power. The actual *use* of this potential labor is something else again, and the actual labor produces more value, surplus value, over and above the value which has been given in exchange for the workers' labor power. The class struggle is stimulated by the *existence* of this anterior surplus and by the effort to control and appropriate it. This conception of the production of the surplus has overtones of Scientific Marxism's economism.

According to Marx, then, while labor power in capitalist society is a commodity like others, it has an extraordinary character not shared by any other commodity: it is a creative, value-producing force, being alone capable of producing more value than it itself has. Because of the capitalist relations of production, all the value produced by the worker belongs to the capitalist, since the latter has bought the workers' labor power. The working class, then, is paid only for its labor power, not for its actual labor, thus receiving only part of what it produces. In this, Marx *like the other political economists*[8] had assumed that labor alone was the source of value, all the other forces and factors—for example, capital or land—simply allowing their owners a *claim* on the surplus produced, but not actually producing it.

Marx's argument is that the "exchange value" of any commodity refers to "the proportional quantities in which it exchanges for all other quantities." Since the value of any commodity can be expressed in terms of many others, "it must be something distinct from and independent of these. . . . We must be able to reduce all of them to an expression common to all, and distinguishing them only by the proportions in which they contain that same and identical measure. . . . What is the common social substance of all these commodities? It is labour ... not only labour, but social labour ... the average amount of labor socially necessary, under any given division of labor to produce it. ... A commodity has value, because it is a crystallization of social labour, which also includes the labor involved in the raw materials and machines and tools consumed during the course of its production."[9]

Upon what, however, does the value of labor power itself depend? This, says Marx, is determined like the value of any other commodity, i.e., by the labor socially necessary to reproduce it which is here the labor necessary to reproduce the working class itself. Marx adds, however, that "the value of labour is in every country determined by a *traditional* standard of life. It is not mere physical life, but it is the satisfaction of certain wants springing from the social conditions in which people are placed and reared up.... This *historical social* element ... may be expanded or contracted."[10]

It is clear that for Marx, however, this *social* element, this symbolic and cultural aspect, is an untheoretized *residual* factor. It is added unsystematically, for the sake of "realism." His central emphasis, however, is on labor power's determination by "the quantity of labour necessary to maintain or reproduce it."[11] Marx thus acknowledges that, quite apart from the economic cost of reproducing labor power, wages include a traditional sociohistorical element, a society's more or less shared notion of a "normal" wage and normal standard of living for workers, that varies from place to place and time to time. But on what does *this* varying historical element itself depend? Marx simply does not confront this, leaving it unasked and unanswered.

In point of fact, however, at least two considerations seem to influence this sociohistorical element: first, there is the development of the forces of production themselves, i.e., the more advanced they are, the higher the wage and standard of living defined as normal for a working class in a given society; second, there is the working class's own militancy and the effectiveness of its own struggles, i.e., the more militantly and effectively it struggles, the higher the wage and standard of living that comes to be defined as "normal" for the working class.

In the first instance, however, if the traditional or "normal" wage is dependent on the development of productivity, wages would rise and class struggle would diminish with industrialization; the more mature the capitalism, the *less*, not the more, class struggle. This, indeed, seems to be what happened historically. In the second case, where the wage that comes to be deemed normal depends on workers' own struggles, it is not that the class struggle derives from a contest over a surplus value already in being; rather, it determines this surplus value itself. There is thus no "law of value" dependent simply on the structural characteristics and blind economic laws of capitalism; instead, the very value (and law of value) of labor depends in part on a political and voluntaristic element, class struggle. When Marx invokes a "traditional" element in the value of labor power, he is in effect hiding his economism under an untheoretized, ad hoc historicism.

If the value of a commodity, for Marx, depends on the amount of socially necessary labor incorporated in it, this "labor" is not simply equivalent to an amount of physical energy. Clearly energy can be expended, as in the explosion of a volcano, in which no work is accomplished and no value accrued. The question, then, is *under what conditions* does energy generate value? Marx maintained that human labor differs from the work of a bee in that it is guided by foresight or a plan. If energy is expended in order to achieve an imagined condition, it is not, however, only because this condition can be *foreseen* but also because it is *desired* or valued. As I will later note, Engels himself remarks that even animals act with foresight and anticipation. Labor is energy expended with the intention of achieving a *desired* future state. Labor, then, is energy expended with a view to achieving a *desired* future condition, an end, which is continuously monitored in terms of the approach to this end; it is a disciplined process of conformity to norms, to valued conditions. Labor, then, is not just energy expended but energy expenditures controlled by value commitments.

It is not simply, however, that there are two independent elements in the equation constituting work—i.e., energy and norms—because the latter themselves are among the things influencing the energies available. Given a commitment to a set of values, energies are *generated* to achieve them. What constitutes labor, then, cannot be defined independent of—but is itself partly dependent on—a symbolic system of culture with its values. As Paul Schrecker has observed, "all work implies the perfectability of the object worked on."[12] Labor, then, is culture dependent and thus culture *constituted*. It is not labor but merely energy that exists apart from culture.

Labor and culture, then, are not independent domains. Without the existence of human purposes defined in terms of some social standard there can only be prehuman "work" which, while producing energy interchanges between organisms and nature, cannot produce *values*. When Marx notes that only the "socially necessary" labor time produces value, this acknowledges that it is not the sheer number of hours worked that determines value, but the conformity of this labor to some value standard, if only to a standard of efficiency. To note that some labor process was *not* socially necessary implies that it could have been otherwise, that there was not only an alternative but one that was *preferable* and which is, indeed, socially used as a standard.

In defining value as labor crystallized in commodities, Marx is saying value does not depend upon what anyone thinks, knows, or believes and that it does not depend on the *utility* imputed by persons to a commodity. Value depends, then, in no way on the "subjective" standpoint of the participants involved, but only on the amount of labor "objectively" incorporated in a commodity. Value is thus, for Marx, *in* the commodity; it is a *substance* that inheres in it and whose effects are not mediated by human judgement, but, rather, shape judgements including those about the prices people are, in the long run, willing to pay. Insofar as Marx holds that this process takes place apart from people's desires, his theory of value forgoes all subject-object interaction; it is a political economy consonant with his structuralism and his philosophical materialism, laying the groundwork for the evolution of an economistic "scientific socialism" out of Marxism.

In defining labor power as a commodity like any other, Marx implies that it will be subject primarily to considerations of cost and to the logic of efficiency, even though it consists of a human being's lifetime. Marx does not think that moral considerations will limit the exploitation of labor any more than it limits the use of oil or wood. For Marx, as political economist, it is not a question of what people may want to do by reason of their moral code but, rather, of what the conditions in which they find themselves will allow or constrain them to do. "The *will* of the capitalist is certainly to take as much as possible," observes Marx. "What we have to do," however, "is not to talk about his will but to enquire into his power, the limits of this *power, and the character of those limits*."[13] Marx as political economist is thus increasingly Marx the "Scientific Marxist," whose theme is the central theme of materialism: i.e., that it is not the consciousness of persons that determines their social being but their social being that determines their consciousness. Here, then, moralities, ideologies, symbol systems, culture, are the shaped rather than the shapers.

One of the most important if masked expressions of this may be found in Marx's theory (or "law") of value, which holds that the ratios in which commodities tend—in some unspecified long run—to be exchanged with one another depends on the differing amounts of labor each incorporates. In principle, if a barrel of crude oil has seven times the value of a bushel of wheat (as at the time I write), this implies that the labor incorporated in the former is considerably greater than that in the latter. If the difficulties here are obvious they are even more burdensome in any attempt to account for the ten-fold increase in the value of oil during the 1970's in terms of the labor theory of value.

Marx, of course, did not hold that value—which he did not equate with price—increased simply when the labor incorporated in commodities increased, for that would make commodities inefficiently produced more valuable than those produced efficiently. Marx, therefore, added that a commodity's value depends on the amount of incorporated labor that was "socially necessary." How, then, does one distinguish necessary from unnecessary labor? For the most part, Marx seems to have assumed that necessary labor was that performed diligently with modern means of production.

This implied that the work process, rather than being governed by guild-imposed traditions, could vary in labor intensity, methods, or machinery, and that producers could and would choose among alternatives. The theory of value, then, premised that a mode of production was not externally imposed but could be scrutinized, selected, and changed in accordance (at least in part) with the will of the capitalist producer. Underneath labor that was socially necessary there was tacit choice and commitment.

Certainly this is implied by Marx's discussion of the manner in which the value of labor itself was determined by an historically evolved customary standard of living. For this means that workers will not exert themselves for less than the customary standard of living and may choose not to work at all—going on strike or on the dole—if wages do not sustain them in a standard of living they deem proper. Thus whether or not labor is "socially necessary" depends partly on whether working enables workers to fullfill their values.

For the most part, however, Marx emphasized that workers labored and capitalists managed as they did because they had to, being pressed in the first case by the invisible threat of starvation and, in the second, by the threat of competition. These extreme cases, however, could also lead to a disinvestment of work or capital. In addition, they divert attention from the larger range of situations in which persons normally seek to compromise various demands made on them, to make time (and other resources) available to meet other obligations (for example, to kin and friends), or to pursue "leisure" interests. Persons are often prepared to continue diseconomies if this allows them room to satisfy some of their other values. Economizing behavior commonly undermines the pursuit of other values, among them, as Marx noted, the most sacred; yet other values correspondingly limit the sphere of economizing behavior. The most strictly economizing behavior is possible and tolerable primarily where person and capital are separated, and when investments of the latter do not involve participation of the person. But if it is possible for a capitalist to invest his money without committing his person, it is not possible for the worker to do so with his time.

Marx's general premise was that economizing behavior is the product of "necessity," because the economizers would squeeze out those who did not. Even under capitalism, however, formal and informal group arrangements—trade unions or cartels—can protect those refusing to economize. Both workers and capitalists seek to split the link between their incomes and their productivity. Economizing is thus only a tendency under capitalism. But is it a tendency of capitalism alone? Apparently not, since all the "socialist" societies we have seen in this century have also been disposed to economize. Indeed, this might be better said as follows: as long as the economizing imperatives of the law of value persist, any society remains "capitalist." This, whether or not it has a bourgeoisie which privately owns the means of production. Continued operation of the law of value in collectivist societies, then, means that capitalism survives beyond the bourgeoisie; it means that there can be capitalism without a bourgeoisie.

The historical role of the bourgeoisie, then, has been to serve as a starting mechanism for capitalism but, at some point, they cease being needed for capitalism's reproduction and maintenance. Most generally, what is useful here is an analytical distinction between culture structure and social structure; more particularly, a distinction is required between the culture of capitalism and its class structure originally dominated by a bourgeoisie. The latent historical function of scientific Marxism has been the destruction only of the latter class structure and the simultaneous *reproduction* of capitalist *culture*.

This is clearly the case where self-described "socialisms" tighten labor discipline, intensify productivity, and inhibit waste, pressing toward cheaper costs of production and lowered unit costs. The culture of capitalism is not transcended but reproduced when socialist societies tighten work discipline and intensify productivity. Indeed, a similar (not identical) social structure is also reproduced by the same process, differentiating between workers who are controlled from above and a management which controls them and which, seeking increased returns on funds invested, intensifies labor's dependence and management's domination—a far cry from any form of democratic self-management by workers.

What Marxists have historically called "socialism" has in fact—although scarcely in their self-understanding—been the perpetuation (and even development) of a capitalist culture from which a proprietary class has been removed but in which the capitalist culture continues to produce a hierarchical system of stratification. Differentiating workers and management through a wage system which pays "each according to his work," it produces systematic differences in their life styles which, having to be justified, are thereby generative of ideological distortions.

The continuing law of value in collectivist societies—their press toward economizing behavior—need not imply that there exist objective laws of socialist development which control its evolution. Yet neither can it be assumed that socialist development depends only on the will of socialists and is subject to no limits. Still these limits are not only economic but also moral. When socialist societies pursue modernization through intensified labor discipline and increased capital investment in the means of production, this commitment to one line of development entails a corresponding disengagement from other, alternative commitments, such, for example, as reducing inequalities of income among social strata of geographic regions. But is such industrial modernization to be understood simply as the result of external necessity? What is defined as necessary depends partly on what is deemed desirable and is therefore wanted.

The imposition of labor discipline may occur partly because this allows larger savings—a "surplus," available for capitalizing mechanization—on the assumption that the workers will not consume it. But what makes this necessary? A controlling group imposing labor discipline will be resisted by those whose work is being economized, and, wanting to control the surplus, it will, for both reasons, exclude workers from decision-making through different authoritarian arrangements. In short, the controlling group is clearly more committed to hightening productivity than to income equality or workers' self-management. It has assigned higher priority to productivity in some part because its theory, scientific Marxism, assigns great importance to increasing productivity and, also partly, because it is committed to maintaining a system of national sovereignty. Its emphasis on productivity derives in part from its nationalist commitments. In the case of Chinese collectivism, however, Maoism entailed a slow-down of mechanization and modernization when this was seen as subjecting the Chinese nation to Russian hegemony.

My object here, however, is clearly not to formulate an account of these complex events but only to exemplify the ways that a decision to pursue socialist development through industrial modernization—or to defer this—depends in part on the system of values the actors are attempting to protect as well as on the theoretical systems influencing their definition of events. Necessity, then, is always a judgement grounded in, and varying with, a specific climate of values. Even scarcity itself—as I develop below—depends not only on what is produced but also on what is wanted and valued, while the effects of scarcity likewise vary with a group's profile of values.

Marxism as a Theory of Indefinite Growth

Marx's socialism seeks to overcome scarcity by freeing the forces of production from the stunting influence of outmoded capitalist property institutions. Marx believes that, with the overthrow of these property relations, production will be liberated and can continue to be revolutionized. Scarcity, Marx believes, can be solved by *producing more*. There is thus the expectation of an indefinite and continuous increase in production. Yet this is unlikely with the vast increase in world population, on the one side, and the dwindling supplies of raw materials, oil supplies, and metals, on the other.

The premise of a continuous and indefinite expansion of production—which Marx's socialism shares with classical political economy and with capitalism—appears less possible with each passing year. Rather than the overcoming of scarcity, which Marx's socialism assumes to be the human prospect, the world struggle for scarce resources appears more likely to intensify and to become more brutal. If there was ever any chance of coping with world scarcity simply by expanding production, with each passing decade's plunderous exploitation of resources that chance and that strategy come to appear as a fast-fading eighteenth-century fantasy.

But was the expectation of dealing with scarcity simply by heightening production *ever* rational? Emile Durkheim's critique of the great utopian socialist, Henri Saint-Simon, had argued that no social system, including socialism, could be stable, nor could the people in it ever be satisfied, unless it had viable moral norms limiting people's consumerism. Without these limits, he said, each improvement in their condition would simply lead people to extend their aspirations anew, and they could achieve no satisfaction as they pursued an ever-receding goal:

> ... it is a general law of all living things that needs and appetites are normal only on condition of being controlled ... an appetite that nothing can appease can never be satisfied. Insatiable thirst can only be a source of suffering ... insatiability is a sign of morbidity.... But how fix the quantity of well-being, comfort, luxury, that a human being ought not to pass? Nothing is found in the organic or psychological constitution of man which sets a limit to such needs ... as there is nothing within an individual which constrains these appetites, they must surely be constrained by some force exterior to him, or else they would become insatiable—that is, morbid ... economic appetites cannot be appeased unless they are limited ... they must be subordinated to some end which surpasses them, and it is only on this condition that they are capable of being satisfied ... there will always be some workers who will receive more and others less ... at the end of a short time the latter find their share meager compared with what goes to the others, and as a result new demands arise ... excited desires will tend naturally to keep outrunning their goals, for the very reason that there will be nothing before them which stops them.[14]

Durkheim's premise, that men are insatiable and that unless otherwise limited will seek ever more consumer satisfactions, is, interestingly enough, also shared by Marx:

> A house may be large or small; as long as the neighboring
> houses are small, it satisfies all social requirements for a resi-
> dence. But let there arise next to the little house a palace and
> the little house shrinks into a hut ... if the neighbouring
> palace rises in equal or greater measure, the occupant of the
> little house will always find himself more uncomfortable,
> more dissatisfied, more cramped within his four walls.[15]

Durkheim himself could not have said it better.

Plainly, Marx and Durkheim share the same assumption concerning human insatiability. To assume, however, as Marx does
that men are insatiable, on the one side, and that scarcity can be
overcome by increased productivity, on the other, are incompatible premises. The problem is particularly acute for Marx because
Marx's political economy rejects a systematic focus on the *subjective* side of "demand" and of "value." For Marx, it is the sheer
amount of labor in it that determines a commodity's value, not the
subjective utility it has to those purchasing it; correspondingly, for
Marx it is the sheer amount of production, the sheer *supply* side of
the equation alone, that will, *without reference to the demand
side,* solve the problem of scarcity.

Durkheim's solution to the problems of scarcity, however, is
radically different because his central concern is not with these in
isolation but with the human *unhappiness or satisfaction* to which
they contribute. "What is needed if social order is to reign," says
Durkheim, "is that the mass of men be content with their lot. But
what is needed for them to be content, is not that they have more
or less, but that they be convinced they have no right to more. And
for this, it is absolutely essential that there be an authority whose
superiority they acknowledge and which tells them what is right
... a moral power is required whose superiority [man] recognizes."[16]

This problem arises in modern society, said Durkheim, because
all the moderating institutions of previous times, especially the
church and guild, have declined, and there are no longer "moral
authorities" whose restrictions persons accept as legitimate. The
entire development of modern industry, noted Durkheim, has
aroused rather than moderated human wants, particularly since
industry became an autonomous force in society, no longer subordinated to forces outside of itself.

The *Communist Manifesto*, indeed, says much the same, noting how capitalism destroyed all relationships between people except the cash nexus and has "drowned the most heavenly ecstasies of religious fervor [and] . . . stripped of its halo every occupation hitherto honored," while it multiplied new wants in people. "In place of the old wants, satisfied by the productions of the country, we find new wants, requiring for their satisfaction the products of distant lands and climes."[17]

When Marx speaks of capitalism as governed by its own blind laws, he converges with Durkheim who noted that the economy has become autonomous, unchecked by other forces in society. For Durkheim, however, the solution lay in eliminating the autonomy of the economy, by bringing it under the governance of *society* and by transforming the consciousness and aspirations of men by subjecting them to moral authorities whose restrictions they accepted as legitimate. For Durkheim, neither capitalism nor socialism can establish a *satisfying* social order insofar as they merely expand productivity; for increased goods alone without a restriction on consumerism which was accepted as legitimate would, he argued, never make people content. Indeed, he indicated, to the extent that capitalism undermined all authorities that could exert a moderating influence, capitalism fosters an *anomie*, a human satiability incapable of satisfaction.

Durkheim seems to be correct. Economic productivity exists to satisfy human beings and is not an end in itself. The proper end of social reconstruction—of socialist emancipation—would seem to be human contentment and satisfaction, not indefinite industrial progress, not the endless revolutionizing of productivity. Durkheim seems correct, also, in noting that unless there is some limit set on consumerism there will never be human contentment, however much living standards increase. As his own fable of the little house and the palace suggests, Marx agreed. Yet he neglected the force of the most basic point Durkheim is making, namely, that productivity exists for man, not man for productivity. As Marx entrenched himself in classical political economy, he absorbed increasingly its problematic and its limits, even as he radicalized it. Economistic, Scientific Marxism means the ritualistic substitution of industrialization for human emancipation as a goal. That is, industrialization, which had first been a *means* to the end of human emancipation, has become an *end* in itself. Stalinism is precisely the not so accidental enactment of *that* potential of Scientific Marxism. Stalinism is a social system in which industrialization becomes the key criterion of socialism's achievement and its legitimacy, and whose aim is the power of the new state rather than the contentment and welfare of its citizenry.

But if Durkheim's work is an effective critique of scientific socialism's economism and its downgrading of the moral, symbolic, cultural, and ideological side of socialism, nonetheless, *Durkheim's theory should not be appropriated uncritically*. For one thing, Durkheim's premise about human insatiability is an ungrounded and authoritarian metaphysic of human nature. Left to their own devices, it holds, men will be insatiable unless controlled and limited from the *outside*.

While it is surely true that what men believe will affect the satisfaction or disappointment they feel with their standard of living, it is also true that (other things, including their beliefs, held constant) persons are more likely to be happy with more rather than less, and certainly with an increasing rather than a declining standard of living, especially if others have more. Surely human contentment is not unaffected by plenty or poverty. If Marx neglected the subjective and symbolic elements on which human contentment was grounded, Durkheim neglected the material and economic side. In his polemical effort to prove that the economists and socialists had one-sidedly overstressed economic poverty, Durkheim lapsed into a no less one-sided neglect of economic poverty, diagnosing the modern malaise simply as due to "poverty of *morality*."

Durkheim mystified the reasons why men submit to moral norms; he accepted the false consciousness which conceives of morality as a thing apart from human making and doing, so that his stress is on the effectiveness of only *external* constraints on persons' appetites. Granted that Durkheim saw such restraining moralities as societally produced and not as god given; granted that he saw religions themselves as the products of society, this is a *reified* Society from which persons are alienated and which towers above them much as the state or religion does.

For Durkheim the moralities needed to moderate human appetites are essentially cultural systems from which persons are alienated. Indeed, it is this very alienation that generates a sense of the unchallengeable external character of these religions or moralities. But why should persons submit to alienation from a culture which is of their own making? And why assume that persons will *not* submit to moralities which they recognize as of their own making? Indeed, at a certain point in the secularization of the modern world, one reason why moralities lose their hold on people is precisely because they are not seen as *theirs;* and one way to restore the hold of morality is to bring it under people's effective control.

Durkheim's critique of Marxism, then, is a critique of only one side of Marx, of only one of the Two Marxisms, of *Scientific* Marxism; his is not a rejection of all socialism or even of "communism."[18] Indeed, Durkheim saw communism (as distinct from socialism) as submitting to the high morality of equality, thus escaping the insatiability of a scientific socialism whose ultimate goal becomes the concentration of state power through industrialization. Durkheim was a guild (or syndicalist) socialist who wanted to bring the means of production under the direct control of viable human communities, rather than have them monopolized by a single, all-embracing state remote from people's everyday lives, ignorant of their daily work, and, correspondingly, unable to influence everyday life except bureaucratically.

With his emphasis upon the importance of revitalizing modern morality, Durkheim was the "pacifist" counterpart of Georges Sorel who, at about the same time in France, also denounced scientific socialism for embodying a moral decay and who called the proletariat even to violence and myth to bring forth their moral revitalization. In his rejection of the capitalist economy's autonomy, Durkheim is also the academic counterpart of the Lukács who interpreted Marxism as a theory of the *totality,* not as a theory of the primacy of the economic, and who understood socialism as a transformation in which the economy would once again serve rather than dominate culture. Sorel and Lukács, of course, are the exponents of the Critical Marxism repressed by the emergence of economistic Scientific Marxism, and I shall have occasion to examine their views in a later volume.

It may suffice for the moment, however, to suggest that one of the historical functions of Critical Marxism is to develop the morality of socialism, or a moral socialism in which the pursuit of human emancipation is not derailed by the industrial build-up of the state's power; in which consumerism is not confused with either culture or contentment; in which there is an enrichment of social structures and of groups autonomous of the state, which can enable people to use rather than be used by the state and which, being close to everyday life, can enforce a living moral code with knowledge and compassion, without a ponderous and plundering bureaucracy. Such, at any rate, would be a Critical Marxism congenial to and convergent with Durkheim's socialism and sociology.

NOTES

1. Karl Marx, *Capital* (Moscow: Foreign Languages Publishing House, 1959), vol. III, pp. 799–800.

2. Jean Baudrillard, *The Mirror of Production*, trans. Mark Poster (St. Louis: Telos Press, 1975).

3. Karl Marx, *Wage-Labour and Capital* (New York: International Publishers, 1933), pp. 29–30. Originally published in 1849 and rewritten by Engels so that it is now "approximately as Marx would have written in 1891" (ibid., p. 6).

4. The preceding quotations are all from Karl Marx, *Value, Price and Profit*, ed. Eleanor Marx Aveling (New York: International Publishers, 1935), pp. 59ff.

5. Ibid.

6. *Capital* III, Foreign Languages ed., p. 772.

7. "The best points in my book are: (1) the *double character of labour,* according to whether it is expressed in use value or exchange value (*all* understanding of the facts depends upon this, it is immediately emphasized in the *first* chapter); (2) the treatment of *surplus value independently of its particular* forms as profit, interest, ground rent, etc." Letter of 24 August 1867 from Marx to Engels. Karl Marx and Frederick Engels, *Selected Correspondence 1846–1895*, trans. Dona Torr (New York: International Publishers, 1942), pp. 226–27.

8. ". . . classical political economy found that the value of a commodity was determined by the value of the labour incorporated in it and requisite for its production. . . . Marx was the first to investigate thoroughly into the value-forming quality of labour and to discover that not all labour which is apparently, or even really, necessary to the production of a commodity, imparts under all circumstances to this a magnitude of value corresponding to the quantity of labor used up." Marx, *Wage-Labour and Capital*, p. 7 of Engels's introduction.

9. Marx, *Value, Price and Profit*, pp. 29ff.

10. Ibid., p. 57. Italics added.

11. Ibid., p. 41.

12. Paul Schrecker, *Work and History* (New York: T. Y. Crowell, 1971), p. 13.

13. Marx, *Value, Price and Profit*, p. 11.

14. Emile Durkheim, *Socialism and Saint-Simon (Le Socialisme)*, ed. Alvin W. Gouldner (Yellow Springs, Oh.: Antioch Press, 1958), pp. 197ff.

15. Marx, *Wage-Labour and Capital,* p. 33.

16. Ibid., p. 200.

17. *Communist Manifesto* by Karl Marx and Friedrich Engels, authorized English edition of 1888, supervised by Engels, published by Charles H. Kerr, Chicago, p. 17.

18. For further discussion of Durkheim's "guild socialism," see my introduction to his *Socialism and Saint-Simon* cited above.

8

"ECONOMIC DETERMINISMS" IN MARXISM

We find ourselves in a situation which is at once remarkable but common: the people whom we are studying are also studying us. As the tale goes, we have put our eye to the keyhole and the first thing we observe is another eye staring back at us. We are not isolated, superior anthropologists studying faraway illiterates, nor industrial sociologists studying supposedly naive factory workers. Those about whom we are reflecting are just as reflective as we, and, sometimes, they disagree with our conclusions.

It is inherent in the situation that, when I portray Marxism as critique, Scientific Marxists will disagree; contrariwise, when I portray Marxism as science, Critical Marxists will object. Had I been writing before 1914, the central disagreement with my analysis would have come from social democrats of the Second International, who conceived Marxism as a scientific socialism and who would have denied vigorously that Marxism was critique. This was essentially the tack that Karl Kautsky took in his review of Karl Korsch's *Marxism and Philosophy*. Indeed, this was also the position that the Communist International—seeking to protect its emerging canonization of "Marxism-Leninism"—also took toward Korsch and toward Georg Lukács's *History and Class Consciousness*. Today, however, affairs are different, and their more Hegelian reading of Marxism has been ascendent. As Norman Levine writes rather inexactly, "a growing literature that rejects the interpretation of Marx as a universal determinist has been forthcoming within the past two decades."[1] He cites the work of Karl Wittfogel, Irving Zeitlin, Henri LeFebvre, Lucien Goldmann, August Cornu, Jean-Paul Sartre, Ihring Fetscher, Theodor Adorno, and Max Horkheimer.

Engels and the Debate
About Economic Determinism(s)

The philosopher Richard Bernstein—adopting an Hegelianizing interpretation of Marxism—holds that *all* of Marx's thinking, including *Capital* itself, aims "not to affirm the impotence of man in the face of impersonal forces but rather to affirm the *real* possibility of a critical understanding of the world which allows man's eventual mastery of his own fate."[2] But in his *Capital*, Marx had rejected the "anthropological" standpoint in which "man" is presumably ever the same in his "species being" and, with insistent historicity, studied men and women in their historical plurality and uniqueness, i.e., as proletarians and capitalists.

Elsewhere Bernstein insists, without offering textual evidence, that "the point of *Capital* is not to sanctify the immutability of 'economic laws' but to reveal their mutability in history."[3] If one reads that statement carefully, one may notice that Bernstein goes to some lengths to present Marx's *Capital* as if it really did not talk about economic laws which were said to operate with an iron immutability. Instead of denying this forthrightly, Bernstein embellishes the issue rhetorically and says that *Capital* does not "sanctify" the immutability of economic laws. But to "sanctify" simply means to make holy and untouchable. The point, however, is that Marx did see such laws—as he plainly said—as controlling people's will and consciousness.

Although Marx does not believe the laws of *capitalism* eternal, he believes them inexorable, asserting the immutability and inexorability of capitalism's "pitiless laws," as he called them, under certain historical conditions. I have already shown, and below will show still further, that a *central* dimension of Marx's work is precisely its general emphasis on the *limits* within which persons make their own history; it is this standpoint—and not the quasi-theological doctrine of "free will" here rechristened as "praxis"—that is historically *innovative* in Marx, although the latter is indeed very much there.

Bernstein writes as if *all* of Marx's works were of one piece, but clearly his *Eighteenth Brumaire* is different from *Capital,* being less deterministic and economistic than the latter. Bernstein is correct, I believe, in holding that the aim of Marx's work is to affirm "man's" ability to achieve a critical understanding of his life that will eventually allow him to master it. This, however, is expected to emerge only with the development of the forces of

production revolutionized by the bourgeoisie, which establishes
the conditions for emancipating society from the realm of scarcity,
particularly when released from the limits imposed by bourgeois
relations of production. Bernstein writes as if "critical understanding" would suffice, in Marx's view, to lay the groundwork of
emancipation; but that reduces Marx to a left Hegelian. It is precisely because capitalism's pitiless, blind, and naturelike laws
make persons impotent, thus denying them what Marx took to be
their human birthright, that he opposed and despised capitalism.
And it is precisely because of this subjugation of persons by
capitalism's iron laws that Marx relies upon the no less inexorable
internal structural contradictions of capitalism to produce
capitalism's doom. It is just this "proof" of ordained doom that
generations of Marxists understood to be the essence of Marxism,
making it a *science* in which historical outcomes did not depend
on mere "will" but on inescapable and certain scientific laws. It is
these laws that were understood as distinguishing Marxism from
moralizing and sentimental humanitarianism and utopianism. It is
exactly *because capitalism imputedly has inexorable laws which
effectively dominate persons* that Marx opposes it, and in which
Marx finds the very guarantee of his victory over it. If we had any
illusion that the difference between Critical and Scientific Marxism corresponds to the difference between those emancipated
from one-sidedness and those in bondage to it, Bernstein's Hegelian reading of Marx must disabuse us.

If the first point that needs to be noted is that Hegelianizing
Marxists are blind to the deterministic (and economistic) *side* of
Marxism, it also needs to be added that what they do see, even if
limited and skewed, is indeed there, truly part of authentic Marxism. Thus I am not asserting that Marxism is reducible to this
economism and determinism; on the contrary, I am arguing that it
is characterized precisely by its contradictory *combination* of determinism and voluntarism, its emphasis on the laws of capitalism
and the struggle to release men from subjugation to them through
their own free practice.

An antideterminist reading of Marxism is, of course, inherent in
Critical Marxism's voluntarism, though scarcely its monopoly.
The most recent defense of an antideterminist reading is offered
by Melvin Rader who cites the familiar passage in Marx's *Preface
to the Critique of Political Economy:* "My investigation led to the
result that legal relations as well as forms of the state . . . are rooted
in the material conditions of life. . . . In the social production
which men carry on they enter into definite relations that are

indispensable and independent of their will. . . . The sum total of these relations of production constitutes the economic structure of society—the real foundation on which rise legal and political superstructures and to which correspond definite forms of social consciousness. The mode of production in material life conditions (*bedingt*) the social, political and intellectual life processes in general (*überhaupt*)."[4] Rader argues that a proper translation of *bedingt*[5] is "conditions" (although acknowledging that many other scholars translate it as "determines") thus softening the determinism of the passage. At the same time, he also acknowledges that *überhaupt* "can be translated 'altogether',," which would *strengthen* the determinism.

Rader rejects this translation, however, because its determinism is presumably at variance with "what Marx says elsewhere." This, of course, implies that Marxism could not embody a contradiction, which is contrary to my own essential contention. Moreover, this contradiction becomes impossible to see precisely with the procedure Rader follows. Besides, if the criterion is consistency, one could have chosen to translate Marx's less deterministic phrasings in ways that assimilate them to the deterministic formulation, rather than as Rader does, in the reverse direction. Rader concludes that in his translation—which already adopts the very assumption that is at issue—"the implication is far from economic determinism."

Yet even the idea of a "condition," as, for example, in necessary condition, refers to that which is *requisite* for the doing or happening of something else, to a circumstance *essential* to the appearance of something else. What condition (*bedingt*) means *here* is grounding or foundation; indeed, it means—as Marx expressly says above—the "real foundation" of the legal and political superstructure and which, like the "foundation" of a building, is that on which everything else rests, is the necessary condition of the structure above it, is that on which the superstructure is *dependent*. Determinism simply means: given X, then Y. Economic determinism means given a certain mode of production, then there will follow a certain superstructure of other social relations. Thus in his critique of Proudhon, Marx wrote: "In acquiring new productive forces men change their mode of production; and in changing their mode of production, in changing their way of earning their living, they change all their social relations. The hand-mill gives you society with the feudal lord, the steam-mill, society with the industrial capitalist."[6] Is this not an economic determinism?

Those cited above by Norman Levine as opposing a determinist reading of Marxism are, it will be noticed, precisely those whom I have called "Critical Marxists." Yet no matter how long their roster and how appealing their seeming antidogmatism, what we have is not a consensus among Marxists but a systematic division and conflict; and it is not a division in which one side embodies all the forces of blindness, while the other is enlightenment incarnate. They are all interested parties joined in sympathy to one another and in antipathy to the other side. On this point as on so many others, Norman Levine oversimplifies where he is not simply wrong. Thus his roster of antideterminist Marxists makes no mention of the substantial French groups around the Centre d'Etudes et de Recherches Marxistes and such journals as *Recherches Internationale à la Lumière du Marxisme* as well as *La Pensée,* who cannot at all be said to have clearly renounced what Levine calls the "universal determinist" or unilinear view of Marx. Such names as Maurice Godelier or Jean Chesneaux or even Jean Suret-Canale are sometimes ambiguous in their position and cannot always be counted against the universal determinists. Levine's picture of Marxist universal determinism overthrown is thus, to understate, somewhat overdrawn. When he marches the troops out for inspection he leaves the opposing forces in the barracks, neglects to mention there is a war going on, and fails altogether to explain why this intellectual conflict has intensified since the turn of the century.

Indeed, Levine is so completely a partisan in this internecine struggle within Marxism that he even denies that Scientific Marxists are Marxists at all. Instead, he calls them adherents of Engels and actually calls their theory, "Engelsism." Engels, Levine tells us "was the first revisionist" and something of an ignoramus, while Marx was a revolutionary genius. "My bias is apparent," acknowledges Levine correctly, "I consider Marx had the most creative, imaginative, and relevant mind"—whatever a "relevant mind" may be. Engels's mind, however, "was of a second order."[7]

In short, rather than confronting Marx's and Marxism's contradictions and attempting to understand them, Levine conceals these by splitting Marx and Engels. Indeed, the central point of splitting them is to deny that there are contradictions *within* Marx and Marxism by dramatizing a contradiction *between* them. Marx and Engels are, in effect, presented as having lived a life of total illusion concerning each other. Each thought the other his closest friend and congenial collaborator, but they were, Levine argues, fundamentally opposed. Well, we shall have to see. In this discussion two distinct matters are commonly confused. (1) Did Marx and Engels disagree, about what, and how important was this? (2) Just which doctrines did Marx in fact espouse? The latter issue has often taken the form of a loud but largely sterile debate about whether Marx was "really" an "economic determinist." In particular, critical Marxists such as Georg Lukács are at pains to deny this. My own concern, however, will be less with Marx's name than with the rules of his game. The important issue is what Marx believed, not the label his beliefs deserved. I shall also hold that this matter cannot be resolved without reflection about what "economic determinism" might mean, and how that term should be used. Not only do we need to think about the meaning of "economic determinism," but we also require more methodological clarity, asking ourselves about the texts being cited, whether from a brief letter or from a carefully developed analysis, from an earlier or later text, and asking ourselves what is implied in comparing certain texts. In short, we shall not only have to consider the concrete issue of Marx's economic determinism but also how arguments concerning this issue are conducted.

In the previous chapters, I documented that in Marx's mature scholarship, his *Capital* above all, Marx repeatedly declared himself a scientist; he clearly regarded his social theory as a social science modeled after the then emerging natural sciences. Like other scientists, Marx assumed that there are inescapable laws of capitalism which controlled persons' purposes and will and which doomed capitalism inexorably.[8] Indeed, in his more general theory—usually called "historical materialism"—Marx held that the mode of production (in *any* society) was an infrastructure that determined (any) society's ideological and political superstructure. There are thus *two* economic determinisms here, one bearing on the historically limited but inexorable laws of *capitalism* that doom it inevitably; the second, consisting of a set of more general premises on which the first was grounded, the more general paradigm of historical materialism, which is indeed a kind of "universal determinism," albeit not necessarily a universal evolutionism.

A Look at Some Texts

In opposition, Critical Marxists and others who deny Marx was any sort of determinist, commonly invoke certain stock quotations. Two sets of quotations are commonly cited. Set one usually includes (a) a letter Marx wrote the Russian socialist Vera Sas-

soulitch some two years before he died, which is usually contrasted with (b) one Engels wrote earlier on the same subject,
which purportedly comes to different conclusions than Marx's, and
(c) a letter Marx wrote to the editor of the Russian journal
Otyecestvenniye Zapisky (*Notes on the Fatherland*) six years before he died. These texts discuss the possible uniqueness of Russia and its capacity to escape capitalism, and thus center on the
issue of Marx's "universal determinism" as a unilinear
evolutionism.

The second set commonly cited to reject the view that Marx was
a determinist bear on another kind of determinism, the universal
determinism of the historical materialism paradigm mentioned
above. This second, equally tired, set of texts were all written by
Engels. Thus they can be relevant only to the question of whether
Marxism (but not Marx himself) was determinist; therefore, they
are cited by those who accept Engels as a cofounder of Marxism
and as an authentic Marxist.

The first set of texts purporting to prove that Marx was not a
unilinear evolutionary determinist are altogether no more than,
say, twenty printed pages, almost all of which are focused on one
delimited issue, the politically heated question of the emerging
revolution in Czarist Russia; second, they were written very late
in Marx's life, just a few years before his death, and lastly, with
one important exception, all are contained in incidental letters
rather than manuscripts. (That one exception is Marx's *Grundrisse*
discussion of the forms of primitive communalism, to which I will
also turn later.) Since I have already considered some of the material in set one I shall feel free to deal briefly with it below.

In set two, the Engels's texts include five letters he wrote following Marx's death in 1883: to Franz Mehring (14 July 1893), to
Conrad Schmidt (27 October and 5 August 1890), to J. Bloch (21
September 1890), and to H. Starkenberg (25 January 1894). These
texts number no more than fifteen printed pages and are rather
casual letters concerning which Engels warns one correspondent,
Starkenberg, "Please do not weigh each word in the above too
carefully."[9]

Marx and Economic Determinism: The Russian Question

During the development of the revolutionary movement in Russia
a key question emerged. Could Russia skip the capitalist stage,

going on directly to the construction of socialism, or must the revolutionary movement reconcile itself to the fact that socioeconomic evolution required that Russia pass through the capitalist stage, in order to develop the industrial requisites of socialism? Jonathan Frankel formulates the implications of this struggle with exceptional clarity:

> anybody hoping to convert the Russian revolutionary movement to Marxism would have to overcome a crucial dilemma. If he emphasized that Russia had to go through the same prolonged stages of capitalist development as the West, he would be accused of weakening the faith of the revolutionaries who were fighting for equality, for socialism, not for political liberty. The revolutionary could hardly be expected to martyr himself in the attempt to overthrow the dictatorship of the Tsar if the only result would be to entrench emergent capitalism. If Marxism meant to postpone all hope of socialism for many decades or even for centuries, then such a doctrine spelt suicide for the revolutionary movement. Yet, as against this, if it was said that Russia could avoid the capitalist stage and so pass directly to socialism, then what was the relevance of Marxism to the Russian revolutionary movement? Nearly all the populist leaders—Lavrov, Tkaschev, even Bakunin—admired Marx's socio-economic analysis of capitalist society, but they all argued that Russia as a feudal and agrarian country could learn from the West only how to avoid its errors and so find a direct road to socialism. Marxism was irrelevant.[10]

In 1874 Tkaschev had written that a social revolution would be easier in Russia than in the West. While Russia had no urban proletariat (on which Marx depended as the agent of socialism) still, Tkaschev says, "we also have no bourgeoisie . . . our workers will have to fight only against the *political power—the power of capital* is with us still only in embryo." And you sir, he says to Engels, "are undoubtedly aware that the fight against the former is much easier than against the latter."[11] Thus Tkaschev argued that the very backwardness of capitalism in Russia was an advantage to the socialist revolution there. Correspondingly, there was the further implication that the stronger capitalism grew in Russia, the more *difficult* it would be to achieve a socialist revolution.[12] Thus the sooner revolutionaries made their bid for power in Russia, the better their prospects, and vice versa.

By this line of reasoning, replied Engels, one ought to seek the reestablishment of savagery and semi-savagery, for in them, he indicates, there are no class distinctions, hence no ruling class, and hence no difficulty at all in establishing a socialist revolution and a society without classes. But, says Engels, "it would not occur to us to reestablish this state, for . . . only at a certain level of development of the productive forces of society, an even very high level for our modern conditions, does it become possible to raise production to such an extent that the abolition of class distinctions can be a real progress, can be lasting without bringing about stagnation or even decline in the mode of social production. But the productive forces have reached this level only in the hands of the bourgeoisie. The bourgeoisie, therefore, in this respect also is just as necessary a precondition of the socialist revolution as the proletariat itself. Hence a man who will say that this revolution can be more easily carried out in a country, because, *although* it has no proletariat, it has no bourgeoisie *either*, only proves that he has still to learn the ABC of socialism."[13]

For Engels, then, the socialist revolution was "the victory of the proletariat over the bourgeoisie, and . . . this requires not only a proletariat that carries out this revolution, but also a bourgeoisie in whose hands the productive forces have developed so far that they allow of the final destruction of class distinctions."[14]

Engels, however, has no doubt that, given the intolerable conditions imposed on the Russian peasantry, the fiscal chaos of the state, and the corruption of its administration, that Russian society was then "held together with great difficulty and only outwardly by an Oriental despotism . . . which not only from day to day comes into more glaring contradiction with the views of the enlightened classes and in particular with those of the rapidly developing bourgeoisie of the capital."[15] For these reasons, then, "Russia undoubtedly is on the eve of a revolution." The communal ownership system in Russian villages, the *mir*, will not allow Russia to skip the prior development of a capitalist phase necessary to socialist development because that communal system is itself already decaying with the emergence of capitalism in Russia, and land is cultivated individually not collectively. Yet, says Engels, it is possible that the *mir could* take on a new lease on life, *could* continue its social development and allow Russian peasants to skip "the intermediary form of bourgeois smallholdings."[16]

"This, however, can only happen," adds Engels, "if before the complete break-up of communal ownership, a proletarian revolution is successfully carried out in Western Europe, creating for the

Russian peasant preconditions requisite for such a transition, particularly the material conditions which he needs if only to carry through the revolution necessarily connected therewith of his whole agricultural system. . . If anything can still save Russian communal ownership and give it a chance of growing into a new, really viable form, it is a proletarian revolution in Western Europe."[17]

In summary: for the most part, Engels here insists that a socialist society premises a mature development of industrial productivity as requisite for the overcoming of scarcity necessary for the institution of a classless socialism. The development of productivity, the great historical mission of the bourgeoisie, is thus as necessary for socialist revolution as is the proletariat. Engels's central thrust here, then, is that skipping the capitalist stage and going directly on to socialism in Russia is an illusion held only by the naive. Engels asks, "is it permissible for one over twelve years of age to imagine the course of a revolution" in the manner that Tkaschev supposes.

Nonetheless, adds Engels, it is conceivable that peasant collectivism might be resuscitated if there were a proletarian revolution in industrially advanced Western Europe. The *main* course of development he anticipated, then, is a continuing development of capitalism in Russia, which will corrupt and deteriorate the *mir* but which would also create the conditions requisite for a classless socialism; an alternative course, secondary but nonetheless considered possible, is that Russia might indeed proceed directly to its own social revolution, on the condition that it is accompanied and helped by a proletarian revolution in the West. While Engels emphasizes the importance of a prior period of bourgeois development, he thus does not altogether exclude the possibility that Russia might skip or compress that stage and move on rapidly, having a kind of permanent revolution in which there is an almost direct transition to social revolution and subsequent socialism in Russia, *given outside help from advanced industrial proletariats.* Thus even here in his most orthodox posture, Engels equivocates; he does not insist that capitalism in Russia is inevitable, and that socialism can only await the mature development of capitalism. Engels, therefore, was *not* an evolutionary determinist, for he did *not* insist on a unilinear evolutionism, in which each society must inescapably go through the same sequence of social states. It is thus mistaken to say, as Jonathan Frankel has, that Engels's reply to Tkaschev embodied a "watertight determinism."[18] Moreover, the central issue here has been whether capitalism was inevitable, especially under Russian conditions; the question was not, whether, once developed, capitalism's laws and *subsequent* evolution and doom were themselves inevitable. *The latter was never challenged.* How, then, does Engels's position compare with Marx's?

Three years later, toward the end of 1877, Marx wrote an unpublished reply to the editor of *Otyecestvenniye Zapisky* dealing with the same issues. Marx then formulated the question as being whether the Russians can "find a path of development for their country which will be different from that which Western Europe pursued and still pursues."[19] Here Marx observed that Chernyshevsky had questioned whether the liberal economists were correct in believing that "Russia must begin by destroying *la commune rurale* in order to pass to the capitalist regime, or whether, on the contrary, she can without experiencing the tortures of this regime, appropriate all its fruits by developing *ses propres données historiques* [the particular historic conditions already given her]."[20]

On this question, Marx then offers it as his own opinion that:

> If Russia continues to pursue the path she has followed since 1861, she will lose the finest chance ever offered by history to a nation, in order to undergo all the fatal vicissitudes of the capitalist regime.[21]

Marx adds, that his chapter on primitive accumulation in *Capital* does no "more than trace the path by which, in Western Europe, the capitalist order of economy emerged from the womb of the feudal order of economy."[22] Marx's point here, then, is to distinguish between (1) the question of the rise of capitalism, which he now clearly indicates need not be inevitable and (2) the question of whether, once this capitalist road has been taken, there was any escape from the "tortures of this regime."

Marx then immediately quotes from *Capital*, arguing that expropriation of workers from their traditional means of production and subsistence "has not yet been radically accomplished except in England . . . but all the countries of Western Europe are going through the same movement."[23] He then observes that, at the end of that chapter in *Capital*, "the historic tendency of production is . . . that it itself begets its own negation with the *inexorability which governs the metamorphoses of nature* . . . capitalist property, resting as it actually does already on a form of collective property, cannot do other than transform itself into social property."[24]

Marx thus clearly distinguished between (1) the problem of the *origin* of capitalism, allowing that this need not always and everywhere be inescapable, that it might be skipped if a nation like Russia fully exploited its unusual opportunities, and he separates this from (2) the internal development of capitalism which, once mature, allows of no escape: "it begets its own negation with . . . inexorability . . . and cannot do other than transform itself into social property." "After once taken to the bosom of the capitalist regime," holds Marx, "she [Russia] will experience its pitiless laws like other profane people."[25]

Marx thus did not assert that capitalism must develop in Russia but only that, *if* it did, it would then be subjected to capitalism's inescapable and pitiless laws. The genesis of capitalism, he insists, is not a universal destiny "imposed by fate upon every people, whatever the historic circumstances in which it finds itself."[26] Marx thus observes that the Roman plebians in antiquity were also expropriated but they did not become wage laborers "but a mob of do-nothings," and Rome did not develop capitalism but slavery. History, then, has no *marche genérale*, says Marx; similar events can, if taking place under different circumstances, produce different results. In summary: Marx rejects the idea that capitalism must arise everywhere. At the same time, he also insists that, once it develops, there is no escaping its laws. If there are differences between Marx and Engels on this they hinge primarily on the *degree* to which each rejected the idea of the inevitability of capitalism, but Engels too allowed that possibility, however reluctantly. If Engels's views seem more deterministic than Marx's judgement three years *after* Engels's reply to Tkaschev, they do not seem more deterministic than Marx's polemic against Bakunin five years earlier. Note, moreover, that Marx's later position also corresponds to the changing situation in Russia, which had grown more revolutionary than when Engels had written. Finally, to say Russia might escape capitalism and pass on directly to revolution is one thing; to say that she would then be passing on to a *socialist* revolution is quite another. Both Marx and Engels are much clearer about Russia's being able to avoid capitalism than they are about the nature of the society that would emerge there if she did, or whether that would be socialist.

In 1882 when the Russian edition of the *Communist Manifesto* was published, Marx and Engels wrote a new preface which again considers whether Russia must pass through capitalism before going on to "the highest communist form of landed property" or whether this communal property must first be disintegrated, as it was in the West. "The only possible answer to this question today is as follows," they reply: "If the Russian Revolution becomes the signal for the workers' revolution in the West, so that one supplements the other, then the present form of land ownership in Russia may be the starting point of communist development."[27]

It should be noted, first, that this reply is essentially similar to Engels's letter to Tkaschev in allowing for the resuscitation of peasant communalism and in specifying the same condition for it, namely, a workers' revolution in Western Europe, here seen as being summoned by possible Russian revolution. Second, this is, after all, a joint new preface *signed by both Engels and Marx,* so there is no indication of their having differing views of that matter. Third, there remains a question as to whether the resuscitation of peasant communalism envisaged in this preface, and in Engels's letter to Tkaschev, implied that a *socialist* society may be started in Russia, which Marx had denied in his 1872 critique of Bakunin. Clearly, however, Marx and Engels never regarded communism in *land,* and land alone, as a *socialist economy,* so that while this text allows for a unique historical (and even communist) development in Russia, allowing it to skip over or compress the development of capitalism, still, they only explictly admit of the possibility of starting on the road to a *socialist society.* Fourth and finally, this new preface to the Russian edition in no way repeals or relents on the determinism of capitalism's own merciless laws, once a nation has started on the development of a capitalist economy.

In February of 1881, two years before his death, Marx received a letter from Vera Sassoulitch, who wanted to know whether Marx could offer any hope for the future of the Russian *mir.* Marx seems to have been very unsure of how to answer, drafting three separate replies before finally sending her a terse answer in which, as above, he reiterates that the emergence of capitalism itself is not inevitable outside of Western Europe, and that the *mir* could be the basis of Russian regeneration, if one could "eliminate the deleterious influences which assail it from every quarter"—including the development of capitalism itself, which was proceeding with increasing speed—"and then to ensure the conditions normal for spontaneous development,"[28] the character of which Marx does not here specify. Again, there remains ambiguity about whether avoidance of capitalism necessarily implies achievement of *socialism*.

On 23 April 1888 Engels once more wrote[29] Vera Sassoulitch, who had inquired about his opinion of Plekhanov's new book which Engels had not read. Replying, he notes that "the Russians are approaching their 1789" and that the revolution could break out there momentarily. So precarious is Russian society that "if ever Blanquism—the phantasy of overturning an entire society through the action of a small conspiracy—had a certain justification for its existence, that is certainly in Petersburg." Engels does not here deliver determinist lectures about the importance of the prior development of proper structural conditions; he acknowledges that even a conspiracy can overturn a society ripe for revolution. He adds, however, that the conspirators will get more than they expected: "the people who laid the spark to the mine will be swept away by the explosion. . . . People who boasted that they had *made* a revolution have always seen the next day that they had no idea what they were doing, that the revolution they *made* did not in the least resemble the one they would have liked to make." Here in these realistic, indeed prophetic comments, Engels argues that it is social structure that ultimately shapes history, whatever men may intend. The general argument is: when structures are precarious and on the brink of explosion, individual intervention can indeed be decisive but, afterwards, the structural drift reasserts itself. Whatever else may be said, Engels is certainly here imposing no unswervable *marche genérale* on history; detours were possible. Engels leans toward a synchronic universal determinism rather than a unilinear evolutionary determination.

Clearly, then, no case has here been established that Marx and Engels differed decisively about the inevitable emergence of capitalism outside of Western Europe; under different conditions both allowed, Engels somewhat less and Marx more, the possibility that Russia could bypass the capitalist stage of development. Under no conditions, however, did either regard the development of a mature capitalism as susceptible to diverse or indeterminate outcomes; both regarded it as inescapably doomed by its own laws.

We may thus conclude that Marx's *Capital* was a study of the origins and functioning of capitalism in Western Europe, mostly based on analysis of examples from one case, that of England, where the condition taken to be essential to its emergence was a primitive accumulation of capital, the expropriation of the peasantry, and, more generally, the expropriation of the means of production from artisans and working people. Marx denies, in the texts cited above, that this model of capitalism's origin applies universally; he denies that capitalism *must* arise outside of Western Europe or that all countries must become capitalist. Marx thus allows for a multilinear evolution. For that matter, so does Engels, if less emphatically. What works itself out "with an iron necessity," then, is not the rise of capitalism itself but the development of its contradictions and the doom they bring, *once capitalism has emerged with any maturity.* Although capitalism *need* not arise outside Western Europe, so far as Marx is concerned, he does *not* say that the laws of capitalism differ fundamentally in the different countries in which it exists or, should capitalism arise elsewhere, that its laws would differ. To the contrary, Marx insists that once having taken the capitalist road, Russia cannot escape the laws of capitalism.

Thus while the origins and rise of capitalism may vary and are not inevitable outside of Western Europe, the laws of capitalism's own functioning remain constant and inexorable for *capitalist societies, once created.* The crux of the matter is that in Marxism, "economic determinism" may have three distinct meanings, and it is only one of these on which Marx and Engels ever wavered. In Marxism, "economic determinism" is not ambiguous but triguous:

1. *Unilinear Evolutionism.* All societies are said to pass through the same sequence of stages, each of which is the inescapable result of the previous stage and the necessary requisite of the next. If Marx ever held this view, it is certainly the one he rejected. But there is no indication at all that he ever rejects either of two other forms of economic determinism: (a) synchronic universal determinism and (b) synchronic particularistic determinism.

2. *Particularistic Determinism.* These are the "pitiless" and inescapable laws of capitalism, and apply only to its historical lifespan; e.g., the increasing misery of the proletariat; the increasing centralization and concentration of capital; the increasing division of labor; the increasingly cooperative form of the labor process; the application of science to technology; the spread of the world market; the "steady intensification of the wrath of the working class . . . with the inexorability of a law of nature, capitalist production begets its own negation."[30]

3. *Universal Determinism.* This involves statements bearing on the universality of the determination of the (ideological and po-

litical) superstructure by the mode of production, i.e., the infrastructure. The nucleus of this is the direct relationship between owners and producers through which the latter's unpaid surplus labor is siphoned to the former. These statements are a *universal* determinism because they are meant to apply to *any* class-exploitative system anywhere, whether or not capitalist. Marx thus writes in the third volume of *Capital* (pp. 770 et seq.): "the specific economic form, in which unpaid surplus labour is pumped out of direct producers, *determines* the relationship of rulers and ruled, as it grows out of production and, in turn, reacts upon it as a *determining* element. Upon this, however, is founded the entire formation of the economic community which grows out of the production relations themselves. . . . It is always the direct relationship of the owners of the conditions of production to the direct producers—a relation always naturally corresponding to a definite stage in the development of the methods of labor and thereby its social productivity—which reveals the innermost secret, the hidden basis, of the entire social structure, and with it the political form of the relation of sovereignty and dependence, in short, the corresponding forms of the State" (My italics).

The universal determinism frequently found in the pages of the *Communist Manifesto* is at the center of Engels's attention when he formulates what he takes to be its "fundamental proposition," its very "nucleus": "in every historical epoch, the prevailing mode of economic production and exchange, and the social organization necessarily following from it, form the basis upon which is built up, and from which alone can be explained, the political and intellectual history of that epoch; that consequently the whole history of mankind (since the dissolution of primitive tribal society, holding land in common ownership) has been the history of class struggles, contests between the exploiting and exploited, ruling and ruled classes; the history of these class struggles forms a series of evolution in which, now-a-days, a stage has been reached where the exploited and oppressed class—the proletariat—cannot attain its emancipation from the sway of the exploiting and ruling class—the bourgeoisie—without at the same time, and once for all, emancipating society at large from all exploitations, class distinctions and class struggles."[31] Engels added that "this proposition is destined to do for history what Darwin's theory has done for biology."

Clearly, then, there were a set of assumptions concerning the dominance of the mode of production for other spheres of society that were *not* meant to apply to capitalism alone. On the contrary,

this universal determinism provides the "covering laws" of which
the laws of capitalism are special cases, and on which they rest. It
is just this universal determinism that came to be called "historical materialism." And it is precisely because they apply to all
class-exploitative societies that even such a friendly and meticulous interpretation of Marxism as that offered by Irving Zeitlin[32]
and Victor Perez-Diaz[33] should feel free, simply in passing, to
characterize it as an "economic determinism."

It is clear that while Marx and Engels issued an easement on
economic determinism *as a unilinear evolutionism,* they never
went all the way. They never relinquished the two synchronic
forms of economic determinism—particular and universal determinism. Moreover, Marx and Engels released themselves from
unilinear evolutionism only by assuming the Russian Revolution
to have a surrogate industrial base in central Europe to compensate for its own lack of one. And even as they take leave of unilinear evolutionism, and from its implication that capitalism was
inevitable everywhere, it is notable that they are not equally emphatic in proclaiming that *socialism could be achieved without a
prior experience with capitalism.* (One can see in this ambiguity
the doctrinal sources of Menshevism, which tended to continue to
emphasize that the bourgeois revolution had to precede the
socialist. Correspondingly, one can also see here some of the doctrinal sources of Trotsky's emphasis on permanent revolution with
its insistence on the importance of central European aid for the
Russian Revolution.) Marx and Engels seem much readier to deny
the inevitability of capitalism, but much more reluctant to come
right out and say that capitalism is *dispensable for socialism.* They
do a good bit of "waffling" and glossing concerning the latter. For
if socialism could be achieved without a prior passage through
capitalism, why stop there? Why could not socialism also be
achieved without a society's prior experience of feudalism or
slavery? Indeed, this was precisely the problem Engels had anticipated in answering Tkaschev that, by the latter's own reasoning, the best basis for socialism was an already classless tribal
society.

In denying capitalism was inevitable, Marx and Engels had
opened up the possibility of a socialism without a prior capitalism,
or had hedged about this; they thereby began to blur the entire
question of the requisites of socialism, whether anything at all
was necessary for achieving socialism—and, if so, what? *The pressure from the revolution in Russia had resulted in Marx and*

Engels unlocking—but not actually opening—the door to a fully voluntaristic and Critical Marxism that might turn its back on the severe structural requirements of their own Scientific Marxism. Opening that now unlocked door, however, remained the historical task of Lenin. And as the possibility arose genielike from the theoretical pressure that any society might at any time opt for socialism, as the requisites for socialism grew suddenly ambiguous, so, also, did the *very nature of socialism itself.* If we have no picture of the parents, we cannot say what the child will be. Socialism's own nature might, therefore, be as multiform as the conditions which might produce it.

Engels: Defining a Paradigm for Marxism

There was, as mentioned earlier, a second set of critical texts, often cited but rarely appreciated. They are all written by Engels and are cited most commonly for "public relations" purposes, i.e., to soften Marxism's image as an economic determinism. If the discussion around the question of the Russian Revolution had released Marxism from determinism as unilinear evolutionism, Engels's later letters can be regarded as an attempt to do something similar *at the level of synchronic universal determinism.* Although Engels does not succeed, it is evident that he was converging on this.

Yet something considerably more important was also afoot in these last letters, which, be it noted, correspond in time to Engels's capsule summary of the *Manifesto's* "fundamental proposition" in its 1888 edition. The really important thing about them is that they exhibit Engels in the very process of explicating Marxism's *paradigm;* they indicate the specific sociological conditions which led to this effort; and, most importantly, they reveal quite clearly the *level* at which he pitched the paradigm. In particular, these letters make it plain that, analytically, Engels chose to center Marxism's paradigm not at the level of either unilinear determinism or synchronic particularistic determinism (capitalism), but at the level of synchronic universal determinism (historical materialism). Thus in Engels's paradigm for Marxism, historical materialism becomes more central, while evolutionism and capitalism's special political economy become less so. In short, the most consequential commitments were made.

Engels's texts to follow are all characterized by much the same features: (1) They are all written by Engels after Marx's death in

1883, as Engels in his loneliness faces his own mortality and gives thought to the image that posterity will have of his work with Marx. These are the letters of a man setting his house in order. They are methodologically reflective efforts at remedying defects, dissociating the Marxist legacy from friendly but vulgar interpretations, sharpening its argument, and, above all, attempting to reduce the dissonance within it without departing from the theory's main commitments. In short, Engels is exhibiting that "imperishable" human motive, namely, trying to gloss over contradictions in the system. Engels never pretended to be god.

(2) These texts uniformly indicate that Marxism is to be understood as a general theory of social *systems* the latter being characterized expressly in terms of the reciprocal influence of different elements of the system upon one another. The formulations of earlier texts, such as their *German Ideology* and *The Communist Manifesto*, had often featured *one*-way connections stressing that social being determines social consciousness or that material conditions determine ideologies. They had not *systematically* emphasized the reciprocal impact of consciousness on "social being" or of ideas on material conditions. These one-way formulations are now replaced by Engels's *systematic* focus on the *two*-way, mutual influence of different social regions on one another.

(3) This interaction effect, however, is invariably qualified by assertions that, in the long run or in the final instance, the economic infrastructure determines all the others, despite the fact that these other superstructural elements react back upon the economic infrastructure.

(4) We are, however, never told how to determine *when* the "final instance" or "the long run" has arrived. One implication is that the insertion of the focus on system interaction is a gloss rationalizing, but not basically changing, the priority formerly given to the economic infrastructure. In this interpretation, Engels leans toward an intransigent "economism." In another interpretation, however, it is precisely because there is no way of knowing when the final instance has arrived in which the economic infrastructure has its last word, that the final instance is an analytic millennium which, hallowed in ritual mention, can now be forgotten in daily theoretical practice. Analysis is thenceforward devoted to the concrete study of the mutual influence of all system elements, and the economic element would simply become a heuristic entering point, resolving the question of where one begins to deal with a system of interacting elements. In this

view, Engels is surreptitiously surrendering economism. What, then, was Engels doing—protecting the priority of the economic, limiting, or undermining it? The systems interaction paradigm Engels crystallized was ambiguous, a symptom of a conflict Engels was striving to contain. Scientific Marxism would interpret this paradigm as asserting the power of the economic in the last instance; Critical Marxism could view it as allowing a new weight to the superstructure and, via its stress on "interaction," as a step toward an emphasis on the "totality." Engels's paradigm thus opened the way for both Scientific *and* Critical Marxism's development.

A few examples from this second set of Engels texts may suffice. In his letter to Conrad Schmidt of 5 August 1890, Engels reminds Schmidt that "the materialist conception of history . . . has a lot of friends to whom it serves as an excuse for *not* studying history. Just as Marx used to say with regard to the French 'Marxists' of the late seventies: 'All I know is that I am not a Marxist.' " Unfortunately, Engels then promptly drops that terribly interesting if now too familiar phrase, treating it as a *bon mot,* rather than as an occasion for serious reflection. Yet how is it possible that a theory comes to be vulgarized in this manner by its very devotees—is it simply because the epigones are lazy? Unless we can develop a serious answer to this I do not think that we can even begin to know what a theory is.

Engels continues in this mood of methodological alertness, unhappy in particular with "many of the younger writers in Germany" to whom the word "materialistic" serves as a mere phrase, as a label to be pasted on their views, and a substitute for further study. "But our conception of history," insists Engels, "is above all a guide to study, not a lever for construction after the manner of the Hegelians." Again, Engels makes it clear that his target is "many of the younger Germans [who] simply make use of the phrase, historical materialism . . . in order to get their own relatively scanty historical knowledge . . . fitted together into a neat system as quickly as possible, and they then think themselves something very tremendous."

Engels is here attempting to induce young German socialists to do serious historical research, to treat the Marxist intellectual legacy as a theory to be applied rather than to be canonized. In a word, Engels has a very good sense of what "normal science" is about, and what would be necessary to make Marxism a normal science. "Only a little has been done here up to now," he complains, "because only a few people have got down to it seriously." That the line between establishing a paradigm and canonizing it is a very fine one is discernible when Engels affirms that "in this field we can utilise masses of help." In other words, what is needed are people willing to work *within* the paradigm and "apply" it, rather than reexamine it critically in its fundamentals. But this is still not the sacralising sentiment of the canonizer; it is only the politics of any scientific innovator who wants to mobilize students to flesh out his rough outline; it is still normal science, or Engels's *effort* to normalize Marxism as science. There is as yet nothing inherently dogmatic about it—seen from the standpoint of normal science. On the contrary, Engels's remarks are cheerfully antidogmatic and disdainful of those who want to build a "neat system" on the cheap. Anyone who works seriously, he promises the young men, can "distinguish himself." There are, then, intellectual careers to be made here; this is always the promise of the paradigm-builder. Engels's antidogmatic insistence on serious scholarship and his skepticism about system always had the danger of fostering a "revisionism" and an Eduard Bernstein— whose mentor Engels was.

In his letter to Schmidt, Engels also comments on their basic intellectual paradigm, "historical materialism," observing that "the conditions of existence of the different formations of society must be individually examined before the attempt is made to deduce from them the political, civil-legal, aesthetic, philosophic, religious, etc., notions corresponding to them." The "conditions of existence" and "formations" are certainly vague enough, but this is a letter to a friend who will understand. Yet there is no sign here of Engels the vulgarizer who presumably reduces everything to technology. Indeed, a few sentences earlier, he had had a chance for that when he stated that how products get divided in society "depends on *how much* there is to divide, and this must surely change with the progress of production and social organization, so that the method of division may also change." In other words, how things get divided, according to Engels, depends on how much there is to divide and the kind of "social organization" there is— not just the technology. Yet while Engels does not appear to be as technologically obsessed as some critics suggest, there is no doubt that he operates within the basic paradigm in which consciousness is to be deduced from (because dependent on) the "conditions of existence."

Engels accepts this; his point is that before you can make such a deduction from the material conditions you must first study and know them. The paradigm still requires an encounter with the concrete history of different social worlds, rather than textual examination and reexaminations of Marx's writings. This, however, is part of what earns Engels the stigma of "positivist"; but those condemning him as such miss the manner in which Engels was attempting to use historical scholarship as a defense against the reification and canonization of Marxism. If this was "positivism," clearly Marxism needed more of it. Moreover, Engels is also at pains to reject dustbowl empiricism, insisting as (in a letter to Schmidt on 17 October 1889) that "only a clear theoretical vision can guide the way through the labyrinth of facts."[34]

Then, there is Engels's much cited letter of 21 September 1890[35] to J. Bloch, in which he holds that "according to the materialist conception of history the determining element (moment) in history is *ultimately* production and reproduction in real life. More than this neither Marx nor I have ever asserted." Above all, this does *not* mean that "the economic element is the *only* determining one." For while "the economic situation is the basis . . . the various elements of the superstructure—political forms of the class struggle and its consequences, constitutions established by the victorious class after a successful battle, etc.,—forms of law— and then even the reflexes of all these actual struggles in the brains of the combatants: political, legal, philosophical theories, religious ideas and their further development into systems of dogma—also exercise their influence upon the course of historical struggles and in many cases preponderate in determining their *form*. There is an endless interaction of all these elements, in which, amid all the endless *host* of accidents . . . the economic movement finally asserts itself as necessary. . . . We make our own history, but in the first place under very definite presuppositions and conditions. Among these the economic ones are finally decisive. But the political, etc., ones, and indeed even the traditions which haunt human minds, also play a part, although not the decisive one."

Clearly, what is being crystallized in this letter is an emphasis on the interaction of all elements within a framework in which the economic remains finally decisive. The latter underscores an essential aspect of the paradigm, and reference to it here is not merely ritualistic. Yet Engels acknowledges his and Marx's overemphasis on the economic which, he says, "we had to emphasize . . . in opposition to our adversaries, who denied it, and we had not always the time, the place or the opportunity to allow the other elements involved in the interaction to come into their rights." The effort here, then, is to underscore the weight of the *other* elements, to defend Marxism from the appearance of being a single factor theory by bringing into focus elements in the superstructure, and by stressing that the relationship among these several different elements was that of "interaction." It is this that is most salient in this letter, not that the economic elements "are finally decisive."

Once again, Engels expresses the sense that somehow things have gone wrong with "the younger writers." Clearly, there was emerging a *generation* problem in the transmission of Marxist theory. The young generation was somehow vulgarizing Marxism, and Engels was using his last letters to set matters straight. He saw the legacy in peril and thought the peril came from young writers and intellectuals who "think they have fully understood a theory and can apply it without more ado from the moment they have mastered its main principles, and those even not always correctly."

Yet it seems odd. Why shouldn't a theory be "fully understood" and successfully applied by those who have "mastered its main principles"? How else does one master a theory; what else is necessary for theoretical mastery? Above all, Engels seems to be saying that a theory cannot be mastered simply by studying the texts in which it is embodied but has to be applied in fresh efforts at understanding new materials. But how could such efforts actually deepen one's understanding of the *theory*, enable one to master it, since after all, the facts—as we saw Engels remarking earlier—are to be viewed from the standpoint of theory, not the theory from the standpoint of the facts? There seems to be an unresolved problem here that is not so much due to the younger generation's intellectual laziness or presumptuousness, but is linked to what a theory is. When we later return to this problem we shall see that, if a theory is to be thought "mastered," it must be *used* in the same way as those judging the persons employing it, rather than by simply reciting it. Thus the problem becomes, Why is the younger generation not using the theory in the same way as Engels (or the older generation) used it, or thought they used it? But we must table this for later exploration.

In another letter of 27 October 1890 to Conrad Schmidt, Engels once more takes up the theme of the relative independence of various social sectors noting that "in the last instance production is the decisive factor. But when trade in products becomes independent of production itself, it follows a movement of its own, which, while it is governed as a whole by production . . . within this general dependence follows particular laws contained in the nature of this new factor." In that connection, Engels notes that conquest of India was first occasioned by the desire for imports, yet there was soon a colossal reaction of the import trades upon industry; "they first created the need for *exports* to these countries and developed large-scale industry." Like Marx, Engels concurred that industry was spurred by commerce, and that the industrial revolution was preceded by a commercial expansion.

Further pursuing the theme of the relative independence of various social sectors, Engels observed that while the state grows out of society the state administration soon acquires "particular interests, distinct . . . from the interests of those who gave them their office; they make themselves independent of the latter and—the state is in being." There is a resultant "interaction of two unequal forces" that is, between the new economic movement and the new political power in "which each strives for as much independence as possible. . . . On the whole, the economic movement gets its way, but it has also to suffer reactions from the political movement."

And again, Engels speaks of "realms of ideology" such as belief in magic and spirits which have a "negative economic basis," as being grounded in "the low economic development of the prehistoric period"; in turn, the low economic development of that period is "also partially conditioned and even caused by the false conceptions of nature." The emergence of science is gradually "clearing away this nonsense" when it is not replacing it with new nonsense "already less absurd." "The people who deal with this belong in their turn to special spheres in the division of labour and appear to themselves to be working in an independent field. And insofar as they form an independent group within the social division of labour, insofar do their productions, including their errors, react back as an influence upon the whole development of society, even on its economic development. But all the same they themselves remain under the dominating influence of economic development."

Again and again: each sector has a measure of independence, yet it is also in interaction with the others, affecting and shaping their development and even the development of the economic infrastructure which remains the dominant sphere. Moreover, there is no uncritical admiration of science which, as Engels observes, sometimes replaces the old nonsense with its own fresh nonsense and is, on the whole, subordinate to the mode of production. Science is the new historically progressive force, but is scarcely the last word in enlightenment. In all this, Engels repeatedly calls attention to Marx's *Eighteenth Brumaire* which (he indicates) exemplifies the proper application of historical materialism, adding curiously that "there are also many allusions in *Capital*."[36]

In his letter of 25 January 1894[37] to Starkenberg, Engels writes that "the economic conditions which we regard as the determining basis of the history of society are the methods by which human beings in a given society produce their means of subsistence and exchange the products among themselves. . . . Thus the *entire technique* of production and transport is here included." Technique, therefore, is included in the determining economic conditions, but the latter are not at all here reduced to technology. Indeed, "under economic conditions are further included the geographical basis on which they operate." So, too, is race itself. Yet while "technique largely depends on the state of science, science depends far more still on the *state* and the *requirements* of technology . . . unfortunately, it has become the custom in Germany to write the history of the sciences as if they had fallen from the sky." Here again, Engels reiterates that ideologies interact with one another and react back upon economic development, but "economic necessity" ultimately asserts itself. Again, Starkenberg is directed to read Marx's *Eighteenth Brumaire* and Engels's own *Anti-Dühring*.

How are we to understand the direction Engels has taken here in these last letters? And what do they and the other texts tell us about the "differences" between Engels and Marx?

NOTES

1. Norman Levine, *The Tragic Deception: Marx contra Engels* (Santa Barbara: Clio Books, 1975), p. 104.

2. Richard J. Bernstein, *Praxis and Action: Contemporary Philosophies of Human Activity* (Philadelphia: University of Pennsylvania Press, 1971), p. 58. This somewhat glowing interpretation of Marxism glosses its internal contradictions and reduces it to a philosophy of

praxis, therby implying that the generations of Marxists, who had viewed it as a scientific socialism, were altogether mistaken. Despite this lopsidedness, in which no textual evidence is offered to justify Bernstein's views, it is refreshingly lucid and of considerable originality. Even more original is his *The Structuring of Social and Political Theory* (London: Basil Blackwell, 1976).

3. Bernstein, *Praxis and Action,* p. 64.

4. Melvin Rader, *Marx's Interpretation of History* (New York: Oxford University Press, 1979). Rader quotes from the Charles Kerr edition of 1904, pp. 11–12, while the last sentence quoted is Rader's own rendition on his p. 15.

5. Moreover, the question is not so much what *bedingt* means today, but how it was used in Marx's own time by educated Germans. The Grimms' dictionary gives us some indication of this (see Jacob Grimm and Wilhelm Grimm, *Deutsches Wörterbuch* [Leipzig: Herzel, 1854]). Although Rader holds that Marx would have used *bestimmt* had he wished to say the mode of production "determines" rather than "conditions" the superstructure, the Grimms, however, note that *bestimmen* was then a synonym for *bedingen*. Moreover, they also note that *bedingt* is grounded in *causa*. Finally, *bedingt* is built upon *ding* which means thing. This suggests that when Marx used *bedingt*, he was implying a mode of influence appropriate to inanimate objects, to produced objects rather than to the actions of persons, or at least likening the doing and action of persons to the making of objects, to which indeed *bedingt* refers. *Bedingt* thus seems to resonate the notion of an external causation imposed on things. It therefore implies strong not weak control over the object made, a binding rather than, say, an inducement. My colleague, Steven Schwarzschild, indicates that his own studies of Hegel's usage of *bestimmt* suggest that this often referred to the *Geist's* control over human affairs. *Bedingt,* then, would have a more mechanistic resonance, while *bestimmt* had a more organicist import, or what Louis Althusser has referred to as the "expressionist" model of Hegel's logic of causation. It may be that Marx's use of *bedingt* was not an effort to tone down determinism, but to avoid Hegel's form of expressionist determinism. *Bedingt* would also be more consistent with *Marx's* theory of alienation, for with its conflation of making and doing and its stress on the former, the sense is that man is now not treated as a proper human "subject" but is controlled as if a thing—is thingified. Moreover, the more mechanistic resonance of *bedingt* would also seem to be more consistent (than *bestimmt*) with Marx's growing convergence with the mechanistic logic of nineteenth-century science's determinism.

6. Karl Marx, *The Poverty of Philosophy* (New York: International Publishers, n.d.), p. 92.

7. Levine, *Tragic Deception,* p. xvii.

8. Much is sometimes made of the fact that Marx once briefly men-

·tioned that one conceivable outcome of the class struggle is that both parties could be ruined; and once Marx said, in passing, that the choice was "socialism or barbarism." These, I take it, are simply different (negative) forms in which the doom of capitalism may come, but not forms in which that doom is escaped. And both are fugitive remarks, not considered and developed statements.

9. Karl Marx and Frederick Engels, *Selected Correspondence, 1846–1895*, trans. Dona Torr (New York: International Publishers, 1942), p. 519.

10. Jonathan Frankel, ed., *Valdimir Akhimov on the Dilemmas of Russian Marxism, 1895–1903* (London & New York: Cambridge University Press, 1969), p. 7.

11. Robert C. Tucker, ed., *The Marx-Engels Reader* (New York: W. W. Norton & Co., 1972), cited by Engels on p. 589.

12. On this see the excellent discussion by Shlomo Avineri, *The Social and Political Thought of Karl Marx* (London and New York: Cambridge University Press, 1968), chapter 6, "The Revolutionary Dialectics of Capitalist Society."

13. Tucker, *Marx-Engels Reader*, p. 590. Engels's reply to Tkaschev was written in 1874 and published as a separate pamphlet in 1875.

14. Ibid., pp. 589–90.

15. Ibid., pp. 599, 592.

16. Ibid., p. 597.

17. Ibid.

18. Frankel, *Vladimir Akhimov*, p. 8.

19. Marx and Engels, *Selected Correspondence*, p. 352. Actually, this formulation is that of N. K. Mickhailovski, the populist to whom he was replying, but Marx adheres here to that problematic. Only five years earlier, Marx had ridiculed Bakunin for expecting "the European social revolution . . . at the level of the Russian or Slavic agricultural or pastoral people."

20. Ibid., p. 352. Marx wrote this letter in French.

21. Ibid., p. 353.

22. Ibid.

23. Ibid.

24. Ibid., pp. 353–54. Italics added.

25. Ibid., p. 354.

26. Ibid.

27. Ibid., p. 355. Dona Torr's translation strangely reads ". . . starting point of an historical development," but David McLellan and Dirk J. Struik also use the wording I follow here. See *Birth of the Communist Manifesto*, ed. D. J. Struik (New York: International Publishers, 1975), p. 132. The German reads: ". . . dann kann das heutige russische Gemeineigentum zum Ausgangspunk einer kommunistischen Entwicklung dienen." Karl Marx and Friedrich Engels, *Das Kommunis-*

tische Manifest, ed. Erich Gleischer (Munich: Verlage der SPO, 1946) p. 7.

28. Karl Marx, *Selected Writings,* ed. David McLellan (New York: Oxford University Press, 1977), p. 577.

29. See ibid., p. 436.

30. Karl Marx, *Capital: A Critique of Political Economy,* vol. I, translated from the 4th German ed. by Eden and Cedar Paul, published in 2 vols with an introduction by G. D. H. Cole (London and Toronto: J. M. Dent & Sons, 1930), vol. 2, p. 846.

31. *Communist Manifesto,* by Karl Marx and Friedrich Engels, authorized English edition of 1888, supervised by Engels, published by Charles H. Kerr, Chicago, pp. 7–8.

32. Irving M. Zeitlin, *Marxism: A Re-Examination* (New York: Van Nostrand Reinhold Co., 1967), p. 81. An intelligent Hegelian and an unaccountably neglected discussion whose serious scope is compressed into an economical and lucid formulation.

33. Victor M. Perez-Diaz, *State, Bureaucracy and Civil Society: A Critical Discussion of the Political Theory of Karl Marx* (London: Macmillan Publishers, 1978), p. 70. A sure-footed and sometimes brilliant contribution of great promise. Perez-Diaz may be in the process of creating a left functionalism.

34. Marx and Engels, *Selected Correspondence,* p. 475. The letter to Schmidt of 5 August 1890 precedes this.

35. Ibid.

36. Ibid., p. 477.

37. Ibid., p. 516.

9

ENGELS AGAINST MARX?
Marxism as Property

The caricature of Engels as the first revisionist and of his work as a *haute vulgarisation* of Marx is not new but began to emerge during and shortly after World War I. One finds it in Erwin Bans, "Engels als Theoretiker," in the issue of *Kommunismus*, 3 December 1920, a journal that Georg Lukács edited for a while after World War I. Even before, it may be found in Rudolfo Mondolfo's *Le Matérialisme Historique d'après F. Engels*, published in Paris in 1917.

The most competent contemporary source of that view is George Lichtheim's learned *Marxism*, which holds that "socialism, as understood by Engels and those who followed in his lead, was above all scientific. . . . Engels's later writings, especially *Socialism: Utopian and Scientific*, are a veritable compendium of the new positivist world-view. . . . Marx gradually came to adopt a standpoint which in some respects resembled the scientism of the age, but he never quite yielded to the temptation to recast his doctrine altogether in evolutionary-materialist terms; Engels had no such inhibition."[1]

Lichtheim does acknowledge, however, that Marx's own development was towards a Scientific Marxism: "The thinking of the mature Marx plainly discloses a growing emphasis upon the scientific study of processes independent of human volition and a corresponding stress upon the concept of 'historical necessity'. . . . Yet the subsequent drift towards positivism and scientism— accelerated after his death and formalized by Kautsky after Engels in his turn had left the scene (1895)—went far beyond anything he could have envisaged."[2] I concur with Lichtheim in the view— expressed earlier by Karl Korsch—that Engels "merely accentuated a tendency that was already present in Marx,"[3] but not with

Lichtheim's speculations about what Marx would have "envisaged." How can anyone know what Marx would have envisaged had he lived twelve years longer, as Engels did, after Marx's death in 1883. I agree entirely with Lichtheim that, first, Marx manifested an increasingly scientific, antivoluntarist position, and, second, that "Marx never relinquished his hold on the two horns of his peculiar dilemma."[4] Which means: he never resolved the contradiction.

To maintain anything more than that, however, makes Engels the scapegoat for Scientific Marxism; to differentiate him radically from Marx is, as I hope to show below, historically dubious and unjust. Given their different life spans; and given Marx's drift toward science,[5] if we extrapolate Marx, and pretend that he had another dozen years of life, i.e., if we draw a line representing his theoretical movement up to 1883 and extend it to 1895, can we be so sure that his reliance on science in 1895 would then have differed from Engels's? Marx's purity, one suspects, depended in part on his earlier death. The difference between Marx and Engels is a complex question, and we must reject all tendencies to replace a "vulgar Marxism" with a vulgar criticism of Engels.

Lichtheim complains that Engels's critique of Dühring was a "veritable compendium of the new positivist world view." But he also mentions, somewhat too quickly, that this was written "with some assistance from Marx." In truth, Engels's *Anti-Dühring*—perhaps the most comprehensive statement of their "system" ever written either by Marx or Engels—involved the close collaboration of the two friends. Marx, in fact, wrote part of one of the chapters and later endorsed the book for party publication. Engels's surrender to "positivism" was hardly done behind Marx's back. Never one to bite his tongue, Marx, we must conclude, countenanced these views. Why did he do so if he did not concur? The most reasonable assumption is that Marx shared Engels's drift toward "positivism" and Scientific Marxism, although, as we shall see, the matter is complex and to understand it we shall have to go beyond that obvious consideration.

Nevertheless, there has been a busy cottage industry of critics who make a scapegoat of Engels as the fount of the positivist heresy in Marxism—best epitomized by Sartre's wreckless reference to Marx's "destructive encounter with Engels."[6] In an interview with Lucio Colletti, the interviewer complains (and correctly) that Colletti tends "to counterpose Marx against Engels in an extremely radical way ... indeed, in one passage, you have gone so far as to speak of 'the gulf between the rigor and complexity which characterizes every page of Marx, and the popular vulgarization and at times dilettantism of the work of Engels'." The interviewer also correctly objects to the "supposed political contrast between the two men—an allegedly pro-reformist Engels set off against an unswervingly radical Marx. Engels, after all, never committed such involuntary blunders as Marx's prediction that the mere introduction of universal suffrage—bourgeois democracy—would ensure the advent of socialism in England, a far more parliamentarist statement than anything to be found in Engels."[7]

The imputation of a radical gulf between Marx and Engels, heedless of the differences in the periods in which they worked, and which fails to see Marx's own movement toward science, survives less because of its intellectual justification than because of the need it serves. What is at work here is the need to deal with the real contradiction within Marxism, its Januslike character as both a Scientific Marxism and Critical Marxism. The critique of Engels, however, seeks to resolve this by denying that there is a contradiction *within* Marxism, insinuating that the contradiction was *between* Marx and Engels, and that the rejected "positivist" side of Marxism was largely an alien heresy somehow smuggled in by Engels behind Marx's back.

The manufacturer's son, Engels, who enjoyed horses, good wine, attractive women, and all song, is not a congenial figure to revolutionary or academic ascetics. My own contrary judgement, however, is emphatically that of Trotsky: "Engels is undoubtedly one of the finest, best integrated and noblest of personalities in the gallery of great men . . . how consciously Engels endeavors to complement Marx: all his life is used up in this task. . . . Against the background of their everyday lives, Engels gains tremendously in stature."[8]

In contrast, the effort to cope with the contradiction in Marxism repeatedly takes the form of a "splitting" mechanism—splitting the young from the old Marx or, as here, splitting Marx from Engels. What splitting (in Anna Freud's sense) does is to *minimize* the similarities between any two objects, declaring them to be essentially two different things, and focusing on their differences. The splitting mechanism makes one thing into two, stresses the virtues of one, while emphasizing the defects of the other. In effect, the contradiction *within* one entity is thus resolved by reconstructing it as *two* entities: one, whose negative character is focalized; a second, whose positive character is stressed. This has the effect of reducing the dissonance of the single "gray" object where strengths and weaknesses are complexly intermingled, by substituting for it, one object, all white, and a second, all black. Ambivalences to the original object are resolved; persons can now whole-heartedly accept one of the objects and unambivalently reject the other. Splitting thus produces both uncritical hero worship and unworthy "scapegoating."

Efforts to resolve differences between Marx and Engels by thus splitting them rest on a most un-Marxist assumption: that Marxism simply cannot be internally contradictory, that there are no real contradictions *within* it, but only differences *between two persons*, Marx and Engels, the latter of whom is downgraded as the first "vulgar" Marxist and an oversimplifying "amateur" to boot.

The differences discernible between Marx's and Engels's work have been largely evaluated from the standpoint of philosophy, from which perspective the son of the cotton mill owner, who never won a college degree, is held to be naive and gauche. Engels's "corruption" of Marxism is tacitly seen as a "sin against philosophy," and it is philosophers rather than economists (or more generally, those in the social sciences) who condemn Engels as a vulgarizer. (One honorable exception is Louis Althusser who, on several occasions, speaks of Engels's theoretical "genius.")

Engels was an empirical genius, which is not the same thing as saying that he was a theory-less empiricist. Not one of the major works that Marx wrote was based on his own systematic, direct, firsthand observation, as was Engels's own early study of 1844 of *The Condition of the Working Class in England*. (Indeed, so far as I know, Marx never set foot in a factory, mine, mill, or shipyard, either as worker or observer.) It was *not* Engels's capacity to write clearly and forcefully (which detractors hold up to contempt as journalistic "popularization") that was his contribution to Marxism, but, rather, his *firsthand* studies of capitalism and urbanism, undertaken *from both sides of the class divide*.

As a student of the new industrial proletariat in Manchester, Engels haunted their streets, drank in their pubs, read their press, talked with their leaders, and came to know them intimately in a way that Marx never did. Indeed, Engels's lover, Mary Burns, was an Irish working-class revolutionary who could not be admitted to the Marx home lest it offend Marx's wife, daughter of the Baron von Westphalen. Engels's personal involvement in his father's cotton-milling business on the Continent and in England, and the connections these opened up, brought him a close acquaintance with the commercial and industrial vanguard of capitalism—an acquaintance Marx never had except through his friendship with Engels. Engels's business involvements thus also acquainted him with life on the other side of the class divide, and both experiences provided intellectual sustenance to the emerging Marxism. Indeed, it was Engels who first placed England and its advanced capitalism at the center of Marxism. It was also Engels's early article, "Outline of a Critique of Political Economy," says Harold Draper, that "was at least one of the important influences, if not the most important one, that turned Marx to the study of political economy."[9]

Engels's field work for his *Conditions of the Working Class in England*, as well as his firsthand business experience, centered his attention on technology, the new technology (and not simply on subsistence-getting activity in general), and on the *ambiguities* of that technology; he viewed it as a new source for the relief of ancient scarcity and, also, as the present but historically transient source of misery among the working class. Engels saw how new fortunes were being made in Manchester and how, at the same time, a new misery was also being mass produced—observations relevant to Marx's subsequent theorizing about the increasing misery of the working class. And it is the young Engels who begins to see the working class as more than a passive object of philanthropy in the manner of the Saint-Simonians, but as an aggressive historical agent with their own power and initiative: "From them will come England's salvation." (Indeed, in the *Condition of the Working Class*, Engels portrayed communism as mitigating the violence of the coming proletarian class struggle.)

Engels also took note of the ramifying effects of the industrial revolution: the spread of social and cultural debris hurtful to workers, such as child labor, disease, slum overcrowding, disrupted families, drunkenness, sexual distortions. Engels's vision of the technological disruption of social life and its resultant human misery is also seen in its association with commerce; on the one side, facilitating the spread of commerce and, on the other, spurred by commercial motives. Engels clearly saw technology, then, in its association with bourgeois commerce.

Engels noted that the industrial revolution's hurtful consequences were hidden, spontaneously and unconsciously, by the bourgeoisie. Speaking of the street layout of Manchester that hides the slums, Engels had remarked in the *Condition*, "I cannot help feeling that the liberal industrialists . . . are not altogether innocent of this bashful style of building." In effect, Engels began developing a notion of the *limits* of bourgeois rationality; the bourgeoisie is seen as concealing the one-sided distribution of gains to itself and of costs of the working class. He is here thus working toward the Marxist notion of ideology.

"While I was in Manchester," reminisced Engels, "it was tangibly brought home to me that the economic facts . . . are, at least in the modern world, a decisive historical force; that they form the basis of the origination of the present-day class antagonisms; that these class antagonisms, in the countries where they have become fully developed . . . are in their turn the basis of the formation of political parties and political struggles, and thus of all political history."[10] Engels thus saw his own Manchester experience as an independent grounding of historical materialism or as an origin of what he calls, in his preface to the 1888 English translation of *The Communist Manifesto*, its "fundamental proposition." In the latter, however, it is not his own Manchester experience, but Marx, whom Engels credits with the idea. Is this modesty or reality? Is it Marx who puts Engels's Manchester experience into words; or is it Engels who provides him, vicariously, with the decisive experiences which Marx distilled theoretically? The evidence of the *Condition of the Working Class in England* strongly suggests that Engels had, at the least, taken his own convergent path to historical materialism. And Marx himself says exactly that, in his *A Contribution to the Critique of Political Economy:* "Friedrich Engels . . . arrived by another road . . . at the same result as I."

Engels, the avid participant observer and roving ethnographer of capitalism, suspected the philosopher's proclivity to erect his ideas as a system. Systems, he says, are the rationalist's false consciousness; they are born because men are continually driven to achieve fictitious consistencies by hiding contradictions. He thus begins his *Anti-Dühring* by lampooning German academicians because "the most insignificant doctor of philosophy and even the student will not go in for anything less than a complete 'system'."

If Engels's Marxism was less philosophically sophisticated, it was the work of a man who had been close to the things he was talking about; it was a critique of capitalism that was achieved by someone who had actually known at first hand *both* workers and capitalists; it was the product of an observer whose suspicions of "system" were in healthy tension with the system he helped to complete.

Unilinear and Multilinear Evolutionism
in Marx and Engels

For Norman Levine, Engels, unlike Marx, "believed in necessitarian stages of development: history moved from the lower to the higher. Capitalism, for Engels, represented the highest stage of productive capacity yet attained by man. . . . If historical laws had any validity, and they did according to Engels, Russia must follow the path of western Europe . . . from primitive society to capitalist society, and the *mir* must be destroyed. Consequently, the revolution that was immanent in Russia was not the proletarian revolution. Rather, it was the bourgeois revolution."[11]

First of all, it must be noted that Levine cites nothing in this discussion about Engels that would in the least justify the conclusions he recites. Levine does, however, earlier[12] cite Engels's polemic against Tkaschev in which he held that a bourgeoisie was as much a necessary condition for a socialist revolution as a proletariat. This, however, bore on only a limited problem and is a very slender basis for Levine's larger and very general conclusion that, while Marx was a multilinear evolutionist, Engels was a unilinear determinist. The former has been clear, at least since the availability of Marx's *Grundrisse* in which he indicated that the oriental path of village development was a very different basis for evolution than the Graeco-Roman city, and hence that Western development was historically unique, rather than a universal template. Nonetheless, there is no evidence that Engels disagreed with Marx's views about Asiatic development or, for that matter, that they had substantial differences about the possibility of skipping stages in Russia. Both found this difficult to come to a conclusion about; but both came to it after much soul-searching.

In Engels's reply to Tkaschev, it must also be remembered that Engels was most vehement in rejecting the latter's views when they are given a *general* formula, namely, when Tkaschev held that the struggle against a developed capitalism is less promising than struggle against an embryo capitalism. There is no doubt that this defied the general position both he and Marx had long held: that development of capitalism would bring a mature proletariat into a society whose contradictions were most intense and is thus the most favorable context to produce a socialism. If Tkaschev was trying to find a way for Russian socialists to keep up their courage, rather than waiting passively for capitalism to come, Engels was, for his part, attempting to defend Western socialism from seeming to face an impregnable foe. In short, Engels's position here, first, reaffirmed the main position he had shared with Marx; second, it was, at its most vehement, a critique to Tkaschev's own different general formula which had accented the advantages of industrial "backwardness"; and, third, it was in important part as much motivated by concrete political considerations as by any metaphysical propensity, of which Levine repeatedly accuses him.

As shown earlier, however, Engels's reply to Tkaschev had considered it possible for the *mir* to take on a new lease on life and might allow Russian peasants to skip "the intermediary form of bourgeois small-holdings." This could happen, said Engels, if before the *mir's* complete dissolution there was a successful workers' revolution in Western Europe which provided the surrogate material basis that Russia's native economic development lacked. According to Engels, then, a proletarian revolution in Western Europe might well give the *mir* "a chance of growing into a new, really viable form." Rather than dogmatically insisting on a deterministic unilinear evolution, Engels exhibited openness toward possible social novelty, while, at the same time, attempting to accommodate (i.e., normalize) this novelty to the essential Marxist paradigm with his inventive idea of a surrogate material basis in the West for a Russian Revolution, an idea that Marx would later endorse in their joint preface to the 1882 edition of the Russian translation of the *Communist Manifesto.*

In addition to the discussion of the Russian *mir,* as the second basis on which Marx's multilinear evolutionism is usually affirmed, there is his discussion in the *Grundrisse* of the Asiatic mode of production.[13] Supposedly, this not only documents Marx's multilinearity but also tacitly demonstrates Engels's vulgarizing unilinearity which presumably ignored this. In this vein, Levine notes that the initial sign that Marx was reading Asian history were his notebooks of 1853, with excerpts from his readings on Indian history, and that by the time he started the *Grundrisse* in 1857, he had conceived the Asiatic form of communal society. "In this socioeconomic totality," writes Levine, "the Oriental despot was the sole proprietor of the land . . . the village was powerless and propertyless, because the land belonged to the despot who formed therein an all-embracing unity. The specific manner in which the Asiatic despot exercised his social control . . . was through his maintenance of public works. Village communities in arid regions needed water to carry on their agriculture, and the Asiatic lord had as his primary social duty the construction and preservation of irrigation canals."[14]

Levine tells us[15] that, on this question, Engels "was in basic agreement with Marx." Levine typically formulates the matter in a distorted way in stating that *Engels had agreed with Marx* on the Asiatic mode of production. This is significantly inexact because it implies that Engels's views were dependent on Marx's. As I shall later show, Marx's "own" views were actually derived from political economists (not to say, Hegel), such as R. Jones, and from Engels's own original ideas. On 6 June 1853 Engels had written the following to Marx from Manchester, which *accounted* for the absence of private property under oriental despotism:

> The absence of property in land is indeed the key to the whole of the East. Here lies its political and religious history. But how does it come about that the Orientals do not arrive at landed property, even in feudal form? I think it is mainly due to the climate, together with the nature of the soil, especially with the great stretches of desert which extend from the Sahara straight across Arabia, Persia, India, and Tartary up to the highest Asiatic plateau. Artificial irrigation is here the first condition of agriculture and this is a matter either for the communes, the provinces, or the central government.[16]

Thus Engels did not "agree with Marx." Rather, and at the very least, they agreed with one another; and Engels undoubtedly had priority in explaining the origins of the unique propertyless character of oriental society. Moreover, and I shall return to this much mooted point shortly, Marx *followed Engels* in attributing importance to the climate and to irrigation technologies.[17]

Too much has been made to rest on Marx's yeasty notes concerning primitive communal forms, often without acknowledging the defective brevity of these seminal remarks which, be it remembered, Marx himself never sought to and never did publish. Their essential contents are to be found in nine printed pages, from page 471 to 479 in a volume of almost 900 printed pages. Of these, Martin Nicolaus, their admiring translator notes, "In 1858 not a single person in the world understood the *Grundrisse* except Marx, and even he had his troubles with it."[18] (Now, of course, everyone understands with complete confidence that they "overthrow the myth that Marx had a rigid historical theory of economic development.") Martin Nicolaus also speaks of "the unfinished quality of the manuscript . . . we have here a *rough draft* . . . [with]

missing elements of grammar, of difficult, sometimes awkward, obscure and even altogether inaccurate formulations, endless sentences and paragraphs, irritating digressions and reiterations, etc. It is a text which proclaims on nearly every page its unripeness for print."[19]

I believe that these nine pages do indeed justify considerable doubt about viewing Marx, *at that period and after,* as a unilinear determinist, although I do not believe they demonstrate that he was not a unilinear determinist *earlier,* in the late forties. These pages also brilliantly hint at the kind of comparative historical scholarship required to document their views, a scholarship to which Max Weber, rather than any proper Marxist, is probably the legitimate heir. On the evidence in hand, not much more can be said. Certainly, it does not in the least justify the *ad hominem* attacks on Engels's supposed intellectual inferiority or contempt for him as a "metaphysical determinist." For the most part, those who have handed in the verdict against Engels have not been a jury of his peers.

One of the less important conclusions which I believe that the discussion above supports is this: the contrast between Engels and Marx, aside from being greatly overstated, is so compulsively invidious and flagrantly tendentious as to suggest that it is grounded in some driving need. The passion for differentiating and degrading Engels is sometimes so powerful that it drives those overcome by it to the plainest internal contradictions, leading them to gloss over the slim textual grounding of their argument, and to a procedure in which it is tacitly assumed that *any* difference between Engels's formulations and Marx's is *prima facie* evidence of the *inferiority* of Engels's text. It never seems to occur to a critic like Norman Levine that some differences may be to Engels's credit, rather than evidence of his vulgarizing corruption of Hegel and Marx, of which Levine accuses him. What is worse, irresponsible comparisons between Engels and Marx have the effect of discrediting even serious efforts to understand such differences as do exist between the two and, also, what these might *mean*—other, that is, than as "evidence" for Marx's superiority. In this eristic, the substantive issues themselves lose value and became mere efforts at public relations, to canonize Marx and protect him from a semblance of the slightest flaw, even if at the cost of abusing his lifetime friend.

Not only is almost any difference exaggerated but—as I have shown in Levine's discussion of Asiatic society—even where there are *no* real differences, even where the two *agree*, this is presented as if it were evidence of Engels's inferiority, of the capitulation of (what is expressly called) his second-rate mind to Marx's genius; we are then told that *Engels agreed with Marx*. Thus where *some* difference in texts is found, it is treated as proof of Engels's vulgarization of Marx and as ipso facto evidence that Engels's views were inferior to his; where *no* difference in texts is found, this is presented as evidence of the fitting subordination of the lesser to the greater mind.

That even the absence of differences is used against Engels may be seen once more in Levine's discussion of Engels's political views on the alliance between the peasantry and the proletariat—a matter of far greater moment, of course, than the use to which is is put here. Levine notes that, in the 1870 edition of *The Peasant War in Germany,* Engels had called for a worker-peasant alliance, since an urban insurrection without it seemed doomed. "A worker-peasant alliance was the correct formula," we are assured by Levine, but the trouble was that "Engels then espoused a policy that made a worker-peasant alliance an impossibility. Land nationalization remained an uncompromisable principle in Engels's socialist platform . . . [consequently] Engels remained the prisoner of the proletarian, urban model of class struggle."[20]

The trouble is that Levine seems to have forgotten that he had discussed the same matter earlier, in connection with Marx who, he tells us, "was willing to accept a proletarian-peasant alliance, where one was possible, as a justifiable revolutionary strategy." But adds Levine, this "is not to say that Marx ever surrendered his belief that the land must be nationalized. Land nationalization remained throughout his life an unshakeable tenet of communism."[21] Now this is a matter of great historical import, and it is regrettable that we must temporarily confine ourselves only to the small implication which shows us that there *was no* difference here between Engels and Marx. Levine uses Marx's espousal of a worker-peasant alliance to prove that he did not view the peasantry as conservative and passive, thus evidencing his revolutionary flexibility. Yet when Engels faithfully adheres to Marx's policy, Levine argues that this shows that *he* was the "prisoner" of an outmoded notion of urban class struggle and *lacking* in revolutionary flexibility and spirit. Clearly, the policy of worker-peasant alliance and of simultaneous land nationalization was a fateful contradiction whose full impact was to be seen only much later in the Soviet Revolution, but it was a contradiction spawned by Marx and shared by Engels, which in no way allows them to be contrasted invidiously.

Levine states that the major difference between Marx and Engels centered on the issue of praxis. "The central idea that distinguished the Marxian from the Engelsian interpretation of nature was the notion of *praxis*. . . . Engels [presumably unlike Marx] described a macrocosmic determinism in which thought was merely the epiphenomenon of physical forces. Marx referred to humanism and dialectical naturalism, the belief that man modified the inorganic world. . . . The Marxian vision was always on man who acted, while the Engelsian was on cosmological determinism."[22]

Although Levine centers his analysis on the idea of praxis he does little to clarify how he understands that basic idea.[23] Yet he says enough to indicate that this involves (for him) an emphasis on the mutability of the world on the basis of human initiative, activity, and power. Yet pages later, and without seeing the contradiction, Levine observes that *both* "Marx and Engels continued to believe in, to extol, the revolutionary nature of the working masses."[24]

The Role of Labor in Evolution

There is a little known but interesting essay that Engels wrote which bears on his conception of praxis, seen within an *evolutionary* framework. It is clear from this essay, written in 1876, that Engels conceived of labor as that everyday praxis in which human beings not only transformed and appropriated external and internal nature—a view which he and Marx both derived from Hegel—but this praxis was also seen as shaping the very formation of the human species. In this essay[25] we see Engels in the role in which his critics most despise him,[26] as the student of science and evolution, and, we may add, as a forerunner of modern ecology with its concern about the destruction of the natural environment. It will be plain from this that Engels's studies of science were not simply a gymnasium for the exercise of his metaphysical proclivities, of which he is paradoxically accused by those (like Levine) who deny he had any talent for philosophy.

In this essay, Engels begins by noting that labor, much more than the source of all wealth, is "the first fundamental condition of all human life, and to such an extent that in a sense we must say: it created man himself."[27] Thus according to the Engels who, allegedly unlike Marx, attributed little importance to human praxis, man made himself. Engels argues that "the decisive step in the transition from ape to man" occurred when tree climbing led to the differentiation between the ape's hands and feet, thus leaving the hands free when walking, and thereby conducive to an upright gait. The hands became specialized for eating, nest building, and physical defense—"they grasp cudgels." Yet "no ape's hand has ever fashioned the crudest stone knife,"[28] a dubious accomplishment reserved for men.

Engels held that the greater flexibility acquired by the ape's hand subsequently evolved into the human hand as a result of its (Lamarckian) transmission and increase over generations, concluding that "thus the [human] hand is not only an organ of labor, *it is also its product.*" It is with the hands' development through labor that man's supremacy over nature begins, for this extends men's mental capacity since the use of hands enables the continual discovery of "new, hitherto unknown properties in natural objects." It permitted labor to be more productive and complex which, in turn, intensified human association and cooperation; thus, "evolving human beings arrived at the point where they had something to say to one another."[29]

For Engels, speech itself emerged "out of and along with labor." "First labor; afterwards, and then along with it, speech" contributes to the evolution of the ape brain into the human brain. The brain's development is in turn accompanied by "the development of all the senses." These reciprocally contributed to the development of both speech and labor. For Engels, then, the key distinction between the ape-horde and the human race was not speech but *labor.* Labor really begins, says Engels, with the "fabrication of tools" for hunting and fishing. For Engels, the use of tools, not premeditated effort, characterized *human* labor, for "it is obvious that we cannot think of denying to animals the capacity for planned, premeditated activity."[30] Use of tools helped diversify and stabilize the human diet, in particular allowing meat to become a staple. "Man did not become what he is without meat," which is associated with the taming of animals and the development of the use of fire.

In the idealistic view, notes Engels, "all the credit for rapidly progressing civilization was ascribed to the head, to the development of the brain . . . even the materialists of the Darwinian school are still unable to formulate a clear idea of the origin of man, because under that ideological influence they cannot recognize the role that labor has played therein."[31] Whatever its merits from the standpoint of contemporary evolutionary science, clearly Engels is affirming the primacy of labor as *praxis* in human evolution, enabling persons not merely to accommodate passively to their environment but actively to transform it to their purposes, to "dominate" it. It is in this praxis whereby man bends nature to his own ends that Engels finds "the ultimate, essential distinction between man and other animals."

Two other points of interest in this essay are worth noting. One concerns Engels's emerging use of a kind of general systems theory, which stresses the mutual interaction of elements, and thus the possibly ramifying effects of one change throughout a system. A second is Engels's observation that human initiatives similarly produce reactions from the natural environment on which they work, reactions which were not expected or intended but were unanticipated consequences of their labor. For Engels, such unanticipated consequences do not necessarily imply the presence of an alienation produced by a system of exploitation. Moreover, Engels here casts a skeptical eye on the human capacity to dominate its environment. With all Engels's emphasis on the importance of man's labor as a self-creating praxis, man is no Promethean standing triumphantly astride the earth. Engels is no proponent of an unreflective view in which man gives himself a charter to dominate the universe and everything in it; he has a sense of human limits and fallibilities.

Engels does indeed seem to differ from his friend who identified himself with Prometheus: "It is Prometheus who remains his [Marx's] favorite hero; for Prometheus is a Satan who suffers, a Job who never assents; and unlike either Job or Satan, he brings liberation to mankind. Prometheus turns up in *Das Kapital* (in Chapter Twenty-three) to represent the proletariat chained to capital. The Light-Bringer was tortured, we remember, by Zeus's eagle's tearing, precisely, his liver, as Karl Marx himself—who is said to have reread Aeschylus every year—was obsessed by the fear that his liver would be eaten like his father's by cancer."[32]

Norman Levine notes that Marx had "begun his doctoral dissertation with a note of veneration for Prometheus. 'The knowledge of Prometheus . . . is his own self-awareness, his own self-consciousness as the highest godhead. There is nothing equal to him'"[33] Levine, of course, again thinks this a great compliment to Marx, just as he thought it marvelous of Marx only to have studied applied science. I, however, rather think that this "How-like-a-God-is-Man (and-I-am-a-man)" Prometheanism, is a naive, transient form of humanistic imperialism which has little to recommend it, least of all history; it is a human imperialism by which man transformed the world into an ecological charnel house for himself and other species. All that recommends such humanistic imperialism is that it opposes the tragic view of history. Yet if the latter consigned humanity to eternal suffering and served as an apology for whatever miserable forms of domination that strutted across the historical stage, its successor, Promethean humanistic imperialism, came perilously close to sanctioning a view of humanity as noble Nietzschean beast of prey, lording it over other species—although this is somewhat unjust to Nietzsche.

As suggested, Engels's own views seem more sober, less intoxicated with delusions of godliness, more aware of human limits without conceding an iota to the tragic view. "Everything acts upon everything else and vice versa," urged Engels, "it is mainly because they forget this universal motion and reciprocal action that our natural scientists cannot see clearly into the simplest things." (Thus Engels, supposedly the ideologist of positivism and of scientific hero worship.)

While stressing that, of all animals, men alone "succeeded in impressing the stamp of their will upon the earth," Engels immediately warns, "Let us not, however, flatter ourselves too much upon our human victories over nature. For every such victory it revenges itself upon us. To be sure each such victory has in the first instance the results upon which we counted, but in the second and third instances it has quite unforeseen effects, which only too often nullify these first results . . . we by no means dominate nature, as a conqueror dominates a foreign people, as one standing outside nature—that we belong to it with flesh and blood and brain and stand in its very midst; and that our entire supremacy over it consists in the fact that we, above all other creatures, are capable of knowing and correctly applying its laws.[34]

Clearly, then, when Engels speaks of technology he means knowledge of nature, not just hardware; and his focus on nature was driven by a dialectical sense of man's unity with and difference from nature, his dependence on nature and his effort to dominate it, his separation from it and his being in its very midst, flesh and mind alike part of one whole. There is a hint of mysticism here in Engels's near rapture, of a communion with the All.

We may, like Levine, decry this as evidence of Engels's abiding search for God and as proof of his remnant religion; or we may extol him as another philosopher of the "totality," akin to the Critical Marxist Lukács, whose links to the Russian mystics Dostoyevsky and Tolstoy[35] surely do not disqualify him as a serious thinker.

Engels's quest for a lost oneness is a central reason for his interest in science—not only his commitment to an instrumental reason—and he remarks that the more science advances "the more will men *once again* not only feel but know themselves to be one with nature" and indeed with himself, destroying that "nonsensical and unnatural notion of an antithesis between mind and matter, man and nature, soul and body."[36] For Engels, then, the point of science was not simply instrumental control by man over nature, but the restoration of *oneness with nature.*

Engels's view of capitalism involves a distinctive, ecologically sensitive critique of its degradation of nature. Capitalism and its social science, political economy, "concerns itself for the most part only with the immediately intended social effects of human activities directed towards production and exchange." Capitalism means a narrowing of attention to market conditions and profit-making activity, and a corresponding neglect of the effects of their actions on nature. "The Spanish planters in Cuba who burned down the forests on the mountainsides and found in the ashes enough fertilizer for *one* generation of extremely profitable coffee trees—what cared they that afterwards the tropical downpours would wash away the new unprotected soil and leave only the bare rocks behind?"[37]

My intention, then, is not to deny that there were differences, even important differences, between Marx and Engels. What I have insisted on, however, is that, first, these not be exaggerated and seized upon to make a scapegoat of Engels or to protect Marx from any taint of error; and I have insisted further that such differences as are textually established should not be tacitly treated as automatic evidence of Engels's intellectual inferiority. Seeing a difference in texts, one ought to question which of the differences is right, rather than using one or the other to fuel Engels's funeral pyre. And seeing a difference in their *texts,* one ought to ask whether this evidences a difference in their individual *views;* and one ought further to consider the premises on which one allows oneself to conclude that it does. I shall return to this last shortly.

On Technology

First, however, I want to consider another difference of considerable import that is often suggested to exist between Engels and
Marx. This has to do with their views about the role of technology
in the development of capitalism in particular, and as an element
in the paradigm of historical materialism more generally. Essentially, I concur with Shlomo Avineri when he notes that "industrial revolution in its technological aspects does not really hold the
centre of Marx's interest. . . . One need only compare the highly
technologically oriented draft of the *Manifesto,* written by Engels
in 1847 . . . with Marx's final version of the *Manifesto* . . ."[38] Avineri
states the issue fairly. Yet a moment later, in the latter part of the
sentence quoted last, he adds that, in the *Manifesto,* "technology
is a mere side issue." No textual reference is cited in support of
this remarkable statement. Worse still, Avineri then proceeds to
compound what one must, in all respect, call a blatant exaggera-
tion, by declaring, again with no textual evidence, that "Marx is
interested in technology *only* because he sees in it the most consequential development of man's relation to his world-shaping
capacity. Hence he sees capitalism itself as a highly developed
stage in the unfolding of man's creative powers—a speculative
element missing from Engels's thought. Marx sees of course that
the development of machinery has been the main technological
achievement of the industrial revolution. But technology is just an
expression of man's creative powers. This power, including the
discovery and development of machinery, would never have come
into being had it not been caused by a human need."[39]

Our discussion of Engels's analysis of the role of labor in human
evolution plainly indicates that Avineri is mistaken in holding that
the idea of capitalism as an unfolding of man's creative power is "a
speculative element missing from Engels's thought." (Engels's
critics complain that Engels is not speculative enough when he
seeks to assimilate modern science, but too speculative when he
tries to assimilate Hegel's metaphysics.) Indeed, Engels is perfectly prepared to speculate even about the *origins* of these creative powers, rather than simply brandishing them in Promethean
romanticism.

But is it really true that in the *Communist Manifesto*—the final
draft of which was a product of *both* Marx *and* Engels and is *not*
just "Marx's version"—that "technology is a mere side issue"?
Clearly, in the *Manifesto* as in their other works of the late 1840s,

the forces of production—including technology—are of decisive importance to them *both*. Even though one should not reduce the "forces of production" to technology, the latter is certainly understood by Marx as a key constituent of the former. Throughout the *Manifesto* there is discussion of technology, directly and indirectly, through frequent references to the growth of industry, navigation, communication. Indeed, after noting that the feudal system of industry was supplanted by the manufacturing system, the *Manifesto* remarks that "modern industry has established the world market, for which the discovery of America paved the way."[40] Does Avineri suppose that Marx thought "modern industry" possible without modern technology? And again, one aspect of the world significance of the bourgeoisie, according to the *Manifesto*, is that they "cannot exist without constantly revolutionizing the instruments of production, and thereby the relations of production."[41] Surely that reference, especially to the "instruments of production," plainly indicates it is a fantasy to think that in the *Manifesto* "technology is a mere side issue." Again, the *Manifesto* refers to "the means of production and of exchange on whose foundation the bourgeoisie built itself up."[42] Surely these means of production relate importantly to technology. Again, the *Manifesto* holds that "with the development of industry the proletariat not only increases in number, it becomes concentrated in greater masses, its strength grows and it feels that strength more . . . machinery obliterates all distinctions of labor, and nearly everywhere reduces wages to the same low level."[43] Does this treat technology as a mere side issue? On the contrary, this makes it plain that modern industrial machine technology was expected by both Marx and Engels to help constitute the proletariat, in strength of numbers and in social character, so that it could fulfill its historical mission of overthrowing capitalism and supplanting it with socialism.

Avineri's contention that Marx sees technology as "just an expression of man's creative power" is only a testimonial to Avineri's creative power. In fact, technology is central to the whole Marxist notion of productive powers or forces which, together with the *relations* of production, largely constitute the economic infrastructure which, according to Marx and Engels, governs society in the last instance. The mutual tensions between these forces and relations of production are the central contradiction that Marx and Engels expected would ultimately overthrow capitalist society.

Just as crucially, Marx and Engels saw modern bourgeois industry, grounded in an advancing technology, as allowing for an escape from want that established the very possibility of socialism. The technological, after all, relates to an increase in productivity grounded in the improvement of machinery. Estrangement or alienation itself, as we have seen, can "only be abolished given two *practical* premises," held Marx and Engels in their *The German Ideology*.

> For it to become an "intolerable" power, i.e., a power against which men make a revolution, it must necessarily have rendered the great mass of humanity "propertyless," and produced, at the same time, the contradiction of an existing world of wealth and culture, both of which conditions presuppose a great increase in productive power, a high degree of its development ... this development of productive forces ... is absolutely necessary as a practical premise: firstly, for the reason that without it only *want* is made general, and with want the struggle for necessities and all the old filthy business would necessarily be reproduced; and because only with this universal development of productive forces is a *universal* intercourse between men established.... Empirically, communism is only possible as the act of the dominant peoples "all at once" or simultaneously which presupposes the universal development of productive forces and the world intercourse bound up with them.[44]

Avineri's idea, then, that for Marx, technology was a trivial issue, is frivolous, born of his insistence on exaggerating the differences between Marx and Engels and of his effort to prove that "here as well as elsewhere the difference between Marx and Engels is significant and striking."[45]

Yet to say that Avineri has grossly and unfairly inflated that difference and to hold that he is totally in error in holding that technology was a trivial issue for Marx (and Engels) in the *Manifesto*, or anywhere else for that matter, are *not* the same as saying there was no difference in the salience of technology for Marx and Engels. While Engels acknowledges, as had Marx, that modern industry and capitalism are born of a commercial interest in profit, he does seem to explore the effects of technological change more insistently than does Marx, particularly in his *The Condition of the Working Class in England in 1844*.

It is perhaps generally correct to suggest that Engels associated capitalism and technology somewhat more closely than did Marx, perhaps attributing more importance than Marx had to technological innovation as a source of larger social change. Levine, too, may be correct in arguing that "when Engels wrote of the economic, the center of gravity of that definition was always the technological."[46] In contrast, Marx tended to accent the ways in which the development of modern industrial technology was *also* called forth by the opportunities for commercial profit.

Thus in a letter to P. V. Annenkov of 28 December 1846, Marx wrote that "the general demands of consumption increased more rapidly than production and the development of machinery was a necessary consequence of the needs of the market. Since 1825, the invention and application of machinery has been simply the result of the war between workers and employers . . . the European nations . . . were driven to adopt machinery owing to English competition." In short, if Engels had stressed technology's role as cause, Marx stressed its role as effect; if Engels overestimated technology's autonomy, Marx may well have underestimated it.

Marx then goes on to make an interesting remark: "The application of machinery in the present day is one of the conditions of our present economic system, but the way in which machinery is utilised is totally distinct from the machinery itself. Powder remains the same whether it is used to wound a man or to dress his wounds."[47] Here Marx makes a distinction between a machine and the use to which it is put, implying a certain neutrality or independence in its character, and that it is not inherently changed by the use to which it is put or the property or economic system within which it is developed; Marx here looks on technology as a brick that can be lugged from one socioeconomic system to another without changing it. The development of technology in bourgeois society thus does indeed provide the basis for socialism precisely because it generates a large-scale and homogenized proletariat and solves the problem of want, so that socialism need not mean making want general, while at the same time technology's neutrality enables it to be transferred to a socialist social system. But whether a technology born of the war between workers and owners would not have built into it features at variance with the liberative intentions of socialism is a question that Marx does not raise. On this important question, I am not aware of any difference between Marx and Engels.

We can see from the above that Marx viewed trade and markets as fostering industry. Indeed, Marx generally argues that capitalism preceded and fostered the industrial revolution. This dissociates capitalism from any necessary connection with industry and machine production, treating capitalism as only implying general commodity production—i.e., as an economy in which things are produced for sale by means of labor, which is both constrained and free to sell its labor power for a wage and which is employed with the object of making a private profit. Now such a system of production had existed for hundreds of years in England before the industrial revolution began there. In itself, it could not have been conceivable by Marx as the grounding for human emancipation through socialism, for it could not have been seen as the culminating class society so fundamentally different from all other forms of class society preceding it.

Capitalism is of decisive moment for Marx because it is a class society which is constrained to revolutionize the means of production. In short, what makes it different from preceding societies is that it is released by capital from the limits of the land. "The bourgeoisie cannot exist without constantly revolutionizing the instruments of production," and it is this, says the *Manifesto*, which transforms the entire bourgeois era and society. This revolution in production starts with a system of manufacture characterized by an increasing division of labor and the assembly of workers and their families (at first doing much the same thing), under the control of a capitalist who may at first only supply the raw materials, but who subsequently gains control over the instruments of production. Precisely as the instruments of production are developed and become more costly they come increasingly under the control of the capitalist, while the worker, alienated from them, is now constrained to work for a wage.

The essential means by which the bourgeoisie "revolutionized" production and gained control over the instruments of production were closely related, though not reduced, to the development of machinery. Without machinery, the bourgeois era would have been just one more class system. Ancient Greece also had wage labor both by freemen and slaves (who were rented out) and commodity production; what it did not have was machinery deliberately developed for and harnessed to production. Conversely, Europe from the twelfth century on had technical innovation, but this operated within a limited framework in which "civil society" and commodity production were circumscribed and in which economic decisions were still highly politicized. Thus while there were surely many factors involved in the outbreak of the industrial revolution in England, certainly two of the most important were (a) an established and already extensive system of commodity production with wage labor, and (b) a period of creative technical innovation (by no means confined to profit-seeking industry) and, above all, the *conjunction* of the two.

What is at issue in this matter, then, is nothing less than an effort to define the character of the modern mode of production. Profit seeking, generalized commodity production with wage labor, and the use of machinery in manufacture seem essential and partially independent elements in (even if not exhausting) the bourgeois mode of production. If this issue brings into focus the question of the characteristics of the capitalist era, it also tacitly raises the question of just what Marx intended to supersede in overthrowing capitalism. That is, what is the nature of the "socialism" he wanted to succeed it? Clearly, what is being overthrown—in the Marxist view—when capitalism is dismantled, is generalized commodity production for private profit, based on the private ownership of the means of production. The central goal of the proletariat when, as the *Manifesto* says, it becomes the "ruling class," is "to centralize all the instruments of production in the hands of the State."[48] Clearly, however, Marx does not intend to abolish machinery in overthrowing capitalism. As evident in their discussion in *The German Ideology,* Marx agreed with Engels in believing that the abolition of private property premised a certain "mass of productive powers and . . . the possibility to increase them infinitely [N. B.] by machinery, chemical, and other means. . . . Communism has only appeared since machines and other inventions made it possible to offer to all members of society the promise of an all-around education, a happy existence."[49]

> There must always be a dominant class controlling the forces of production and a poverty-stricken, oppressed class, so long as there is not enough produced to supply the immediate wants of all members of society, but also a surplus of products for the increase of social capital and for the further development of the forces of production. . . . Private property will be abolished only when the means of production have become available in sufficient quantities. . . . Once liberated from the yoke of private ownership, large scale industry will develop on a new scale that will dwarf the present machine industry as conspicuously as this has dwarfed the manufacturing system of earlier days. The growth of industry will provide a quantity of products sufficient to gratify the need of all.

> The same will be true for agricultural production. . . . Here
> scientific methods and improvements of all sorts will soon
> result in a totally new leap forward, which will provide amply
> for society's needs. . . . The division of society into various
> antagonistic classes will then become superfluous.[50]

If socialism premises a release from scarcity based on increased
productivity, it therefore premises the requisites of that increase.
These include continued use and development of advanced
technology in industry, the continued existence of the very division
of labor and the entire system of authority and subordination
on which the application of technology to industry depends and,
with this, the very human stultification that machinery and that
division of labor imply. It is only in a more remote, vaguely
sketched communist society beyond socialism that removal of this
stunting division of labor is contemplated. In expropriating private
ownership of the means of production, then, there was never
any intention by Marx or Engels of eliminating machine manufacture
and the division of labor in which it was grounded—that
"instrument of civilised and refined exploitation," as Marx called
it[51]—for this refined exploitation was the very premise of the escape
from want that their socialism promised. The long march to
the cornucopia of communism was to wind through the valley of
socialist exploitation.

The retention under socialism of the manufacturing division of
labor, and, with it, of the authority of man over man, was always a
premise of their socialism. Indeed, in an article written in October
1872 (and published in 1874)—in short, when Marx was still very
much alive—Engels decried those socialists who waged a "regular
crusade against what they call the principle of authority."[52]
Authority, said Engels, means that the will of one is imposed on
another and presupposes the latter's subordination. Engels denies
the possibility of creating a social system in which authority
would cease to exist. "A certain authority, no matter how delegated,
and, on the other hand, a certain subordination, are things
which, independently of all social organisation, are imposed on us
together with the material conditions under which we produce
and make products circulate."[53]

Indeed, "the material conditions of production and circulation
inevitably develop along with large-scale industry and large-scale
agriculture, and increasingly tend to enlarge the scope of this authority."[54] People will have to come to work on time even under

socialism, says Engels. Once fixed, whether by majority vote or by a delegate, these hours "must be observed without question." The "will of the single individual will always have to subordinate itself, which means that questions are settled in an authoritarian way. The automatic machinery is more despotic than the small capitalists. . . . If man, by dint of his knowledge and inventive genius, has subdued the forces of nature, the latter avenge themselves upon him by subjecting him, insofar as he employs them, to a veritable despotism independent of all social organisation. Wanting to abolish authority in large-scale industry is tantamount to wanting to abolish industry itself, to destroy the power loom in order to return to the spinning wheel."[55]

So long as the reduction or elimination of want is a requisite of socialism, and so long as this premises the use of advanced industry to optimize product output and the efficient use of scarce resources, then the division of labor and with it a system of authority needed to coordinate it are required. Moreover, the increase of plenty and productivity are tacitly looked upon in a "Promethean" way—that is as *endless* and *insatiable*. Engels speaks of the "possibility to increase them infinitely,"[56] in discussing "the final abolition of private ownership":

> Crises will cease to be; the increase of production, which in the present order of society spells overproduction and is such a great cause of suffering, will then not even suffice to meet the need and will have to be greatly stimulated. Instead of bringing wretchedness in its wake, over-production beyond the immediate wants of society will satisfy the needs of all, and create new needs, and at the same time the means of their gratification.

Given this premise of an endless increase in plenty, combined with the assumption that the available means of production are not limitless and costless, the drive toward Promethean abundance generates pressures to economize and use limited resources, including human labor, efficiently, thus retaining if not intensifying the division of labor and "imperious authority" (as Engels called it) even under socialism. At this point, then, the differences between capitalism and socialism become blurred, particularly from the standpoint of ordinary workers in advanced industry.

In short, the differences between Engels's and Marx's account of the role of the forces of production, and especially of technology, can now be seen to express a real intellectual (not to say political) problem. We can now begin to see why it was that Marx, even if attributing somewhat less importance to technology than Engels, does *not* make an issue of it with Engels. It is not, as Levine imagines,[57] that Marx did not want these intellectual differences to interfere with their friendship, but, rather that, since Marx himself assumed that socialism required the development of advanced forces of production, he also saw advanced industry and technology as critically important for socialism. It is not, as I indicated, that Marx did not see that the system of machine manufacture entailed exploitation and suffering; he simply saw no way forward to socialism without this exploitation and suffering.

The differences between Marx and Engels, then, are not an oversight; nor are they simply due to their agreed-upon division of labor; nor do they express only the differences inevitable between any two human beings; nor, again, are they evidence of Engels's corruption of Marx's genius. Their differences were, in part, produced by certain unresolved theoretical problems they shared.

One problem was that they had assumed that socialism meant the elimination of poverty and had further assumed that this primarily required strengthening the forces of production, which included both technology and the division of labor. But the division of labor also meant the crippling of human potentialities— alienation. The problem was: how could socialism escape want without, however, utilising the old crippling division of labor? Engels is drawn to technology because this might allow a "clean" solution to the problem of want; and might one day yield a technology that allowed abolition of the old division of labor.

For both Marx and Engels, however, the important thing was the escape from want, and neither could reject anything that promised this. If Engels was overly sanguine about using technology to accomplish this, Marx, for his part, was obscure about how he intended to escape want and yet avoid the alienating division of labor. Focusing on capitalism as general commodity production directed attention to the importance of expropriating the bourgeoisie. Yet expropriation did not mean that the old division of labor was scrapped. Moreover, they still needed technology's productivity. Thus while Engels might have accented technology more than Marx would have wished, Engels at least addressed a problem of the theory they shared. Recognizing this, Marx could not very well berate him for it, all the more so since he himself had no better solution to their common problem. Bound to the conquest of want, Marx could not very well reject anything that promised to accomplish it. The differences between them are thus expressive of *the internal needs and tensions of their intellectual system as a whole.*

An example: one person in a family may become the group's "economy bloc," reminding the others of their limited funds, while others, in turn, may be less disposed to mention this. This can become part of the division of social labor within the family, with the wife alert to its limited resources, and, indeed, the rest of the family relying on her to be so. Their own more spendthrift impulses, therefore, need not be curbed; they can now be expressed in the confidence that they will be checked by the wife. If the wife were absent, however, then the "spendthrift" husband might be forced to assume her role himself and speak for the economy bloc. For the group has a real problem—its income is, in fact, limited. These "differences" between husband and wife, then, are not generated simply by their personal differences but are role differences in part grounded in circumstances they share.

This is essentially my view of the textual differences (such as they are) between Marx and Engels, of how they are generated, and what they mean. They signify the presence of unresolved problems in their system of thought. These differences themselves were the expression of incipient efforts to develop solutions for problems in the mode of analysis they shared. Their very differences, then, testify to their intellectual kinship and contributed to their solidarity precisely because they were an effort to solve a common problem.

Authorship as Fiction and Literary Property

The point of comparing Marx and Engels's texts is not—nor should it be—to thrust them into a posthumous contest. Still less should it be to portray Marx as a demigod incapable of error and Engels as a vulgar positivist responsible for all the defects of Marxism. The sound reasons for examining their differences include the clarification of certain unresolved problems in their theory and its evolution, and to exhibit a method of analyzing theories having application to other social theories as well.

Underlying the usual invidious contrast of Marx-Engels texts is an entire meta-theory concerning theory production; but it is a theory which itself remains untheoretized. Basically, those invidiously contrasting Marx and Engels tacitly assume that social theory is the product of a single "creator" who is taken to be an individual person. The tacit meta-theory (or, better still, tacit rules of analysis) are atomistic and individualistic, partly romantic and partly bourgeois in character. The tacit but dubious methodological assumption is that we can properly impute differences between "Marxism" and "Engelsism" by comparing texts which bear Marx's name with those bearing Engels's. Differences between the two texts are then attributed to differences between the two persons because it is assumed that the names on each text indicate its *true* and *full* authorship, *and* that each of these is *independent* of the other, because their named authors are different.

Actually, however, "authorship"—i.e., placing a name on a text—is a conventional way of formulating a condensed account of the origins of the text. In short, "authorship" is in part a societally standardized myth of origins. It is convincing within a secular cultural framework in which it is held that individuals make things, thus normalizing the origin of the text for those believing this. At the same time, the text is also presented as a moral production produced in conformity with certain prescriptions, so that the text may not only be understood but evaluated. The naming of an individual as author specifies—in an individualistic culture— who may be held *accountable* for a text. It makes a text something for which *person(s)* are accountable.

"Authorship" is also part of the political economy of culture. Authorship conventionally assigns a text to the person named as author as his property; since about the seventeenth century it is a claim to incomes produced by the text. Conventionally defining the text as belonging to the person named on it as its author, it entails the assumption that, since he created or wrote it, it is deservedly and truly his, because expressive of his work and personality. The conclusions reached in comparing texts presented under the names of Marx and Engels are thus grounded in an unexamined meta-theory of literary property[58]—i.e., in a *pre*-text— which treats cultural objects as if they were merely individual products.

Authorship is the use of a segment of a collectively developed culture for private incomes (whether in money or repute); it is the transformation of culture into an income-producing, individually controlled stock of goods. To some extent—and, often, to a considerable extent—authorship has become a conventional fiction or pre-text, minimizing the larger cultural origins while emphasizing the individual origin of a text. It is a socially sanctioned illusion, for there may be assistants who helped do the "research," find resources, think through, and, indeed, sometimes actually "write-up" the text in question; there may be colleagues and comrades who have helped, students to whom new texts are presented in "tryouts" because they are less threatening, as well as spouses,[59] lovers, friends with whom there is constant communication about the ideas involved. Although not usually seen as part of the work group producing the textual product, they are indeed members of it and who, because conventionally neglected, I shall call the shadow group.

Whether enshadowed or not, however, all theory work is not simply influenced by but is always the product of some collective group. In the case of Marx and Engels, the latter was surely not part of Marx's shadow group, being widely known in his lifetime as Marx's colleague and was even called (by Kugelmann) Marx's "twin star"; Engels was almost the "Pope" of Marxism (as he has also been called) after Marx died. Among those more properly considered part of Marx and Engels's shadow group was Helene Demuth—"our faithful Lenchen"—a feudal gift from Mrs. Marx's mother to the newly married Marxes as a housemaid. Helene Demuth, later mother of Marx's illegitimate son and herself buried in the Marx family gravesite at Highgate, became Engels's housekeeper after Marx died and "acted for Engels, as she had done for Marx, 'as his housekeeper and his trusted counsellor and advisor, not only in matters of daily life, but even in politics.'"[60]

Beyond those with whom he has face-to-face relations, an author of course also derives help from countless other scholars or artists (living or dead) whom he has read or whose work he has seen. Behind each theory product, then, there is not merely the person whose name appears as author, but an entire group and tradition for whom the assigned author is merely the emblem. This is obviously true of Marx and Engels's "own" publications, each work often being discussed frequently and closely with the other. An author's name, it might be said, is actually not the name of an individual person but of an intellectual work group. The author's name, however, overshadows the group or tradition involved in a text's production and serves authoritatively to resolve its paternity (or maternity) putting aside all questions, much as a father's name on a birth certificate does. Yet it is obvious that there are such things as plagiarism and ghost writing, the first being authorship of one man's work that is claimed by another without his permis-

sion; the second, where authorship is claimed and used by one
with the permission of another. Thus it was long unknown that
many of the articles which appeared in the *New York Herald
Tribune* under Marx's name were actually written by Engels as a
contribution to Marx's support.[61] Engels was, in this connection,
part of Marx's "shadow group." There is also, of course, a larger
sense in which he was "overshadowed," for the theory to which
they both contributed came to be called (often by Marx's foes),
"Marxism." When Marx had blurted, in criticism of some French
Marxists whom he thought vulgarizing his work, "I am not a
Marxist," this is in part the effort of a theory's owner to assert his
control over his theoretical property (to protect the "brand"
name), and to prevent others from using it improperly. The very
idea of a "Marxism" thus manifests the compelling fiction of individual authorship, whether made by Marx's Bakunist adversaries or
by his Guesdist admirers. Marx's daughter Laura had a finer sense
of tact and property—and perhaps also of Engels's own expectations—when writing to him (2 January 1893) she declared:
"As for me, my dear General, you know that it's enough to be
marxiste et engelsiste to stay young forever."

An otherwise extremely careful scholar, Marian Sawer makes
reference to the supposed fact that "by June 1853 Marx had already developed the distinctive Marxian model of Oriental society." This model, notes Sawer, had two elements: (1) "the central
feature was seen as the governmental monopoly of land," and (2)
the oriental state's dominance was grounded in "the need for the
central power to provide the conditions of production such as
irrigation and communication." But the first, as Sawer herself acknowledges, "was similar to that employed by political
economists" such as Richard Jones. Actually, more than similar, it
was almost identical. The second element was suggested to Marx
by Engels (in his letter of 6 June 1853), and Sawer acknowledges
that also. Despite this, she still speaks of *Marx* developing "the
distinctive Marxian model of Oriental society."[62] Clearly, the con-
ventionalized fictions on which her account rests are compelling.
It is called the "Marxian" model even though Marx simply appropriated from others *both* of the ideas on which it is based.

From the standpoint of a political economy of culture, a theory
is also the product of unpaid theory work by members of the
working group. It entails a situation in which the named author
literally appropriates the product of an entire group, and a larger
culture—and the incomes it produces—for himself while, con-

versely, members of the shadow group, receiving neither income nor repute, have truly been alienated from their labor by the author. Often compensation is given through footnotes or other acknowledgements of the property rights or contributions of others. Yet footnotes are inherently ambiguous, on the one side, acknowledging the existence of a debt, but on the other, delimiting and discharging it, allowing the author to claim that he is debt free and now has a freehold on his intellectual property. A footnote honorably discharging a debt can, in effect, become a quitclaim which the author has given to himself, relinquishing the other's interests in his work and placing himself in sole possession.

If the "author" is in part the conventional emblem of the creativity of the collectivity, he is, nonetheless, not the inanimate puppet of the work group, and his voice is not simply the group's ventriloquistic projection. The work group is stratified and has leadership. For the author recruits and discharges members from his work group, taking initiatives of his own, and responding actively and selectively to their criticisms and suggestions. While individual authorship is always to some extent fictional and conventional, it may also in part express the real initiatives of an individual theorist whose collaboration with a work group helps produce those theoretical performances traditionally termed authorship (and scholarship).

Authorship, moreover, is not only dependent on the *work* but on the *tact* of the work group; which is to say, it is not merely a system of domination but a *hegemony* in which the author's special position is accepted by the dominated as legitimate. It is well known that, great gentleman that he was, Engels once said that the essential ideas of Marxism were largely the creation of Marx and that, while Marx could have produced them without him, he, Engels, could not have produced them without Marx. Engels accepted the conventions of authorship; by which I mean that while his humility correctly conveys the reality of Marx's *leadership* of their work group, Engels is surely mistaken in maintaining that he was not *necessary* to the production of Marxism, or that Marx could have accomplished his work without him. For Engels participated in their agreed upon division of labor (focusing on military history and science); he provided Marx with intellectual stimulation and consensual validation in the precarious years before his work won outside recognition; and, of course, he gave material support without which Marx would have had to divert himself from his scholarship to earn a living for his family.

Edmund Wilson puts it well:

> Marx and Engels in relation to one another were like the
> electrodes of the voltaic cell . . . Marx was to play the part of
> the metal of the positive electrode, which gives out hydrogen
> and remains unchanged, while Engels was to be the negative
> electrode, which gradually gets used up. "There's nothing I
> long for more," Engels wrote Marx, April 27, 1867, just after
> the last pages of the first volume of *Das Kapital* had finally
> been got off to the printer, "than to escape from this miserable
> commerce, which is demoralizing me completely by reason of
> the time it makes me waste. . . ." He is going to give it up, he
> says; but then his income will be very much reduced, "and
> what I always have on my mind is what are we going to do
> about you?" Marx replies on a note of contrition: "I confi-
> dently hope and believe that I shall be within a year's time
> enough of a made man so that I can fundamentally reform my
> economic situation and stand finally on my own feet again. If
> it had not been for you, I should never have been able to bring
> this work to completion, and I assure you that it has always
> weighed like an incubus on my conscience that it should have
> been principally on account of me that you have been allow-
> ing your splendid abilities to be wasted and rusted in busi-
> ness and have had, besides, to live through all my *petites
> misères* with me."[63]

Marx thus acknowledges that his work could not have been completed without Engels's help and without the waste of his "splendid abilities."

Bearing in mind the constant and intimate communication between Marx and Engels, it is clear there are few texts we can
confidently label as exclusively the product of one or the other.
The entire enterprise of denigrating Engels assumes, however,
just the opposite without any real reflection on the *methodological* problems and the dubious theoretical premises involved in making that invidious comparison. Together with
others, including "dear faithful Lenchen," Marx and Engels comprised a theory-producing work group, a small community of critical theorists, and for the most part, each of "their" texts represents the views, work, and sacrifice of other, often anonymous,
members of their theoretical community. "Their" texts are by no
means the product of their individual work alone but of an often
invisible group and larger tradition whose unpaid contributions

the authors appropriated for themselves. This supportive group is important under all conditions but, most especially, when theory work seeks to elude conventional views and for which, therefore, authors all the more require protection from the demand for conformity to the prevailing paradigm or to the common sense.[64]

One final thought about the relations of Marx and Engels. I have stressed the consensus and the functional differentiation of their intellectual contributions—partly a deliberate division of labor and partly an unplanned differentiation which was a response to the unresolved problems of their common theory. I have, too, of course acknowledged that they were different personalities and therefore incapable of having identical views, but my accent has been on their consensus and collaboration. I want to acknowledge, however, that (given my own assumptions about contradiction and conflict in social affairs) I would be astonished if their difference never took the form of conflicts and tensions, open or repressed. Here I wish to add only two things. First, that even conflicts premise a sharing among the conflicting parties, and second, that the sheer premise of possible conflict does not absolve us of the obligation to *prove* it. It would have been a near miracle if Engels's subordination of his own life to Marx's did not leave some resentment. Yet this is a conjecture in which we tacitly liken Engels's feelings to our own. But "ever-laughing Engels" was a remarkable man. Whether anything *might be* or even *should* have been is one thing; whether it was in fact, is quite another. Although it is true that Marx was often an abrasive person who finally broke with almost everyone with whom he had once been friendly, we know of only one notable quarrel between Engels and Marx, and that was when Mary Burns (Engels's lover) died and when, in the midst of Engels's desolation, all Marx could think of was the press of his own needs. We do know, however, that after Marx died, Engels—as Helene Demuth told Eleanor Marx— "'burnt lots of letters referring to himself.'"[65] We may, therefore, never learn much more.

NOTES

1. George Lichtheim, *Marxism*, 2nd ed. (London: Routledge & Kegan Paul, 1964), pp. 235, 238, 243.

2. Ibid., pp. 236, 238.

3. Karl Korsch, *Marxism and Philosophy* (London: New Left Books, 1970), p. 80.

4. Lichtheim, *Marxism*, p. 236.

5. Levine, too, accepts this trend line. See his *The Tragic Deception: Marx Contra Engels* (Santa Barbara: Clio Books, 1975), p. 6. As Marx became "deeply immersed in his economic studies . . . even though the basic theme of human activity remained persistent, it again appeared in a different form . . . as labor . . . the making of things necessary for human subsistence, replaced the political revolutionizing *praxis* of the 'theses on Feurbach' . . . a shift has taken place. . . . By 1858, history for Marx, had become the story of the expansion of social production powers . . . a reflection of industrial capacity."

6. J.-P. Sartre, *Situations* (Paris: Gallimard, 1949), vol. 3, p. 213n.

7. Interview with Lucio Colletti, *New Left Review*, July/August 1974, pp. 13–14. It is far from clear that Marx's "blunder" about universal suffrage was "involuntary." His statements on this were measured and reiterated.

8. Irving Howe, ed., *Basic Writings of Trotsky* (New York: Random House, 1963), pp. 401–02.

9. Hal Draper, *Karl Marx's Theory of Revolution, Part 1: The State and Bureaucracy* (New York: Monthly Review Press, 1977), vol. 1, p. 16.

10. Frederick Engels, "On the History of the Communist League," Marx-Engels, *Werke*, Institut für Marxismus-Leninismus (Berlin: Dietz Verlag, 1956–68), vol. 21, p. 211.

11. Levine, *Tragic Deception*, pp. 192–93.

12. Ibid., p. 171.

13. Richard Bernstein, too, emphasizes that "Marx's views on the Asiatic Mode of Production not only have intrinsic importance, they help to overthrow the myth that Marx had a rigid historical theory of economic development applicable to all societies." Richard J. Bernstein, *Praxis and Action: Contemporary Philosophies of Human Activity* (Philadelphia: University of Pennsylvania Press, 1971), p. 63.

14. Levine, *Tragic Deception*, pp. 92–99. This cannot fail to remind one of the great importance that the first Cambodian communist government attributed to irrigation works and dams.

15. Ibid., p. 201.

16. Karl Marx and Frederick Engels, *Selected Correspondence, 1846–1895*, trans. Dona Torr (New York: International Publishers, 1942), pp. 66–67.

17. Karl Marx, *Grundrisse: Introduction to the Critique of Political Economy*, trans. Martin Nicolaus (Harmondsworth: Penguin Books, 1973), p. 474. ". . . *aqueducts*, very important among the Asiatic peoples . . ."

18. Ibid., p. 61.

19. Ibid., pp. 24–25.

20. Levine, *Tragic Deception*, p. 197.

21. Ibid., p. 71.

22. Ibid., p. 152.

23. For serious discussion, see Bernstein, *Praxis and Action;* Nicholas Lobkowicz, *Theory and Practice: History of a Concept from Aristotle to Marx* (South Bend, Ind.: University of Notre Dame Press, 1967); Shlomo Avineri, *The Social and Political Thought of Karl Marx* (London and New York: Cambridge University Press, 1969).

24. Levine, *Tragic Deception*, p. 181. Subsequently, however, Levine purports to show that Engels became increasingly reformist, non-revolutionary, the first revisionist. But at the last congress of the First International at the Hague in 1872, just one year after the disaster of the Paris Commune, Marx held that America, England, and Holland might achieve socialism through parliamentary and peaceful means. This, however, seemed to embarrass Engels who (in the preface to the first English translation of *Capital*) insisted that, in saying this, Marx "never forgot to add that he hardly expected the English ruling classes to submit, without a 'pro-slavery rebellion,' [in the manner of the American confederacy] to this peaceful and legal revolution." Karl Marx, *Capital: A Critique of Political Economy*, vol. I, translated from the 4th German edition by Eden and Cedar Paul, published in 2 vols., with an introduction by G. D. H. Cole (London and Toronto: J. M. Dent & Sons, 1930), vol. 2, p. 887. Was Engels more reformist than Marx, or was it the other way around?

25. The essay, which plays no role in Levine's work on Engels, is "The Role of Labor in the Ape's Evolution into Man," *Dialectics: A Marxist Literary Journal*, no. 8, pp. 1–14. Translated by Morris Goldenberg with the assistance of Leonard Mims, n.d.

26. Levine, *Tragic Deception*, p. 2. Levine makes the strange remark that "Marx never treated the inorganic world as having a separate and distinct existence apart from man," as if this was a compliment to Marx. Yet this sentence is not merely wrong but downright silly if meant to imply that Marx the materialist did not acknowledge the priority and independence of the world before men. It is typical of Levine, however, that his formulations are not merely inexact but ludicrous. For why make a special point about insensate, "inorganic" nature? Wasn't there also sensate and organic life before men evolved? Did Marx discuss *this* in its own right or only in relationship to men? Obviously Marx thought Darwin decisive and, he said, as having provided the basis in natural philosophy for his own work. It seems that it is this that is embarrassing to Levine who tries to squeeze out of it with his bizarre reference to "inorganic" nature. Darwinianism conventionally looked on *homo sapiens* as *produced* beings derivative of natural selection and survival. In the essay on the role of labor in man's evolution from the ape, what Engels is doing is actually stressing the role of *man's praxis* even in that natural evolution-

ary process, stressing that man was not simply a product made by a natural environment but was also *self*-produced. Levine says some of the most mind-boggling things on this subject, such as: "When Marx did become involved in science, it was always in terms of applied science" (ibid., p. 237). Were this true, one could only say, too bad for Marx. Levine attributes idiotic behavior to Marx, as if complimenting him; fortunately, Marx was not an idiot. He obviously spent much time studying not merely the findings but the methods of several of the sciences, and on top of that worked creatively in mathematics. Levine condemns Engels for his supposed emphasis on technology and then applauds Marx for having attended to applied science—i.e., technology—rather than pure science. Once again, Engels is put in a no-win situation and Marx in a no-lose situation. When Engels studies technology and emphasizes its importance he presumably evidences his second-rate, positivistic mind; but when Marx does so he evidences his Promethean humanism, aiming at a "science that could be used to improve and enhance human productivity . . . and enlarge the productive powers of man" (Ibid). In 1863 Marx actually took a course on technology given by a Professor Willis at the Geological Institute in London.

27. Engels, "Role of Labor," p. 1.

28. Ibid., p. 2.

29. Ibid., p. 4.

30. Ibid., p. 9. So much for Marx's bee and foresightful architect.

31. Ibid., p. 8.

32. Edmund Wilson, *To the Finland Station* (Garden City, N.Y.: Doubleday & Co., 1940), p. 317.

33. Levine, *Tragic Deception*, p. 6.

34. Engels, "Role of Labor," pp. 10, 11.

35. Concerning these links, see Michael Löwy, *Pour une Sociologie des Intellectuals Revolutionnaires: L'Evolution Politique de Lukács, 1909–1929* (Paris: Presses Universitaires du France, 1976).

36. Engels, "Role of Labor," p. 11. Italics added.

37. Ibid., p. 13.

38. Avineri, *Social and Political Thought*, p. 153.

39. Ibid., p. 153. This unfortunately evokes Levine. A recent discussion stressing the importance of technology in Marxism is to be found in Ramesh Mishra, "Technology and Social Structure in Marx's Theory," *Science and Society*, Summer 1979, pp. 132-58. Mishra appears to accept E. Balibar's conception of industrial technology as entailing both the separation of the worker from the means of production and his transformation into an appendage. Mishra adds that these "are, in a certain sense, inherent in technology itself quite independent of the relations of production." He is therefore led to ask: "Does not industrial technology . . . provide a fertile soil for the institutionalization of inequality and class relations in 'socialist' societies" (p. 149).

40. *Communist Manifesto* by Karl Marx and Friedrich Engels, authorized Engish edition of 1888, supervised by Engels, published by Charles H. Kerr, Chicago, p. 14.

41. Ibid., p. 16.

42. Ibid., p. 19.

43. Ibid., p. 24.

44. Karl Marx and Friedrich Engels, *The German Ideology* trans. W. Lough and C. P. Magill, ed. R. Pascal (New York: International Publishers, n.d.), pp. 24–25.

45. Avineri, *Social and Political Thought*, p. 153.

46. Levine, *Tragic Deception*, p. 159.

47. Marx and Engels, *Selected Correspondence*, pp. 10–11.

48. *Communist Manifesto*, p. 141.

49. F. Engels, "1847 Draft of the Communist Confession of Faith," in *Birth of the Communist Manifesto*, ed. D. J. Struik (New York: International Publishers, 1971), pp. 163, 167.

50. Ibid., pp. 178, 180, 183. Nowhere does Marx challenge any of this.

51. *Capital I*, Dent ed. 1:380.

52. Robert C. Tucker, ed., *The Marx-Engels Reader* (New York: W. W. Norton & Co., 1972), p. 662.

53. Ibid., p. 664.

54. Ibid.

55. Ibid., p. 663.

56. Engels, "The Communist Credos," in *Birth of Communist Manifesto*, p. 183.

57. Levine, *Tragic Deception*, p. 240.

58. For an introductory yet valuable discussion of property in knowledge, see W. W. Sharock, "On Owning Knowledge," in *Ethnomethodology*, ed. Roy Turner (Harmondsworth: Penguin Books, 1974), pp. 45–53. See also Lewis Mumford: "Pascal pointed out that people often spoke of 'my ideas' as complacently as middle-class people talked of 'my house' or 'my paintings,' but that it would be more honest to speak of 'our ideas.' This trait became so deeply a mark of the finer scientific mind that my own master, Patrick Geddes, was pleased rather than offended when others put forth his most original ideas as their own. He gleefully described his habitual practice as that of the cuckoo bird who lay her eggs in other birds' nests, and gives them the trouble of hatching and caring for the offspring." Lewis Mumford, *The Myth of the Machine* (New York: Harcourt Brace Jovanovich, 1964), vol. 2, *The Pentagon of Power*, p. 122. Patrick Geddes (like Mumford) was of course the exception, not the rule, which is why the history of modern science is littered with disputes about "priority." For fuller discussion of my own related views, see Gouldner, *The Future of Intellectuals and the Rise of the New Class* (New York: Seabury Press, 1979), pp. 18ff.

59. A curious instance was the posthumous review of the life and work

of Oscar Lewis the anthropologist by John Womack, Jr., in which the latter decided to award Ruth Lewis credit for the literary merit of her husband's work. (Notice how ingrained the fiction of individual authorship is: even as I criticize it, I am constrained to use it—"her husband's work.") Womack does this even though Ruth Lewis's contribution is usually indicated on the title page of this work or is elsewhere acknowledged. Thus one member of Oscar Lewis's production group is here presented by Womack as an unmasking of an unusual situation when, in fact, it is standard. See the review by Womack in the *New York Review of Books*, Aug. 4, 1977, pp. 25ff.

60. From Edward Aveling, "Frederick Engels at Home," cited in Chuschichi Tsuzuki, *The Life of Eleanor Marx, 1855–1898, A Socialist Tragedy* (London and New York: Oxford University Press, 1967), p. 240. See also Stefan Grossman's work *Lenschen Demuth und andere Novellin* (Berlin, 1925).

61. See Gustav Meyer: "in 1851 *The New York Herald Tribune* . . . offered him [Marx] the post as regular correspondent. But Marx had not sufficient command of English as yet and was therefore forced to depend on Engels, to write, or at least translate, his articles. For years, indeed, countless articles which were sent under his name were actually written by his friend. . . . When his first articles were due, Marx was deep in his economic studies and asked Engels if he could write a series for him on the German revolution. Accordingly between August 1851 and October 1852 he wrote a group of articles called *Germany, Revolution and Counter-Revolution,* which were issued in book form after his death by Kautsky, with Marx's name on the title page. . . . From 1851 till 1859 none of Engels's writings appeared under his own name. His sole purpose was to enable Marx to support his family." Gustav Meyer, *Friedrich Engels, A Biography* (New York: A. A. Knopf, 1936), pp. 144, 155.

62. Marian Sawer, *Marxism and the Question of the Asiatic Mode of Production* (The Hague: Martinus Nijhoff, 1977), p. 44.

63. Wilson, *To the Finland Station*, pp. 309–10.

64. Compare Alvin W. Gouldner, *Enter Plato: Classical Greece and the Origins of Social Theory* (New York: Basic Books, 1965), pp. 177ff.

65. Yvonne Kapp, *Eleanor Marx* (London: Lawrence & Wishart, 1972), vol. 1, *Family Life (1853–1883)*, p. 278.

PART III

Paradigms and Anomalies in Marxism
The Ordeal of Aborted Creativity

In theoretical work as in art, I value only the simple, the tranquil and the bold.

Rosa Luxemburg

Rereading your book has made me regretfully aware of our increasing age. How freshly passionate, with what bold anticipations, and without learned and systematic, scholarly doubts, is the thing dealt with here ... compared with which the later "gray on gray" makes a damned unpleasant contrast.

Marx to Engels (in 1863) about the latter's *Condition of the Working Class in England:*

10

ANOMALIES AND THE EVOLUTION OF EARLY MARXISM

It is one thing when a system is young, still forming its boundaries, and when its principal adversaries are outside of it, but quite another when it becomes old enough to have a past containing commitments which it has made and with which it must somehow live. In this chapter, a view in three stages of the evolution of Marxism in the lifetimes of its founders is offered, which devolves around this transition.

Before discussing each of these stages, however, it will be necessary to characterize what I shall call the primary paradigm of Marxism that came to be called "historical materialism." This paradigm constitutes the basic rules of social analysis with which Marxism at first sought to understand information bearing on its central problematics, alienation and capitalism, and other historical developments.

The Primary Paradigm: Historical Materialism

In starkest outline, the paradigm includes the following interrelated elements:

1. *A Model of unilinear social development* in five stages. Human society is viewed as a progression from (a) the tribal or primitive commune in which land is held in common to class divided societies, i.e., (b) the slavery of classical antiquity, (c) feudal society, (d) bourgeois, capitalist society, culminating in (e) a classless socialist society where once again property will be held in common, but at a higher, industrial level of productivity.

2. *The Industrial Revolution* as the culmination, but not the cause, of capitalism. The bourgeoisie are seen as constituting a sharp historical break with all previous land-based modes of pro-

duction. Basing themselves on capital rather than land, the bourgeoisie revolutionize the forces of production continually, thereby laying the basis for overcoming scarcity and for achieving a socialism that will continue capitalism's drive toward abundance, thus making a classless society feasible.

3. *A class conflict model* in which class struggle is the central driving force of history and takes place between the ruling class, which consists of those who have private ownership of the dominant means of production and the direct producers they exploit. They struggle with one another during slave, feudal, and bourgeois societies, until the proletariat's struggle succeeds in achieving socialism.

4. *Revolution* as the means through which socialism will be established by the proletariat. It will be a revolution in which the latter violently and forcibly vanquish the bourgeoisie (unless they ruin one another) and brings the old order crashing down.

5. *Socialist revolution will also be multi-national*, occuring simultaneously in the most advanced nations. Socialism in one country is expressly rejected.[1]

6. *Internal contradictions of capitalism.* The proletariat's revolutionary efforts are the active or subjective side of the *objective, structural contradictions between the forces and relations of production*—the latter blocking the former—which ensure the doom of capitalism.

7. *The class state.* The capitalist class uses the state to dominate the majority of society for its own class advantage; the state is thus the planning committee and the repressive arm of the ruling class as a whole.

8. *Ideological Hegemony.* The bourgeoisie maintain themselves and dominate the proletariat not only through the power of the state but, additionally, through their control of the instruments of communication and, generally, because they are able to impose their own ideas, making these dominant in society; they thus have cultural and intellectual hegemony as well as power.

9. *Superstructure and infrastructure.* The state and the realm of politics more generally, as well as the ideologies of the various groups, constitute a superstructure; this is largely controlled by the social system growing up around the mode of production—the infrastructure—consisting centrally of the forces and the relations of production, in their growing contradiction. Politics, generally, is grounded in economics.

10. *Materialism.* Consciousness is thus dependent on social being.

11. *Expropriation and state control of economy.* After the proletariat comes to power and takes over the state, it abolishes private property in the means of production, it nationalizes the means of production, and turns them over to the state to administer.

12. *Working class as ruling class.* With the expropriation of the bourgeoisie, the working class becomes the ruling class in society.

13. *Withering away of the state.* Since the state is then no longer needed as the instrument of a minority class to exploit a majority, and since the social revolution will have occurred *simultaneously* in the world's strongest nations, the state is not needed as an instrument of national defense or class exploitation and it begins to wither away.

I reiterate: this is intended only as the briefest outline of the first paradigm—its elemental rules of social analysis—with which Marx and Engels inaugurate Marxism, and is presented above primarily as a preface to the following three-stage model of the evolution of Marxism during its founders' lifetimes.

A Model of the Evolution of Primary Marxism

Stage I: Paradigm Coalescence

During this stage there is the emergence of Marxism's first, most elemental analytic rules—regulative and constitutive—outlined above—i.e., of historical materialism. Marx and Engels themselves begin to view these rules as "their own," as identity-defining. During this period they self-consciously distinguish their own ideas from others: they launch a critique of bourgeois society; they differentiate their own views from those of the philosophical idealists and vulgar materialists; they seek to transcend philosophy, moving toward science and empirical study; they seek to transcend "interpretation" with action; they differentiate their own views from those of competing socialists. This, then, is a period of Marxism's most comprehensive character-defining attachments and rejections. The boundaries are formed. This stage was fully in evidence by 1848, having been developed during the period of economic distress culminating in the depression of that year in Marx and Engels's *Communist Manifesto;* in their earlier

The German Ideology (completed in the summer of 1846); in Marx's polemic against Proudhon, *The Poverty of Philosophy,* published in French in 1847; as well as in Engels's own *The Condition of the Working Class in England in 1844.*

Stage I is also a period when Marx and Engels are both very highly resource oriented, addressing substantial energies to the "critique" of others' views, and focusing greatly on the study of *texts.* In this seminal period they articulate their most general rules of analysis which are, briefly, in a kind of "equilibrium."

Stage II: The Paradigm Applied

This takes two main forms: (A.) Historical journalism such as *The Eighteenth Brumaire of Louis Bonaparte* (1852) and *The Class Struggles in France* (1852); (B.) Technical work in political economy; e.g., the so-called *Grundrisse* (1857–59); *The Critique of Political Economy* (1859); culminating in *Capital* (1867). This technical work in political economy is done by Marx "alone."

This stage, which runs roughly from 1849 to (possibly) 1871, is for the most part a period of economic development and growth. Intellectually, this is a period of the *application* of the paradigm to "concrete" historical, journalistic, and "technical" economic studies. In neither journalistic nor technical studies does the primary paradigm itself above become focally *problematic.* This is a period when the *focus* is less philosophical, "anthropological," and less centered on their own intellectual "resources" than on their intellectual "topics." It is thus not an identity-defining period of "birth." Much journalism is written during this phase which, too, is largely topic centered (for example, for the *New York Herald Tribune*) and involves relatively less exegesis or critique of texts.

During this phase Marx is passionately given over to complex, detailed technical work in political economics with which his notes (e.g., the *Grundrisse*) and even his letters to Engels are saturated. This is not at all an "empiricist" phase, however, but is at first an effort to fuse their basic paradigm with and apply it to a technical economics, and to the illumination of contemporary events or historical developments. Engels, also, develops his own kind of technical studies: of military history and of various physical sciences. This, then, is a time when the primary paradigm is de-focalized; application, not development, of the paradigm is central; energies center on the critical appropriation of new technical traditions (economics and cultural anthropology), new intellectual resources such as languages and mathematics, and new bodies of concrete historical information and sociological data.

The second stage differs from the first in that Marx and Engels had by now made intellectual commitments which constrained them. In the first period they were heir to others' work—to Hegel, the utopian socialists, the political economists—but now, in the second period, they faced a legacy they could not refuse. They were limited by their own by-now established identity and by the need to be consistent with their own rules. If the first stage had produced their paradigm in a burst of creative intensity, the second seemed to require cooler reflection, facing them with the task of accommodating continued development with consistency and fidelity to their own past. During this period, the paradigm begins to undergo a kind of entropy and several important paradigm anomalies begin to emerge, although not focally defined by them as such:

1. The unilinear model of social evolution begins, partly tacitly and partly overtly, to be undermined both by the political discussion of the prospects of socialism in Russia and by historical studies of the dissolution of the primitive communes and the various forms—including the Asiatic Mode of Production—to which these can lead.

2. The emphasis on the universal importance of class struggles is undermined by their growing research on the primitive (i.e., tribal) commune, and the growing importance it assumes in their studies, as is their idea that the ruling class is the class that owns the dominant means of production.

3. Marx is beginning to doubt that forcible revolution will be necessary in all societies and will express this publicly in 1872, holding that some countries may take a parliamentary path to socialism.

4. Marx's views on the class state grow more complex in the course of his journalistic-historical studies of *The Eighteenth Brumaire* and *The Class Struggles in France* which place more emphasis on the state's autonomy, the importance of nationalism and political legitimacy, of politics in general, and of the moral grounding of politics in particular. The state's relative autonomy is asserted even more emphatically in their view of "Oriental Despotism" and the Asiatic Mode of Production.

5. The relative importance of *ideological* hegemony as a basis of bourgeois control grows in importance and, indeed, much of Marx's political economy focuses on the problem of *mystification*

and concealment of social reality through the hidden extraction of surplus value under capitalism.

6. The assumption of the unambiguous dominance of infrastructure over superstructure, of economics over politics and the state, is thus being undermined and challenged as must, indeed, the original philosophical materialism. Marxism moves tacitly from materialism-as-contrary to materialism-as-negation of idealism.

7. Any assumption that the old, bourgeois state could be taken over by socialists and used for their purposes is further undermined by the conclusions Marx drew from the Paris Commune in *The Civil War in France* (1871). Yet this conclusion is in tension, if not in downright conflict, with the assumption (number three above) about the possibility of a parliamentary accession to power. Thus at one level, Marxism is becoming more revolutionary; but, at another, it is becoming more reformist. The internal contradictions grow.

Stage III: Normalizing the Paradigm

This period, *roughly* from 1872 to 1883 (Marx's death) and 1895 (Engels's) is largely centered on efforts to curb the vulgarizations of Marxism that grow with its successful spread and the growing interest of a younger generation of socialists. Beginning even in Marx's own lifetime, the problem of maintaining Marxism's identity and boundaries intensifies.

There are two main tasks with which this period is faced: (1) boundary maintenance in the face of the threat of "vulgarization" and (2) coping with growing paradigm anomalies. The first task tends to provoke merely defensive reassertion of the old paradigm; the second, however, requires candid discussion of the paradigm's internal difficulties. The two tasks may thus be mutually inhibitive. In the end, the boundary maintenance and socialization task, that is, the mere reproduction of the primary paradigm, becomes the central commitment Engels makes, after he is left alone by Marx's death. In short, serious critical rethinking of the primary paradigm is put aside in favor of a defensive reassertion which papers over its contradictions. The consolidation of the Marxist paradigm by Engels during this period involves the concise and explicit formulation of elements already in the primary paradigm with additional emphasis on the interaction of super- and infrastructural elements, thus making the paradigm explicit, facilitating its transmission, correcting for tendencies toward vulgarization, yet glossing the inherent difficulties of the paradigm.

Engels as Marxism's Paradigm-Definer

Gareth Stedman Jones has noted that Engels's synthesis embodied "a theoretical limit": "The confusions of some of Engels's later texts reflect . . . a theoretical limit to the unfinished work of Marx and Engels." That is, one could not have expected Engels's formalization of the paradigm to be much superior to the materials it synthesizes. This difficulty centers on Engels's contention that the economy is determining in the "final instance" but that, nonetheless, the ideological superstructure reacts back on the economic infrastructure and cannot be reduced to it. The problem is not, as Jones seems to think,[2] that Marx failed to specify "the precise structural mechanism connecting" economic base and ideological superstructure, but elsewhere. To acknowledge a role for the ideological, to recognize its reciprocal impact on the economic base, makes the latter, "objective" conditions, themselves conditioned, and that, to an *unknown* degree. *This, therefore, makes problematic the important question of the extent to which "objective conditions" truly limit action.* There *is* a gap here, and it was into this gap that Lenin would later plunge the vanguard initiatives of the Bolshevik Party.

Engels's efforts, then, consolidate and identify the primary Marxist paradigm: in the vast edifice of texts and ideas, Engels selectively points to those he defines as central. Indeed, it is this very pointing which is paradigm defining. For a paradigm is not just some inherently excellent body of work or ideas; paradigms are constituted as such when *persons of authority* in some intellectual community selectively define what is excellent from among a larger body of work, and their very selection installs their choice as exemplary and thus as a point of orientation for others in their community. It is inherent in paradigm defining that it focuses on some body of work as excellent, highlighting its originality, power, and productivity, and recommending it to others. In such a process of sponsorship, the limits, defects, and contradictions of a work will therefore tend to be glossed over. Thus the very process of paradigm construction tends to be a one-sided dramaturgy, highlighting virtues but remaining discreetly silent about intellectual limits, and thus covering up, protecting, and *transmitting* the work's limits and contradictions; and, in covering them up, making it difficult to solve and transcend them. To make something paradigmatic, then, is to transmit an achievement and, at the same time, to conceal its Achilles' heel. Yet this is normal in paradigm making anywhere and certainly not, as his detractors would have it, a sign of Engels's second-rate mind or his proclivity to vulgarization. Much of what is called Engels's vulgarization of Marx is little more than Marxism's normal effort to define its paradigm and to center effort on it.

Engels's formalization of the Marxist paradigm thus aims to correct vulgarizations of Marxism which sought to substitute mere invocation of Marxism for empirical historical scholarship, and which had overemphasized Marxism's economistic side, while underestimating the relative autonomy of superstructural elements, perhaps especially the ideological. Engels's formalization of the paradigm accents the reciprocal interaction of infra- and superstructures, nudging the paradigm toward a generalized form of systems analysis. The technical political economy of *Capital*, however, is not taken as intellectually problematic, but as definitively established and as sufficient to ground the political strategies of the Second International which understood it as proving the necessary and inevitable collapse of capitalism.

Engels's admonitions to the young socialists is not, therefore, to go forth and develop that political economy, as is plain from his last letters, but rather to ponder Marx's *Eighteenth Brumaire* with its manifest escape from vulgar economism, and its compelling concern with the powerful role of the state and of politics. Engels encourages economic and social history, conceived not as an application of *Capital* but of the primary paradigm. Engels then largely defines himself as the keeper of the primary paradigm, rather than of the *Capital*'s political economy. This is the part of Marxism which, in one sense, is more fundamental and which, in another, is also pretechnical; it is also that part of Marxism in which Engels's own interests and intellectual investments were greatest.

Paradigm Simplification and the Stasis of Marxism

Faced with the task of transmitting Marxism to growing numbers of young socialists with a tendency to "vulgarize" it, Engels is constrained to accept and simplify the primary paradigm, to paper over its difficulties, and to define concisely rather than appraise critically its essentials, thus to facilitate their transmission. This is surely a task that Marx, too, would have faced, had he lived, and we really have little basis for imputing that he would have done it very differently than Engels. Engels, then, selectively defines Marxism as an intellectual and political position after Marx's death; he is its paradigm-definer.

To make an intellectual standpoint paradigmatic is essentially what any *textbook* does; it is to treat a set of theories as so secured that they then become things to be transmitted to minds less sophisticated than those whose labors formulated them and who are expected to use it as their point of departure. A paradigm, then, is essentially a mechanism stabilizing intellectual hegemony: of founders over epigones, of an older over a younger generation. The paradigm, as is plain from Engels's admonitions to young socialists, is intended as a work-assigning charter, allocating tasks for young apprentice and journeymen intellectuals, constituting them as members of a school who must uphold the collective paradigm as the emblem and property of their community, demarcating the intellectual boundaries which define it and which need to be protected.

The dogmatism which subsequently mushrooms among Marxists is thus already half-prepared by the stasis of critical thought inherent in the paradigm form; but this is only a *potential* for dogmatism that Marxism shares even with conventional and normal science. If Marxist dogmatism is not a development alien to science itself but a potential it shares with it,[3] why does this potentiality blossom so fully in Marxism?

In part this happens because Marxism is not simply an interpretation of the world—as it pledged it would *not* be—but an effort to change it. Precisely because it is an effort to unite theory and practice to change the world, there is great pressure to present "theory" as a *secured* basis for action, rather than as problematic and in need of further development. One cannot ask people to undertake great risks on behalf of uncertain theories. Marxist theory tends to be taken as given rather than problematic, all the more because its efforts to change the world proceed uniquely through dangerous conflict against powerful forces, and this induces anxiety in those undertaking the struggle. These anxieties heighten rigidities and increase the need for theoretical certainty to justify the costs suffered.

The theory, moreover, tends to become a doctrinal source of group solidarity—i.e., a set of shared beliefs which hold the group together against external threat and internal anxiety, because they are held in *common;* but insofar as diversity in belief appears, their capacity to fortify group solidarity is impaired. The very combat setting, then, exerts great pressure to suspend critical evaluation of Marxism, thus freezing it; it fosters a view of the theory as already secured and needing only to be applied, rather than as requiring new researches. If "normal" academic social science is paralyzed by its need for certainty, never acting because it never knows enough, so that each research ends with a plea for a new one, Marxism satisfies action's need for certainty by declaring itself an already proven product and by canonizing its theory, thereby leading to the gloss of anomalies and thus crippling the theory's capacity for further development. Most members of Marxist combat groups will, moreover, be rewarded for their political successes in winning power, or for their steadfastness, loyalty, and ability to control their anxieties, while struggling for power, rather than for their theoretical sophistication. As Marxism becomes involved in the struggle for power, the theory itself becomes the property of a political party, being a basis of its solidarity, and theory becomes subject to *authoritative* interpretation by party leaders (who may be but who are often not theorists).

Theorists are thus alienated from their theoretical property; they can no longer speak the theory independently of party leaders even though the latter may have little or no theoretical competence. It is notable that Marx and Engels often had sharp differences with the leadership of the German workers parties, and many of their differences with Lassalle may be so interpreted. They refused to accept party discipline and to submit to political considerations in their own theory work, which, as Engels related,[4] was why they refused to edit socialist party newspapers.

Party control over the paradigm heightens theory's vulnerability to dogmatism, subjecting it to an icy immobilism. Party control narrows Marxism down to an instrumental technology for mobilizing power, intensifying the paradigm's native impulse to resist critical examination of basic issues. Insofar as the party leadership grounds its authority in its theoretical competence, any critique of theory must imply a critique of its authority and decisions. And insofar as the leadership's authority is grounded in its political success, the theory will either be disregarded or molded to suit leadership purposes. Precisely because Marxism had vaunted theory, noting it gave communism one of its great advantages[5] Marxist party leaders have—far more than leaders of other political parties—sought to present themselves as theoretically competent, if not gifted; therefore, they use their party prestige and organizational power to resolve theoretical issues in favor of their own interpretations. Insofar as theorists remain expropriated from theory by party leaders, which means that changes in the paradigm must first be sanctioned by party leaders, then the paradigm will be canonized and stunted, will learn little from historical research, and be closed to·cumulative growth and development.[6]

Anomalies as Illicit Creativity

Our explorations of the early evolution of Marxism have turned up two interesting problems. One is the way the crystallization of Marxism's paradigm was stimulated by the encounter with the younger generation of socialist followers. Like the pearl in the oyster surrounding the irritating grain of sand, paradigm formation proceeded partly in response to that irritation. The problem this confronts us with is "classic." Why do such intergenerational encounters come to be defined (by elders, of course) as evidencing a "vulgarization" (by the young, of course)?

The second problem hatched here is the "anomaly problem." Again, it is classic, recurrently manifesting itself in all manner of ongoing intellectual efforts, including the "real" sciences as Thomas Kuhn has patiently told us since 1962. "Anomalies," we might say, are the bland form contradiction takes within institutionalized intellectual life. Here "anomaly" means differences between the expectations of the primary Marxist paradigm and those other assumptions or conclusions to which Marx later comes when he deals with new materials which are sometimes (and I think too narrowly) called his "research." Anomalies have to do with how we get trapped by our past, by our previous commitments or even learnings, and how these first energizing triumphs of our existence come to hang like an albatross around our necks as we wander off trying to continue our growth, and repeat those successes. The classical site of the anomaly problem in Marxism is, of course, Marx's *Eighteenth Brumaire of Louis Bonaparte* in which, as already noted, he accents the relative autonomy of ideology and of the political sphere, at some appreciable remove from the more economistic stipulations of the primary paradigm.

It would be wrong though if we made too much of the particularism of that book and isolated it from others. For if we pay

attention to dates, we will notice it was written shortly before
Marx also developed his studies of Oriental Despotism and the
Asiatic Mode of Production (AMP) which, as we have seen, have
their own yeasty anomaly and, before that curious letter he wrote
to Engels on 27 July 1854. This letter to Engels broached and
burrowed toward (but never really tunneled to) the problem of
"Civil Society" and how this was implicated in the rise of the
bourgeoisie, mulling over Thierry's observation that "the word
'catalla, capitalia'—appears with the rise of the communes."

Marx's anomaly-fertile period thus began (but only began) about
the time he started the *Eighteenth Brumaire* in 1852 and intensified around 1853 to 1854; its lingering resonance may be noticed
in the second edition of the *Eighteenth Brumaire* in 1868, and the
changes he made in it. The year that Marx began the *Eighteenth
Brumaire*—this season of illicit intellectual pregnancy—was (we
may note) also the year that the Marxes' housekeeper, Helene
Demuth, bore and gave birth to Marx's illegitimate son, Freddy.
Marx's disruptive illicit thoughts, his paradigm anomalies, were,
like his illegitimate son, ordered from his house soon after birth. It
was then, in that fertile span, that Marx had a new burst of creativity but then wrenched himself away from its untidy new beginnings.

In his *Eighteenth Brumaire,* Marx noted that the bourgeois re-
publicans were "not a faction of the bourgeoisie held together by
common interests and marked-off by specific conditions of production," but were united by their republican *ideology* whose
influence was due "above all, however, to French nationalism."[7]
In short, ample room is allowed here for the impact of political
ideology on events, and "idealistic" motives are neither ignored
nor repressed. The point is that the importance attributed to them
here is distant from the primary paradigm's emphasis (that consciousness does not determine social being but, rather, that social
being determines social consciousness), although this, too, is reiterated in *The Eighteenth Brumaire.* Moreover, people are not
simply seen as defending economically grounded material interests but also as seeking power; Louis Bonaparte is presented as
driven, not by wealth, but by power hunger. Marx similarly distinguishes between the parliamentary and extraparliamentary
bourgeoisie, holding that the latter "appear to act on the basis of
pure power interests." While Marx's primary paradigm normally
stressed the influence of class position or economic interests on

politics, in the *Eighteenth Brumaire* he amply indicated the link-
ages between politics and *morality*, bringing into focus the influence of political legitimacy. In that vein, Marx emphasizes that
in contrast to the National Assembly, where votes are divided and
the nation's collective will is dispersed, the election of the president concentrates the will of the nation: "In the President this
national spirit finds its incarnation";[8] being the very embodiment
of the principle of popular sovereignty, he is especially powerful:
i.e., "he possesses a sort of divine right."

This historical study thus repeatedly exhibits the fact that Marx
attributed importance to moral and normative elements for the
events he was then attempting to understand. Yet while repeatedly acknowledging them in this concrete empirical context,
he also never swerved from emphasizing the priority of the economic when he theoretized explicitly. That is, as Marx pauses to
gather in the importance of these superstructural elements, he
also attempts to reduce their dissonance with his paradigm's
theoretized focus on the priority of the economic, seeking to accommodate and fold the ideological and political back into his
theoretical system, accommodating it to the economic: he normalizes the anomalies.

There is one area in this historical study that is particularly
dissonant with Marx's theoretical system, and that is the emphasis
he attributes to the state and to its vast influence over society.
Usually, Marx's theoretized conception of the state's role is that it
is derivative of class relations and economic arrangements. In his
theoretized paradigm, Marx emphasizes the dependence of the
state, of its repressive apparatus and its personnel, on the ruling
class. Marxism makes an important contribution by recovering the
state as a *part* of society, by seeing it in its relations with other
social forces, rather than treating it as uniquely above societal
influence. The rationality of Marx's view of the state resides in his
persistent effort to recontextualize it, to see it in its relations to the
societal whole. Yet rather than accepting the lofty Hegelian view
of the state as an embodiment of society's rationality, and as inte-
grating and useful for society-as-whole, Marx recovers the partiality
of the state, its interested character rather than its disinterested-
ness, its special openness to the ruling class and its use against the
working class. Above all, Marx seeks to demystify the state in a
way that parallels his critique of philosophical idealism. To do
this, he relates the state to the class system and insists on its

service to the ruling bourgeoisie. "The executive of the modern State," declares the *Communist Manifesto*,[9] "is but a committee for managing the common affairs of the whole bourgeoisie."

It is therefore essential to the consistency of Marx's theory that the state be a relatively passive, secondary force in society, reflecting the will, obeying the policies, amenable to the interests, of the ruling proprietary class.

In Paul Sweezy's lucid summary, "classes are distinguished by their differing relations to the means of production and defined by a property system which gives to the society a legally sanctioned and enforceable structure. The primary and overriding function of the state is to maintain and protect this property system, which is equivalent to saying that the state is the instrument of the property-owning class or classes to guarantee the social structure of which they are the beneficiaries . . . the class(es) owning the means of production exploit the propertyless class(es) and are able to do so because of their control of the state."[10]

Marxism, then, clearly entails a critique of the liberal view of the state as a neutral instrument for maintaining social order. It recovers the *private* advantage accruing to the state's conduct of public business, focalizing an aspect of the state which the liberal view had repressed, inverting the conventional view not only by denying that the state is lordly master above society, but by insisting that it is the servant of one of the parties to the class struggle, the ruling class. (Marx, it seems, could not withstand the temptation of the contrary.)

That, at any rate, was the *theory*. Yet in Marx's historical studies, things are, as we have seen, quite otherwise. If in the paradigm and theory (and in the historical researches as well) politics and state are derivatives of the class system and obey the ruling class, the historical researches also present the state as *dominating society and even the class system*. Marx thus holds that in a country like France with a bureaucracy of more than half a million, "the state enmeshes, controls, regulates, superintends and tutors civil society from its most comprehensive manifestations of life down to its most insignificant stirrings, from its most general modes of being to the private existence of individuals; where through the most extraordinary centralization this parasitic body acquires a ubiquity, an omniscience, a capacity for accelerated mobility and an elasticity which finds a counterpart only in the helpless dependence, in the loose shapelessness of the actual body politic."[11]

In a statement that applies equally to later collectivizing "socialist" revolutions in the twentieth century, Marx observed that "all revolutions perfected this machine instead of smashing it. The parties that contended in turn for domination regarded the possession of this huge state edifice as the principal spoils of the victor."[12] Alongside of what Marx significantly calls "the *actual* classes of society," Bonaparte he says, "is forced to create an *artificial* caste, for which the maintenance of his regime becomes a bread-and-butter question."[13]

In the end, Marx makes a valiant effort to normalize the Bonapartist state by relating it to the class system and by seeing it as the representative of a class: "Only under the second Bonaparte does the state seem to have made itself completely independent. . . . And yet the state power is not suspended in the air. Bonaparte represented a class." But which class does Marx claim Bonaparte's state represented? Not the bankers, industrial magnates, or the big bourgeoisie; indeed, "the same bourgeoisie now cries out against the stupidity of the masses, the vile multitude that betrayed it to Bonaparte." Marx claims that Bonaparte's state represented "the most numerous class of French society . . . the *small-holding peasants*." In short, here the state is not the representative of a minority class which uses it to exploit the vast majority but, rather, "the Bonapartes are the dynasty of the peasants, that is, the French masses."

Marx's effort at normalizing his own analysis of the Bonapartist state thus only generated a new wave of anomalies for the Marxist *theory* of the state as agency of a minority exploiting class. Marx's account grows even more confused when he observes that, if the Bonapartist state is actually representative of the masses of peasants, "what about the peasant uprisings in half of France, the raids of the army on the peasants, the mass incarceration and transportation of peasants? Since Louis XIV, France has experienced no similar persecution of the peasants." Marx again veers course, now cautioning "let us not misunderstand. The Bonaparte dynasty represents not the revolutionary but the conservative peasant . . . the one who wants to consolidate his holding. . . . It represents not the enlightenment but the superstition of the peasant."

Marx then reiterates his view of Bonaparte's state as "the executive which has made itself independent," even though representative of some of the peasantry. The confusion of Marx's account of Bonapartism is complete when he drops the peasantry and suddenly claims that Bonaparte is actually representative of the *lumpen proletariat:* "the representative of the lumpen proletariat to which he himself, his entourage, his government, and his army belong, and whose main object is to benefit himself."

Marx concludes the *Eighteenth Brumaire* by observing that "Bonaparte throws the whole bourgeois economy into confusion." Apparently, however, it was not only the bourgeois economy but the revolutionary theorist himself who was also thrown into confusion. Indeed, it is not only the Marxist theory of the state, as executive committee of the ruling class, that has here become a shambles, but the entire analysis careens and staggers. Reality had dealt theory a dizzying blow.

The tension between Marx's historical materialism, which plainly assigns a derivative role to the state, and the relative autonomy of the state in society—evident to Marx as political journalist—was never resolved systematically at the level of *theory*. It remains a troublesome difficulty leading generations of Marxists to attempt to salvage the theory with countless, ingenious but ad hoc glosses.

Normalizing Marx's Theory of the State

Thus despite excellent discussions of Marx's analysis of the state in various contexts, Hal Draper's study of Marx's political theory, which offers an exquisite distinction between the "independence" and the "autonomy" of the state, must finally acknowledge the growing "autonomization" of the state executive. The latter, Draper notes, can cut itself free of dependence on "every other section of society including those . . . dominant economically." The state is finally described as playing "Caliban" to the ruling class's "Prospero"; i.e., the state is akin to the churlish, unwilling slave, Caliban, who seeks his own profit and is able to do so precisely because his master, the ruling class, is also dependent on it. The Caliban-state, while normally kept in check, may in abnormal times get out of hand, rising to power over its former master.

Draper finally attempts to normalize Marx's theory of the state by claiming it is *two* theories, a general and a special theory, each applicable to different times. The special theory, "the state as the managing committee of a ruling class," applies only in normal times. This operates within a larger "general theory of the State" which holds that in abnormal times the state is only the "executor of the economic necessities of the national situation" (Engels) and "is always the organizer of society in the interests of the class (exploitative) structure taken as a whole." "The more rapid the change—the more revolutionary the times . . . the more does the special theory begin to warp away from a close match with reality, and the more does the general theory of the state become applicable in order to explain the pattern of political power in the process of social transformation."[14]

The state, then, remains the executive committee of the ruling class, except during abnormal revolutionary times. The trouble is, times are so often abnormal. And they are revolutionary precisely when the state is experiencing some sort of political crisis of its own. The state's condition, then, is not simply dependent on revolutionary times, but its own political crises also determine when times may be revolutionary.

Draper's formulation obscures the fact that the state's autonomy in the modern Western world does not simply vary cyclically, going up and down with revolutionary surges and declines, but has also manifested a long-range increase over time, despite cyclical variations. The state thus enters into growing tension with the proprietary class. Marx's focus on the state as part of society, and especially of its dependence on the class system, premised the then relatively limited states in contrast with the gargantuan state apparatuses that subsequently appear. (If early socialists were—according to Marx—"utopians" because they wrote before the full emergence of the modern proletariat, what shall we say of a Marxism written before the appearance of the modern, full-grown state?)

Marx's focus on the state's dependence on the class system thus produced a new intellectual repression; it concealed (for some Marxists) the increasing power and autonomy of the state, and hence its systematic tension with the proprietary or any other class. Marxism thus led to the glossing over of what every political journalist, and even the common sense, knows: that the modern state does not simply serve the proprietary class but often (and increasingly) towers over it. In this case, what might it mean to call proprietors a "ruling class," let alone to call the Soviet working class a ruling class? The modern Western state does not simply serve the ruling (or any) class, but contests with it for resources. The Western state bureaucracy siphons off the economic surplus available to other classes and can do so because it has continually expanding powers of its own, which are not simply delegated to it by a proprietary class. At any rate, the state now competes with the "actual" classes for economic resources during "normal" times; during exceptional times, however, it extracts such resources from the classes by command and sometimes with force and terror. That is the real difference between the state in "normal" and "abnormal" periods.

Marxism's theoretical distortions concerning the state—the uniquely Marxist form of utopianism—contributed profoundly to the failure of Marxist practice, and nowhere more profoundly than in the USSR. At the very moment of Marxism's success, when it wins the struggle for power and takes control of a state, when it sees itself on the brink of an emancipating socialism, what it is in fact creating is the vastly expanded power of a new state, confirming Marx's statement that "all revolutions perfected this machine instead of smashing it."

In a paradigm that distinguished "actual classes" (including the ruling class) from the state bureaucracy, it is not expected that the latter can become a new ruling class and it is defined as an "artificial" caste. The theory mythologizes that the proletariat is the new ruling class,[15] even though the proletariat has never been more thoroughly humiliated than in certain Marxist states. Marxism thus leaves socialists intellectually bewildered before the growing power of the state and, in particular, gives them no purchase on understanding the class character of a Marxist state such as the USSR. Marxist theory, which entailed an intellectual emancipation from the old mystique of the state, now eventuates in a new "Darkness at Noon."

How shall we understand the failure of this theory? Of a theory that, starting out to produce emancipation, ends by nourishing a new false consciousness, inferior even to the common sense? It needs to be emphasized that I am not saying that it was the "logic" of Marxist theory that inevitably produced the political monstrosities of Stalinism and Eastern Europe. Certainly, many factors contributed to that unique catastrophe, not least among them the cultural particularities and industrial backwardness of Eastern Europe. Yet Marxist theory surely, especially its defective theory of the state, did play *a* role.

For in emphasizing that socialism required the expropriation of private property, it was led to turn the management of that property over to the state. The new state then develops a vast managerial bureaucracy to control both the economic *and* the political spheres. The bureaucracy effectively becomes a new *stand*, i.e., a ruling class whose political and personal privileges are united, whose actual power is disguised by an ideology that asserts that a bureaucracy is not an "actual" class, but only a creature of such actual classes, and then decorates this new false consciousness with the outrageous myth that the new "actual" ruling class (under socialism) is the humiliated proletariat itself.

Overstating its valuable insight into the class-state nexus, Marxism forgot the common sense of its time. Narcissistically dwelling on the limited circle of illumination it had contributed, Marxism let the learning of—and the common sense—of its time lapse into a darkness penetrable only in an ad hoc way. The capacity of theorists to remain in touch with and to articulate the rules they actually employ in working is here impaired by a background rule peculiar to the theorist's community. This tacit rule discourages the speaking of the commonplace, defines this as banalization and as evidencing a lack of creative originality. Even though that commonplace may actually refer to something decisive, if it is already known it is given less emphasis than something less important but less widely known. To this extent, then, the needs of theorists are at variance with that of theory.

Coping with Theoretical Anomalies: Showing without Telling

It should now be plain that there are crucial anomalies in Marxism which, in part, center on its analysis of politics in general and the state in particular. The primary paradigm presents the latter as superstructural elements dependent on the proprietary class and the mode of production, while the analyses of the *Eighteenth Brumaire* and of the Asiatic Mode of Production present the state and the political sphere as relatively more autonomous and even dominant.

Such differences are, needless to say, given very different interpretations by Marxists and their critics. The former self-righteously define them not as anomalies but as "proof" that Marxism is not a narrow, economistic theory. Marxism's critics, however, interpret such differences as true anomalies and as evidence that Marxism is self-contradictory. Having presented their "verdict" they then retire. Each view, I believe, has elements of value but each is somewhat sterilized by its polemical animus.

The Marxists are correct in that Marxism, especially in stage two of the paradigm, does indeed increasingly manifest an effort to go beyond economism and to give new weight to the state, to the political and to ideological elements—i.e., to the "superstructural." But they are also wrong in that, while this *is* found in Marx's scholarship, it is not present at the *theoretical* level. The new role of the superstructure is not really theoretized; the paradigm, rather than really being changed to accommodate the anomalies, is only normalized. Thus it is often argued in the *Eighteenth Brumaire* that this newly accented role of the superstructure actually fits into the old paradigm. This is "normalization." (It is rather like the good magician who encourages his audience to think that he has accidentally allowed them to glimpse how he does his trick, but who then finishes by showing them that this solution, which he had in any event put in their minds, was wrong, and they are doubly "tricked.") In brief, the anomalies are not defined as anomalies. The contradiction is denied and *the theorist can "show" that he has taken account of what is not in his theory while still adhering to it*. Basically, this theoretical maneuver is managed by glossing over the differences between "showing" and "telling," and pretending that the two are equal. The theorist in effect *shows* the reader that he does, indeed, take account of what his theory omits, thus insinuating that this is actually incorporated in what his theory expressly "tells," although it is not.

As for the anti-Marxists: they are right in sensing an inconsistency (if not worse) between what Marx shows in the *Eighteenth Brumaire* and what he tells (in his theory), but wrong in viewing this "showing" as a mere inadvertence that will not be repeated, or in implying that this difference between showing and telling is a vice peculiar to Marxism. Marxists are surely wrong in denying the difference or in making light of it; anti-Marxists are no less wrong in noting it but simply using the occasion to score points. What is happening here deserves to be understood better, precisely because it is not peculiar to Marxism and because it tells us something generally important about theory construction.

Analytic: Theory Plus Background Assumptions

To begin with, we need to work our way toward a deeper understanding of what theory is (and, therefore, what it is not). In short, we need a meta-theory about theory and we can best develop this by contrasting theory with something frequently mistaken for it, which I call, "analysis." All theorists, indeed all thinkers, have their characteristic ways of processing information, their typical intellectual *modus operandi.* To know a thinker is (at least) to know his analytic, his *modus operandi.* Analytics are the ideal types (or typifications) of the rules—regulative and constitutive—of problem solving and of information processing, employed by different theorists or schools of theory.

Analytics have an interface in two different directions: on the one side, they rise toward theory itself, which is the salient prominence of the analytic plain; on the other side, an analytic embodies the deeper, less articulate elements—i.e., the background assumptions and the infrastructure of sentiments held by a theorist. Both of these—assumptions and sentiments—link him to the subculture of some social group and to the culture of the larger society. An analytic, then, encompasses both latent background assumptions[16] and articulate theory.

Theory consists of those analytic rules—rules of procedure and constituent rules (ontologies)—which are only (1) *part* of the rules and typifications constituting the analytic; they are *some but not all* the rules a theorist uses in analyzing something and (2) of which the theorist is *focally aware.* Other rules, not part of his theory but still part of his analytic, are viewed with (what Michael Polanyi[17] has called) *auxiliary* awareness. The theory, then, is the explicit part of the analytic; background assumptions are the tacit infrastructure of theory. Theory is articulate analysis; background assumptions are silent partner in the analytic. Theory is the head of the hammer; background assumptions are the handle on which the hammer's head rests, without which it could not be wielded, but of which we have only tacit awareness.

The distinction between theory and background assumptions offered here is partially, but only partially, convergent with the distinction that Jean Piaget makes in his *Development of Thought* between the "scheme" and the "accommodations" of the scheme. For Piaget, the scheme is the most basic pattern by means of which a system assimilates—i.e., destructures and incorporates—its environment, or, here, by which a theoretical system assimilates information. A scheme has a momentum of its own, and tends to absorb and rework material in its environment to reproduce itself; like it, a theory is not simply reactive or responsive to the information flow passing through it. A theory *resists* information. In order to be applied, a scheme, being very general, must be "accommodated" or customized to cope with the diverse, concrete materials it encounters, thereby opening the scheme to pressures that may change it. While scheme-versus-accommodation thus parallels theory-versus-background assumption, it omits the crucial distinction I have stressed between the two, the focalized awareness of theory and the auxiliary awareness of background assumptions (which, together, constitute the analytic). It is precisely that distinction in awareness that led Alfred North Whitehead to make his famous observation that "to come very near to a true theory, and to grasp its precise application, are two very different things, as the history of science teaches us. Everything of importance has been said before by somebody who did not discover it."

Put another way, a theory never actually *describes* theory work, never describes the theorist's actual *modus operandi,* because theory is only the theorist's *self*-understanding, i.e., a *selective, limited* part of his *modus operandi* of which he is aware and for which, presumably, he will take responsibility. If theory is the theorist's self-understanding, it is also, however, his self-*mis*understanding. That is, theory is also the "false consciousness" of theorists, premising as it does that they are acting only in conformity with the rules to which they say they conform, when, in fact, they also and always follow other rules as well—implicit and tacit rules, their background assumptions.

Theorists, then, follow and use many more and different rules (procedural and constitutive) than those they can articulate as "their" theory. Theory is only a limited set of the rules of analysis used. There remain other, inarticulate rules of consequence: the theoretical silence, the theoretical subtext, the theoretical other: the tacit background.

Theory, then, is articulate analysis, is analysis that knows and can say what it is doing. As such, it is precisely the paradigm of *rationality* with which we began this trilogy in *The Dialectic of Ideology and Technology,*[18] and was there called the "culture of critical discourse." That is, this historically emergent notion of the rational, insists that an analytic should be capable of speaking the rules it follows. Rationality thus prizes "theoreticity." Rationality like theory, then, is also in part always something of a false consciousness, pretending to know the rules it follows, pretending it has only followed rules it can and has spoken, when it must always follow other unspeakable rules as well.

The view of theory to which we have been led here differs from that held by many theorists who, precisely when operating *against* a dominant positivism, conceive theory only in its relationship to "research" and to "fact." While Talcott Parsons attempted to show that social facts and social science depended on theory, he ignored the *analytic* of which theory was only a part. Parsons had made theory problematic only within the context of theory-and-research but failed to explore theory's relationship to more tacit parts of analytic.[19]

Waging war against an empiricism which imagined that it could be theory free, Parsons (and other functionalists) took the tack that even empiricists have a "tacit" theory. This had the effect of conflating the distinction between theory and analytic. In centering his critique on the limits of empiricism, Parsons never systematically explored the limits of theory. Focusing on theory's connection with research, with the latter's factual findings, Parsons's central thesis was that the historical development of social theory converged because of its relation to research, and that this nexus controlled theory's evolution. Social theory, then, came to be defined only in its relationship to science, while its other linkage, never systematically clarified, remained a conflated set of "extrascientific" factors.

The more that the focus came to be on what, during the late 1930s and '40s, sociologists expectantly called "the marriage of theory and research," theory's other involvements were treated as illicit liaisons. Theory's relationship to the analytic, to deeper background assumptions, to structures of sentiment, and to society and culture more broadly, became occluded; the practice and practitioners of the sociology of knowledge came to be suspect, and philosophy was ignored.

There was, therefore, a tacit endorsement of theory's self-understanding that it can be value free, free of all but technical interests, and independent of societal pressures. In short, social theory's struggle against empiricism put it in the position of dwelling upon its own scientific credentials, of stressing the scientific character of theory itself, thus assimilating social theory to science, making it a "science-thing." This endorsed social theory's consciousness that it (like science) was situation free, field independent, a virgin birth untouched by society. The struggle against empiricism, then, had the unfortunate effect of scientizing theory, even antipositivist theory, of oversimplifying theory, and of reinforcing theorists' false consciousness. Ironically, the more theory ingratiated itself with science, the less it was capable of the very autonomy that it prized.

The "Vulgarization" of Marxism

We may now return to the two specific questions with which we began discussing theory as articulate analytic, beginning with the problem of "vulgarization," i.e., the difficulties in transmitting theory to a younger generation. Here we must remember that theory is no isolated island; it rests on a variety of infrastructures, background assumptions, and is linked to structures of sentiments—ultimately the larger society and culture. It is inherent in socializing a new generation into a paradigm that the theory communicated to it will inevitably focus on only a *limited* part of the previous generation's *modus operandi*. To transmit a theory, then, is not to transmit the whole working *modus operandi* (i.e., the analytic) but only its most visible part. The next generation will, inevitably, not be given all it needs to proceed. The younger generation will have to customize the theory it receives to fit new conditions and will have to improvise new background assumptions. Since the analytic is linked to the larger society and culture, it shifts and changes with new historical developments so that young theorists must either improvise new background assumptions, to make an older theory workable, or "reinterpret" the theory it inherits, to make it fit new background assumptions it has developed.

In the last case, the younger generation may be seen (by the older) as "distorting" the theory, where this means *adding* something improper to it. When, however, a younger generation attempts to understand a theory literally, that is, by limiting its interpretation to the articulate theory offered, and without adding the usual (but to them often unknown) tacit elements in the analytic, they are then seen as "vulgarizing" the theory—i.e., oversimplifying, *omitting* something proper. This was essentially Engels's charge against the younger generation; they had not, he complained, given sufficient weight to superstructural elements and had omitted the reciprocal interaction of these elements with the infrastructure.

Theory thus gets vulgarized precisely because it is only part of analysis, the articulate part, and precisely when other, tacit elements lodged in the analytic—and on which theory is grounded—are somehow not simultaneously conveyed. Insofar as

Marxism was bent on "abolishing" philosophy, some of its own deepest premises became enshadowed, as Louis Althusser has correctly seen. These were thrust into the tacit analytic which was, nonetheless, available to Marx and Engels who had devalued it. Younger socialists, however, who accepted the masters' injunction to "abolish" philosophy as sanctioning their avoidance of it, were then radically cut off from access to much of the analytic background on which historical materialism was grounded, and without which it became a mechanical and, indeed, vulgar project.

Where theory is bound up with a practice of "research" that entails highly explicated behaviors—i.e., "operations"—under controlled conditions, many of the inarticulate elements in the analytic get transmitted informally without either side, transmitters or receivers, knowing it. There is here both a telling of the theory and a showing of the analytic in the course of a working "apprenticeship," so that the gap between showing and telling is reduced, even if not eliminated.

It is in these terms we may develop our interpretation of the problem of anomalies in Marx's work, that is, of the differences between his theory and what is usually called his "research." Actually, the differences are not between his theory paradigm and his "research" but between the *assumptions tacitly exhibited in the course of his research;* in short, the difference is between his theory paradigm and his background assumptions. In this perspective, then, works such as Marx's *Eighteenth Brumaire* which show the importance he attached to the autonomy of the political, the state, and to ideological elements are best understood as exhibiting more tacit elements in Marx's analytic. These are *shown* in the course of his investigations but are not *told* as elements in his theory paradigm, historical materialism. From our perspective, then, this difference exemplifies the inevitable gap that exists between all theory and analytic; it implies no special culpability in Marx's work. If our view of such differences "normalizes" them, it should not, however, tranquilize our curiosity about them. For it leaves an important question unanswered: *which* analytic rules come to be articulated as "theory" and *which* remain silent, locked into the analytic only as a tacit presence.

In this context I can only sketch a few of the more obvious factors that affect this: an element is moved from the silence of background assumptions to the speech of the theory if an author defines it as his literary property. An author is more likely to articulate a rule if he defines it as "his," as exhibiting his originality; in this instance, articulating the rule is a way of protecting his property in it. To anticipate: theory-making is the generation of cultural capital; it is an effort to capitalize an analytic, transforming parts of it into private property. For Marx, the crucial consideration here is that the *dominant* tradition in political theory, in German philosophy (and, indeed, in political journalism) tended to stress the autonomy of the political, of the state, and of ideologies and ideas. The alternative, dominant view of politics and ideologies was, in short, already someone else's property. Moreover, allowing these elements that are shared to remain in the inarticulate analytic, while focusing theory on the *unshared* elements, sharpens the differences between the new paradigm and its older competitors, overemphasizing its own originality and drawing identity-clarifying boundaries around it more strongly. Repressing shared rules into the analytic allows the theorist to draw a line between his own and competing paradigms and to establish the difference his theory makes, thus justifying the intellectual war to be launched against the others. If the former consideration bears on the economics of theory, this latter bears on its politics.

One also suspects that any rule that provides a clearer view of relatively new historical events or research findings will, more than rules enabling the understanding of long-familiar events or findings, more likely surface from tacit assumption to explicit theory. Again, rules enabling anomalies to be accounted for—i.e., explaining things at variance with the expectations of already "appropriated" theory—will also more likely become focal and be installed in theory.

It must not be supposed, however, that rules remain tacit simply because they have never been brought into focus in one of the above ways. The problem is not only what raises elements of tacit analytic up into focal theory but also what keeps them down; in short, what *prevents* them from being raised into focal theory? Elements of an analytic may under certain conditions be actively repressed, rather than simply ignored. Most basically, analytic elements will be repressed, and kept at the level of the tacit, *to the extent that they are dissonant with components of the articulated theory.*

Insofar as a theory is grounded in an interest that is not universal, i.e., is linked more closely to the interests of some social groups rather than others, then it has an interest that it will refuse to put into question and will resist making focal. It thereby generates a silence concerning itself and about the limits that curtail its own rationality. Unable to recognize and make problematic its own grounds, such a theory has ideological elements. Elements in the tacit analytic dissonant with the theory's presentation of itself as autonomous or neutral—i.e., which embarrass and exhibit the theory as someone's ideology—are more likely to remain tacit within the analytic.

Marxism is interesting in this regard because it confronts this issue head-on, dealing with it not by denying that it is committed to the interests of some special group, the proletariat, but by affirming that this group's interests are *universal,* and hence that its commitment to the proletariat does not subvert its knowledge interests; therefore, that it—unlike its adversaries—is presumably ideology free. Actually , however, as I will show in a later volume on the social origins of Marxism, this "candid" view of Marxism as the theory of the proletariat is, at least, a much oversimplified self-understanding; for Marxism, like other social theories, is silent about at least some of the groups for which it speaks. Marxism's group alliances go beyond the proletariat and these generate the symptoms of all ideologies: an inability to speak and make problematic its own grounding. To some extent, then, analytics remain inarticulate when they have an ideological character that, if visible, would generate dissonance with theory's presentation of itself as "autonomous."

Finally, elements may remain in the analytic not only because they are at variance with a theory's portrayal of *itself* but also with its portrayal *of the world.* The tacit analytic is left tacit when it differs from or contradicts claims made expressly in the theory. This is essentially the case with the kinds of tacit assumptions that were made in the *Eighteenth Brumaire* about the importance of the political. Victor Perez-Diaz puts the matter succinctly. Noting that Marx developed no "explicit, complete, fully coherent theory of politics and bureaucracy under capitalist conditions," he explains that "the reason for this lies deeper than in a mere lack of attention to the subject on the part of Marx. To make explicit and develop the theory which was implicit in his political analysis would have run counter to some of Marx's basic generalizations and also to some key points of his economics, and this inhibited Marx from developing such a political theory . . . the absence of a fully explicit political theory should be treated as a 'lapse'—that is, as a symptom of an internal theoretical conflict."[20]

Perez-Diaz notes that, in the *Eighteenth Brumaire,* Marx was thus led to normalize the importance he there attributed to political and ideological considerations, which is to say, ultimately accommodating the background assumptions of his analytic to the postulations of his explicit theory paradigm: "Marx certainly looks at the strictly political and cultural developments included in the process of production of the Bonapartist Regime. But he tends to consider this outcome as a 'necessity' arising out of a given set of economic and social conditions."

Paradigm Rebels versus Paradigm Patriarchs

Under what conditions will anomalies surface, become salient and be made "theory"? It is certainly not just because of their intrinsic intellectual worth. It is not simply that anomalies—being at variance with prior expectation—become visible and this visibility is then stabilized as explicated theory. For when anomalies diverge from, impair, or threaten the value of intellectual property held by some group or persons they may normalize it, impugn its intellectual validity, importance, relevance, or interest. The career of an anomaly, then, depends importantly on its implication for the existing distribution of cultural and intellectual property.

Correspondingly, discovery of something anomalous has different consequences, depending on *whose* theory it violates. When an anomaly threatens our intellectual competitor's theory, far from being suppressed or neglected, it will be seized upon and paraded triumphantly. Scientific development, then, is not a form of progress in which new facts, theories, or anomalies are always given ready and generous acceptance. We would, rather, expect a mean resistance to new facts and theories that are anomalous to some established theory precisely because it *belongs* to someone and is intellectual, career-fostering property.

The most common form of this resistance is to make a methodological counterattack, impugning the procedure employed by those whose work generated the imputed novelty, thus tacitly arguing that the anomaly is only seemingly such and denying its reality. Theories thus do not collapse at the drop of an anomaly. It commonly takes *repeated and cumulative anomalies* to discredit an established theory, not simply because it has so much in favor of it, though this is certainly a factor, but also because there are so many having property interests in it.

Nor do anomalies speak for themselves. If anomalies are to shake or overturn paradigms, there must also be those, an agent or agency, who identify the anomalies as "theirs" and who struggle on their behalf because their career prospects and property interests are advanced by them. If a theory without an advocate is a flimsy thing indeed, an anomaly without an advocate is an embarrassment that soon passes. In both cases, such advocacy is bound up with the advocates' property interests or prospects in some cultural intellectual object. The crucial agent of much intellectual creativity or theoretical novelty, then, is those to whom the *established* theory does not already belong, a group having few or no property interests in the dominant paradigm.

Paradigm rebels, then, are not Prometheans storming the intellectual heavens in the service of mankind, but intellectual guerrillas seeking to rearrange an existing system of intellectual property to their own advantage. The decisive agent of intellectual development, therefore, is not the theory itself but some specific group who speaks on its behalf, giving it a sociological mooring, because the theory advances its own property interests. This agent, of course, is most commonly the *younger* cohort of theorists. It is they who are often an intellectual proletariat, supporting anomalies even when they do not discover them.

A view of theory as cultural property not only helps explain what happens to anomalies once discovered, but how and why they are generated, who is more likely to do the kind of work that yields anomalies, and who is more open to them once they are produced, readier to see, as well as to speak on their behalf. In our own historical period, intellectual creativity is produced in the course of a struggle about cultural property within the framework of a zero-sum game; for the property and repute of a younger generation necessarily undermines that of the paradigm patriarchs. The younger generation's milestones are the older's tombstones. Intellectual life, in our time, is a contest for the protection or reallocation of cultural and intellectual property between competing generations.

The older generation seeks to muffle and defuse this contest by controlling the education and careers of the younger, by advancing only those whose work promises to support the property and career interests of the older generation, winnowing out doubting Thomases who resist the old paradigm. Here, of course, are those whose careers may be mangled because of their very intellectual originality, for this may threaten the older generation's property interests in the established paradigm.

This system of property in knowledge, however, has the seeds of its own destruction or, more accurately, of the destruction of any established paradigm allocated as property. For the more that the younger generation succumbs to the pressure of the paradigm patriarchs, the more the former grow as a mutually competitive cohort, more or less indistinguishable from one another—or only marginally so—and the more the value of their own intellectual holdings and career chances is impaired. Each additional recruit successfully socialized into the swelling ranks of the conformers undermines the motivation of later recruits to conform to the pressures of the paradigm patriarchs. This, then, is another source of the gap between intellectual generations. Having less or no property in the established paradigm, having little or nothing to lose but their faceless anonymity, and a world of creativity to win, they are motivated to stray from the paradigm in search of greener pastures and to keep a sharp eye open for signs of more remunerative intellectual action elsewhere. Anomalies and their fate, then, do not just depend on their phenomenological interest to some group—whether technical or lay. For this "interest" in itself is grounded in groups advocating or opposing anomalies, in part because of the implication they have for the existing distribution of intellectual property and the incomes, power, and repute of the groups involved.[21]

The Ambiguous Archeology of the Two Marxisms

Theory, I have argued, is part (but only part) of a larger, more encompassing set of rules for processing information and, indeed, for defining what information is. Theory, in short, is only *part* of the analytic and rests on other more tacit rules—also part of the analytic—the background assumptions. It is in these terms that our distinction between Critical and Scientific Marxisms may be formulated: both are part of Marxism's analytic, but Scientific Marxism was (at first) Marxism's *theory,* while Critical Marxism then became lodged in its background assumptions. It is thus relevant to note that *the texts most typical of Critical Marxism were never published by Marx,* i.e., the philosophical and economic manuscripts of 1844, the theses on Feuerbach, and the *Grundrisse.* Marx's public life as a scholar was increasingly "scientific" although he remained a critical theorist at a different, perhaps deeper part of his intellectual life. The rules of social analysis came, during Marx's lifetime, increasingly to center on the display and proprieties of science, while other analytics, including those of philosophy, came to be defined as premodern, became enshadowed, and sank into his analytic's background assumptions.

So both Scientific and Critical Marxisms are, indeed, part of and basic to Marxism. Nevertheless, the way they were inserted at different levels of the Marxist analytic is not a universal, true in all periods of Marxism's development. Marxism at first established itself in competition against other theories, bourgeois and socialist, by repressing millenarianism, utopianism, idealism, philosophy, interpretation, and art, not to speak of the importance of the voluntaristic component of politics and social life generally. They are, indeed, all part of Marx's analytic, but they are not part of his *theory*. In repressing them, they are not then without consequence; their presence is felt in the strains they sometimes produce but, more than that, their presence is *required* in order to make "scientific" Marxism work, so that although dissonant and contradictory they cannot be expelled.

Marxism, then, at first matured and lived at two levels. There was Marxism's manifest level as theory, as technical and extraordinary language, focused on working class self-emancipation. Marxism, however, also lived at another, deeper level, which was at first not easily spoken in its own community. It lived at the level of the background assumptions of an analytic in which there remained an abiding commitment to the importance of the voluntaristic element, of philosophy, of theory, of ideology, of consciousness and rational persuasion, and beyond these to the *social strata* whose special work they are, the intelligentsia.

It is precisely the simultaneous existence of these two levels that aided Marxism to survive failures of its manifest, technical theory and to accommodate to falsified predictions—e.g., the expectation of revolution in the advanced capitalist nations of the west—without a demoralizing sense of its inauthenticity. Marxism's archeology as a symbol system at first involved a specific *hierarchy:* an articulate theory of Scientific Marxism superimposed on and repressing the latent analytic of Critical Marxism, yet also grounded in and depending on the latter as background assumption. If at some point this deeper level in Marxism becomes infrastructure that cannot be self-reflected upon, it is also Marxism's final survival system, containing the last immanent code for interpreting messages on the technical level of articulate theory, for resolving ambiguities churned up there, and for dealing with dissonance that could not be resolved on that technical level. In short, the background assumptions were the analytic of last resort, unscrambling, by-passing, or devaluing the manifest's theory's cumulating anomalies and historical surprises.

The successful Marxist revolutionaries—Lenin, Mao, Castro— are all commonly characterized by their ability to get beneath the manifest theoretical level of Scientific Marxism, to work their way down to and recover the latent, repressed elements of the Marxist analytic, and to establish a revitalizing contact with its background assumptions. Most especially they mobilize the latent voluntarism of the Marxist analytic, reassert the strategic importance of ideas and ideology, and the potency of the subjective. In effect, successful Marxist revolution is made only by those who broke with Marxist *theory,* with Scientific Marxism, who began to elaborate articulately the dissonant voluntarism of the once-repressed Marxist *analytic* and to generate Critical Marxisms, which are most systematically elaborated by Georg Lukács and Antonio Gramsci. But they and their doctrines must wait for another volume.

Here, however, we reclaim our topic, the distinction between Scientific and Critical Marxisms, but now move beyond our initial formulation to a more archeological view and see them as occupying different positions in this archeology at different times. As Marxism achieved its first paradigm and perhaps until the Second International, these different layers had a distinct relationship to one another. In *that* structuring of Marxism, Scientific Marxism was the dominant layer and served to impose a repressive silence upon Critical Marxism. That—i.e., both layers *and their hierarchy*—was Scientific Marxism. With the emergence of Leninism—and our fuller discussion of this must also await a later volume—that specific structure of Marxist theory began to crack. By the time of Mao's China and Castro's Cuba, the bottom rail has become the top, Critical Marxism surfaces, becoming the controlling and dominant theory, especially in less developed nations, and there is then a new zone of analytic silence; some of what had earlier been Scientific Marxism's salient theory is now thrust into the background assumptions of Critical Marxism's analytic.

It needs remembering, however, that Scientific Marxism itself had a history. It grew out of the inhibition—not the removal—of a still earlier problematic, utopianism-idealism-voluntarism. Critical Marxism, then, has an archeological ambiguity. In some perspectives, it is late Marxism or neo-Marxism—Marxism$_2$—that succeeds Scientific Marxism, i.e., Marxism$_1$. In another historical perspective, however, Critical Marxism, or important elements of it, *pre*cedes Scientific Marxism, is a kind of Marxism$_0$ or even a pre-Marxism. At its center there is the very socialism that Marx and Engels had patronizingly termed "utopian."

Our archeological perspective on the Two Marxisms also helps explain how they are able to survive the contradiction each represented for the other. Scientific Marxism—Marxism$_1$ on which most discussions of Marxism had traditionally centered—always consisted of a hierarchical ordering of two layers: (1) a dominant focalized theory centered on the constraints imposed by socioeconomic structures, which is superimposed upon (2) a lower layer, a more voluntaristic analytic that allowed for political persuasion and tacitly premised that persons' commitments did indeed matter. It is precisely because these two different aspects of Marxism$_1$ were on different levels—one atop the other, the theory on the background assumptions—that they did not come into continual, open tensions. Their mutual dissonance could be managed, and Marxism$_1$ could for a while live with its contradictions.

NOTES

1. "United action of the leading civilized countries at least, is one of the first conditions for the emancipation of the proletariat." *Communist Manifesto* by Karl Marx and Friedrich Engels, authorized English edition of 1888, supervised by Engels, published by Charles H. Kerr, Chicago, p. 38; "Can such a revolution take place in one country alone? Answer: No. Large-scale industry, by creating a world market, has so linked up the peoples of the earth, and especially the civilized peoples, that each of them is dependent on what happens in other lands. . . . The communist revolution will, therefore, not be a national revolution alone; it will take place in all civilized countries, or at least in England, America, France and Germany at one and the same time." F. Engels, "The Communist Credos," in *The Birth of the Communist Manifesto*, ed. D. J. Struik (New York: International Publishers, 1971), p. 182. "Empirically, communism is only possible as the act of the dominant peoples 'all at once' or simultaneously." Marx and Engels, *The German Ideology*, trans. W. Lough and C. P. Magill, ed. R. Pascal (New York: International Publishers, n.d.), p. 25. This rejection of socialism in one country was so well known and taken for granted among all socialists, including the Bolsheviks, that when Stalin adopted Bukharin's policy of "socialism in one country" he never attempted to deny that he was departing from the original formulations, but proceeded rather in two other ways: first, by adopting a rationalist antitraditionalist tone, namely, by arguing that one should not adhere rigidly to the formulae of the past under new conditions, and, second, by intimating that the policy against socialism in one country was largely Engels's. Stalin, too, was attempting to make a scapegoat of Engels. See, for example, J. V. Stalin, "The Social Democratic Deviation in

Our Party," in which Stalin argues that "in the fifties and sixties of the last century . . . all of us, Marxists, beginning with Marx and Engels, were of the opinion that the victory of socialism in one country was impossible." Stalin then goes on to discuss Engels's "Principles of Communism" (found in *Birth of Communist Manifesto*) and stresses this was written before the era of monopoly capitalism, that Lenin adapted it to the post-monopoly era, and that his greatness "consists precisely in the fact that he was never a slave to the letter of Marxism." J. V. Stalin, *On the Opposition* (Peking: Foreign Languages Press, 1974), pp. 395ff. While acknowledging Marx's concurrence, Stalin never, as far as I am aware, actually quotes something *he* authored or coauthored that rejected socialism in one country. Engels alone is cited and quoted. Later, on p. 443, Stalin mentions only Engels as the author of the policy rejecting socialism in one country, and quotes extensively from him. See also pp. 446–47 where, by now, this policy has become Engels's alone.

2. See Gareth Stedman Jones, "Engels and the End of Classical German Philosophy," *New Left Review*, May/June, 1973. On the contradiction itself, see also the neglected but still very useful piece by Robert V. Daniels, "Fate and Will in the Marxian Philosophy of History," *Journal of the History of Ideas* 21 October/December, 1960.

3. For an interesting and close study of dogmatism in science, see Robert McAulay, "Velikovsky and the Infrastructure of Science," *Theory and Society*, November 1978, pp. 313–42.

4. F. Engels, *Briefe an Bebel* (Berlin: Dietz Verlag, 1958). See especially the letter of 18 November 1892 in which Engels remarks: "It is a barren position for anyone with initiative to be the editor of a party journal. Marx and I always agreed that we would never accept such a position and could only work for a journal financially independent even of the Party itself." For fuller development of my position on the autonomy of the theorists' community, see my "Politics of the Mind," in *For Sociology: Renewal and Critique in Sociology Today* (Harmondsworth: Penguin Books, 1975), esp. pp. 120–23.

5. *Communist Manifesto*, p. 30, where it is noted that theory enables communists to have a superior understanding of "the line of march."

6. This means there is no way of protecting the cumulative development of Marxist social theory, nor of any other, than by setting it in a specific group context, i.e., a relatively *autonomous community of theorists*. Again, see my "The Politics of the Mind." And one must add immediately that even the university today is only a faint and unsatisfactory semblance of what is needed, for the university itself is subject to political and market pressures. It thus seems likely that Marx's own eccentric career and marginal life, his failure to get the university post he had coveted, his refusal to take a routine job to make a living, and the lifelong help of his friend Engels—contributed powerfully to his escape from the intellectual conventions of his time.

7. Karl Marx, *The Eighteenth Brumaire of Louis Bonaparte* (New York: International Publishers, 1964), p. 27.

8. Ibid., pp. 32–33.

9. *Communist Manifesto,* p. 15. Here once more, Engels is trying to make Marx less vulnerable; the original German had not referred to the "executive" but to the "modern state power."

10. Paul Sweezy, "Is There a Ruling Class in the USSR?" *Monthly Review,* October, 1978, p. 2.

11. Marx, *Eighteenth Brumaire,* pp. 61–62. See also p. 18.

12. Ibid., p. 122.

13. Ibid., p. 129. Italics added.

14. Hal Draper, *Karl Marx's Theory of Revolution, Part I: The State and Bureaucracy* (New York: Monthly Review Press, 1977), vol. 2, p. 587. See also vol. 1, pp. 318ff.

15. Since the revolution is defined by Marxists as the proletariat's seizure of state power and the destruction of the old ruling class's economic base, then, following such a revolution, the proletariat has presumably taken power in the state itself. As Paul Sweezy summarizes: "Since, however, there could be no question of dividing up the means of production among individual workers, the new property system would necessarily have to be collective. And since the only institution representing the working class as a whole would be the new state, this meant the erstwhile private property of the bourgeoisie would become the property of the state. Thus, the proletariat would become the new ruling class." Sweezy, "Is There a Ruling Class," p. 4.

16. Since I have analyzed these at length in my *The Coming Crisis of Western Sociology* (New York: Basic Books, 1970), I shall not repeat that discussion here. See especially pp. 29ff.

17. See Michael Polanyi, *The Tacit Dimension* (New York: Doubleday & Co., Anchor Books, 1967).

18. See my *The Dialectic of Ideology and Technology* (New York: Seabury Press, 1976), especially chap. 2, "Ideological Discourse as Rationality and False Consciousness."

19. The classical locus of Parsons's position on this remains his *Structure of Social Action* (New York: McGraw Hill & Co., 1937), esp. chap. 1. Although fundamentally mistaken in its main thesis about the origins of voluntaristic theory, this book emancipated American sociology from empiricism, as much as any one book could.

20. Victor Perez-Diaz, *State, Bureaucracy and Civil Society: A Critical Discussion of the Political Theory of Karl Marx* (London: Macmillan Publishers, 1978), pp. 86ff.

21. For an excellent discussion of factors contributing to the phenomenological interest of some theory, see Murray S. Davis, "That's Interesting!" *Philosophy of Social Science,* 1971 1:309–44.

11

STATE AND CLASS IN MARXISM

I want to begin here by reexamining the Asiatic Mode of Production (AMP) as an anomaly—that is, as a moment of aborted creativity—in Marxism. I have earlier indicated that the texts bearing on the AMP, and the other social forms developed after the dissolution of the primitive (tribal) commune, are extremely skimpy. I am neither the first to suggest this, nor does this view go unchallenged in discussion among Marxists and "Marxologists." Thus, for example, M. Shapiro[1] has also stressed the brevity with which Marx treats the AMP which, in turn, has drawn a dissenting rejoinder from Umberto Melotti. Melotti argues, however, not without certain internal contradictions, that "Marx did not make just a single stray reference to the Asiatic Mode but actually dealt with it quite extensively." One may take this as typical of the level with which such discussions are pursued. Having set up a straw man—i.e., "a single stray reference"—which he correctly rejects, Melotti then proceeds to draw a patently false conclusion, i.e., claiming Marx "dealt with it quite extensively." There are "many passages" (left uncited) which Melotti claims "presuppose" such a concept; then, he adds, Engels "uses it in several letters."[2] Even Melotti's avid defense of the textual basis of the AMP is not precisely overwhelming. Melotti subsequently cites Rodinson, who speaks of "the text in which Marx sought to examine closely and to define precapitalist formations, and that is the relevant section of the *Grundrisse*," i.e., the few pages I cited earlier. When mentioning Maxine Rodinson's opinion,[3] however, Melotti does not challenge the former's clear indication of the brevity of the textual basis. Apart from the few pages in the *Grundrisse*, the most sustained discussion is Marx's article, "The British Rule in India."[4] If one adds Marx's, "The Future Results of British Rule in India,"[5] then we have perhaps added another twelve pages to the relevant texts. One should remember that the *Grundrisse* discussion is Marx's unpublished notes and that the above two articles are pieces of journalism, both published in *The New York Herald Tribune*. Then there are the letters Marx sent Engels, in which he cites Bernier on 2 June 1853, and that Engels sent Marx, on 6 June 1853, offering an explanation of the absence of private property in land in the AMP. The textual foundation in Marx and Engels's own work for this vast discussion[6] of the AMP, then is thin, consisting of skimpy unpublished notes, letters, and newspaper articles. (For my purposes, however, that very skimpiness is theoretically relevant.) Indeed, to add the *Grundrisse* discussion to the letters and newspaper articles is much like adding together first and second drafts of one and the same article. In short, essentially the same material is being added twice. So desperate are those committed to establishing a textual foundation for the AMP in Marx's writings that they sometimes even cite Marx's scribbles on the margins of books he read! Thus Sawer soberly refers to "Marginal notes by Marx on H. C. Irwin's, *The Garden of India*."

The Asiatic Mode of Production (AMP) as Anomaly in Marxism

In examining the textual foundation of Marx's views on the AMP, let me be clear that my object in noting their thinness is not to suggest that they lack importance in understanding Third World societies or in understanding Marx's views about them or Marx's views more generally. Rather, my point is that *denial* of the skimpiness of this textual basis makes it impossible to ask the interesting (theoretical) question: *Why did Marx leave his views on the AMP so underdeveloped?* I shall argue that this textual skimpiness is symptomatic of the *repression* of the AMP as a topic. Without seeing that skimpiness, one cannot ask why the topic was repressed.[7]

In what follows, I suggest that the AMP as a topic was repressed because it was anomalous, from the standpoint of Marx's primary paradigm. The import of the AMP, then, is essentially akin to that of the *Eighteenth Brumaire* and, indeed, the anomalies both exhibit are similar. The latter was published in two installments in the first half of 1852, shortly before Marx and Engels's studies led them to the AMP. Scholarly consensus agrees with Marian Sawer that "Marx and Engels took no specific interest in the nature of non-Western thought before 1853."[8] Until then, they generally agreed with Hegel's view, which saw the orient as a stagnant relic of the past, destined to lose to the dynamic West. Indeed, a case might be argued that, even after Marx and Engels took up their own study of oriental societies, their judgement still remained largely within Hegel's framework. Insofar as their view of the AMP attributed great power to its state apparatus, it is continuous with conclusions indicated in the *Eighteenth Brumaire*. The AMP researches thus simply intensified the anomaly that had surfaced in the earlier work, contradicting Marx's primary paradigm even more sharply.

The AMP was not, therefore, subsequently neglected by the world Marxist movement because, as is sometimes implied, Engels failed to reintegrate it back into the primary paradigm. In part, what happened was that Lenin's theory of imperialism diverted attention from the AMP, normalizing the condition of undeveloped oriental societies by viewing them as having the same evolution as Western societies, until subjected to the distorting exploitation of imperialism. Thus the AMP is, from Lenin's standpoint, no longer necessary to account for the special character of Asian societies. (Stated differently, Lenin's study of imperialism veers back toward a unilinear evolutionism and is in that sense a normalization of Marxism.) But the core difficulty faced by the AMP was not of Lenin's or Engels's making but, rather, was resident in anomalies within Marx's own work. It is these anomalies that led to the neglect of the AMP in Marx's *own* work, as well as in the subsequent world Marxist movement. Until the split between the USSR and the People's Republic of China, Marxists—with the important exception of Karl Wittfogel—largely ignored the AMP. Since 1964, however, as Marian Sawer writes, "and the deepening of the Sino-Soviet rift, Soviet historiography has become much more receptive to the idea that Chinese history represents an alternative to, and not just an Asiatic version of, Western European history."[9]

To explore the anomalies that the AMP generated it is first necessary to sketch a model of what Marx had incorporated in it, although this itself changed occasionally. Without allowing ourselves to imply more rigor and definitiveness in these views than they attain, the following are included in Marx's concept of the AMP:

(1) The Asiatic Mode of Production was defined as a social formation comparable to feudalism or slavery, but uniquely characterized by the state-sovereign's control over the mode of production; this rested partly on

(2) the state's control over the building and maintenance of large-scale irrigation systems needed in arid climates, and the state's

(3) legal monopoly or title to the land, making it the ultimate landlord which

(4) gave the state unusual control over the local economy's surplus product,

(5) although local communes retained communal possession and traditional rights in the land and its fruits, and individual persons possessed land only in their capacity as commune members;

(6) the communes are enclosed, quasi-isolated communities, based on an almost self-sufficient combination of agriculture and craft industries.

The mode of production described provides an accounting of the economic stagnation of oriental societies; in effect, it provides a political economy for Hegel's dim view of Asia—in his lectures on the philosophy of history—as a rigid, immobile society. Marx, indeed, is less interested in these societies' despotic political character than in their failure to develop a dynamic economy—i.e., their economic backwardness. The state in the Asiatic Mode of Production is not characterized by Marx in terms of its role as agent for some other "actual" ruling class, but as itself having control over all classes. It is characterized not merely by its possession of the means of repression, but by the economic and social functions it performs for the entire society and its system of production. The state of the AMP, then, is not portrayed in the manner of the primary paradigm—i.e., as an element in the superstructure—but, rather, as decisive for the entire economic *infra*structure, building and managing the water supply essential for agriculture in these arid climates.

The role of the state as portrayed in the primary paradigm is thus reversed; far from being dependent on classes controlling the dominant means of production, the state itself controls these and other classes are dependent on it. In the East, economic and social privileges depended (here in the AMP) on one's service to the state and not, as in the West—whether in slavery, feudalism, or capitalism—on private individual ownership of property. In the primary paradigm, it was a system of private ownership of the means of production that (was said to) lay at the basis of society; which controlled the surplus produced; and which, indeed, controlled the state itself, making it the executive committee of the dominant economic class.

In the AMP, however, all this was reversed. It presumably had no private ownership of production, which constituted (as in the West) a propertied ruling class apart from (and standing over) the state. If in the West the ruling proprietary class intervened between the state and the economy, in the East there was no powerful proprietary class with its own independent loci of power that might serve as a buffer between the state and the community, or which might provide a cover under which a "civil society" or community, relatively independent of the state, might develop.

The anomalous character of the AMP thus centers on (1) the preponderant role of its state and (2) the correspondingly stunted role of proprietary classes in the economy, and in relation to the surplus product. As Umberto Melotti cogently observes: "it cannot really be said that the class structure of Asiatic society emerges with full clarity from Marx's analysis. The exploited class consists of almost all the inhabitants of the village community, reduced to 'general slavery' by the higher power." Melotti adds that Marx sees the Asiatic state as "culminating in the despot or his satraps, but it would be ridiculous to assume that, by contrast, with every other class society [in the West] the exploiting class in Asia would consist of a single individual, even if officially he is the sole landowner."[10]

Thus the AMP is sharply anomalous, so far as Marxism's primary paradigm is concerned, in respect to the dominant role it assigns to the state over classes and to the relatively undeveloped role of the entire class system. The AMP plainly contradicted the *Manifesto*'s ringing declaration that all history was a history of class struggles; characterized by stunted class development and by blunted class struggles, the AMP and its state was clearly central to the economic infrastructure rather than, as the paradigm had it, part of the superstructure. Politics, far from being the handmaid of economics, was (under the AMP) now its overlord, while the ruling group was not a class characterized by private ownership of the means of production.

Engels and the State

The most serious effort to contain these anomalies was precisely made in what is held, by George Lichtheim, to be the fount of the positivist heresy in Marxism, Engels's *Anti-Dühring*. Here Engels simultaneously develops an analysis of the origins of the class system which fully allows a ruling class to be *state* generated, and which systematically focuses on the state's role in performing functions for the society as a *whole.* In effect, the *Anti-Dühring* presents *two* parallel theories of the origins of social classes: one based on spontaneous development of the mode of production, internal to the community; the second, explains classes as deriving from differentiation produced by development of the state.

1. *State-Based Classes.* "How are we to explain the origin of classes and relations based on domination. . . . They arose in two ways. As men first emerged from the animal world . . . [they were] as poor as the animals and hardly more productive . . . there prevailed a certain equality in the conditions of existence, and for the heads of families also a kind of equality of social position—at least an absence of social classes. . . . In each such community there were from the beginning certain common interests the safeguarding of which had to be handed over to individuals, even though under the control of the community as a whole: such were the adjudication of disputes, control of water supplies, especially in hot countries . . . religious functions. Such offices . . . are naturally endowed with a certain measure of authority and the beginnings of state power." Thus far, Engels has a straightforward functional account of the origin of the state; the state and its personnel deriving from the common needs of society as a *whole,* and the state's authority being grounded in its functional contribution to these common needs. Note, by the way, Engels's prominent mention of the state's control of water supplies.

As productive forces develop, adds Engels, the separate communes are grouped together and there is "the setting up of organs to safeguard common interests and to guard against conflicting interests. These organs . . . soon make themselves even more independent, partly through heredity of function . . . and partly because they become more and more indispensable owing to the increasing number of conflicts within the other groups. . . . Here we are only concerned with establishing the fact that the exercise of a social function was everywhere the basis of political supremacy; and further that political supremacy has existed for any length of time only when it fulfilled its social functions. However great the number of despotic governments which rose and fell in India and Persia, each was fully aware that its first duty was the general maintenance of irrigation [sic] throughout the valleys, without which no agriculture was possible."[11] (Clearly, in discussing the origins of classes in *state* formation, Engels has the Asiatic Mode of Production very much on his mind.) He then adds that "alongside this development of classes another was also taking place."

2. *Classes Based on the Mode of Production.* "The natural division of labour within the family cultivating the soil made possible, at a certain level of well-being, the introduction of one or more strangers as additional labor forces," especially where the old common ownership of land had dissolved. As productivity developed, and men could produce more than they required, the means of maintaining a labor force came about. This was supplied through prisoners of war who had previously been economically useless and could not be enslaved: "the introduction of slavery under the conditions of that time was a great step forward. . . . The ancient communes, where they continued to exist, have for thousands of years formed the basis of the most barbarous form of state, oriental despotism, from India to Russia [sic]. It was only where these communities dissolved that the peoples made progress of themselves, and their first economic advance consisted in the increase and development of production by means of slave labour."

There were, then, two parallel if interacting origins of the ruling class: (1) those who performed social functions and who acquired independence from and domination over the community for whom they were performing them—in short, this is a two-class system of state officials and the state's subjects; (2) economic differentiation through the division of labor into something like a three- or four-class system, (a) manual laborers, (b) proprietors directing work and trading goods, (c) public officials, (d) intelligentsia (artists and scientists). While this at first seems to be an analytic distinction between state and economy-based classes, it soon becomes clear that these distinctions are only a slightly more generalized version of, respectively, Eastern (AMP) and Western systems of social stratification. The economy-based class system is actually the class and state system premised in their primary paradigm, characterized by powerful proprietary classes grounded in the economy who are not at all overshadowed by the state's "public officials."

It thus appears that Engels began this formulation in an effort to provide a generalized theory of state and class origins which could encompass the anomalous AMP, but he ends it with the two systems still very much apart, kept together more by editorial devices than analytic transcendence. Engels is simply saying that differentiations of incomes and power can be grounded in either the state's development or in the development of the means of production. While this seems correct enough, it does not, however, produce the reconciliation he had sought between the primary paradigm's view that *the state was the product* of irreconcilable class differences and the AMP's implication that *these class differences were the product of the state*. The two parallel sources of stratification remained.

With their discovery of the AMP, Marx and Engels required a theory which allows the state, and its personnel, to assume dominance over other, proprietary ruling classes and which could explain how that dominance came about. They needed a theory that permitted the political to escape the dominance of the economy and, indeed, to account for its dominance over the economic. The clear addition made here in the *Anti-Dühring* was that, somehow, the state could in its own right be a center for the formation of a real ruling class; any theory that ignored this ignored the clear implication of the AMP. Yet a theory which also said this outright clashed with the primary paradigm which places society's center of gravity in the economic sphere. Thus Engels's theory focused on the state's role in class formation *in very early societies* but it did not say outright that the state's bureaucracy could *at any time* be a *society's ruling class*. Engels is still attempting to do justice to the historical reality of the AMP, on the one hand, while not discarding the primary paradigm, on the other.

In the end, therefore, Engels makes another effort to transcend the difficulties. He moves to unify his account of the origins of social classes in a way that normalizes it. That is, he proposes a common source of both lines of class development, grounding them both in the *level of productivity*. "We may add at this point," he says, "that all historical antagonism between exploiting and exploited, ruling and oppressed classes to this very day find their explanation in this same relatively undeveloped productivity of human labour. So long as the really working population was so much occupied in their necessary labour that they had no time left for looking after the common affairs of society—the direction of labour, affairs of the state, legal matters, art, science, etc.—so long was it always necessary that there should exist a special class, free from actual labour, to manage these affairs; and this special class never failed to impose a greater and greater burden of labour, for its own advantage, on the working masses." Only large-scale industry has so increased productivity as to enable all to "have enough free time left to take part in the general—both theoretical and practical—affairs of society. It is only now, therefore, that any ruling and exploiting class has become superfluous and indeed a hindrance to social development."[12]

This account glosses over the fact that the state itself—as amply evidenced by Marx and Engels's account of the AMP—was a major factor in productivity, might foster or dampen it. Thus Engels's effort to normalize the origins of stratification by referring to the level of productivity, is ambiguous since that very productivity might itself be fostered by the state. The level of productivity is thus not a stable stopping point to account for classes, even though Engels uses it as such, but an arbitrary one; for it, in turn, may depend on the activity of the state.

Engels's argument assumed that the state arose and produced a ruling class, standing over and exploiting the rest of society, when the level of productivity was still too low for everyone to have time for those common activities with which the state is concerned, with the result that these are monopolized by a small, special class. But since a modest increase in productivity permitted the introduction of slavery—rather than being used to allow *everyone to work a bit less*—why wouldn't a *substantial* increase in productivity simply provide a larger surplus to be used to support a larger, nonproductive bureaucracy, rather than eliminating all classes? A fundamental issue glossed here, moreover, is how much productivity is too little, and how much, enough? That is, at what point in the growth of the surplus product will it be defined as sufficient, so that all may be free to participate in managing the community's common affairs? Does this depend solely on the *size* of the surplus itself, as Marx and Engels plainly assume? Does it not also depend on the *sumptuary* norms and expectations of the consumer, *in addition to* (not in place of) the size of the surplus? Part of what made it possible for almost all male citizens of ancient Athens to participate actively in civic management was, first, that they had great numbers of slaves whose product they appropriated, and, second, but no less important, that the citizens had very modest expectations of consumption. By modern standards, they ate, drank, and dressed with simplicity and they found ways to express their individuality through costless aesthetic variability, such as how they folded their toga or how long they wore it.

Engels's discussion of the role of limited productivity in generating both types of ruling classes also provides no clear account of *how* a state bureaucracy (or a proprietary class) becomes a ruling class. We are told that they are "naturally" endowed with a measure of authority, because they contribute to the satisfaction of society's collective needs. That is, because of the social function they perform, society presumably awards them (or consents to their) dominance. They become powerful, then, because they are useful, because society needs them, because they "serve the people." There is a parallel to this among the proprietary classes, for they, too, service social needs, the bourgeoisie, as Marx relates, revolutionizing production, at least for a time. Both bureaucratic officials and proprietary classes, then, are seen as becoming ruling classes because they satisfy society's needs.

Toward a Theory of Ruling Classes

But is every group that satisfies a social need a ruling class? Obviously not. What makes a group into a ruling class is in part the needs it satisfies, how acute (or nondeferrable) and widespread they are, on the one hand, and *their ability to exclude others from satisfying this need,* on the other. What makes a group a ruling class is its ability to *monopolize* a necessary service, to inhibit others from providing this service, and, above all, *to prevent those receiving help from helping themselves and satisfying their own needs.* What makes a group a ruling class is that it can satisfy acute and recurrent mass needs, and that *it can prevent others from doing so.* In satisfying a need in this exclusive manner, a new need is generated: a need is generated for the group supplying the need.

The power of a ruling class, then, does not derive simply from its capacity to satisfy acute mass needs. Its power also entails its ability to exclude competitors supplying the same needs (a struggle very similar to that occurring among *Mafiosi* to control the provision of "illicit" needs). Since competitors already have their own supplies, they cannot be controlled by servicing their needs. At some point, therefore, competitors must be excluded by force and violence or the threat of it. But if the ability to satisfy needs is a center around which a group's power develops, this means that the state's capacity to service the ruling class's need for force and violence is a basis of the ruling class's dependence on the state, and of the latter's influence over the ruling class. A ruling class's power thus rests partly on the social needs it services and on its ability to monopolize this service. The latter, in turn, is based on power as force and violence or, as the phrase has it, grows out of the "barrel of a gun" or other more or less sophisticated weapons.

A group becomes a *ruling class,* then, not merely because it satisfies "basic" needs, but only when it can prevent others, *including the needy themselves,* from doing so. Marx was saying precisely this when he emphasized that a necessary condition for the development of capitalism itself was the expropriation of peasants and other workers, i.e., their loss of control over the instruments of production, so that they were then constrained to sell their labor power for a wage. All that I have done above is to generalize this point and to see that it is, indeed, generalizable.

Proprietors' control over a "surplus" is, in part, based on their exclusive control over the instruments of production, monopolizing a decisive requisite of production. Through the control thus acquired, proprietors are in turn able to satisfy an enormous variety of mass needs and thereby become a dominant social class. Yet if control over the surplus, based on control of the instruments of production, helps establish the hegemony of the proprietary class, consistency suggests that, when the state officialdom has a similar control over the instruments of production—whether hydraulic systems or industrial technology—they, too, become a ruling class. A state-generated ruling class, the bureaucracy, acquires authority for the same reason that proprietors do: both satisfy nondeferrable mass needs by acquiring exclusive control over resources that satisfy them and by making others dependent on them. The state's claim to a monopoly of legitimate violence allows it to monopolize the production of "order" and to satisfy other acute mass needs. In satisfying the need for order it, at the same time, prevents others from doing so, by disarming its own population.

The provision of group needs through control over the means of production, or the surplus, is thus not the only grounding of a ruling class. Under some circumstances a priesthood can be a ruling class, as can a military group or a bureaucracy. A ruling class can be developed around *any acute, i.e., nondeferrable mass need,* if the group supplying it can successfully prevent competitors from providing alternative sources of need satisfaction, and if they can succeed in making the persons receiving the need satisfaction incompetent or unable to satisfy their own needs—i.e., *if it can transform them into dependents.*

Every ruling class, then, does satisfy "its" society's needs, but only on the condition that others become its dependents. A ruling class is thus not a military conqueror but is, rather, committed to the maintenance and reproduction of those under them and is involved in reciprocities with them, providing them certain provisions and protections in exchange for hegemony. It is inherent in this hierarchical arrangement, however, that not everyone's needs will be met *equally;* those who control the supplying of needs will be able to advantage themselves; those dependent, will not.

The reason that a class seeks to monopolize its power, thus making itself into a ruling class, is indeed related to Engels's point about the low level of productivity. In short, needs outrun the ability to satisfy them, and there is scarcity. If there was "enough" for everyone, the drive to monopolize control of these goods and services would be diminished. Engels is half-right: scarcity induces efforts to monopolize and control scarce goods. The other half, which he omitted, however, was that scarcity is an equation in which there are two elements, the supply of goods and services and *the expectations they seek to satisfy.* As suggested earlier, without morally internalized limits on consumption expectations (sumptuary norms), nothing will ever be "enough." Scarcity, then, is indeed important in fostering the process from which a ruling class emerges; but "scarcity" itself is also produced *both* by the supply of provisions and protections, and by *anything that shapes persons' appetites for them, either limiting or enlargening them.*

Insofar as protections and provisions are scarce or precarious, when any group seeks to extend its own share of them, it enters into competition with others, and the more powerful it is the more pressure it can exert on other groups. Proprietors and bureaucratic officials are each in a position to exert considerable pressure on one another; each is in a position to threaten and encroach seriously upon the other. One way to reduce that competition is for them to specialize, each providing certain needs the other does not. Essentially, the "liberal state/economy" in the West pursued that strategy. The liberal state offers proprietors exclusive control over capital and capital accumulation, in exchange for exclusive control over order maintenance by the state. This division of labor, however, breaks down as the proprietary class becomes increasingly dependent on the state's help in capital accumulation and reproduction.

Under late capitalism there has, since the 1930s, been a rapid extension of the state's powers and of dependency upon it, and a continuing limitation of the powers of the proprietary class. Under late capitalism, the number and proportion of persons who are direct dependents of the state grows with the increase of those on welfare, with the growth of the military force, and through the state's direct employment of a labor force and bureaucracy. An ever larger part of the goods and services produced by the proprietary sector is destined for the state. "The most recent figures published by the OECD [Organization for Economic Development], which includes the main industrialized countries show that public spending spurted from an average of 28 percent of national output in 1955–57 to 34 percent 12 years later, and to 41 percent by the mid-1970s."[13] Without this state market, the production of other goods and services would be undermined and limited; the entire level of production and of the surplus produced now depends increasingly on the action of the state, and the process of capital accumulation itself would now be crippled without it.

The crucial mechanism centers on the state's role in the circulation of goods and money. It begins with the state advancing billions to purchase goods and services from the proprietors; it then replaces or meets this advance from revenues obtained from taxes, by borrowing on interest-bearing bonds, and by printing new money, which inflates the currency. In effect, the bonds offered on the money market by the government become a kind of capital akin to that used in the proprietary economy, while this state bond market becomes a major investment outlet for private capital, keeping up the floor under the proprietary rate of profit. Having total control over the issuance of money, the state's power in the commodity and bond market is enormous, while its ability to tax shapes the incomes produced.

This new political economy intensifies the fusion between the proprietary class and the state, but it did not produce it. The very power of the state always made it important for the proprietary class to have access to and influence on the state, which in liberal capitalist societies is mediated by the political parties. That proprietors have advantaged access to the surplus, means, in one part, that they will have more resources to seek and to hold positions in the state, or to prepare their children to do so, or to sponsor a political elite who do this on a full-time basis, and to pay (i.e., bribe) officials for assistance they seek. Recruitment to the state officialdom and influence on it, or on the political parties who (among other things) serve as brokers between proprietors and the state, was thus always particularly available to the proprietary class. Since, however, the state claims to represent the community as a whole, since it satisfies acute mass needs, its uniquely close ties with the proprietary group must be masked.

At the same time, however, insofar as services supplied by the state also satisfy acute nondeferrable mass needs, as they do when there is a threat of external invasion, internal disruption, or a crisis in subsistence getting and distributing; insofar as the state acquires a monopoly of legitimate violence and the armed forces grow along with conscription of citizens; insofar as there is increasing control through taxation over the surplus produced in the proprietary sector, or increased direct control over surpluses of goods produced by its own economic activities; and insofar as the state acquires control over money, capital, labor, rents, or interest rates, education, transport, and communication, the state officialdom becomes a powerful class capable of exerting great reciprocal pressure upon the proprietary class, becoming a competitor class, if not dominating or sometimes destroying the proprietary class.

In this formulation, then, the state and its bureaucracy may, indeed, be or become the ruling class. It is clearly not the puppet of the proprietary class as a general rule. Depending on their relative powers at any one moment, either class can dominate the other. Commonly, however, proprietors and officials compete with one another for the society's scarce resources and surplus. At the same time, the state is not seen here as a neutral force standing impartially above the rest of society; in part, because it is often closely aligned with the proprietary class; and, in part, because it itself may be a ruling class with partisan vested interests of its own, especially in maintaining its control over the needs it supplies and the resources it uses to do so. The state officialdom will, moreover, also be most closely aligned with whatever classes help it to perform its special role in the social division of labor.

The size of the surplus available to the state bureaucracy depends on several factors. It is, to repeat, never just a function of the level of productivity in the economy but also of sumptuary norms that limit consumption. The size of the surplus also depends on the sheer power and ruthlessness of the bureaucracy, for this determines how much it can extract from the proprietary (or any other) class. Essentially, the same is true of the proprietary class. A "surplus," then, is not simply out-there, already in existence, waiting to be appropriated by the bureaucracy, or proprietors. A surplus is produced not only by "labor" but also by the relative power of the contending parties. The state may thus generate the surplus just as much as the economy; and it can do this as much by its exercise of power as by any contribution it makes to the productivity of the economy as, for instance, through building and maintaining irrigation systems.

The size of the surplus depends also on the proportion of the goods and services that are consumed, and the proportion reserved to produce other goods and services—i.e., capitalized. Once encumbered by the state, however, substantial amounts of surplus goods and services are withdrawn from use as production resources because they are used for war or military upkeep, for welfare purposes, or for the sovereign's or bureaucracy's style of life. The state, moreover, need not economize in using its resources since the functions it performs are its monopoly and are not distributed among competitors. Finally, even the modern state usually budgets its resources in an essentially "feudal" manner: i.e., it starts with an estimate of what it wants to spend and then seeks incomes to match this, rather than first calculating its incomes and limiting its expenditures to these.

It has been obvious (since Oriental Despotisms and their "hydraulic" economies) that states can and do contribute to their economy's productivity. Nonetheless, states are never as exclusively committed to increasing productivity as are proprietary classes, because the latter's social functions are more specialized and because their interests are narrower and private. As a result, proprietary classes can more readily extract and build surpluses and *keep them available for reinvestment* in new and improved instruments of production that heighten productivity. It is, therefore, to be expected that economies under the control of proprietary groups will be more dynamically expansive and productive than those more fully under the control of a state bureaucracy (which does not imply these must be the only two alternatives).

The suggestions offered above, on how ruling classes become such, differ from three other theories accounting for this process: the functionalist conception of stratification, the hegemonic view of authority, and the "Machiavellian" focus on force and fraud as the pillars of power. The latter fails partly because it begs the question of how power is mobilized, taking this as a given, and further, it underestimates the vulnerabilities of a power that is neither defined as legitimate nor rests on some mutual provision of gratifications. The functionalist view, in contrast, accounts for the mobilization of power as that which the ruling class gets in return for its contribution to society, but it ignores the fact that, once accumulated, the power of the ruling class then enables it to ignore others' needs. It can thus protect its privileges and perquisites even when it is unable or unwilling to offer reciprocal satisfactions to others. Hegemony theory, for its part, sees a ruling class as protected by the legitimacy others confer on it but never explains why the lowly confer such legitimacy or accept the legitimacy claimed by the dominant.

In my own view, the power of the ruling class is grounded ultimately in its functions, i.e., what it contributes to others. Precisely because of this, however, the ability to satisfy the needs of others or of society is an advantage-conferring position for which there is competition and struggle, so that power is used to secure control over resources required to satisfy needs. Those satisfying social and individual needs are thus more likely to be the powerful, partly because others become dependent on them and partly because the powerful use their power to monopolize need-satisfying resources, and may thus remain in power without using force and violence. It is not simply legitimacy but dependency (which may exist without legitimacy) that bolsters power. The conferral of legitimacy by subordinates is grounded in part in their very dependency; in part by the satisfaction of their practical needs; and in part from the coercive persuasion that power permits a ruling class to exercise routinely. This legitimacy, once conferred, then of course reciprocally reinforces the power and dependency on which it is grounded.

Marxism as a Theory of Proprietary Classes

Western economies have been characterized by proprietary classes whose direct access to a surplus gave them substantial power to resist state officialdom. In Western societies, proprietary classes constituted one of the nodes around which the social networks of a relatively independent "civil society" developed. It is precisely such a relatively independent "civil society" that was lacking in the AMP and which contributed to its stagnation, while it was its presence in Western Europe that contributed much to the dynamism of capital.

One reason that Marxism failed in Eastern European societies, failing especially to achieve its own emancipatory ambitions, is in part because this was a culture-area in which proprietary classes, whether peasantry or nobility, were stunted by the state. In their study of East European intelligentsia (*The Road of Intellectuals to Class Power*) (New York: Harcourt, 1979), George Konrad and Ivan Szelenyi hold that, about the time of the twelfth century, Eastern Europe—Kiev, Novgorad, Poland, or Hungary—were simply poorer than Western Europe rather than differing pro-

foundly in other ways. Later, however, under the pressure of
seminomadic military empires that is, Tartar and Turkish expan-
sionism, East European society became more militarized; its
bureaucratic, central state organs became overdeveloped; and
there was a corresponding barrier to the growth of groups centering
on private property and a stunting of civil society. The central
state in Moscow refused to share power with a feudal nobility
based on patrimonial holdings and curbed them by cultivating a
"service nobility" whose land tenure depended on their loyalty
and service to the state, and whose estates could be and were
sometimes reshuffled. Neither nobility nor peasantry could here
develop their autonomy around private property, nor could they
limit the power of the central state. The resultant societies were
thus much more nearly like the Asiatic Mode of Production,
examples of that ideal type where the state's domination rested
in this case on the society's acute need for military protection
rather than for irrigation; and, indeed, Lenin and other Bolsheviks
themselves referred to Russia as semi-Asiatic despotism.

At this point there appear to be certain potential internal contradictions in Marxism. On the one hand, Marxism is committed to
the expropriation of the proprietary class—in the West, the
bourgeoisie or capitalist class. On the other hand, however, the
socialist future it envisages is inconceivable without that class and
its vast expansion of productivity. It seems as if Marxism is bent on
killing the very goose which (Marxism itself recognizes) has laid
the golden eggs. It does this in two ways: first, by eliminating this
historically most productive class and, second, by investing control over production in the state, which—as Marxism saw in the
AMP—threatens the economy with stagnation. There is no doubt
that Marxism means to eliminate the bourgeoisie, and no doubt
also that Marxism premises a high level of productivity. Yet Marxism would say this is only a seeming, not a real contradiction,
because the bourgeoisie will not be eliminable until after they
have revolutionized production, and only when the private relations of production become a barrier to further increases in productivity. Thus socialism will release productivity from this barrier and will not impair but heighten productivity. But if socialist
economy is managed by the state with a powerful bureaucracy,
will this not impose severe limits on productivity? More than that,
will they not themselves become a powerful new ruling class
which plunges the rest of society into a new and more debilitating
dependence, crippling the liberative intent of socialism?

Moreover, Marxists have so far come to power only where the bourgeoisie was weak and before it had gone very far in revolutionizing production.

Even if the elimination of the bourgeoisie does not threaten future productivity it will, however, have powerful *political* repercussions; it will leave socialist "civil society" profoundly weakened vis-a-vis the state. For there will now be no class of proprietors whose independent powers enabled it to fortify civil society and to counterbalance the power of the state bureaucracy. In short, socialism seems to imply a culmination of state power, making the state under socialism a center of domination for which there is no force independent of it. If this is so, then in Marx's own view of the AMP, such a newly powerful state will ultimately limit productivity and must defeat socialism's emancipatory aspirations. It remains only to be added that this appears to be exactly what has happened in those collectivist states that claim a Marxist inspiration: their bureaucracy soon becomes a new ruling class, controlling workers far more totally than any capitalist state (except the fascist) ever did; eviscerating civil society; developing a highly inefficient economy greatly dependent on technology transfers from the West; rigidly curbing the liberties of its citizens, and closely superintending every sphere of life.

The development of a vast, overtowering bureaucracy in Marxist states is not, however, to be understood as due to the "statist" aspirations of Marx and Engels. That is to say, domination of the state in Marxist societies is not due to the fact that Marx and Engels's theory valued the state as an end in itself. To the contrary, their *ultimate* ambition was the withering away of the state. The vast expansion of collectivist states is, nonetheless, connected with the theoretical assumptions that were made. If the growth of the state under socialism was unintended, it was, nonetheless, in part *structured* by Marxism's theoretical commitments.

It is first to be noted that we have it on the authority of the *Communist Manifesto* itself that, when the working-class revolution occurs and when the proprietary class is expropriated, it is the *state* which will then own and run the means of production: "the proletariat will use its political supremacy to wrest, by degrees, all capital from the bourgeoisie, to centralize all instruments of production in the hands of the State, i.e., of the proletariat organized as the ruling class; and to increase the total of productive forces as quickly as possible."[14]

There will further be the "centralization of credit in the hands

of the state. . . . Centralization of the means of communication and
transport in the hands of the State. . . . Extension of factories and
instruments of production owned by the State." Moreover, all land
will also be nationalized: that is, there will be "abolition of property in land."[15] Thus the object was elimination of the entire proprietary class in agriculture and the countryside, no less than in
manufacture and the city, and the ownership of their means of
production was to be transferred to the state. Since the state will
now control all means of violence and repression, as well as all
instruments of production, control of the social surplus would,
under the socialism contemplated by Marx and Engels, be under
the undivided control of the state.

Under these conditions, what could it possibly mean to call the
working class the "new ruling class." To speak of the state, as the
Manifesto does, as "the proletariat organized as the ruling class"
is, at best, a total false consciousness or, at worst, an impenetrable
mystification serving as an ideology to mask the reality that the
bureaucracy has become a new ruling class.

Marx and Engels were aware that there is a contradiction between their pursuit of socialism as a human emancipation, and
their endowment of the socialist state with greater power than any
Western state had hitherto achieved. Indeed, they themselves describe the state of the AMP, having just such a total domination of
society without a counterbalancing proprietary class, as an Oriental Despotism. They see the anomaly they have perpetrated, but
only with a fugitive glimpse, quickly thrusting it back into the
shadows of their merely auxiliary attention. Thus after endowing
the state with all the means of production, credit, communication,
transport, after giving it total power, the *Manifesto* then draws
back and promises that this new most powerful state will someday
wither away. Why? The argument is that, since all classes will be
eliminated, no state will be needed: "When, in the course of development, class distinctions have disappeared, and all production has been concentrated in the hands of a vast association of the
whole nation, the public power will lose its political character."
Yet communal possession of the land under the AMP did not prevent the state from being a despotism. It was not that public power
had lost its political character, but that the political power lost or
never had a public character. The *Manifesto* adds, "Political
power, properly so-called, is merely the organized power of one
class for oppressing another. If the proletariat . . . by means of a
revolution . . . makes itself the ruling class . . . then it will . . . have

swept away the conditions for the existence of class antagonism, and of classes generally," and this will therefore eliminate the state as a political force at the disposal of one class for exploitation of another class.

The entire presupposition here, however, was that a ruling class could only be a *proprietary* class, i.e., a class that owned the dominant means of production *privately*. But it was precisely that assumption which was undermined by discovery of the AMP. It was for just that reason that Engels sought in the *Anti-Dühring* to reconstruct the Marxist theory of classes in order to allow for a ruling class grounded in the state. The central and defining impulse of Marxism's primary paradigm, however, had defined a ruling class as a proprietary class. Thus the *Manifesto* expects that the "public" power will ultimately not serve a class exploitative character and, therefore, that the state bureaucracy *could* not constitute a ruling class exploiting others. The primary paradigm of Marxism thus does not bring the class character of a state bureaucracy into focus but, rather, occludes this. This is a major reason why the AMP in particular, and the theory of the state in general, remained undeveloped in the work of Marx and Engels. It explains why the AMP is discussed only in brief fugitive glosses, notes, in letters not intended for publication, or in brief newspaper articles. This explains why the AMP sinks into invisibility in the subsequent history of the world Marxist movement, and is most especially repressed in the Soviet Union between 1931 and 1964, when the concept is drummed out of the Soviet reading of Marxism. As E. Iolk, one of the Soviet scholars in the debates that repressed the AMP, remarks: "The concept of a special 'asiatic' mode of production . . . is theoretically unfounded, because it contradicts the foundations of the Marxist-Leninist teaching on classes and the state."[16] That the AMP was recognized as anomalous is here made explicit; the resulting strategy of normalizing such an anomaly, by denying the reality of one half of the contradiction, could not be made more visible. What Iolk forgets, of course, is that by exactly that same reasoning one is led with equal force to conclude that, given the AMP, it is "the Marxist-Leninist teachings on classes and the state" that are "unfounded."

The AMP was "rehabilitated" by Soviet Marxists after the Sino-Soviet break intensified, testifying to the new ideological uses it is now made to serve. If Soviet scholars now point the AMP at the Chinese, as a kind of accusation and explanation, it is not, however, to be supposed that they are blind to its critical import for Soviet society itself. This, however, is left in silence, partly because it is too dangerous to voice and partly because they can count on tacit understanding of this among colleagues. Indeed it is precisely the AMP's applicability to the USSR itself that provides another motive for the contemporary resurfacing of that concept among some Marxists in the West. This standpoint argues that the USSR has become a "bureaucratic collectivism" only because of Russia's semi-Asiatic character, thereby dissociating Marxism and socialism from the political liability of association with the USSR. The implication is that what happened in semi-Asiatic Russia was peculiar to it but would not happen in socialisms in advanced industrial societies. The AMP is thus used to justify future applications of Marxism. This highly tendentious use of the AMP, however, can persuade only if one assumes that a civil society of some power would survive in the West and could counterbalance a newly powerful socialist state. This, in turn, premises that a socialist state in the West would have neither the ability nor the motive to smash civil society, reducing it to the Russian "semi-Asiatic" level. In short, the argument assumes that the impoverishment and weakness of civil society of Russian life was altogether due to its unique cultural inheritance, and it underestimates the extent to which the Stalinist state smashed or immobilized even those social structures which did exist and had been strong, including new organizations such as trade unions and old structures such as the family.[17]

The most dangerous ideological use today of the AMP, however, is that to which Soviet ideologists seem ready to put it, namely, as a basis for defining China as having a development that sets it off uniquely from the West, that defines it as uniquely inferior economically or politically backward and antiindividualistic. In effect, then, this Soviet use of the AMP offers to provide an ideological groundwork for *détente* between the Soviet Union and the United States, whose main object would be the political isolation of "barbaric" China.

It is paradoxical that the old unilinear Marxism, which indeed saw Asia as stagnant, barbaric, and backward, nonetheless saw it as developing on the same track as the West, and thus as at one with Western development; multilinear readings of Marxism, however, which seek to make Marxism less dogmatically determinist, have the paradoxical consequence of stressing the uniqueness of the orient and the fundamental nature of its difference from the West.

Current reinterpretations of the AMP, by writers such as Umberto Melotti, in turn, seek to deal with this by defining both the AMP and the classical societies from which the West evolved as being on a par, the latter issuing in modern capitalist society, the former in what Melotti (following Bruno Rizzi) calls "bureaucratic collectivism." Capitalism and bureaucratic collectivism, then, are defined as on the same level of development, and both are treated as precursors of socialism; the model thus constitutes an intermediary multilinearism culminating in unilinearism.

I have suggested, then, that the hyper-development of the state in Marxist collectivism is not to be understood simply as a result of Marx and Engels's statism. It results, in part, from a kind of default; that is, some agency is needed to manage the property expropriated from the proprietary class. Since the state is defined (in the primary paradigm) as the instrument of the ruling class—then, when the bourgeoisie is overthrown and replaced by the working class, the latter are now defined as the new proprietary class. The state is then seen as the proletariat's "executive committee," as the agency of the majority class in society and, thus, as not needing to exploit the majority. The state then presumably loses its partisan political character and becomes a fully public realm devoid of its own special exploitative interests. The Marxist view, then, is that someone must manage the newly expropriated property and that the state is not only a technically feasible agency to do so but, having been sociologically decontaminated, its use is now compatible with Marxists' hopes for a socialist emancipation. In effect, the Marxist theory of the state and of the ruling class, here interwoven, had misled Marxist politics by profoundly underestimating the dangers to human emancipation inherent in the state bureaucracy and its capacity to be a new ruling class.

There is, however, at least a second characteristic of Marx's theory conducive to the same hyper-development of the state under socialism. This relates to Marxism's deemphasis upon semi-autonomous social structures in consequence of its tendency to see almost all social organization as dependent on the mode of production. In short, inherent in Marxism's "economism" there is not only a tendency to underemphasize the role of the ideology and of "consciousness" but also of almost all social structures not directly implicated in the mode of production. This, in turn, entails a tendency to view society as if it were a factory run by a state. Marx assumed that this left the forces of production free to develop; in point of fact, what it does is to leave the state free to

develop unchecked, placing at its disposal increasing forces of
production.

Economism as the Surrender of Social Structure

Marxism's critique of utopian socialism, which had wanted to proceed at once, even in the midst of the old society, to the development of small communities prefiguring its vision of a better society, inhibited Marxism's own prefigurative impulse, channeling it
into the purely instrumental politics of both the Second and Third
Internationals. In particular, Scientific Marxism's impulse is to
reduce politics to the struggle for power in the state. It thus neglects the importance of protecting and rebuilding the dense infrastructure of communities, institutions, organizations, and
groups within which the working class presently lives and
through which, even now, some of its own needs could be
supplied through self-help and mutual aid, by which its own anxieties can be controlled, and its dependency reduced. Marx sees
such institutions, however, very largely as a transmission belt for
ruling-class values and as mechanisms for the control of the
working class. He believes, for example, that trade unions can
divert energy from the need for a total social reconstruction and
can accommodate the working class to society as it is. Marx failed
to see that, without viable working-class institutions, communities, and groups within capitalism, the dependency and passivity of the working class are heightened, its vulnerability to the
regressive politics of fascism and authoritarianism is in modern
times intensified, and the working class is unable to cultivate the
skills and self-reliance needed to manage its own existence. Without prefigurative working class communities and groups committed to self-help, even "soviets" have little future as a method of
political self-management by the working class. A fundamental
expression of Marxism's "economism," then, is thus not just the
theory of the automatic crash; it is Marxism's surrender of social
structures, its uncritical acceptance of the deterioration of the entire fabric of social structure required to sustain working class life,
and its tendency to understand the problem of working-class dependency merely as "false consciousness."

The Communist Manifesto had clearly seen, yet never focused
theoretically on, the diffuse deterioration of old social structures
among the working class. But it never clearly saw the special

contribution they make in helping persons cope with their own suffering through practical mutual aid or self-help. Marxism noted that workers had no country, no family, no claim on human help from any but themselves and thus had nothing to lose but their chains. "The working men have no country . . . national differences and antagonisms between people are daily more and more vanishing." Only the bourgeoisie have the family "in its completely developed form." "This state of things finds its complement in the practical absence of the family among the proletarians." Their work environment, instead of sheltering them only exploits them. "The bourgeoisie . . . has left remaining no other nexus between man and man than naked self-interest, than callous 'cash payment.' . . . The bourgeoisie has stripped of its halo every occupation hitherto honored." Indeed, even "differences of age and sex have no longer any distinctive validity," since all workers under capitalism are primarily instruments of labor. Thus, the *Communist Manifesto.*

Marx and Engels, then, were fully aware of the advanced deterioration of the social structure experienced by the emerging working classes. This, however, simply becomes one other item in their long bill of indictment against capitalism. Their attitude is that these ancient solidarities neither need to be nor can be restored. "The bourgeois family will vanish . . . with the vanishing of capital," they say with an air of, good riddance! What is conveyed is that all these older solidarities of family, guild, neighborhood, nation are archaic, blocking the requisite class and international solidarity of the proletariat.

For Marx's socialism, all these other institutions and groups are just appendages of production and of persons associated primarily as producers. Apart from economic institutions, the only other that clearly has a future in Marx's socialism is the state. The need for a rich, complex set of social structures in civil society that might resist the state's domination is ignored because of the myth that the new socialist state would be the obedient instrument of the new ruling class, the proletariat. Presumably, therefore, the working class would not need social structures to help defend it against its "own" state. Marxism thus once again contributed—and not unwittingly—to the continuation of the growth of the Western state which, developing with the absolute monarchy, had been extended by the powerful centralizing impulse of the French Revolution, culminating in the effort to eliminate groups standing between individuals and the revolutionary state, and which regarded civil society's organizational structure as compromising its own sovereignty.

In Marx's 1850 address to the Central Committee to the Communist League, he discusses the "coming" bourgeois democratic revolution in Germany and the dangers it represents to the working class: "As in the first French Revolution the petty bourgeois will give the feudal lands to the peasant, as free property." The workers, Marx warns, must oppose this plan and "demand that the confiscated feudal property remain *state* property and be converted into *workers' colonies* cultivated by the associated rural proletariat with all the advantages of large-scale production." Furthermore, Marx adds, "the democrats will either work directly for a federated republic, or . . . will at least attempt to cripple the central government by the utmost autonomy and independence for the communities and provinces. The workers in opposition to this plan, must not only strive for a single and indivisible German republic, but also within this republic *for the most determined centralization of power in the hands of the state authority. They must not allow themselves to be misguided by the democratic talk of freedom for the communities, of self-government,* etc. . . . it must under no circumstances be permitted that every village, every town, and every province should put a new obstacle in the path of revolutionary activity, *which can proceed with full force only from the center.*" That the French Revolution's centralization was a model is plainly indicated in the very last sentence: "As in France in 1793, so today in Germany it is the task of the revolutionary party to carry through the strictest centralization."[18]

As the influence of French culture was tempered with his experience of English institutions, Marx's emphasis on the state and its centralization temporarily receded (although never as much as suggested by those wishing to exculpate Marxism from any taint of responsibility for Stalinism). The decisive text here is *The Civil War in France,* which was presented shortly after the fall of the Paris Commune as an address to the General Council of the First International on 30 May 1871. While an analysis of the Commune, it was inevitably a tribute to the Communards, bound to express sympathy with most of what they had done, especially as they were just being brutally massacred and many still lay unburied in Paris streets.

Marx observes in *The Civil War in France* that the working class cannot simply seize and use governmental power for its own purposes. The centralized state power, centering on the standing army, police, bureaucracy, clergy, and judiciary had been developed to serve "nascent middle class society as a mighty weapon in its struggles against feudalism."[19] Yet even this state apparatus, complained Marx, was still limited by various interests: "its development remained clogged by all manner of medieval rubbish, seignorial rights, local privileges, municipal and guild monopolies and provincial constitutions."[20] Any decentralizing limits on the central state power, whether municipal constitutions or seignorial rights, are lumped together as historical "relics." Marx is thus happy to note that "the gigantic broom of the French Revolution of the eighteenth century swept away all these relics of bygone times, thus clearing simultaneously the social soil of its last hindrances to the superstructure of the modern state edifice raised under the First Empire."

This state subsequently becomes "the national power of capital over labor . . . a public force organised for social enslavement, . . . an engine of class despotism . . . the purely repressive character of the state power stands out in bolder and bolder relief." Thus it is that this state cannot be seized by the working class and used for its own purposes but must be destroyed. Clearly, however, Marx saw the growing centralization of the state as having at first a progressive character, eliminating the old "medieval rubbish" of localism; only later, as it becomes the chief instrument for the domination of the working class, does it become reactionary and need to be eliminated. But his emphasis here is on eliminating the centralized state of the bourgeoisie, not necessarily on eliminating *all* such states, and not necessarily endorsing this as a program for a *socialist* state. Indeed, Marx did not define the Commune as socialist.

By now, Marx had also increasingly normalized his diagnosis of Louis Bonaparte's government, no longer seeing it as a government of the peasantry at large, the conservative peasantry, or the lumpen proletariat, and he now remarks that it only "professed to rest upon the peasantry." Under its sway, he says, "bourgeois society, freed from political cares, attained a development unexpected even by itself. Its industry and commerce expanded into colossal dimensions."[21] In other words, the bourgeoisie's political powerlessness was presumably a blessing in disguise, allowing them to devote their energies to money-making. In contrast to this Bonapartist state "apparently soaring high above society," the Commune restored the republic to society and sought to remove all class rule. Marx thus notes that the Paris Commune "got rid of the army, and replaced it by National Guard, the bulk of which consisted of working men,"[22] substituting the armed people for the standing army. The Commune also eliminated a specialized parliament, substituting recallable municipal counsellors selected by universal suffrage who were to be a working body not just a talking assembly, combining both legislative and executive functions. "Public functions ceased to be the private property of the tools of the Central Government . . . the whole initiative hitherto exercised by the state was laid into the hands of the Commune." Similarly, the Commune eliminated the power of the police, disestablished and disendowed all churches as proprietary bodies, and established free education clear of interference from church and state.

There seems little question that Marx sympathizes with these provisions of the Commune. The "merely repressive organs of the old governmental power were to be amputated," he observes, while "its legitimate functions were wrested from an authority usurping pre-eminence over society itself, and restored to the responsible agents of society."[23] Even then, however, Marx is careful to add that this new Commune is not a reproduction of the medieval commune, nor is it "an attempt to break up into a confederation of small states. . . . The antagonism of the Commune against the state power has been mistaken for an exaggerated form of the ancient struggle against over-centralization." This, Marx claims, was not the case. "In reality, the Communal Constitution brought the rural producers under the intellectual lead of the central towns of their districts, and there secured to them, in the working men, the natural trustees of their interests. The very existence of the Commune involved . . . local municipal liberty, but no longer as a check upon the superseded state power." Marx thus resists a view of the Commune as a radically decentralising force, in a manner consistent with his 1850 address to the Central Committee of the Communist League. At the economic level, Marx also spoke of "united cooperative societies" that were to "regulate national production upon a common plan."[24] Whether this means that the state would no longer manage the expropriated properties, as specified in the *Communist Manifesto*, will be discussed further below. Clearly, however, Marx has here qualified the extreme centralizing drive, which had earlier led him to accent the importance of the socialist state, though rejecting any general tendency toward an anticentralized autonomy at the local level.

Marx's posture toward the antistatist program of the Commune seems to have been that its "heart" was in the right place. But did he think that, in its antistatism, the Commune's "head" was also in the right place? Marx's diagnosis of the Commune's weaknesses, of why it would lose, suggests not. This diagnosis indicates that the Commune's vulnerabilities lay in its sentimentality and "conscientious scruples" and in its failure to mobilize power with sufficient decisiveness and centralization. Marx thus writes his friend, Kugelmann, on 12 April 1871 that, apart from being too easy-going and scrupulous, their "second mistake" was that "the Central Committee surrendered its power too soon, to make way for the Commune." In short, Marx distinguished between the Commune's demolition of the old bourgeois state, which he endorsed and wished it had gone further, and its "scruples" which had impaired its effective concentration of power against the bourgeois class enemy. This last, then, implies that Marx believed that the Commune should have strengthened not weakened its own state apparatus. Thus the dictates of the heart and the head were not consistent. Marx's impulse, we may say, entailed an anticentralizing anarchism of the "heart," contradicted by a procentralizing statism of the intelligence. Indeed, he criticized the Commune for its failure to build its own instrument of state repression.

This is visible in his more sober diagnosis of the Paris Commune a decade later. In a letter of 22 February 1881—two years before his death—Marx wrote to the Dutch socialist Domela Neiuwenhuis, emphasizing that "a socialist government does not come into power in a country unless conditions are so developed that it can above all take the necessary measures for intimidating the mass of the bourgeoisie sufficiently to gain time—the first *desirderatum*—for lasting action."[25] Marx then goes directly on to say, "Perhaps you will point to the Paris Commune; but apart from the fact that this was merely the rising of a town under exceptional circumstances, the majority of the Commune was in no sense socialist, nor could it be."

One can observe how much less significance Marx attributes here to the Commune, as well as how much less glowing was his later judgement of it: "with a small amount of sound common sense [which he apparently thinks it lacked], however, they could have reached a compromise with Versailles useful to the whole mass of the people—the only thing that could be reached at the time." Clearly Marx has returned to his "normal" view, stressing the need for a powerful state apparatus to terrorize the class enemy and, also, reemphasizing a deterministic economism, which he likens expressly to Christian millenarianism: "The dream that the end of the world was at hand inspired the early Christians in their struggle with the Roman Empire and gave them confidence in victory. Scientific insight into the *inevitable* disintegration of the dominant order of society continually proceeding before our eyes, and the ever-growing passion into which the masses are scourged by the ghosts of government— while at the same time the positive development of the means of production advances with giant strides—all this is a sufficient guarantee that with the moment of a real proletarian revolution there will also be given the conditions (though these are certain not to be idyllic) of its next *modus operandi.*"[26]

Clearly, Marx held that the Communards had been too soft, and they and all socialists required a state to intimidate their class enemies. But do they, in Marx's view, also need the state to administer the forces of production which they will have expropriated from private owners, or is it his view now that they are to be administered by "co-operative societies"? On 3 August 1871 *The New York Herald* published an interview with Marx in which he directly addressed this question. Asked what the first step would be, if the International came to power in England, Marx insisted that: "we would proceed to the transformation of all great properties, such as manufactures—all the land, in favor of the state."[27] Thus, immediately upon the heels of *The Civil War in France,* sometimes assumed to be evidence of Marx's departure from statism, Marx returned, as if without change, to the plainly statist formula of the *Communist Manifesto.*

NOTES

1. See M. Shapiro, "Stages of Social Development," *Marxism Today,* September 1962, p. 283.

2. See Umberto Melotti, *Marx and the Third World* (London: Macmillan Publishers, 1977), p. 11.

3. See Maxine Rodinson, *Islam and Capitalism* (Harmondsworth: Penguin Books, 1974), p. 59.

4. See Robert Tucker, ed., *The Marx-Engels Reader* (New York: W. W. Norton & Co., 1972), pp. 577–82. The article is dated 10 June 1853.

5. Ibid., pp. 583–88. The article is dated 22 July 1853.

6. See for instance Marian Sawer's useful book, *Marxism and the Question of the Asiatic Mode of Production* (The Hague: Martinus Nijhoff, 1977); Perry Anderson, *Passages from Antiquity to Feudalism* (London: New Left Books, 1974) and his *Lineages of the Abolutist State* (London: New Left Books, 1974); Anderson drops the AMP on the empirical grounds that the two elements central to it, common ownership of land and a centralized system of irrigation are not usually found together historically but are on different levels of development; but here our own concerns are with the internal dynamics of Marx and Engels's theory; Jean Chesneaux, "Le mode de production asiatique," *La Pensée*, January/February 1964; M. Godelier, ed., *Sur les sociétés précapitalistes: textes choisis de Marx, Engels, Lenine* (Paris: C.R.M., 1970); Lawrence Krader, *The Asiatic Mode of Production* (Assen: Van Gorcum, 1975); there is also the work of Karl Wittfogel whose complete bibliography is given in the prematurely hagiographical work by G. L. Ulmen, *The Science of Society: Toward an Understanding of the Life and Work of Karl August Wittfogel* (Paris: Mouton, 1978); see also the comprehensive bibliography by Ulmen, surely the best part of the volume, pp. 625–91.

7. To reiterate: *my* topic here is the evolution of Marx's *theory* of the AMP, *not its empirical adequacy;* for the latter, see the empirically grounded objections of Perry Anderson, *Passages from Antiquity* and Barrington Moore's *Social Origins of Dictatorship and Democracy* (London: Allen Lane, 1967).

8. Sawer, *Marxism and Asiatic Production,* p. 40.

9. Ibid., p. 100.

10. Melotti, *Marx and the Third World,* pp. 59–60.

11. Frederick Engels, *Herr Eugen Dühring's Revolution in Science,* *(Anti-Dühring),* trans. Emile Burns, ed. C. P. Dutt (New York: International Publishers, 1939), pp. 197ff.

12. Ibid., p. 201.

13. *International Herald Tribune,* February 3–4, 1979, p. 9. From 1962 to 1975, government spending (as a percent of gross domestic product) increased from 34.2% to 44.4% in Britain; from 36.3% to 40.3% in France; from 32.4% to 41.9% in Italy; from 19.0% to 23.4% in Japan; from 34.4% to 51.2% in the Netherlands; from 32.7% to 49.4% in Sweden; from 29.5% to 34.0% in the United States; and from 33.6% to 42.1% in West Germany. Speaking of the military alone, in the United States, Sidney Willhelm notes: " . . . the military pays $15 billion annually to the civilians it hires directly, more than $35 billion to military personnel, and billions more indirectly through military contracts with civilian businesses. Of course, personnel costs do not cease with salaries; medical benefits, housing facilities, food and clothing allowances, commissary privileges, transportation provisions, and many other emoluments are financed. Military housing subsidies exceed the sum spent for public housing to assist the millions of Americans in poverty. In 1968, the Penta-

gon allocated $44 billion for purchase of goods and services, making it the largest single purchaser in the nation. . . . In mid-1969, the Department of Defense held direct ownership of 29 million acres, and by 1970, its total equipment, material, etc., amounted to $214 billion, 38% of the 554 billion in total assets for all U.S. manufacturing corporations." See Sidney M. Willhelm, "The Rise of State Rule," *Catalyst*, no. 9, 1977, p. 16. In an analysis of data about California, Willhelm reports that "from a total 1969 population of 19,834,000, there were 7,278,041 persons institutionalized under state control; another 647,988 persons are employed by the state of California to care for the institutionalized people—a total of almost 8 million, i.e., approximately 40% of all Californians are either clients or employees of institutionalized state agencies of care and control with respect to education, social welfare, health and penology." Ibid., p. 48.

14. *Communist Manifesto* by Karl Marx and Friedrich Engels, authorized English edition of 1888, supervised by Engels, published by Charles H. Kerr, Chicago, p. 41.

15. See Marx and Engels, "Über die Nationalisierung des Grund und Boden," Marx-Engels, *Werke*, Institut für Marxismus-Leninismus (Berlin: Dietz Verlag, 1956–68), vol. 17, pp. 59–62. F. Engels, "The Peasant Question in France and Germany," in K. Marx and F. Engels, *Selected Works* (Moscow: Progress Pub., 1955) vol. 2, p. 395. Marx and Engels were adamant on the nationalization of land.

16. Sawer, *Marxism and Asiatic Production,* p. 52.

17. For fuller development, see Alvin W. Gouldner, "Stalinism: A Study of Internal Colonialism," *Telos*, Winter 1977–78, pp. 5–48.

18. Saul K. Padover, *Karl Marx on Revolution* (New York: McGraw-Hill Book Co., 1972).

19. Karl Marx, *The Civil War in France* (New York: International Publishers, 1940), p. 54.

20. Ibid.

21. Ibid.

22. Ibid., p. 57.

23. Ibid., pp. 58–59.

24. Ibid., p. 61.

25. Karl Marx and Frederick Engels, *Selected Correspondence, 1846–1895*, trans. Dona Torr (New York: International Publishers, 1942), p. 386.

26. Ibid., p. 387. Italics added.

27. Cited in Saul K. Padover, *Karl Marx, An Intimate Biography* (New York: McGraw-Hill Book Co., 1978), p. 488. Marx subsequently repudiated this interview, but this is likely to have been because of its impolitic remarks about some of the Commune's leaders, having referred to one as an ass and traitor, and another as a blowhard and coward.

12

CIVIL SOCIETY IN CAPITALISM AND SOCIALISM

The more Marx ignored and devalued civil society the more he formulated a socialism without safeguards, a socialism whose rise to power could only take the form of centralization. Marx had inherited the idea of civil society as one of a pair of concepts, the other being, of course, the state. We are told that Marx himself even noticed civil society's importance for capitalist development, although, once again, if we look at the texts they seem pretty modest to support such a heavy hypothesis. The most important is a letter Marx wrote Engels on 27 July 1854.

Schlomo Avineri contrives to find in this letter a veritable theory of the origins of capitalism in which Marx supposedly asserts that the accumulation of capital and the industrial revolution were made possible by a preceding "socio-political revolution in late medieval Europe; the emergence of a civil society, *bürgerliche Gesellschaft*, i.e., an autonomous sphere of economic activity, unimpeded by political and religious restrictions. . . . Marx ascribes the emergence of civil society to the communal movement of the late Middle Ages, which emancipated the urban corporations and communes from their dependence on the political arrangements of the feudal structure. According to Marx, the communal movement created a sphere of autonomous economic activity, unrestricted by political and religious tutelage which might limit its freedom of economic choice. . . . Only the late medieval town developed, in the wake of the communal movement, a concept of property free from feudal, i.e., political and community-oriented limitations. Not only did this development justify morally the accumulation of property; it also separated the political sphere from the economic and gave rise to legal and institutional arrangements that made the accumulation of capital possible and socially acceptable."[1]

If this is a proper understanding of Marx, he did indeed see civil society as significant in the origin of capitalism. The first thing to note and reiterate, however, is that this insight is, if it exists at all, even more fugitive than the insight Marx had into the AMP. The problem that most concerns me here is why, in general, are Marx's studies of civil society aborted? The answer is largely that Marx normally emphasized that the social structures of civil society were *not* independent entities generating bourgeois society but were, rather, forms in which bourgeois society had emerged; that is, *they were the products rather than the producers of the bourgeois class.*

Marx thus speaks (in the letter of 27 July) of the corporations and guilds as "the forms, in short, in which the industrial bourgeoisie developed." He does not stress here that these social organizations are independent causes, but dependent effects, of the rise of the bourgeoisie. The emphasis is, at most, on the association or correlation of the two, not on the independence and priority of the civil society.

More than that, a main focus in the primary Marxist paradigm is on the way economic relations govern the political, rather than on the kinds of social structure (civil society) which are not reducible to economic classes or relationships. Thus civil society, for Marx, normally implies "forms" in which, essentially, economic developments take place. The primary paradigm of Marxism tends to dichotomize social structures, reducing all social relations either to economic or to political (and ideological) relations, i.e., infra- or superstructural elements. But in this impulse to dichotomize social relationships where, for example, did the kinship, the age, and the sex systems fit—were they infra- or superstructural? The insistent distinction between infra- and superstructures tended to focus on some concrete social spheres, while others fall between the two and, at the same time, neglected the fact that both political and economic spheres were differentiations of a more basic *social* material and, therefore, shared certain things in common, rather than simply being distinct from one another.

An essential aspect of civil society is that it is a sphere autonomous of the state, that it is not determined by the state or politics, but has a life of its own. The concept of the civil society that Marx encountered was thus largely a residual concept, being that which was *not* the state, and what was *left over* in society after the state was "excluded." Its essential point was to establish that the state did not encompass society, that there was something more of importance—but what exactly this was remained unclear. Marx filled that basket with (and reduced it to) economic activities and classes. In the preface to his *Critique of Political Economy,* he characterizes civil society as the sum total of the material conditions of life, and he maintains that "the anatomy of civil society is to be sought in political economy."[2]

In the *Grundrisse,* Marx sees civil society historically, as the corruption of society's "natural bonds" by bourgeois competition and egoism, observing that "only in the eighteenth century, in 'civil society,' do the various forms of social connectedness confront the individual as a mere means toward his private purposes, as external necessity."[3] In that discussion, as Marx speaks of production as being inherently "social," part of what he refers to is, clearly, the larger whole encompassing the production of individuals, so that "social" here means totality. In another part, however, it also clearly means a form of human "connectedness," something quite apart from the differentiated political or economic specialization this connectedness may develop.

Civil society, then, was regarded by Marx as a development, indeed a corruption, of the social whole which, at first, entailed "natural bonds," that is, family and other traditional ties. Civil society was thus a stage in the evolution of social bonds, a corrupted connectedness in which social relationships are used and viewed only instrumentally. (Marx has here moved toward the brink of a distinction between the natural *Gemeinschaft* and the rational *Gesellschaft* that was to be a center of Ferdinand Tönnies's sociology.) Marx has seen—i.e., glimpsed but never analyzed—that common character shared by both the political and the economic, i.e., the "social" as the totality of "connectedness" which has an evolution of its own. His focus, however, is on the "anatomy" of the social, which he takes to be its material base and political economy. In short, for Marx, the focus is first on the economic, and then on the political as a sphere shaped by the former; while the social and, indeed, civil society itself thus slips away, remaining an undeveloped, residual concept.

Engels says all this quite plainly in the framework of his own remarks about the origins of the bourgeoisie. For him, too, the essential content of civil society, i.e., its anatomy, is clearly its political economy. Civil society was the product, not the condition, of capitalism and bourgeois development. The central thrust

of Engels's argument was to deny Dühring's contention that "political conditions are the decisive cause of the economic order."
Engels counters that "everyone knows that what took place was
the opposite. . . . The burghers conquered one position after another
in continuous struggle with the nobility. . . . And how did it accomplish this? Simply through a change in the economic order
which sooner or later, voluntarily or as the outcome of a struggle,
was followed by a change in the political conditions . . . the decisive weapon of the burghers in this struggle was their *economic*
power. . . . In all their production the burghers had remained
hemmed in by the feudal political forms of the Middle Ages. . . .
The bourgeois revolution put an end to this. Not, however, by
adjusting the economic order to suit the political conditions . . .
but by doing the opposite, by casting aside the old mouldering
political rubbish and creating political conditions in which the
new 'economic order' could exist and develop."[4]

In this account of the origins of the bourgeoisie, there is not one
word about the independence or priority of civil society. It is all a
matter of economic development. In the primary paradigm, only
the economic had its own natural and spontaneous development;
it was the source of initiative and action, the other spheres were
sites of *re*-action. The sphere of human connectedness, of society
and the social, shared by both the economic and the political, was
shunted aside by the imperative need to *distinguish* the two and
demonstrate the hegemony of the economic.

Marx is thus operating with the tacit metaphor that the economic is the "content" and social organization is the "form." He is
thus never able to consider that the capacity to organize effectively was a necessary condition of the "conspiratorial and revolutionary character of the municipal movement in the twelfth
century," in which the Western bourgeoisie began to emerge.
Their development greatly depended on their ingenuity and success in creating and maintaining a variety of new organizations
which provided supportive structures to protect their new economic forms, preventing them from being overwhelmed and assimilated back into the feudal system.

Far from being, as Marx held, a corruption and dissolution of the
natural social bond, civil society actually marked the rise of vital
new modes of social organization. The natural bond whose dissolution Marx decried was often only the traditional social organization of *feudalism* which maintained the domination of nobility
over the serfs and peasantry. While that "natural bond" of domi-

nation was being dissolved, this was not merely accomplished by society's atomization, i.e., by the egoism of competitive individuals; it involved new modes of social connectedness and organization, the shift from traditional to planned organizations, rather than just the dissolution of "natural" organization into sheer atomization. It was precisely this efflorescence of organizational creativity, rather than the emerging bourgeoisie's economic activities as such, that sovereigns saw as dangerous.

Marx himself thus cites (in the letter of 27 July) the energetic efforts made by the Emperors Frederick I and Frederick II to abolish precisely these new "forms"—the *Communiones, conspirationes, conjurations,* consulates. Frederick II thus declares: "It has recently come to our knowledge that the guilds of certain cities, market-towns and other places, have, of their own will, constituted tribunals, authorities, offices, administrations and certain other institutions of this kind . . . and because among many of them . . . such things have already developed into abuse and malpractices . . . we hereby in virtue of our imperial power revoke these jurisdictions. . . . We prohibit, also, all conventions and sworn confederacies within and without cities: between city and city, between person and person or between city and person of whatsoever kind they may be." Again, Marx cites King Henry's decree against city communes requiring that "no city and no market-town may organise communes, unions, leagues or sworn confederacies of any kind."

All this marked the eruption of new social organizations which contributed to the extrication of secular social structure from the old "natural" bonds, that is, from domination by the feudal authorities. It provided organizational facilities which persons could use to pursue ends of their own choosing and resist feudal impositions upon their interests. These new organizations, however, were not simply limited-purpose associations for economic pursuits, i.e., *Gesellschaften,* but were, also, new *communities, Gemeinschaften,* within which persons' entire lives might escape feudal dominion. City air, as the saying went, "makes men free," not just rich; in it, they learned self-help and self-respect. Even ordinary peasants, not simply merchants or craftsmen, were invited to take up a new life in the city and were promised its protection. A new civil society, nucleated with these energetic new organizations, thus arose, enabling a sector of the population to escape feudalism's constant and close supervision, and to develop a new independence.

It is difficult to say whether experience acquired in managing their own small businesses gave craftsmen or merchants experience in running other kinds of organizations, whether it was the other way around, or, as seems most likely, whether each contributed to the other. Both were probably fostered by the more diffuse opportunities for ·self-help and self-management found in the cities. In this new community, a new economy was gradually established in which persons' economic obligations were now less likely to vary with their incomes; in which fixed, hence predictable rents and taxes allowed more economic rationality; in which merchants and craftsmen were less dependent on only local buyers and could, therefore, negotiate better terms of trade for themselves, with the result that capital accumulation, at least among some, could develop faster. The new organizational infrastructure included political instruments that edged the balance of power in favor of townspeople and, at the same time, constituted protected enclaves within which (not only economic activities but also) the larger reach of the everyday life could be lived according to new standards, even when deviant from the claims of feudalism.

At the same time, however, organizational competence and effectiveness was scarcely the monopoly of townsmen in Western Europe but was also an important characteristic of villagers as well. Robert Brenner, for example, argues that in Western Germany of the later middle ages peasant organizations resisting the lord were "closely bound up with the very development of the quasi-communal character of peasant economy. Most fundamental was the need to regulate co-operatively the village commons and to struggle against the lords to establish and to protect their common rights—common lands (for grazing and so on) and the common-field organization of agriculture. . . . The peasants organized themselves in order to fix rents and to ensure rights of inheritance . . . they fought successfully to replace the old landlord-installed village mayor (*Schultheis*) by their own elected village magistrates. In some villages they even won the right to choose the village priest. All these rights the peasants forced the lords to recognize in countless village charters (*Weistumer*)."[5]

In East Germany, however, self-governing peasant villages did not develop to the same extent, and the peasants could not so readily displace the lord's *Schultheis*. This different development, suggests Brenner, derives from the East's more colonialized character, the underdevelopment of communal activities and land that might have formed a center of peasant collaboration and organization. In the East, the landlord came first as a colonizer, bringing the peasant into a social framework he established; the village's single lord confronted a relatively sparser village population and he was, therefore, relatively stronger than in the West, where a village might be divided between two lords.

Independent self-managed social organization outside of the feudal structure thus developed in the West both in the villages and in the towns. Far from deriving strength from a prior capitalist agriculture, they were often grounded in the communal aspects of the economy. The origins of civil society in the West, then, do not seem to be reducible to a prior development of trade or crafts or prior emergence of the bourgeoisie; civil society seems to contribute as much to bourgeois development as it derives from it. It was, moreover, not simply the prior development of trade and tradesmen that undermined the feudal structure but, at least just as much, the undermining of the feudal system through the prior development of organizations permitting self-help in the villages and town, that helped open the way for the bourgeois mode of production.

In the decline of serfdom, as in the rise of the bourgeoisie—and they are not two sides of one coin—Western Europeans' organizational competence, collective traditions of organization, and resulting experience of autonomy and mastery, in short, their collective capacity to use organization for self-help, yielded a quasi-independent civil society that played a distinct role in events. Civil society was not simply a "form" through which the bourgeoisie made their history, but a necessary condition of that history. It was conducive to the development of habits of independence, and to the accumulation (and retention) of surpluses necessary for the advent of the bourgeoisie.

In his important study, Michael Walzer has also shown how organizational zeal and competence were fostered by Calvinism which, he says, led to a view of politics as "a kind of conscientious and continuous labor," which developed new types of men. Seeing themselves as divine instruments, they could escape total involvement with their families and seek "brethren" who shared their ideas and zeal; "thus there arose the leagues and covenants, conferences and congregations which are the prototype of revolutionary zeal. [There was] the formation of groups specifically and deliberately designed to implement these demands, groups based on the principle of voluntary association and requiring proof of

ideological commitment but not of blood ties, aristocratic patron-
age, or local residence . . . oriented not toward acquisition so
much as toward contention, struggle, destruction, and rebuilding
. . . [Calvin] relied above all on organizations, and imparted to his
followers an extraordinary organizational initiative and stamina.
There have been few men in history who loved meetings
more. . . . Medieval Catholics had also organized the faithful, but
they had done so without removing them in any way from the
existing political and feudal worlds, or from the complex bonds of
local and patriarchical connection."[6]

With the development of the new organizations, of new towns
walled off from the feudal countryside, of new local politics
enabling villagers to elect their own mayors and pastors, and of
new leagues, conferences, and confederations, there was created,
on the one hand, a set of special-purpose organizations able to
concentrate resources and discharge them on behalf of focused
goals, concentrations of power with which new purposes could be
pursued and by which they might be defended from feudal
backlash; and, on the other, there also arose new communities in
which people were insulated from older authorities, were able to
discourage old values and permit new ways of life and values to be
internalized in persons during the course of an enveloping everyday socialization.

It is during the Middle Ages, then, that the organizational foundations were laid for the democratic revolutions of the seventeenth and eighteenth centuries. Scholars such as Emile Lousse
and Robert R. Palmer have stressed the importance of "constituted bodies," "most of them predominantly aristocratic in 1760,
and including parliaments, councils, assemblies, and magistracies
of various kinds,"[7] for the development of these democratic revolutions. Palmer holds that these revolutions were in part grounded
in "the attempts of these constituted bodies to defend their corporate liberties and their independence." They also provided arenas
within which various classes—and not only the bourgeoisie—
acquired organizational competence, political experience, and
developed leaders. Typically, these organizations were absent in
Russia until fairly late in the eighteenth century and it was only in
1785 that the Empress Catherine issued a Charter of the Nobility.
"The absence from Russia of bodies of the kind described is only
one of the signs that Russia, at the middle of the eighteenth century, did not belong to the region of Western Civilization,"[8] although moving in that direction.

In contrast to the views of Walzer, Brenner, and Palmer cited above, stressing the importance of organizational competence as a special element in the development of both the economy and politics of Western Europe, Marxism lacked a systematic focus on social organization as a distinct level of social structures, whether of limited-purpose organizations or multi-bonded communities, and these tend to be assimilated in Marx to the mode of production, or to the political region of the superstructure, constituting mere "forms" through which the bourgeoisie developed. For Marx, then, civil society remained a residual concept that never came into focus.

Civil Society as Sociology's Object and Historical Mission

While civil society was only a residual concept for Marxism it was focal for sociology; if it was a given for Marxism, civil society was sociology's central problematic, the main scientific object to which it has devoted itself. Indeed, civil society has been sociology's principal scientific object since its beginnings in the positivistic sociology of Auguste Comte, the putative "father" of sociology, as well as of the man whose protegé he was, positivism's founder, Henri Saint-Simon.

The emergence of sociology was in part shaped by its critique of three main preceding intellectual commitments, and it is these that help to define it and establish civil society as sociology's scientific object. First, sociology developed a critique of political economy's emphasis on a competitive, market individualism. Second, early sociology opposed institutionalized religions, including both Catholicism and Protestantism, regarded the critique of deism as a necessary foundation of the sciences, and saw the sciences as the necessary basis of modern society. In short, the critique of conventional and established religion was, for early sociologists (particularly Saint-Simon) as for Marxism, the beginning of all critique. Third, and finally, early sociology rejected the dominance of society by the state, saw the state as undermining society and as essentially archaic insofar as its characteristic form was domination by force. Sociology viewed the modern period as one whose enlightenment and productivity no longer required the repression characteristic of the state, and which it thus expected (and encouraged) to "wither" away. Among the foundations of sociology then are, first, its antiindividualism; second, its suspicion and critique of traditional religions, of religious authority as a basis of knowledge, and its strongly secularizing epistemology; third, and finally, sociology was antistatist and, more generally, defocalized the importance of politics.

Sociology's concern with civil society, however, was also still largely residual, including at the largest remove all groups and institutions not directly part of the state. At another, more analytical level, however, sociology also associated civil society with elements contributing to the maintenance of order and stability in society that spontaneously and "naturally" developed; that is, without the planful initiative of the state or anyone else. The central problem of modern society, to the sociology that arose on the heels of the French Revolution, was the threat to social order— whether anarchy or revolution—seen as partly exacerbated by the growing division of labor, by the Protestant principle of individual responsibility for decisions, by unbridled individualism (Comte), the greediness of the state, or the dangers of the discontented and hungry proletariat (Saint-Simon). It was the maintenance of social order, the prevention of another 1789, that was a fundamental impetus behind the new sociology. It wanted a group life that limited individualism while serving as a buffer between persons and the state, as the crucial desideratum. *The voluntary group, whose members come together spontaneously and voluntarily, is seen as the healthy social unit.* The new sociology, then, thus emphasized the group as a distinctive type of system with its own requirements and placed this at its center. For Comte, for example, the family was the basic unit of society, while (new and critically purified) religion was to be the basis of social regulation and integration.

Unlike Saint-Simon who was at times more mechanistic, Comte emphasized that social order was to be maintained, like an organism, that is, through its own naturally emergent elements or organs. He conceived society as possessing a natural, built-in tendency toward order and equilibrium, regarding a naturally derived order as superior to that which had been imposed legally. He assumed that reason and rationality in daily life are somehow less "natural" than "spontaneous" reactions governed by unplanned tradition, habit, or feeling and that spontaneous methods of maintaining order were superior to others. There is no doubt, however, that Comte left room for planful intervention in the event of severe social disruptions, such as those he believed the new division of labor was generating for the social consensus.

There is also no doubt, however, that he held that "the final order which arises spontaneously is always superior to that which human combination had, by anticipation, constructed."

There was, then, a polemical preference in early sociology's search for the spontaneous maintenance of social order, for social order that was homeostatic, that is, *self*-maintained. (This converges with, but is not the same as, the view advanced by Eisenstadt and Curelaru that sociology's "most important characteristic" was the scientific analysis of "the general problem of social order"[9] and of developmental trends.) It is precisely because of its focus on spontaneous, homeostatic social order that Comte was critical of rational and planned programs of legal, political, or constitutional reform. It is the last that Comte considers the paradigm of the "unnatural" and against which he inveighs: "The multitude of the so-called Constitutions produced by the people since the beginning of the crisis . . . would alone suffice to convince every capable intellect how entirely the nature and difficulty of forming a plan for Social Reorganisation have hitherto been misunderstood." And again, Comte insists that "no jealous, legal provision against the selfish use of wealth, and no mischievous intervention, paralyzing social activity by political prohibition can be very effective." Similarly, Comte never suggested any constitutional guarantees of freedom or legal safeguards against tyranny. Essentially, what Comte is saying is that before political reforms can have effect, sentiments must be changed so that persons are disposed spontaneously to conform with them. He held that legal change cannot effect modifications in the beliefs and morals of a people but, rather, presupposes them. The illiberal and conservative import of much of this is plain and has been commented on at length in my *Coming Crisis of Western Sociology*.

Sociologists, since Comte's time (although scarcely of one single disposition), have been congenial to a conception of society and of the groups in it, that views them as a *natural system*. In this model, explicit, articulated policies (or goals) are but one of many needs the group is seen as attempting to satisfy. Internally, the group's component structures are seen as emergent organs, understandable only in relationship to the various needs of the group and not simply in terms of its articulate policies. Groups (and societies) are seen as striving to survive, to maintain their own equilibrium; this effort may persist even after the group's explicitly stated goals have been achieved. Indeed, the impulse toward survival may on occasion even lead to the neglect or distortion of the group's goals. Whatever the plans of their creators—if any creators are nameable—group maintenance may become an end in itself; groups possess their own distinctive needs which press toward satisfaction.

Once established, the structures and institutions of groups generate new goals that constrain subsequent decision-making, limiting the manner in which the groups' initial goals can be pursued. Group structures and institutions, then, are viewed as spontaneously maintained and as spontaneously changed. Changes in group arrangements are viewed as the result of cumulative, unplanned, adaptive responses to problems or threats (which may or may not be seen as mediated by its elite or dominant figures). Responses to group problems are thought of as taking the form of increasingly developed defense mechanisms, importantly shaped by shared values internalized in group members. The focus is thus on the spontaneously emergent and normatively sanctioned structures, on deviations from group stability or equilibrium rather than from rational plans, and, particularly, on mechanisms by which group structures are defended spontaneously. When departures from planned purposes are considered, they are viewed not so much as due to ignorance or human error but as arising from constraints imposed by existing social structures. Indeed, in given situations, it is assumed that ignorance may not always be disruptive of but may be useful to group structures and arrangements.

Being viewed as a connected system of parts, on the model of an organism, the focus is on their mutual interdependence, on how, therefore, even planned changes may produce ramifying, unanticipated consequences for the group or the planner. When "unanticipated consequences" occur they are usually seen as divergent from, rather than as supportive of, the planner's intentions. Society and groups in it are, then, seen as "growing" organically with their own "natural history" which is planfully modifiable only at considerable peril. Such long range change as takes place, is thus regarded not as conforming to any planner's intentions but as an evolution in conformity with "natural laws." This is modern sociology's most general model of the character of a civil society and its component groups.

In sociology's developing treatment of civil society, then, several trends are to be observed: one is an analytical focus on the problem of a homeostatically, spontaneously maintained social order; the second is its focus on "natural," that is, unplanned social regularities and changes in group life which are counter-posed (invidiously) to planned arrangements and changes; and the third is its focus, at the *concrete* level, on all groups except the state. Comte's emphasis was on overcoming the effects of the revolution which, he felt, had laid siege to the family and church, in its efforts to bar all impediments between person and state. He complained that the revolutionary state had devoured the functions properly belonging to such small groups, had hollowed out society, leaving a sandlike pile of atomized individuals. In its natural condition, Comte averred, society is an integrated assemblage of small groups unified by a common set of beliefs tempered by a religion.

Comte's mentor (and *bête noir*), Saint-Simon, similarly stressed antistatist views. Saint-Simon observed that "those who control public affairs share between them every year one-half of the taxes, and they do not even use a third of what they do not pocket personally in a way which benefits the citizen." Saint-Simon held that *pre*-modern social organization had to be on authoritarian military lines because the masses had earlier been uneducated, incapable of self-management, and were hungry. This, however, is no longer necessary because "the majority have become used to work (which eliminates disorder) and now consists of men who have recently proved that they are capable of administering property, whether in land or money." The men who made the revolution of 1789, he says, "have all sought to improve the governmental machine, whereas they should have subordinated it and put administration in the first place . . . it was with the aim of being governed less, and less expensively, that the nation embarked on revolution. Up to the present it has achieved as a result more government, and more expensive government, than it had before the revolution . . . the imposition of government on top of administration produced harmful effects at the present day, when the mass of the nation consists of men who no longer require to be closely supervised, since they have shown themselves capable of administering all kinds of property. Today the proletarian class can only become dangerous to public order, if the administrators of the national interests are so inept or selfish as to let them become unemployed."[10]

Since Comte, the sociological tradition has been anchored in its emphasis on civil society, particularly in sociology's development within French, English, and American society. Civil society is important also for German sociology, although somewhat more ambiguously, considering the great importance that Max Weber attributed to the nation-state. Yet there is no mistaking its significance in the sociology of Ferdinand Tönnies, with its distinction between traditional social organization (*Gemeinschaft*) and rationally planned social organization (*Gesellschaft*) at the level of the everyday life, or in the sociology of Georg Simmel with its focus on formal structures of relationships.

The French tradition culminates, at one landing, in the work of Emile Durkheim whose lectures on *Professional Ethics and Civic Morals*[11]—as does the preface to the second edition of his *Division of Labor in Society*—indicate the convergence of his sociology with a syndicalist (but nonrevolutionary) socialism. Durkheim held that class differences made it impossible for "just" contracts to be negotiated and led to an unequal exchange of goods and services, being thus conducive to a sense of injustice which had socially unstabilizing effects. These unstabilizing power disparities, Durkheim held, were grounded in the institution of inheritance. Durkheim thus regards inheritance as in tension with modern contractual and individualistic views, anticipates its ultimate elimination, and conceives it possible that property will no longer be transmitted through the family. To whom, then, is property to go after the death of its private owner, especially since the state is blundering and wasteful? Durkheim replied that the *occupational organization* was to be its recipient and manager.

In his second preface to *The Division of Labor*, Durkheim also stressed the importance of such occupational communities, seeing them as ultimately supplanting the state and as constituting the focus for the revitalization of modern morality, the "poverty" which he held central to the modern malaise. It is clear, however, that these syndicates did not only have a morality-building function for Durkheim but also had important economic functions. They were to be Durkheim's equivalent for Marxist nationalization of property by the state.

Durkheim's central concern, however, was the decline of civil society; the dissolution of group structures were, he feared, conducive to various social pathologies, among them suicide and, more generally, to a kind of Hobbesian war of each against all. New self-maintaining social groups were needed to administer and control modern social life that could be coordinated with its newly industrial character. In industrial society, it no longer suffices to organize society in terms of family, church, or territorial units. Moreover, "the state is poorly equipped to supervise these very specialized economic tasks." Durkheim concluded that the new groups appropriate for modern industrial life would be corporations organized around different industries, constituting a focus of common interests and social interaction, from which he expected to arise a new and effective social morality to which persons would give voluntary consent.

In like manner, Talcott Parsons's more recent work has been concerned to explore those factors that contribute to social system equilibrium which is seen as dependent on persons' readiness to conform voluntarily with one another's expectations. For Parsons as for Durkheim, voluntary conformity was important, for without it external restraints are required, and these are always vulnerable to avoidances and hostile coalitions, if they do not coincide with what is desired by the actors. Thus spontaneous and voluntary conformity with the expectations of others—as distinct from that externally coerced or forced—is the only basis of a stable social system and this, in turn, is seen as needing to be grounded in a consensus of moral beliefs and norms. Actors sharing the same moral beliefs would know what to expect from one another and would comply readily with one another's expectations.

In this sociological tradition, the question becomes, on what basis can such shared moral beliefs come into being, so that education and socialization become central. In the positivist tradition beginning with Comte it was also supposed that science, by authoritatively establishing the requirements of modern life, could win consent from persons in society, and thus reestablish the requisite voluntary consensus in morality.

Durkheim's own position came to stress that sheer interaction, centering around common activities, would in time generate a new and shared morality. If for Durkheim the pathology of modern life premised a "poverty of morality," he increasingly doubted that it could be discovered and established by science or social science, as Comte and Saint-Simon had supposed. Durkheim surmises that a scientific ethic might emerge someday but, in the meanwhile, social science cannot provide it. The new morality, for him, must therefore be naturally or spontaneously developed around sustained patterns of social interaction. Patterns of social interaction would provide the focus around which moral beliefs emerge and develop. In his *Suicide*, Durkheim took a strongly antivoluntaristic position, insisting that you cannot simply "will" away the problem; that is, ways of thinking and acting cannot be changed without changing social structure.

Here Durkheim was converging with Marx's materialism, which saw consciousness as grounded in social being. But instead of focusing on the manner in which class relations or position shape consciousness, Durkheim held that more diversified social (not merely economic) relations influence the development of beliefs. In this vein, Durkheim had also held, in his *Division of Labor*, that society is the necessary condition of the moral world, and "cannot exist if its parts are not solidary, but solidarity is only *one* of the conditions of its existence. There are many others which are no less necessary but *which are not moral.*"[12]

Since Comte, then, one major stream of sociology has focused on the sources of a self-maintaining social order grounded in shared moral values and beliefs. Its focus on these has not, however, been as an end in itself but as a source of spontaneous and voluntary choices and social solidarity—i.e., of self-maintenance— thus avoiding (and devaluing) external constraint, including impositions by the state. In short, the problem of morality becomes important in this intellectual tradition in a utilitarian way, i.e., precisely because *useful* to the autonomy and vitality of civil society and its solidarity.

While this sociological tradition may be conceived as a generalization of a market system, thus embodying an ideology (at least) latently liberal or even conservative, yet it is precisely in this focus that modern sociology developed certain of its most abiding elements of rationality. It is seeking an alternative, third way, to the atomization of a competitive market society, on the one side, and to a state dominated existence, on the other. Sociology conceives of civil society as a haven and support for individual persons, i.e., as de-atomizing; as a medium through which they can pursue their own projects in the course of their everyday lives; and as ways of avoiding dependence on the domination by the state. Sociology thus focused on and took as problematic precisely the civil society Marxism took as given.

At the same time, sociology has largely failed to pursue its studies of civil society in the context of the limits imposed by the growing state apparatus and, more generally, in its connection with the state. In this respect, however, sociology only shares Marxism's tendency to treat politics and, indeed, the state, as epiphenomenal. Sociology, however, has been much more consistently prepared to oppose the state or to avoid reliance upon it. Sociology thus continues to supply insight into the working of the civil society that Marxism neglected. Although both traditions are deficient in their analyses of the state, sociology's knowledge of civil society becomes increasingly important, perhaps especially to Marxists whose own liberative ambitions for society have been crushed under the reality of the collectivist state.

In socialist, no less than capitalist societies, then, a central and increasingly urgent problem is how may persons avoid dependence on the state; how may patterns of mutual and self-help—and of the self-management that is *part* of this—be strengthened; how may society resist the enveloping superintendence by the state? From a Marxist standpoint, the growing question is how may civil society be fortified, so that Marxism's own liberative aspirations can be realized? Essentially, sociology's traditions—precisely because they have been *conservative*—have centered on the problems connected with developing a *self*-maintaining civil society, social organizations, and social systems. Deepened knowledge of this is certainly indispensable for any social movement, such as Marxism, which seeks workers' control (when this is not understood as equivalent to nationalization), or which seeks a responsible and competent citizenry, and hopes to develop persons capable of mutual aid and independence, and to retain a viable "public" sphere. Marxism has proven incompetent to deliver on its pledge to usher in an emancipatory society; it is, instead, encouraging authoritarian societies with bloated repressive states and paranoiac bureaucracies.

Insofar as sociologists continue to explore this problem, rather than sinking into routine market research for the welfare-warfare state—thereby transforming themselves into administrative tools of the state bureaucracy—they can play an historically emancipatory role. I have in my *Coming Crisis of Western Sociology* examined at some length the constraints on sociology that may distort its liberative potential. I have also stressed sociology's contradictory character. Civil society as infrastructure of the public sphere thus remains an important focus for at least some sociologists associated together in communities supportive of a critical theory. While it is far from sure that sociology is destined to fulfill its liberative potential, still this surely remains the object of some groups among them. Sociology's liberative potential is, in any event, no more uncertain that that of Marxism, which is already associated with immense political catastrophes. No emancipation is possible in the modern world, however, without a strong civil society that can strengthen the public sphere and can provide a haven from and a center of resistance to the Behemoth state. An understanding of this has been central to the sociological project, though systematically neglected by Marxism.

One part of the liberative potential of sociology—i.e., its rational kernel—was brought to focus by Max Weber's theory of bureaucracy. At a time when German Social Democrats were developing a burgeoning bureaucracy, Weber's somber but penetrating analysis warned that bureaucracy was on the march, in the new Soviet state as elsewhere in Europe. Weber warned that "socialism"—i.e., the kind of scientific socialism he saw around him in Germany—did not mean the dictatorship of the proletariat but, rather, "the dictatorship of the official." The subsequent development of Stalinism would seem to substantiate the profundity of Weber's critique. Indeed, even the Althusserian Scientific Marxist, Göran Therborn, acknowledges that Weber's "analysis of bureaucracy and other administrative apparatuses is far superior in depth and detail to that of either Marx, Engels or Lenin."[13]

NOTES

1. Shlomo Avineri, *The Social and Political Thought of Karl Marx* (London and New York: Cambridge University Press, 1969), p. 155. I use Avineri's reading of this letter because it is the most generous possible interpretation of it, attributing insights to it that less imaginative scholars might not find. My own reading sees Marx saying considerably less; and my own reading of Avineri sees him as transforming Marx into Weber. Here I think Avineri makes a mountain out of a molehill as he had earlier reduced a mountain to a molehill in discussing the Marxist position on technology.

2. For a good discussion, see Hal Draper, *Karl Marx's Theory of Revolution, Part I: The State and Bureaucracy* (New York: Monthly Review Press, 1977), vol. 1, pp. 32ff.

3. Karl Marx, *Grundrisse: Introduction to the Critique of Political Economy,* trans. Martin Nicolaus (Harmondsworth: Penguin Books, 1973), pp. 83–84.

4. Frederick Engels, *Herr Eugen Dühring's Revolution in Science, (Anti-Dühring),* trans. Emile Burns, ed. C. P. Dutt (New York: International Publishers, 1939), pp. 182–83.

5. Robert Brenner, "Agrarian Class Structure and Economic Development in Pre-Industrial Europe," *Past and Present,* February 1976, pp. 56–57.

6. Michael Walzer, *The Revolution of the Saints: A Study in the Origins of Radical Politics* (Cambridge: Harvard University Press, 1965), pp. 2, 3, 10, 13, 29.

7. Robert R. Palmer, *The Age of the Democratic Revolution: A Political History of Europe and America, 1760–1800* (Princeton: Princeton University Press, 1959), p. 23.

8. Ibid., p. 30.

9. S. N. Eisenstadt with M. Curelaru, *The Form of Sociology: Paradigms and Crises* (New York: John Wiley, 1976), p. 16.

10. Henri Comte de Saint-Simon, *Selected Writings (1760–1825)*, ed. F. M. H. Markham (Oxford: Basil Blackwell, 1952), pp. 74, 76, 78, 79.

11. Emile Durkheim, *Professional Ethics and Civic Morals* (Glencoe, Ill.: Free Press, 1958), pp. 213ff.

12. Emile Durkheim, *The Division of Labor in Society* (Glencoe, Ill.: Free Press, 1947), p. 399. Italics added.

13. Göran Therborn, *Science, Class and Society* (London: New Left Books, 1976), p. 302.

APPENDIX
Göran Therborn's Conception of Sociology

Göran Therborn suggests a rather different view of sociology's historical role than that offered here. Instead of viewing it as centered on civil society, Therborn regards sociology as primarily committed to the study of the "ideological community" and as emphasizing the importance of shared moralities and values.

At first, says Therborn, sociology took its inspiration from the naturalistic tradition, especially the biological sciences. Beginning with a confident evolutionary determinism, however, it subsequently turned into a "desperate elitist voluntarism in the age of imperialism."[1]

This conception of sociology's development is borrowed, without critical evaluation or for that matter without indicating its source, from Talcott Parsons's main thesis[2] concerning sociology's evolution in his *The Structure of Social Action* (1937). Therborn adds correctly that "in its naturalistic emphasis sociology paralleled the efforts of Marx and Engels, who were also working toward a natural science of society, were also admirers of Darwin, and were also hostile to theology and moral philosophy."[3] Therborn, however, overemphasizes the importance of the biological sciences, misses the early importance of the Newtonian *mechanical* model for French sociological positivism, and how it contrived to conflate the mechanical with the organismic models.

Therborn is also historically disoriented, arguing that early sociology's deterministic naturalism "paralleled" Marxism. Rather, the reverse is the case; Saint-Simon's naturalism *preceded* that of Marx and Engels. Indeed, Saint-Simon's own path-breaking "Essay on the Science of Man" was written in 1813, five years before Marx was born. As Lenin noted, Marx's work was grounded, in part, on utopian socialists such as Saint-Simon. Through his father-in-law, Baron von Westphalen, and through the lectures of Eduard Gans at the University of Berlin, Marx was early exposed to Saint-Simonian doctrine. In short, Marxism stood on the shoulders of Saint-Simon, not the other way around. Therborn maintains a stony silence about the fact that Marxism and sociology thus have at least one ancestor in common, Henri Saint-Simon.

The unexpected outcome of sociology's early naturalism, claims Therborn, was the reassertion of traditional idealism, which he mistakenly equates with (desperate, elitist) voluntarism. Citing Durkheim, Westermarck, and Max Weber, Therborn argues that sociology then made "the community of values and norms the basic phenomenon of every society."[4] One notes again Therborn's repeated (but unacknowledged) reliance upon the prior scholarship of sociologists. (Since Therborn's entire discussion hinges on his polemical effort to draw a line between sociology and Marxism, invidiously condemning the former as an idealism and exalting the latter as a materialism, he remains silent about his own borrowing from sociologists.) As he had earlier but discreetly borrowed from Parsons, concerning sociology's turn to voluntarism, Therborn here borrows from my own *Coming Crisis of Western Sociology*. One of the central, repeated, and carefully documented claims of this volume is that sociology made the study of values central, although *The Coming Crisis* scarcely reduced sociology to this, as Therborn is prone to do.

As I have shown above, even though Durkheim accented the importance of value elements in society, he also emphasized that *morality was grounded in society*. Durkheim's studies of primitive societies, for example, held that the tribal totem, god, or godhead, was the symbol or flag of the clan that worships it, and that religious ideas emerge out of society. It was Durkheim's central object to show the factors that shape and sustain moral or religious beliefs, and not only what they in turn sustain. This accounting system, I have shown elsewhere[5] is fundamentally convergent with Marx's basic model, premising a social infrastructure from which moralities and religions arise. I have also shown above that Durkheim acknowledged that there were *various* requisites of society, many of which were *not moral*. Both Saint-Simon and Durkheim attached considerable importance to the division of labor as a distinct source of social solidarity, and only one of Durkheim's two basic forms of social solidarity (i.e. "mechanical solidarity") is grounded in the existence of common values.

Therborn also fails to focus on the most obvious interest of early French sociologists: being militant positivists, they saw modern society as defined by the emergence of modern *science*. Saint-Simon's whole object in calling for a social science, which Comte took over from him, was to release modern society from remnant, old regime traditionalism; to establish the basis for a scientific politics; to bring popular thinking about society into line with modern scientific thought; and to establish a new, scientifically grounded belief system which—being scientific, hence certain, hence "positive"—would be given consent voluntarily by persons and which would, therefore, be consensual, hence serving as the new basis of social order. It was Saint-Simon who first began to use science and technology as the basis of a new ideology; but his new ideology and morality was to rest on the new *science*. For Saint-Simon, then, the key to modern society was its new system of knowledge, founded on science's secular new epistemology which rejected religious and other traditional authorities' control over beliefs, and which promised a new technology to release society from ancient scarcities. It was precisely this that was taken to define the new, modern, "positivist" era.

Therborn, however, is prone to a "Freudian forgetting" about the central nature of sociological "positivism," and he argues that early sociology did not see society as having a self-healing principle. Obviously, however, these sociologists (like any positivist) saw that self-healing principle as *science*. If it was naive of them to think so, it remains a fact that the positivists expected a new morality appropriate to the new industrialism to be grounded in the new sciences. In their new positive society, however, science was not only to be the grounding of morality but the basis of a greater economic productivity which, eliminating hunger, would newly reintegrate society, dissolving the animosity of the poor.

Therborn vacillates between asserting that sociology was only later corrupted with idealism, and a different view which holds that this was its original sin: "Indeed, the first two sociologists even founded new religions, the New Christianity of Saint-Simon and Comte's religion of humanity."[6] What this formulation hides is that the foundation of the new religions was to be science, and its new priests were to be scientists. Therborn never mentions that the new sociological religions were sharp *critiques* of conventional religions, especially Catholicism and Protestantism in its various sects. Saint-Simon regarded them as once useful but now obsolescent institutions, out of tune with the new industrial civilization. Arguing that the old church had been founded on the principle of "rendering unto Caesar," Saint-Simon states that his new church would have a new social base, one seeking the "improvement of the conditions of the poorest classes."

In short, Saint-Simon begins to resituate social theory in the *proletariat*, beginning that historically radical break with theory's former reliance on the "prince" that Marx accentuates. Saint-Simon thus not only sought a new epistemological, but a new class base for religion. None of this, however, makes any appearance in Therborn's inflated account of the differences between sociology and Marxism.

Like his analysis of Durkheim and the early French positivists, Therborn's critique of Max Weber as an "idealist" is greatly oversimplified. There are at least three things wrong with it.

First, Therborn conflates idealism and voluntarism, and does not seem to grasp their difference. Voluntarism stresses the importance of internalized norms and values in determining outcomes but *only in interaction with other conditions of action,* while the idealist does not and tends to drop the latter and rely more exclusively on the former. Weber's *Gen-*

eral Economic History with its complex and painstaking discussion of the great variety of conditions entering into economic development in general, and the rise of capitalism in particular, indicates that Weber was a voluntarist not an idealist.

Second, Therborn appears to think that Weber surrendered evolutionary thinking when, in fact, there were various levels on which he clearly manifested a neoevolutionism which, while not determinist, was no less evolutionary and multilinear at that. Thus Western European societies were seen as relinquishing passivity for the assumption of active control of the environment, moving from given "natural" bonds, kin or traditional, to chosen universalistic relationships in the modern purpose-centered association, and moving away from the coercively dominated patriarchy. "This society-wide movement toward voluntarism constitutes one major reference for Weber's concept of 'rationalization,'" observes Jeffrey Alexander, which involves "the ability for groups and individuals to assert self-conscious control in the modern world."[7]

Third and finally, Therborn misses the distinction between the voluntaristic assumptions, often important in Weber's historical studies of *earlier* societies, and the quite different premises of much of his analysis of *contemporary* society. Far from stressing the importance or even existence of communal ethics, moralities, or values today, Weber stresses their *decline* and this is the basis of his pessimism about modernity. Therborn forgets Weber's well-known remark that "the Puritans wanted to work in a calling, we are forced to do so." In short, voluntary and spontaneous commitment is being supplanted by externalized constraint, and the social system has become a juggernaut, an "iron cage," overriding individual purpose rather than expressing it, and society is increasingly held together by impersonal bureaucracies dominated by gray faceless men. Rather than affirming the importance of values and moralities in the modern world, Weber argued that "technical and economic conditions . . . determine the lives of all the individuals . . . with irresistible force."[8]

Having bowdlerized sociology, Therborn summons his final indictment, concluding that "sociology thus became in many ways a modern, scientifically oriented equivalent to theology and moral philosophy." It would seem, however, that those who dwell in the glass steeples of a churchly Marxism should not play bull-in-the-china-shop with others' religions.[9] The essential point he ignores is that sociology's focus on common values was aimed at understanding the spontaneous, *self*-maintaining (i.e., self-healing) mechanisms of civil society, partly as a way of limiting the spreading powers of the modern state and externally imposed political solutions. In the latter nineteenth century, sociology's attention to moral beliefs was, also, an effort to counter Marxism's accent on "material" conditions. In short, sociology's "idealism" emerged partly as a counter to the state and as an effort to oppose Scientific Marxism's economism and its neglect of ideology and consciousness.

Indeed, that economism is repeatedly exhibited in Therborn's own work. For example, there is his offhand definition of "Society" as those "social arrangements determined in the last instance by a specific combination of forces and relations of production."[10] Needless to add, Therborn never provides a clue as to how we may know when that fateful "last instance" has struck.

One may also note Therborn's economism in his discussion of how capitalist societies maintain themselves, which he says depends mainly on their *economies:* "the relative political success to date of the rulers of this world *has been basically determined by the elasticity and capacity for the growth of the advanced capitalist economies,* which has rendered the mechanisms of the economic and social integration of the ruled unexpectedly pervasive and powerful." Therborn adds that "the most important political institution of advanced capitalist societies has proved to be . . . bourgeois democracy. Yet a true theory of bourgeois democracy has never been developed in sociology—nor even for that matter in what is called 'political science.' Even in historical materialism there are only a few general and crude beginnings of one."[11] Be it noted, however, that Therborn will not allow political science or sociology even these few "crude beginnings."

It is also characteristic that Therborn fails to mention that his critique of sociology is no less applicable to Critical Marxism, which (like sociology) accents the role of ideology. Therborn's critique of sociology thus has an invisible mooring: it is grounded in the vendetta of his Scientific Marxism against its traditional foe, Critical Marxism.

Sociology's own critique of Marxism—for almost a century now—has not, it needs stressing, been aimed at Marxism-in-general but, far more specifically, at a more limited reading of Marxism, at Therborn's economistic brand; and, conversely, sociology's own development has tacitly converged with the Critical Marxism that is Therborn's adversary. Thus, one of the founts of Critical Marxism, Georg Lukács, learned much (and not always for the better) from his intimate association with Max Weber, his studies under Georg Simmel, and his close connection with Karl Mannheim. Therborn is thus misguided in persistently obscuring the convergences between Marxism and sociology, in jeering at suggestions concerning such convergences, and in ignoring the fact that Marxism and sociology had a common ancestor in Saint-Simon, who was not only father of positivist sociology but of utopian socialism.

As an economizing Scientific Marxist, Therborn is committed to the view that the mode of production dominates society, in the magic "last instance," of course. He is, therefore, confident that the elimination of the proprietary class will automatically suffice to solve social ills, that no special efforts need to be developed to cultivate persons' consciousness, or to strengthen a civil society that might defend the working class and others from "their own" state.

NOTES

1. Ibid., p. 219.

2. See Talcott Parsons, *The Structure of Social Action* (New York: McGraw-Hill & Co., 1937), esp. pp. 81–82. "Interest will be focused in the process of emergence of a particular theoretical system, that of the 'voluntaristic theory of action'" (p. 12). "This study is meant to be a monographic study of one particular problem in the history of recent social thought . . . the 'voluntaristic theory of action'" (p. 14). Moreover, and as distinct from idealistic social theories, "the voluntaristic system does not in the least deny an important role to conditional and other non-normative elements, but considers these as interdependent with the normative" (p. 82).

3. Therborn, *Science, Class and Society*, p. 22.

4. Ibid., p. 221.

5. Emile Durkheim, *Socialism and Saint-Simon (Le Socialism)*, ed. Alvin W. Gouldner (New York: Collier Books, 1958), esp. pp. 22ff.

6. Therborn, *Science, Class and Society*, p. 221.

7. Jeffrey C. Alexander, "Theoretical Logic in Sociological Thought," (to be published in 2 vols. by the University of California Press, Berkeley, in 1979). Part 2 of vol. 1 contains what is in effect a thorough answer to Therborn's bowdlerization of Weber as idealist. I have drawn heavily on the manuscript in my remarks here.

8. Max Weber, *The Protestant Ethic and the Spirit of Capitalism*, trans. Talcott Parsons (New York: Charles Scribner's Sons, 1958). This and the previous quotation from Weber are from p. 181.

9. Even in this Therborn again relies upon the prior (but unacknowledged) analysis of sociologists. Thus *The Coming Crisis of Western Sociology* had, six years earlier than Therborn's *Science, Class and Society*, pointedly noted "the muted religious impulse of sociology, its present piety as well as its earlier full-fledged religious form" and had critically discussed sociology's link to church and religion. Therborn never asks *why* sociology focuses on shared values and moralities. See my *The Coming Crisis of Western Sociology* (New York: Basic Books, 1970), p. 260, 258ff. See also Eisenstadt, *Form of Sociology*, p. 68.

10. Therborn, *Science, Class and Society*, p. 73.

11. Ibid., p. 218.

13

NIGHTMARE MARXISM

Every theoretical system has another system inside it struggling to get out. And every system has a nightmare: that the caged system will break out.

In conceiving theories as having a natural history—as distinct from the methodologies, proprieties, and moralities of theory making—we have viewed theory not simply as a response to "data" or "facts" but as developing also in an historical landscape of other theories. A theory establishes itself not only by accounting for or predicting facts but also by *drawing lines* and separating itself from its theoretical enemies and, sometimes even more emphatically, from competitor theories with which it might be confused. At some point, however, a theory makes its own positive commitments, moving toward an authoritative paradigm, and it then faces the problem of fidelity to its own past, of consistency with the commitments it has made, and therefore of coping with "anomalies" generated either by its own researches or imposed by history.

If a system does not make room for these anomalies, it becomes dogma; but, at the same time, if a theoretical system simply opened itself to them all and acknowledged every anomaly it encounters as soon as it appeared, its boundaries would soon become unclear, and its identity or character would dissolve. It would cease to be.

Having constituted itself by drawing a line separating it from its enemies and competitors—in the case of Marxism, by drawing a line (critique) between itself and bourgeois society, mechanical materialism, idealism, or alternative socialisms such as utopian socialism—any theory must therefore do repressive work to maintain itself. For a theoretical system can be something only on the condition that it forgo alternatives and not be something else. A system becomes what it is as much by what it excludes and represses as by what it admits and makes salient. Both establish its boundaries and define its identity.

A system's enemies, then, are not only outside of but also within it. There are always other, alternative systems within it having varying degrees of vitality and development. In short, there is usually not only one but several other systems struggling to get out, and not just one but several nightmares that trouble any system.

The systems struggling to get out are not only threats to the parent system's identity but are also necessary to it. The cage and the caged help form one another; the repressed systems also help make the repressor system what it is. One is reminded of ancient Sparta whose entire society was warped in every pore by the need for eternal vigilance against her own restive helots.

What, then, are Marxism's nightmares? There are at least two. Implicit in its repression of idealism and utopianism, as well as in its sublimation of millenarianism into scientism, there is the lurking fear that it is not a truly "scientific socialism," not a theory about society or of the objective conditions that will change it, but only another disguise of the political will, an old utopian project masquerading as new science. In other words, one nightmare of Marxism is that it is another religion of the oppressed—a revolutionary messianism, as Georg Lukács once described his own Marxism. This nightmare broke into the theorizing of Critical Marxism, which is nucleated with utopianism, and, at the political level, emerged openly in Maoism.

Yet there is another Marxist nightmare, an even deeper dragon of the mind that stirs fitfully within it. It is, most basically, this: Marxism emerged in a society whose middle classes had proudly insisted that private property and those having it were the foundation of civilization itself and that, as the *Communist Manifesto* summarizes their view, property is "the fruit of man's own labor . . . the ground work of all personal freedom, activity and independence."[1] This is the nuclear contention—the "first commandment" of bourgeois life—*against which* Marxism was developed and which its theoretical system seeks to encage. The nuclear importance of the issue for communism is also plainly asserted in the *Manifesto* which replies: "The distinguishing feature of Communism is . . . the abolition of bourgeois property. . . . In this sense, the theory of the Communists may be summed up in the single sentence: Abolition of private property."[2]

As usual, most important things are out in the open; but the task, as Whitehead said, is to take hold of what is there in front of us, "to grasp its precise application," to *discover* what we see. The bourgeoisie said private property was the very foundation of civilization. Marxism is a system that creates itself in opposition to that contention. It is precisely this thought that Marxism holds in scornful contempt; it is this private property against which its most basic policies are directed, which it seeks to "annihilate." Marxism argues the *contrary* (not the negation) of the bourgeois first commandment, asserting instead that private property is now *blocking* the forces of production, has become an obstacle to civilization, and must therefore be expropriated. Far from private property being the basis of civilization, says Marxism, the bourgeoisie have destroyed everything once hallowed. The reality, said Marx, is that bourgeois private property itself has now become the most basic threat to civilization and we must either have "socialism or barbarism."

But where is the nightmare in this? Not in the possibility that barbarism will really triumph, which Marx mentions only parenthetically, but in the possibility that the bourgeoisie were right all along and that he was wrong. Now *that* is really a nightmare for a theorist. In the nightmare, what happens is: private property *really* turns out to be the basis of civilization; in the nightmare it is the *rise* of the bourgeoisie that is the turning point of history, not their expropriation; in the nightmare, socialism does not mean that the proletariat becomes the ruling class, but that the state becomes the dominant force—the infrastructure—and its bureaucracy the new ruling class; in the nightmare this new collectivist state brings a new stagnation to the economy, rather than a new productivity; in the nightmare the expropriation of the bourgeoisie is not the basis of a new emancipation but of a new, many times worse, domination. (The sleeper awakes gasping, drenched in sweat.)

It is precisely through its anomalies that Marxism comes close indeed to that very nightmare. The *Eighteenth Brumaire* was a nightmare, exhibiting the independence of the state and its domination of the classes. Marx careens back and forth to find a proper class basis for it, first, in the masses of peasants, then in the conservative peasants, then in the lumpen proletariat. A state representing the lumpen proletariat, the demi-monde and "scum" of society! Is it really farfetched to call this a Marxist nightmare?

If Marxism does not maintain that property as such is the foundation of all civilization, it borders on that idea. It does, after all, emphasize that the relationship between direct producers and owners, is the "innermost secret" of every class society. The property system is a central part of the mode of production and the latter, for Marx, is indeed the infrastructure of civilization. Still, that is not the same as, but only converges with, the bourgeoisie's first commandment: *private* property is the foundation of civilization.

Marx is *ambivalent* about the role of private property; not just hating it, he has a love-hate relationship to it. On the one side, he attributes great importance—great power and, indeed, great value—to the emergence of all the proprietary classes—to slave owners, feudal lords, and especially the bourgeoisie. Consider the judgement passed on the early common ownership of land. "While all civilised people begin with the common ownership of land," says Engels, "in the course of development this common ownership becomes a fetter on production ... is turned into private property," which, he carefully adds, "by no means makes its appearance as the result of slavery or violence."[3] And then consider the paeans with which he greets even slavery: "Without slavery, no Greek state, no Greek art, and science; without slavery, no Roman Empire. But without Hellenism and the Roman Empire as a base, also no modern Europe. We should never forget that our whole economic, political and intellectual development has as its presupposition a state of things in which slavery was as necessary as it was universally recognised. In this sense we are entitled to say: Without the slavery of antiquity, no modern socialism."[4] The very flower and highest hope of Western civilization is, indeed, said to rest not just on private property in general but on vile *slavery* itself. Is not this kith and kin to the bourgeoisie's first commandment?

Consider, further, Marx's own attitude toward the bourgeoisie themselves. Marshall Berman has seen the point here with exceptional clarity, and recognized the power of Marx's ambivalent admiration of them. Speaking of the *Manifesto*, Berman observed that what is startling about it "is that he seems to have come not to bury the bourgeoisie but to praise it. He writes an impassioned, enthusiastic, often lyrical celebration of bourgeois works, ideas, and achievements. Indeed, in these pages he manages to praise the bourgeoisie more powerfully and profoundly than its members have ever known how to praise themselves."[5] The *Manifesto* celebrates the bourgeoisie which, "in its reign of barely a hundred years, has created more massive and more colossal productive powers than have all previous generations put together. Subjection of nature's forces to man, machinery, application of chemistry to agriculture and industry, steam navigation, railways, electric telegraphs, clearing of whole continents for cultivation, canalization of rivers, whole populations conjured out of the ground."

The bourgeoisie are the center of modern exploitation; but they are also a veritable colossus striding the earth, hooping it with world commerce, throwing the dross of centuries into history's dust bin, bringing the most backward of people onto the stage of history, waking them from centuries of long slumber. The bourgeoisie has brought into existence forces that ultimately spell its own destruction; it has conjured up forces that it cannot control; it mass produces misery as it mass produces cotton, but it is also the historical embodiment of Prometheus, laying the basis of mankind's ultimate emancipation from want, producing the very marvels of which artists have only dreamed. Indeed, it is the bourgeoisie who, with their ceaseless accumulation of capital, uninterrupted disturbance and agitation, who with their constant revolutionizing of productivity, who are the very paradigm of *revolution en permanence.* The proletariat's own "permanent revolution," its insistence (or hoped for insistence) on carrying forward the revolution from the bourgeois to the socialist revolution, its refusal to allow the bourgeoisie to call a halt to revolution or to allow bourgeois relations of production to stop this *revolution en permanence,* are only an extension of the Prometheanism of the bourgeoisie. Marx saw the bourgeoisie as the battering ram of history and parted company with them when, and only because, their juggernaut momentum was stalled by their own property system. He would and did allow them anything, denying that they could be swept off the historical stage, so long as they fueled the forces of production. The proletariat, then, are to carry forward the torch of permanent revolution, wresting it from the hands of the bourgeoisie, as the latter begins to falter; but Marx had no doubt that it was the bourgeoisie who had first lit that torch and put the flame to human progress.

Marxism, then, is grounded in the most profound and radical ambivalence to proprietary classes, and its passionate admiration for the bourgeoisie could be controlled only by a theoretical system in which its condemnation of them was equally thunderous, seeing and *needing* to see them as the possessors of a demonic force akin to "that hideous pagan idol, who would not drink the nectar but from the skulls of the slain."[6] The Promethean power and activism of the bourgeoisie, the swath of creative destruction they unceasingly cut in the world, fascinated Marx and he could have resisted their attraction only with the most energetic exorcisms. He is surely drawn to his own nightmare.

As Marx extended his comparative studies to include Asia, and discovered the AMP and Oriental Despotism, proprietary classes could only have become more attractive to him. In contrast with the AMP, all exploitative societies and ruling classes in the West now seem uniquely progressive. Marx believes that however exploitative Western societies were, all were far more preferable than the AMP. He is at bottom a modernizer. The Western track of development as a whole, then, comes to be seen as having a uniquely progressive historical character. In contrast to oriental backwardness, even the West's colonial domination of Asia—and its uncivilized "barbarian" societies—was seen as having a progressive import. My point here, however, does not bear on Marx's chauvinism (on which, more in a later volume). The dilemma, for Marxism, went deeper.

It had to do with where the dividing line in Western history was to be drawn. Certainly, Marxism speaks directly to that question, unambiguously affirming that Europe's basic turning point was the emergence of a *propertyless* class who, it is promised, will produce a socialist culmination precisely *because it is propertyless*. Having "nothing to lose but its chains," the proletariat is imputedly free to usher in the new classless society. This is surely the dominant commitment of Marxism's primary paradigm. Marx and Engels's later studies of Asia, however, were profoundly anomalous, implying a profoundly different periodization and perspective. These suggest that the watershed in world history was the *emergence of proprietary classes* (for they were more economically dynamic than the state ruling class of the AMP). These studies also brought into focus the epochal significance of the proprietary class's shift from land to capital.

While Marxism states unequivocally that Europe's turning point was the emergence of a proletariat, as the revolutionary agent of a classless socialism, nonetheless, there is another, profoundly different layer in Marx's views. From this standpoint, Europe's turning point had already arrived and its social evolution culminates not with socialism but with capitalism. There is, indeed, the further implication that socialism is only a special case of societies that have freed themselves from a land-dominated mode of production through use of capital. In this latter perspective, "socialism" seems to be a variant of capitalism. That is, "socialism" here seems to be a society that relies increasingly on capital, and which wants to do so still more (but which unlike Western capitalisms remains limited by its encompassing and unproductive agricultural system). The real Prometheans, then, were not of the future but had already come: they were men of capital.

Discussion of Marx's AMP commonly fails to mention that he was interested in it (and other forms of primitive communalism), largely because they helped him understand modern *Western* capitalism. Having held that wage labor—the sale of labor power for a price—was one of the preconditions of capitalism, the section of the *Grundrisse* (analyzing primitive communalism) begins by exploring the requisites of wage labor. One of these, says Marx here, is the existence of free labor and its exchange for money; another is the separation of the worker from his own means of production, the means and material of labor. This above all involves the "release of the workers from the soil . . . hence dissolution of small, landed property as well as of communal land ownership resting on the Oriental commune."[7]

Marx concludes his *Grundrisse* discussion of the three forms of the primitive commune (the oriental, the Graeco-Roman city, and the Germanic land system) by stressing *the unique importance for the West of both cities and private property in land:*

> The history of [Western] classical antiquity is the history of cities, but of cities founded on landed property and on agriculture; Asiatic society is a kind of indifferent unity of town and countryside (the really large cities must be regarded here merely as royal camps, as works of artifice [*superfötation*] erected over the economic construction proper); the Middle Ages (Germanic period) begins with the land as the seat of history, whose further development then moves forward in the contradiction between town and countryside; the modern [age] is the urbanization of the countryside; not ruralization of the city as in antiquity.[8]

This discussion brought Marx's analysis to the point that what was required was a vast *comparative* and *historical* scholarship; something quite different from his quick forays into political analysis, or his densely detailed technical political economy, with examples drawn from only one country, England. In the *Grundrisse*'s pages, Marx arrived at the point where the next logical development was the comparative scholarship of Max Weber. In one part, then, Weber's was one of the "nightmare systems" struggling to escape from Marxism.

Marx's analyses of the AMP, then, do much more than certify he had escaped unilinear evolutionary determinism. They suggest with no less force, that Marx, following Hegel, saw Western society as a dynamic entity profoundly contrasted with the stagnant orient. In this perspective, Marx and Engels—followed by Lenin—repeatedly held that imperial Russia to the East was a semi-Asiatic society alien to Western Europe—even if then lately entering its orbit—and, more than that, was a threat to the socialist development that lay growing in the West's historical womb.

With its cities, its private property in land, its dynamic proprietary classes, Western Europe and its culture—Marx saw but did not "discover"—was a unique center of historical development of world scope. Marx's analysis of the ancient city-state or Germanic communalism suggests that the bourgeoisie *was only the recent expression of a larger Western dynamism,* inescapably grounded in this unique past. The materials on early communal forms undermine a vision of Marx as the prophet of a universal *"marche genérale"*; but they offer another, nightmare vision of him as an emerging theorist of the West's manifest destiny and of socialism as the heir to that unique destiny, at which point Marx has developed another interface with Max Weber.

The bourgeoisie, says the *Manifesto,* "creates a world in its own image," compelling all nations to adopt its revolutionary civilization, to renounce their backwardness and to enter the stream of world history. "The bourgeoisie . . . draws all, even the most barbarian, nations into civilization . . . it has made barbarian and semi-barbarian countries dependent on the civilized ones, nations of peasants on nations of bourgeois, the East on the West."[9] This is plainly the language of Western superiority over Eastern "barbarianism," of a bourgeois manifest destiny blindly preparing the ground for the next, higher stage of Western development, to which the proletariat is heir.

There is an ambiguity in Marx's work, then, as to which break in history was really decisive. For while the focus of Marx's *early* work on socialism and the proletariat affirms that this is the important dividing line in history, Marx's *later* work, after his studies of oriental history, suggest that the real watersheds may have been the irruption of proprietary classes in general and of the bourgeoisie in particular. As Umberto Melotti notes (quoting from Marx's 1857 *Introduction to the Critique of Political Economy*), "only capitalism, in Marx's view, constituted a real qualitative jump in the process of man's historical development, by breaking the stranglehold of nature: 'In all forms in which landed property is the decisive factor, natural relations still predominate; in the forms in which the decisive factor is capital, social, historically produced elements predominate.'"[10]

Underneath Marxism's primary paradigm, then, there was another very dim scenario; there was a stifled embryo Marxism whose profound divergence from the paradigm's public posture required that it remain unborn. From a standpoint that assigns strategic significance to the shift from landed property to capital, the expropriation of the bourgeoisie may not be as historically significant as the emergence of capitalism; from a comparative perspective on the stagnant Asiatic Mode of Production, the expropriation of the bourgeoisie may appear to be a perilous experiment threatening a new stagnation. In all this there is a rising redolence, faint but pungent, of an ethnocentrism exalting the West as embodying a unique promise for the world's future development.

In this nightmare scenario, it is the West that is the true agent of historical development; the proletariat, caught in the cunning of history, is the servant of that higher destiny. I have called this, nightmare Marxism; yet nightmares are real and some have them. It is likely that this nightmare flitted through more than one dream of German social democracy and its Scientific Marxism. As one observes the Russians glumly counting their growing Moslem population, or seized with anger against the Chinese and scanning for a theoretical basis for *détente* with the West, it sometimes seems as if they too may be drawn into this nightmare Marxism.

NOTES

1. *Communist Manifesto* by Karl Marx and Friedrich Engels, authorized English edition of 1888, supervised by Engels, published by Charles H. Kerr, Chicago, p. 31.

2. Ibid.

3. Friedrick Engels, *Herr Eugen Dühring's Revolution in Science (Anti-Dühring)*, trans. Emile Burns, ed. C. P. Dutt (New York: International Publishers, 1939), pp. 150, 179.

4. Ibid., p. 200

5. Marshall Berman, "All that Is Solid Melts into Air," *Dissent,* Winter 1978, p. 56. See also Paul Sweezy, "There are . . . in all literature probably no passages which paint the achievements of capitalism in more glowing terms than those devoted to the subject in the *Manifesto.*" *Science and Society,* Winter 1948, p. 80.

6. Karl Marx, *Selected Writings,* ed. David McLellan (New York: Oxford University Press, 1977), p. 336.

7. Karl Marx, *Grundrisse: Introduction to the Critique of Political Economy,* trans. Martin Nicolaus (Harmondsworth: Penguin Books, 1973), p. 471.

8. Ibid., p. 479.

9. *Communist Manifesto,* p. 18. Despite this and much other straightforward evidence, Norman Levine assures us that, unlike Engels "Marx never made a value judgement as to the relationship between Western and non-Western societies." Norman Levine, *The Tragic Deception: Marx Contra Engels* (Santa Barbara: Clio Books, 1975), p. 20.

10. Umberto Melotti, *Marx and the Third World* (London: Macmillan Publishers, 1977), p. 27. Melotti's study is a critique of the Marxist discussion of the problem of unilinear and multilinear evolution in general, and of Marx's analysis of Asiatic society, in particular.

INDEX OF NAMES

INDEX OF SUBJECTS